TRAVEL THROUGH

THE OLD TESTAMENT

Volume Two

Thomas L. Hiegel

Other Books by Author

Travel Through Ephesians

Travel Through The Old Testament Vol 1

Travel Through The Old Testament Vol 2

An extensive Old Testament Study and Reference Source
..............now in two volumes

TRAVEL THROUGH

THE OLD TESTAMENT
REVISED AND EXPANDED

Volume Two

Thomas L. Hiegel

Travel Through the Old Testament Volume Two
Copyright © 2017 by Thomas L. Hiegel
TLH CREATIONS, Dayton OH

Revised and Updated from the original 3-volume work, 2010

All rights reserved. No part of this publication may be reproduced, stored in a retrieval system, or transmitted in any form or by any means-electronic, mechanical, photocopy, recording, or any other—except for brief quotations in printed reviews, without the prior permission of the copyright owner.

All Scripture quotations, unless otherwise indicated, are taken from the NEW AMERICAN STANDARD BIBLE®, Copyright © 1960, 1962, 1963, 1968, 1971, 1972, 1973, 1975, 1977, 1995 by The Lockman Foundation. Used by permission. (www.Lockman.org)

Scripture quotations marked (AMP), "Scripture quotations taken from THE AMPLIFIED BIBLE, copyright © 1954, 1958, 1962, 1964, 1965, 1987, by The Lockman Foundation. All rights reserved. Used by permission, (www.Lockman.org)."

Some Scripture quotations are from the "ESV Bible (The Holy Bible, English Standard Version®), copyright © 2001 by Crossway, a publishing ministry of Good News Publishers. Used by permission. All rights reserved.

Scripture taken from the New King James Version® (NKJV) Copyright © 1982 by Thomas Nelson. Used by permission. All rights reserved.

Scripture quotations marked HCSB have been taken from the Holman Christian Standard Bible®, Copyright © 1999, 2000, 2002, 2003, 2009 by Holman Bible Publishers. Used by permission. Holman Christian Standard Bibles®, Holman CSB®, and HCSB® are federally registered trademarks of Holman Bible Publishers.

Scripture quoted by permission. Quotations designated (NET) are from the NET Bible® copyright ©1996-2016 by Biblical Studies Press, L.L.C. http://netbible.com All rights reserved.

Scripture taken from the HOLY BIBLE, NEW INTERNATIONAL VERSION®, Copyright © 1973, 1978, 1984 BY International Bible Society. Used by permission of Zondervan. All rights reserved.

Scripture quotations marked (NLT) are taken from the *Holy Bible* New Living Translation, copyright © 1996. Used by permission of Tyndale House Publishers, Inc., Wheaton, Illinois 60189. All rights reserved.

ISBN 978-0-9982861-1-2

Printed in the United States of America.

TO THE MEMORY

Of my mentors

Warren J. Campbell

Walter Ellis Swartz

Table of Contents

ABBREVIATIONS ix

AUTHOR'S PREFACE TO REVISED EDITION 10

SECTION 1 Hebrew Poetry and Psalms
ONE: Hebrew Poetry 16

TWO: Psalms 20

SECTION 2 Wisdom
THREE: Wisdom From Proverbs 45

FOUR: Wisdom From Ecclesiastes and Song of Solomon 55

SECTION 3 The Northern Kingdom: Israel
FIVE: The Kings of Israel 72

SIX: The Prophets to Israel 84
Elijah and Elisha
Jonah, Amos, Hosea

SECTION 4 The Southern Kingdom: Judah Begins
SEVEN: Judah Begins 109
Joel
The Day of the Lord

SECTION 5 The Golden Age of Prophecy
EIGHT: Isaiah and Micah 136

SECTION 6: Judah Falls
NINE: Judah in Decline 161

TEN: Judah Falls 174

Nahum, Zephaniah, Jeremiah, Habakkuk, Obadiah, Lamentations

SECTION 7 Captivity
ELEVEN: Babylonia and Persia 200

TWELVE: Daniel and Ezekiel 210

SECTION 8 Restoring and Rebuilding
THIRTEEN: Restoration and Rebuilding 240
Ezra, Esther, Nehemiah

FOURTEEN: Prophets of the Restoration 258
Haggai, Zechariah, Malachi

SECTION 9 Between the Old and New Testaments
FIFTEEN: Silence 277
Six historical divisions

SIXTEEN: The High Priests 292
High Priests of the 400 silent years

Appendix: Chronology of Old Testament History 301

Consolidated Index of Persons, Key Words, Depth of Words and Places, Keys to Books, Outlines, Expanded Help Papers, etc 327

Scripture Index... 336

LIST OF ABBREVIATIONS

OLD TESTAMENT ABBREVIATIONS

Gen	Genesis	SS	Song of Solomon
Ex	Exodus	Isa	Isaiah
Lev	Leviticus	Jer	Jeremiah
Num	Numbers	Lam	Lamentations
Deut	Deuteronomy	Ezek	Ezekiel
Josh	Joshua	Dan	Daniel
Judg	Judges	Hos	Hosea
Ruth	Ruth	Joel	Joel
1, 2 Sam	Samuel	Amos	Amos
1, 2 Kings	Kings	Obad	Obadiah
1, 2 Chron	Chronicles	Jon	Jonah
Ezra	Ezra	Mic	Micah
Neh	Nehemiah	Nah	Nahum
Est	Esther	Hab	Habakkuk
Job	Job	Zeph	Zephaniah
Ps	Psalms	Hag	Haggai
Prov	Proverbs	Zech	Zechariah
Eccl	Ecclesiastes	Mal	Malachi

GENERAL ABBREVIATIONS

AMP	Amplified Bible
BCE	Before the Common Era (B.C.)
CE	Common Era (A.D.)
cp, cps	Chapter, chapters
i.e.	"that is"
e.g.	"for example"
ESV	English Standard Version
HCSB	Holman Christian Standard Bible
NASB	New American Standard Version
NET	New English Translation NET Bible
NIV	New International Version
NLT	New Living Translation
NT	New Testament
OT	Old Testament
vol	In this Volume
v, vv	Verse (s)

AUTHOR'S PREFACE TO REVISED EDITION
Volume Two

The two-volume edition of *Travel Through the Old Testament* is the complete teaching course (revised, expanded, and updated), previously printed in three smaller volumes. It is the author's intent to present a basic, and yet thorough study course on the entire thirty-nine books of the Old Testament. The author maintains a conservative Bible-centered view of Bible interpretation. *The author suggests* you review the first several pages of Volume One which include information about the Bible: (1) Why Study the Bible? (2) The Uniqueness of the Bible, and (3) Structure of The Old Testament.

In this survey and teaching course, we will "travel" through the thirty-nine books called The Old Testament. Volume One included God's original creation in the dateless past, through a visit with the Patriarchs, the deliverance and forming of a special people, Joshua leading God's people into the Promised Land, and the periods of Judges and Kings. Volume Two includes Hebrew poetry, dividing of the Promised Land into Israel and Judah, the exile of both nations, and the return to the Promised Land. Also included is Section 9, **Between the Old and New Testaments**.

Our journey will generally be chronological, with an emphasis on history. Therefore, some of the Old Testament books will be referenced in more than one Section. The full index of word studies, Expanded Help Papers, Depth of Bible Words and Places, and outlines and keys for each book, will assist in locating the material for your in-depth study.

If you are thirsty for the water of the Word, you will benefit from this study. It is my desire for you to grow spiritually strong. To read and understand the Old Testament is the primary need of our generation and the generation to follow. This work will serve as a small library of Old Testament information. Both the scholar and the student will discover truths in this course that will assist in personal growth. In addition, the author's in-depth **Chronology of Old Testament History** may be found at the back of both volumes (The Chronology in Vol. Two has been updated).

The course could be utilized in most settings:
>   Universities and Colleges

Preface

    Sunday School and Seminars
    Home Groups and Personal Studies
    Mid-week gatherings

The author may be contacted at ThomasLHiegel @ thomaslhiegel.com.

Will you join with me in the following prayer while "traveling" through this Course?

    Every breath I take...is by Your grace
    Every step I take...is directed by You
    Every word I speak...is for Your glory
    Everyone I meet...is a neighbor to be loved

Any claims, on my part, to be capable of deploying all, or most, of the methods of textual and historical criticism that are needed for this work, would be unwarrantable. All that I offer is this man's research and view of the declarations, which the Old Testament writings illuminate.

Many sources were used in preparing the general outline during the four weeks following a heart attack in June 2007. The work was completed in three volumes and printed in color during the following year. In 2016 (Vol One) and 2017 (Vol Two), the three original volumes were completely edited, greatly expanded, and combined into two black and white volumes.

Acknowledgments

The following are many of the sources of information used in preparing Vols. One and Two in addition to my personal commentary notes. These sources are given full appreciation for their contributions, many used with permission. Footnotes are included for additional recognition. The author owes a debt of gratitude to the following:

Allis, Oswald T., *God Spake By Moses,* Presbyterian and Reformed Publishing Co, Nutley, NJ, 1972

Anderson, Bernhard W., *Understanding The Old Testament,* Prentice-Hall, Inc, Englewood Cliffs, New Jersey, 1957

Berquist, Jon L., *Judaism in Persia's Shadow,* Fortress Press, Minneapolis, 1995

Bickerman, Elias, From Ezra to the Last of the Maccabees, Schocken Books, NYC, 1949

Brier, Bob, *Great Pharaohs of Ancient Egypt* (transcript of class), The Teaching Company, Chantilly, Virginia, 2004

Brown, William, *The Tabernacle: Its Priests and Its Services,* Hendrickson Publishers, Inc., Peabody, Mass, 1996

Carmody, John and Denise, and Robert L. Cohn, Exploring the Hebrew Bible, Prentice Hall, Englewood Cliffs, NJ, 1988

TRAVEL THOUGH THE OLD TESTAMENT

Dobson, Kent, *Teachings of the Torah*, Zondervan, Grand Rapids, Michigan, 2014

Edersheim, Alfred, Bible *History Old Testament*, Hendrickson Publishers, Inc., Peabody, Massachusetts, 2009

Feiler, Bruce, *Walking The Bible*, HarperCollins Publishers, New York, 2

Geisler, Norman L, *A Popular Survey of the Old Testament,* Grand Rapids, Baker Books, 1977

Grant, Michael, *The History of Ancient Israel,* Michael Grant Publications Limited, 1984

Harris, Katharine, *Nelson's Foundational Bible Dictionary,* Thomas Nelson, Nashville Tennessee, 2004

Harris, Stephen L., *Understanding the Bible,* The McGraw-Hill Companies, Inc., 2003

Hayford, Jack W., Thomas Nelson Publishers: *Hayford's Bible Handbook.* Nashville: Thomas Nelson Publishers, 1995

International Standard Bible Encyclopedia, revised edition, Copyright © 1979 by Wm. B. Eerdmans Publishing Co. All rights reserved.

Ironside, H. A., *Joshua,* Loizeaux Brothers, Neptune, New Jersey, 1950

Ironside, H. A., *Esther,* Loizeaux Brothers, Neptune, New Jersey, 1905

Ironside, H. A., *The 400 Silent Years,* Loizeaux Brothers, Neptune, New Jersey, 1914

Jones, Floyd Nolen, *The Chronology of the Old Testament*, Master Books, Green Forest, AR, 1993

Keller, Werner, *The Bible As History,* Barnes & Noble, Inc., 1995

KJV Bible Commentary, Nashville: Thomas Nelson, 1997, 1994

MacArthur, John, *The MacArthur Bible Handbook.* Nashville, Tenn.: Thomas Nelson Publishers, 2003

MacArthur, John, *The MacArthur Study Bible: New American Standard Bible.* Nashville: Thomas Nelson Publishers, 2006

MacDonald, W., *Believer's Bible Commentary,* Thomas Nelson Publishers, Nashville, 1990

McDowell, Josh: *Josh McDowell's Handbook on Apologetics* electronic ed. Nashville: Thomas Nelson, 1997

McClintock and Strong Encyclopedia, Electronic Database. Copyright © 2000, 2003, 2005, 2006 by Biblesoft, Inc. All rights reserved

Mears, Henrietta, *What The Bible Is All About,* Regal Books/Gospel Light, Angus Hudson London, 1999

Preface

Nelson's Illustrated Bible Dictionary, Copyright © 1986, Thomas Nelson Publishers

New American Standard Bible: 1995 Update. LaHabra, CA: The Lockman Foundation, 1995

NIV Archaeological Study Bible, Copyright © 2005, Grand Rapids, Zondervan

The Pulpit Commentary, Electronic Database. Copyright © 2001, 2003, 2005, 2006 by Biblesoft, Inc.

Purkiser, W.T. Demaray, C.E., Metz, D.C., & Stuneck, M.A., *Exploring The Old Testament,* Beacon Hill Press, Kansas City, 1955

Radmacher, Earl D.; Allen, Ronald Barclay; House, H. Wayne: *The Nelson Study Bible: New King James Version.* Nashville: T. Nelson Publishers, 1997

Richards, Larry: *Every Name of God in the Bible.* Nashville, Tenn.: Thomas Nelson, 2001 (Everything in the Bible Series)

Schultz, Samuel J, Smith, Gary V, *Exploring The Old Testament,* Crossway Books, Wheaton ILL, 2001

Stedman, Ray C., *Adventuring Through the Bible,* Discovery House Publishers, Grand Rapids, MI, 1997

Surburg, Raymond F., *Introduction to the Intertestamental Period,* Concordia, St. Louis, 1975

Swindoll, Charles, *Job,* Copyright © 2004 Charles R. Swindoll, Inc., The W Publishing Group, Nashville

Thomas Nelson Publishers: *Nelson's Complete Book of Bible Maps & Charts: Old and New Testaments.* Rev. and updated ed. Nashville, Tenn.: Thomas Nelson, 1996

Ussher, James, *The Annals of the World*, 1658

Vine, W. E.; Unger, Merrill F.; White, William: *Vine's Complete Expository Dictionary of Old and New Testament Words.* Nashville: T. Nelson, 1996

Vos, H. F. (1999). *Nelson's new illustrated Bible Manners & Customs: How the people of the Bible really lived* (1). Nashville, Tenn.: T. Nelson Publishers.

Willmington, Harold L., *Willmington's Guide to the Bible,* Tyndale House Publishers, Inc., Carol Stream, Illinois, 1984

Wilkinson, B., & Boa, K., *Talk thru the Bible,* Nashville: T. Nelson, 1983

SECTION 1
Hebrew Poetry and Psalms

Psalms and other examples of poetry in the Bible. The period from approximately 1050 to 500 BCE

Theme Statement: *"...the sweet Psalmist of Israel."* (2 Samuel 23:1)

THE KEYS IN SECTION ONE

Section 7: Hebrew Poetry and Psalms

Keys to Psalms—

A Key Word: Praise

The Key Verses (19:14; 145:21)

19:14 *Let the words of my mouth and the meditation of my heart Be acceptable in Your sight, O Lord, my rock and my Redeemer.*

145:21 *My mouth will speak the praise of the Lord, And all flesh will bless His holy name forever and ever.*

The Key Chapter (100)

The Key People in Psalms

David—King of Israel; called a man after God's own heart by God Himself (Psalms 2–41; 51–70; 72:20; 78:70, 71; 86; 89; 96; 101; 103; 105; 108–110; 122; 124; 131–133; 138–145)

Approximate Dates of Key Events in Section 1	
C.1500-538 BCE	Events in Psalms

ONE

Hebrew Poetry

1. The first two Sections of Volume Two will have a slightly different "feel" from Volume One. That is because the books of Psalms, Proverbs, Ecclesiastes, and Song of Solomon ARE different. The first Volume was creation and beginning of all things followed by the beginning and history of God's Kingdom. These next two Sections will "Travel Through" books of wisdom.
   1.1. Much of these two volumes have been written in the approximate date of the events. However, with these two Sections of poetry, wisdom, and Psalms, we are unable to assign exact dates. Each of these topics is scattered throughout the Scriptures. Psalms were written over an approximate period of 1,000 years. This section and the next, are almost dateless but may be considered close to the 1000 BCE period. The theme of this Section is a statement from 2 Samuel 23:1 *the sweet Psalmist of Israel.*

A Basic Outline of Psalms
FIVE DIVISIONS
1. Book I (Genesis) MAN 1-41
2. Book II (Exodus) ISRAEL 42-72
3. Book III (Leviticus) THE SANCTUARY 73-89
4. Book IV (Numbers) THE EARTH 90-106
5. Book V (Deuteronomy) THE WORD OF GOD 107-150

> Jesus in Psalms...He is your Shepherd

   1.2. In Section One, we will look at a few examples of Old Testament poetry, and the book of Psalms. We immediately note that Psalms is the greatest expression of spiritual song and poetry in any writing ever produced.

1.3. Before we review Psalms, we briefly mention some of the early examples of Hebrew poetry in the Old Testament. At an early date, poetry became a part of the literature of the Hebrew people.

1.4. Approximately 40% of the Old Testament is written in poetry. The entire books of Job, Proverbs, Song of Solomon, and Lamentations are Hebrew poetry. There are only seven Old Testament books, which do not contain poetry.

    1.4.1. The very first example of Hebrew poetry in the Old Testament is not an uplifting passage—found in Genesis 4:23-24.[1] A man named Lamech is mentioned in early genealogies, and the two verses written about him are Hebrew poetry.

    1.4.2. Other passages of early Hebrew poetry include:
        1.4.2.1. The prophecy of Noah in Genesis 9:6-7
        1.4.2.2. The blessing of Isaac in Genesis 27:27-29
        1.4.2.3. Jacob's words of Genesis 49:2-27 are poetic in style. This was a prophecy concerning the future of his twelve sons and their descendants.
        1.4.2.4. The wonderful Song of Moses and Miriam following the crossing of the Red Sea in Exodus 15. This is wonderful early Hebrew poetry, which I suggest you read and visualize the words.[2]

    1.4.3. Three of the greatest poetic masterpieces of the Old Testament are:
        1.4.3.1. The Song of Deborah in Judges 5
        1.4.3.2. The Song of the Bow, David's lament over the death of Saul and Jonathan in 2 Samuel 1:19-21
        1.4.3.3. A long passage which begins the book of Nahum, "the Burden of Nineveh."

    1.4.4. There are many other Scriptures, which are expressed poetically:
        1.4.4.1. The Psalms of Hezekiah (Isaiah 38:10-20)
        1.4.4.2. The prayer of Jonah (Jonah 2:2-9)
        1.4.4.3. The prayer of Habakkuk (Habakkuk 3:2-19)

---

[1] Lamech said to his wives, 23 *"Adah and Zillah, Listen to my voice, You wives of Lamech, Give heed to my speech, For I have killed a man for wounding me;*
And a boy for striking me; 24 If Cain is avenged sevenfold, Then Lamech seventy-sevenfold."

[2] *Moses begins: The Lord is my strength and song, And He has become my salvation; This is my God, and I will praise Him; My father's God, and I will extol Him. 3 " The Lord is a warrior; The Lord is His name.*

And Miriam responds back: *"Sing to the Lord, for He is highly exalted; The horse and his rider He has hurled into the sea."* Moses also wrote the 90th Psalms.

TRAVEL THROUGH THE OLD TESTAMENT

    1.4.4.4. The lamentations of Jeremiah (Lamentations)
 1.4.5. One last example is the beautiful passage in 1 Samuel 2, "a prayer of Hannah." The entire example of inspirational poetry is printed for your reading.

1 Samuel 2:1-10
Then Hannah prayed and said,
"My heart exults in the Lord;
My horn is exalted in the Lord,
My mouth speaks boldly against my enemies,
Because I rejoice in Your salvation.
2 " There is no one holy like the Lord,
Indeed, there is no one besides You,
Nor is there any rock like our God.
3 " Boast no more so very proudly,
Do not let arrogance come out of your mouth;
For the Lord is a God of knowledge,
And with Him actions are weighed.
4 " The bows of the mighty are shattered,
But the feeble gird on strength.
5 "Those who were full hire themselves out for bread,
But those who were hungry cease to hunger.
Even the barren gives birth to seven,
But she who has many children languishes.
6 " The Lord kills and makes alive;
He brings down to Sheol and raises up.
7 " The Lord makes poor and rich;
He brings low, He also exalts.
8 " He raises the poor from the dust,
He lifts the needy from the ash heap
To make them sit with nobles,
And inherit a seat of honor;
For the pillars of the earth are the Lord's,
And He set the world on them.
9 " He keeps the feet of His godly ones,
But the wicked ones are silenced in darkness;
For not by might shall a man prevail.
10 " Those who contend with the Lord will be shattered;
Against them He will thunder in the heavens,
The Lord will judge the ends of the earth;
And He will give strength to His king,
And will exalt the horn of His anointed."

1.5. By now you realize from the examples offered, Hebrew poetry was not in rhyme, of which we are familiar. We think of something similar to:

Hebrew Poetry

    1.5.1.   One, *two*, buckle my *shoe*,
    1.5.2.   Three, *four*, shut the *door*,
    1.5.3.   Five, *six*, pick up *sticks*,
    1.5.4.   Seven, *eight*, lay them *straight*.

1.6. Hebrew poetry was the rhythm of thought and usually with quite graphic language. It has beauty and charm all its own, expressed in various arrangements including repetition, amplification, and contrast. Sound or syllable was not a component of Hebrew poetry.

    1.6.1.   Much of it was called Parallelism; the first line or two expressing a thought, the next lines a variation or amplification of the first two (Psalms 19:1, Exodus 15:4). In other poetry, the second line was in opposition to the first.[1]

1.7. There are four types of Hebrew poetry in the Scriptures:

    1.7.1.   The most loved by many is the *Song or Lyric type*. Most of the Psalms written by David, who is called Israel's *"beloved singer of songs"* in 2 Samuel 23:1 are **Lyric Type**. In fact, after David died, this type of Hebrew Poetry also ceased.

    1.7.2.   The second type of Hebrew poetry was a **Teaching Type** called *didactic poetry*.[2] Proverbs and Ecclesiastes have numerous examples of this type.

        1.7.2.1.   This teaching type included observations about life, duties, and moral principles expressed in poetry. This type included the well-known alphabetical method of teaching called acrostic.

        1.7.2.2.   An acrostic is a set of letters or sequence of letters, as the first letters of a line. Preachers use this quite often. The best example in the Old Testament is Psalms 119. This Psalms has 176 verses, 8 verses for each of the twenty-two Hebrew letters. Also, the 34th Psalms uses this same type. Each of the last 22 verses of Proverbs 31 begins with the twenty-two Hebrew letters.

    1.7.3.   The third type is found in Job and Song of Solomon, appropriately called **Dramatic Type.** The style includes a development of ideas rather than centering on persons or events.

    1.7.4.   The fourth type is a funeral song such as Lamentations, which we will review in Section 6.

---

[1] Proverbs 11:17 *The merciful man does himself good, But the cruel man does himself harm.*
[2] Didactic means "instructive."

TWO

Psalms

1 Now we explore the wonderful Book of Psalms—originally the songbook of the Hebrew nation. Someone rightfully said, "It's also the songbook of the church." Perhaps more of our songs should be written with Psalms as the pattern. Music and religion are inseparable.
- 1.1. When you are burdened with grief or sorrow, pour out a song from you inmost being.
- 1.2. We realize many of our older hymns and choruses were from this book of Psalms. In years past, we had an entire service singing only Psalms (of course, we all had the KJV at that time). Many years ago, as a song leader, I recall chorus' such as
    - 1.2.1. "The Horse and Rider Thrown Into the Sea"
    - 1.2.2. "They That Wait Upon the Lord"
    - 1.2.3. "Fear Not For I Have Redeemed You"
    - 1.2.4. "Holy, Holy, Holy"
    - 1.2.5. "Bless the Lord Oh My Soul"
- 1.3. Psalms are a mirror into which anyone can look and see himself and his emotions. In this book, we can find almost every problem, along with the way out. The Psalms have a wonderful capacity to capture the reality of our human experience.
    - 1.3.1. The Hebrew title of this book is a wonderful word, which I have thoroughly studied. For example, the Hebrew word "Tehillim" is *Praises*. One of the studies I prepared was **"Seven Hebrew Words of Praise"** which is summarized as an Expanded Help Paper in this volume. Each of the seven words expresses a different element of true praise—the completeness of praise. They really tell us what our praise should be today....I have no doubt, each element is needed for complete praise.
- 1.4. The Psalms, the closest thing to a biblical prayer book, were collected over a long period, probably coming between 1000 and

Psalms

1.5. 400 BCE. At various times, new groupings were added to the collection.

Depth of Bible Words and Locations
Selah
This word appears seventy-one times in the Psalms and means "to lift up," possibly a musical sign, to pause. It also appears three times in the Book of Habakkuk. To guess at its exact meaning would only be conjecture.

1.5.1. The authorship of Psalms has probably occupied every Bible student's research. It is probably wise to go with the most accepted conclusions: Even though we sometimes say that David is the author of Psalms, in fact, he wrote "only" seventy-three of the 150; we know this from the inspired headings that we have. The headings are at the top of many of the Psalms. We learn from those:

    1.5.1.1. Moses wrote Psalms 90
    1.5.1.2. Solomon wrote both Psalms 72 and 127
    1.5.1.3. Asaph wrote twelve Psalms
    1.5.1.4. Eleven were written by "the sons of Korah"
    1.5.1.5. One by a musician named Heman (88)
    1.5.1.6. One by Ehan (89)
    1.5.1.7. And forty-nine of the Psalms include no mention of its author.

1.5.2. Both Asaph and Heman are noted as authors. They were two of David's chief musicians. We know they both performed music with cymbals. Four of Asaph's sons, the "sons of Asaph" formed a musical guild and were prominent in temple worship, especially as singers. Asaph is said to have "prophesied under the direction of the king," through his music (1 Chronicles 25:2). In addition, we note the "sons of Korah" served as musicians in the temple according to 1 Chronicles 6:31. Ehan we know nothing about.

    1.5.2.1. My dear friend Colleen wrote many songs that have been a blessing to others. I always considered her music as prophetic worship. She is a Psalmist.

1.5.3. The book of Psalms has five divisions (not inspired, however, are from ancient tradition), which most of our English versions utilize. We really do not know the exact reason for the divisions.

    1.5.3.1. Some believe it was because of the length of a scroll

- 1.5.3.2. Some have compared the first section with Genesis, the second with Exodus, etc, (as shown in the basic outline of Psalms), believing they parallel the Pentateuch.
    - 1.5.3.2.1. Genesis and the 1st section of Psalms are concerning MAN
    - 1.5.3.2.2. Exodus and the 2nd section of Psalms are concerning ISRAEL AS A NATION
    - 1.5.3.2.3. Leviticus and the 3rd section of Psalms are concerning THE SANCTUARY
    - 1.5.3.2.4. Numbers and the 4th section of Psalms are concerning ISRAEL AND THE NATION
    - 1.5.3.2.5. Deuteronomy and the 5th section of Psalms are concerning GOD AND HIS WORD
- 1.5.4. Each book ends with a closing or doxology, which comprise a rewarding personal study.
- 1.6. I have taught many times on the last few Psalms, which are wonderful praise, ending with these words *Let everything that has breath praise the Lord. Praise the Lord!* (Psalms 150:6). And I alwarys ask: "Do *you* have breath?" Simple...but a dynamic for every person in the world to think about!
    - 1.6.1. There are many types of praise. Let me offer seven distinct Hebrew words**,** which we translate "praise." Together they give us a very full and rich picture of Bible praise. Praise is also the **KEY WORD** of Psalms.

EXPANDED HELP PAPER
Seven Hebrew Words of Praise

Praise is God's method to bind together His family. Everything else falls into insignificance in the midst of praise.

1. In 2 Chronicles 20:19 we see first the Hebrew word HALAL. It means "to make a clear boast, to rave, to be shiny, to celebrate, or to be clamorously foolish."
    a. A young man came to me one time, he met his first love.
    b. His words were "Oh my! She's the one!" "She will complete my life." He went on and on about her, exploring her tiny earlobes, caverns of her dimples, and the pools of her deep eyes.
    c. This guy was convinced, clamorously foolish, boasting.
    d. I dare you to boast for God, brag on Him, boast of Him.

Psalms

      e. Concerning David in 1 Chron 23:30 *They are to stand every morning to thank and to praise (HALAL) the Lord, and likewise at evening;* and in 2 Chron 23:13 *And all the people of the land rejoiced and blew trumpets, the singers with their musical instruments leading the praise (HALAL);* Neh 5:13 *And all the assembly said, "Amen!" And they praised (HALAL) the Lord.*

2. In Psalms 50:23 we find TOWDAH. TOWDAH has some HALAL inside—celebration. It means, "To extend the hand in thanksgiving." It is the lifting of hands with acceptance of fact. It is thanking God for things not yet manifested. Receiving a promise of God, believe it before you experience the result.

3. Found in Psalms 63:3, SHABACH, "to address in a loud tone, to shout." Praise is to include a shout unto the Lord. The emphasis in this word in the volume.
      a. Includes elements of HALAL, but the SHAVBACH voices the celebration loudly. Ps 47:1 *Shout to God with the voice of joy;* Zech 4:7 *he will bring forth the top stone with shouts of "Grace, grace to it!"*
      b. Sometimes we need to look at the mountain in our life and SHABACH. When the enemy comes in like a flood, praise is one of the first places he steals from you. He will attempt to turn HALAL and SHABACH to himself.

4. We find another praise in Ps 72:15, BARAK (baw-rak'). It means "to bow down in worship as an act of adoration." *Let them bless him all day long.*
      a. Praise is certainly not only loudness and boasting and lifting of hands in celebration. This BARAK is bowing down to Him in worship.
      b. An added note of interest, which I discovered years ago: Praise is found in 250 Bible Scriptures. 4 times it is TOWDAH, 3 times it is BARAK. So I concluded, 2% of my time should be TOWDAH, 2% BARAK, and the remaining is to be HALAL and YADAH.

5. Psalms 57:7, ZAMAR, meaning "to rejoice in music before the Lord." It is used "to touch the strings."
      a. God was the originator of the great variety of percussion, wind, brass, and strings. It is glorious to ZAMAR Him with instruments.
      b. Ps 98:5-65 *Sing praises to the Lord with the lyre, With the lyre and the sound of melody. 6 With trumpets and*

the sound of the horn Shout joyfully before the King, the Lord.
- c. Ps 150:3 *Praise Him with trumpet sound; Praise His with harp and lyre. 4. Praise Him with timbrel and dancing; Praise him with stringed instruments and pipe. 5 Praise Him with loud cymbals....*
- d. David *spoke to the chiefs of the Levites to appoint their relatives the singers, with instruments of music, harps, lyres, loud-sounding cymbals, to raise sounds of joy* (1 Chron 15:16)
- e. Each of us is not a professional musician. However, why not fill a jar with stones and shake it to the Lord? Jesus said the very rocks would cry out.
6. Ps 22:3 *Yet You are holy, O You who are enthroned upon the praises of Israel*. TEHILLAH, "to sing you HALAL; a song from your spirit."
7. Ps 134:2, YADAH, "to worship with extended hands."
    - a. Your hands will show forth praises, one way, or another. The opposite of YADAH is a word meaning "to wring the hands in whimpering defeat."
    - b. So you have a choice to make in worship; Use them in praise, extending them to God, or let them hang down in defeat! Ps 47:1 *O clap your hands, all peoples*; Ps 63:4 *I will lift up my hands in Your name.*

1.8. The book of Psalms includes many types of Psalms and a variety of teachings. Let me offer a few of the types:

1.8.1. There are Psalms concerning **nature**, such as Psalms 8 and 19. Perhaps the most complete of the nature Psalms is 104. It could be read along with Genesis 1. The order of the days of creation is observed, with only one exception (life in the sea after that on dry land). Read this vivid description in the note.[1]

---

[1] *1 You are clothed with splendor and majesty,*
2 Covering Yourself with light as with a cloak,
Stretching out heaven like a tent curtain.
3 He lays the beams of His upper chambers in the waters;
He makes the clouds His chariot;
He walks upon the wings of the wind;
4 He makes the winds His messengers,
5 He established the earth upon its foundations,
So that it will not totter forever and ever.

Psalms

1.8.2. There are Psalms, which are **national**; to the Hebrews, religion and politics were inseparable. What a shame we separate the two in our day. It was not the intention of the founders of our nation.

    1.8.2.1. Can you imagine if we would have let it alone? Can't you just see our country where true worship was a part of every "House of Representatives" session?

    1.8.2.2. National Psalms such as 46. The opening line *"God is our refuge and strength,"* inspired Martin Luther's great hymn *"A Mighty Fortress Is Our God."*

    1.8.2.3. Martin Luther began his career lecturing on Psalms 118. Later at the point of death, he sang out these words: "God is our refuge and strength." Read the words of his inspiring hymn:

---

1 A mighty fortress is our God,
A bulwark never failing;
Our helper He amid the flood
Of mortal ills prevailing.
For still our ancient foe
Doth seek to work us woe --
His craft and pow'r are great,
And armed with cruel hate,
On earth is not his equal.

---

2 Did we in our own strength confide
Our striving would be losing,
Were not the right Man on our side,
The Man of God's own choosing.
Dost ask who that may be?
Christ Jesus, it is He --
Lord Sabaoth His name,
From age to age the same --
And He must win the battle.

---

3 And tho this world, with devils filled,
Should threaten to undo us,
We will not fear, for God hath willed
His truth to triumph thru us.
The prince of darkness grim --
We tremble not for him;
His rage we can endure,
For lo! his doom is sure --
One little word shall fell him.

---

4 That word above all earthly pow'rs --
No thanks to them abideth;
The Spirit and the gifts are ours
Thru Him who with us sideth.
Let goods and kindred go,
This mortal life also;
The body they may kill:
God's truth abideth still --
His kingdom is forever.

The mountains rose; the valleys sank down
To the place which You established for them.
He sends forth springs in the valleys;
He causes the grass to grow for the cattle,
And vegetation for the labor of man

1.8.2.4. John Calvin suffering from asthma and being down-hearted at the suffering of his friends quoted Psalms 39:9.[1]

1.8.2.5. Later he said, *"I may truly call the book of Psalms an anatomy of all the parts of the soul, for no one can describe a movement of the Spirit which is not reflected in this mirror."*

1.8.3. Another type of Psalms was called **penitential**.[2] Sometimes, in our current day, we do not completely understand the Psalmist's concern with sin. *Sin was called sin*. We find the Psalmist looking honestly into the depths of his being, not enjoying what he sees, and asking God for forgiveness.

1.8.3.1. In our day we call drunkenness *a disease*, divorce is *maladjustment*, ill temper is *frustration*, and immortality is *self-expression*. However, in the Psalmists' day, sin was sin. Three words permeate the penitential Psalms along with three companion words of pardon:

1.8.3.1.1. *Transgression*, a revolt against God's instructions. "Blot out" means to erase the transgression.

1.8.3.1.2. *Iniquity*, the state of an evil presence, which will destroy all good qualities. "Purge" and "wash" which will purify from all iniquity. Resist the enemy, he will flee.

1.8.3.1.3. *Sin*, falling short of the goal, missing His mark for us. "Cleanse me" will create a new life, forgiven of the sin.

1.8.3.2. Examples of Penitential Psalms include Psalms 6, 32 and 38.[3]

---

[1] Psalms 39:9 *I have become mute, I do not open my mouth, 10 Remove Your plague from me; Because of the opposition of Your hand I am perishing.*
[2] Repentance
[3] Psalms 6:4 *Return, O Lord, rescue my soul;*
Save me because of Your lovingkindness.
Psalms 38:18 *For I confess my iniquity;*
I am full of anxiety because of my sin.
And I love the forgiveness and love of God in Psalms 40:1-3
I waited patiently for the Lord;
And He inclined to me and heard my cry.
2 He brought me up out of the pit of destruction, out of the miry clay,
And He set my feet upon a rock making my footsteps firm.
3 He put a new song in my mouth, a song of praise to our God;
Many will see and fear
And will trust in the Lord.

Psalms

1.8.4. Then a final type of Psalms, which is quite interesting and enlightening: The **Royal** *or Messianic Psalms*.

    1.8.4.1. We could take quite an extended journey through the whole book of Psalms noticing and thinking ...about Jesus and providing details of His life.

    1.8.4.2. Psalms 22:16 sees the piercing of Christ's hands and feet.

    1.8.4.3. The gambling of soldiers for Christ's garments is foretold in Psalms 22:18.

    1.8.4.4. His cry of distress is an echo of Psalms 22:1

    1.8.4.5. Psalms 110 is a striking Psalms with reference to a Messianic King. Jesus used it in argument with the Jews of His day.[1]

    1.8.4.6. We see in this Psalm, The Messiah, the Anointed One, is to occupy a seat of honor at the right hand of God, sharing His glory, victorious over His enemies.

EXPANDED HELP PAPER
Information on Psalms

Refer to the following lists to assist in the study of Psalms.

(1) From Wilkinson and Boa (*Talk thru the Bible*) showing **Christ in Psalms**

(2) Prophecies of Christ (**Messianic Prophecies**)

(3) **Images of God in the Psalms**

(4) A **theme** for each of the 150 Psalms, which will allow you to refer quickly to a Psalms you might need. This is an excellent study in its self

(1) Christ in Psalms

Many of the Psalms specifically anticipated the life and ministry of Jesus Christ, the One who came centuries later as Israel's promised Messiah ("anointed one"). The Psalms, like the four Gospels, give several perspectives on the person and work of Christ:

- **Psalms:** *Jesus Christ, the King* **(portrayed in Matthew)**

---

[1] Psalms 110:1-2 *The Lord says to my Lord:*
"Sit at My right hand Until I make Your enemies a footstool for Your feet."
2 *The Lord will stretch forth Your strong scepter from Zion, saying,*
"Rule in the midst of Your enemies."

Psalms 2: Christ rejected as King by the nations	Psalms 24: Christ is King of Glory
Psalms 18: Christ is Protector and Deliverer	Psalms 47: Christ rules in His kingdom
Psalms 20: Christ provides salvation	Psalms 110: Christ is King-Priest
Psalms 21: Christ is given glory by God	Psalms 132: Christ is enthroned

- **Psalms: *Jesus Christ, the Servant* (portrayed in Mark)**

Psalms 17: Christ is Intercessor	Psalms 41: Christ is betrayed by a close friend
Psalms 22: Christ is the dying Savior	Psalms 69: Christ is hated without a cause
Psalms 23: Christ is Shepherd	Psalms 109: Christ loves those who reject Him
Psalms 40: Christ is obedient unto death	

- **Psalms: *Jesus Christ, the Son of God* (portrayed in Luke)**

Psalms 8: Christ is made a little lower than angels	Psalms 40: Christ's resurrection is realized
Psalms 16: Christ's resurrection is promised	

- **Psalms: *Jesus Christ, the Son of God* (portrayed in John)**

Psalms 19: Christ is Creator	Psalms 118: Christ is the Chief Cornerstone
Psalms 102: Christ is eternal	

(2) Messianic Prophecies In Psalms

There are five different kinds of messianic Psalms: (1) *Typical messianic*. The subject of the Psalms is in some feature a type of Christ (34:20; 69:4, 9). (2) *Typical prophetic*. The Psalmist uses language to describe his present experience, which points beyond his own life and becomes historically true only in Christ (22). (3) *Indirectly messianic*. At the time of composition, the Psalms referred to a king or the house of David in general but awaits final fulfillment in Christ (2, 45, and 72). (4) *Purely prophetic*. Refers solely to Christ without reference to any other son of David (110). (5) *Enthronement*. Anticipates the coming of Yahweh and the consummation of His kingdom—will be fulfilled in the person of Christ (96–99).

The following table summarized from Bruce Wilkinson and Kenneth Boa, *Talk Thru the Bible*. Nashville: T. Nelson, 1983, p. 155

Psalms	Prophecy	Fulfillment
2:7	God will declare Him to be His Son	Matthew 3:17
8:6	All things will be put under His feet	Hebrews 2:8
16:10	He will be resurrected from the dead	Mark 16:6–7
22:1	God will forsake Him in His hour of need	Matthew 27:46
22:7–8	He will be scorned and mocked	Luke 23:35
22:16	His hands and feet will be pierced	John 20:25, 27
22:18	Others will gamble for His clothes	Matthew 27:35–36
34:20	Not one of His bones will be broken	John 19:32–33, 36
35:11	He will be accused by false witnesses	Mark 14:57
35:19	He will be hated without a cause	John 15:25
40:7–8	He will come to do God's will	Hebrews 10:7
41:9	He will be betrayed by a friend	Luke 22:47
45:6	His throne will be forever	Hebrews 1:8
68:18	He will ascend to God's right hand	Mark 16:19
69:9	Zeal for God's house will consume Him	John 2:17
69:21	He will be given vinegar and gall to drink	Matthew 27:34
109:4	He will pray for His enemies	Luke 23:34
109:8	His betrayer's office will be fulfilled by another	Acts 1:20
110:1	His enemies will be made subject to Him	Matthew 22:44
110:4	He will be a priest like	Hebrews 5:6

	Melchizedek	
118:22	He will be the chief cornerstone	Matthew 21:42
118:26	He will come in the name of the LORD	Matthew 21:9

Note that Jesus referred to the Psalms on several occasions:
- ✓ The Beatitudes, Matthew 21:42 from Psalms 118:2
- ✓ John 2:17 from Psalms 89:9
- ✓ Matthew 13:35 from Psalms 78:2
- ✓ He closed His ministry with Psalms 22:1

(3) Images of God in Psalms

Images of God as	Reference in Psalms
Shield	3:3; 28:7; 119:114
Rock	18:2; 42:9; 95:1
King	5:2; 44:4; 74:12
Shepherd	23:1; 80:1
Judge	7:11
Refuge	46:1; 62:7
Fortress	31:3; 71:3
Avenger	26:1
Creator	8:1, 6
Deliverer	37:39, 40
Healer	30:2
Protector	5:11
Provider	78:23–29
Redeemer	107:2

(4) Theme of Each Psalm

Book One: Psalms 1–41

Psalms

1. Two Ways of Life Contrasted
2. Coronation of the Lord's Anointed
3. Victory in the Face of Defeat
4. Evening Prayer for Deliverance
5. Morning Prayer for Guidance
6. Prayer for God's Mercy
7. Wickedness Justly Rewarded
8. God's Glory and Man's Dominion
9. Praise for Victory over Enemies
10. Petition for God's Judgment
11. God Tests the Sons of Men
12. The Pure Words of the Lord
13. The Prayer for God's Answer—Now
14. The Characteristics of the Godless
15. The Characteristics of the Godly
16. Eternal Life for One Who Trusts
17. "Hide Me Under the Shadow of Your Wings"
18. Thanksgiving for Deliverance by God
19. The Works and Words of God
20. Trust Not in Chariots and Horses but in God
21. Triumph of the King
22. Psalms of the Cross

23. Psalms of the Divine Shepherd

24. Psalms of the King of Glory

25. Acrostic Prayer for Instruction

26. "Examine Me, O Lord, and Prove Me

27. Trust in the Lord and Be Not Afraid

28. Rejoice Because of Answered Prayer

29. The Powerful Voice of God

30. Praise for Dramatic Deliverance

31. "Be of Good Courage"

32. The Blessedness of Forgiveness

33. God Considers All Man's Works

34. Seek the Lord

35. Petition for God's Intervention

36. The Excellent Lovingkindness of God

37. "Rest in the Lord"

38. The Heavy Burden of Sin

39. Know the Measure of Man's Days

40. Delight to Do God's Will

41. The Blessedness of Helping the Poor

Book Two: Psalms 42–72

42. Seek After the Lord

43. "Hope in God!"

Psalms

44. Prayer for Deliverance by God

45. The Psalms of the Great King

46. "God Is Our Refuge and Strength"

47. The Lord Shall Subdue All Nations

48. The Praise of Mount Zion

49. Riches Cannot Redeem

50. The Lord Shall Judge All People

51. Confession and Forgiveness of Sin

52. The Lord Shall Judge the Deceitful

53. A Portrait of the Godless

54. The Lord Is Our Helper

55. "Cast Your Burden on the Lord"

56. Fears in the Midst of Trials

57. Prayers in the Midst of Perils

58. Wicked Judges Will Be Judged

59. Petition for Deliverance from Violent Men

60. A Prayer for Deliverance of the Nation

61. A Prayer When Overwhelmed

62. Wait for God

63. Thirst for God

64. A Prayer for God's Protection

65. God's Provision Through Nature

TRAVEL THROUGH THE OLD TESTAMENT

66. Remember What God Has Done

67. God Shall Govern the Earth

68. God Is the Father of the Fatherless

69. Petition for God to Draw Near

70. Prayer for the Poor and Needy

71. Prayer for the Aged

72. The Reign of the Messiah

Book Three: Psalms 73–89

73. The Perspective of Eternity

74. Request for God to Remember His Covenant

75. "God Is the Judge"

76. The Glorious Might of God

77. When Overwhelmed, Remember God's Greatness

78. God's Continued Guidance in Spite of Unbelief

79. Avenge the Defilement of Jerusalem

80. Israel's Plea for God's Mercy

81. God's Plea for Israel's Obedience

82. Rebuke of Israel's Unjust Judges

83. Plea for God to Destroy Israel's Enemies

84. The Joy of Dwelling with God

85. Prayer for Revival

86. "Teach Me Your Way, O Lord"

Psalms

87. Glorious Zion, City of God

88. Crying from Deepest Affliction

89. Claiming God's Promises in Affliction

Book Four: Psalms 90–106

90. "Teach Us to Number Our Days"

91. Abiding in "the Shadow of the Almighty

92. It Is Good to Praise the Lord

93. The Majesty of God

94. Vengeance Belongs Only to God

95. Call to Worship the Lord

96. Declare the Glory of God

97. Rejoice! The Lord Reigns!

98. Sing a New Song to the Lord

99. "Exalt the Lord Our God"

100. "Serve the Lord with Gladness"

101. Commitments of a Holy Life

102. Prayer of an Overwhelmed Saint

103. Bless the Lord, All You People!

104. Psalms Rehearsing Creation

105. Remember, God Keeps His Promises

106. "We Have Sinned"

Book Five: Psalms 107–150

TRAVEL THROUGH THE OLD TESTAMENT

107. God Satisfies the Longing Soul

108. Awake Early and Praise the Lord

109. Song of the Slandered

110. The Coming of the Priest-King-Judge

111. Praise for God's Tender Care

112. The Blessings of Those Who Fear God

113. The Condescending Grace of God

114. In Praise for the Exodus

115. To God Alone Be the Glory

116. Love the Lord for What He Has Done

117. The Praise of All Peoples

118. Better to Trust God than Man

119. An Acrostic in Praise of the Scriptures

120. A Cry in Distress

121. God Is Our Keeper

122. "Pray for the Peace of Jerusalem"

123. Plea for the Mercy of God

124. God Is on Our Side

125. Trust in the Lord and Abide Forever

126. "Sow in Tears … Reap in Joy"

127. Children Are God's Heritage

128. Blessing on the House of the God-Fearing

Psalms

129. Plea of the Persecuted

130. "My Soul Waits for the Lord"

131. A Childlike Faith

132. Trust in the God of David

133. Beauty of the Unity of the Brethren

134. Praise the Lord in the Evening

135. God Has Done Great Things!

136. God's Mercy Endures Forever

137. Tears in Exile

138. God Answered My Prayer

139. "Search Me, O God"

140. Preserve Me from Violence

141. "Set a Guard, O Lord, over My Mouth"

142. "No One Cares for My Soul"

143. "Teach Me to Do Your Will"

144. "What Is Man?"

145. Testify to God's Great Acts

146. "Do Not Put Your Trust in Princes"

147. God Heals the Brokenhearted

148. All Creation Praises the Lord

149. "The Lord Takes Pleasure in His People"

150. "Praise the Lord"

1.9. The teachings included in Psalms are amazing. Most believers have referred to this book for encouragement. For example, [1]

    1.9.1. Teachings about the nature and existence of God such as Psalms 94:9-10. The God of the Psalmist is a personal God. He knows us, feels our hurts, sees our life, fellowships with us, and listens to us.

    1.9.2. Teaching about God as a personal God, Psalms 139:17-18.

    1.9.3. His help to each of us, Psalms 34:15. He is our refuge, Psalms 46:1.

    1.9.4. They also teach us about the nature of man, such as Psalms 51. Nowhere did the Hebrews make any attempt to justify the sins and flaws of their national heroes. Abraham, Moses, and David are seen in a factual, realistic manner; shocking some times, but truthful. The Psalmist knew human nature, including himself.[2]

    1.9.5. He and his parents are part of human inherited sin. Conception or birth is not an act of sin.

    1.9.6. Fellowship with God, Psalms 42:1 and 63:1. A craving for fellowship with the Father is repeated over and over is the book.

    1.9.7. Delight in public worship and fellowship is expressed in Psalms 84. It is full of phrases describing the joy of spiritual worship and the strength, which flows into the life of the worshipper.[3]

    1.9.8. And future life is dealt with in Psalms 6:5, 30:9 and 16:10-11

    1.9.9. On and on are the teachings in this great Song Book of Israel. We know of the education we receive by daily reading this book. The Psalms are timeless in their appeal and universal of their influence. Their use is extensive.

    1.9.10. "Pilgrim Songs" of Israel were sung while traveling to Jerusalem for festivals. Psalms 120-134 are a collection of these songs. One of the most appealing is Psalms 126

---

[1] Psalms 23:4 *I fear no evil, for You are with me; Your rod and Your staff, they comfort me.*
[2] Psalms 51:5 *Behold, I was brought forth in iniquity,*
And in sin my mother conceived me.
[3] Psalms 84:3-4-5 *My King and my God.*
4 How blessed are those who dwell in Your house!
They are ever praising You.
5 How blessed is the man whose strength is in You,

Psalms

expressing the spirit of exiles returning to their native land. Their memories were stirred as they sang:[1]

1.9.11. "Temple Worship"; The Temple was the center of worship. Imagine Psalms 24 being sung in responsive hymn.

1.9.12. "Private Worship" in the Temple was encouraged. Imagine a worshipper singing Psalms 66:16-20.

1.9.13. Carlyle in referring to Psalms said *"one of the grandest things every written with the pen."*[2]

2. In summary, we emphasize the vital place of Psalms in the life of every believer.

2.1. There are over four hundred quotations or indirect references to the Psalms in the New Testament.

2.1.1. Jesus quoted from the book of Psalms on many occasions (e.g. Matt 5:5/Ps 37:11; John 15:25/Ps 69:4)

2.1.2. His assistance was issued from Psalms when the new church chose a new apostle (Acts 1:15; Ps 69:25; 109:8).

2.1.3. The new church also used the Psalms to reinforce their preaching (Acts 2:31; Ps 16:10) and to find encouragement in times of persecution (Acts 4:23–31; Ps 2). Singing selected Psalms was a part of their worship (Eph 5:19; Col 3:16; 1 Cor 14:26)

2.2. It is quite beneficial to study Bible history from the viewpoint of the Psalmists:

2.2.1. Creation (8)
2.2.2. The flood (29)
2.2.3. The patriarchs (47:9, 105:9, 47:4)
2.2.4. The exodus (114)
2.2.5. The wilderness wanderings (68:7, 106)
2.2.6. The captivity (85, 137)

---

[1] *Psalms 126:1 When the Lord brought back the captive ones of Zion,*
We were like those who dream.
2 Then our mouth was filled with laughter
And our tongue with joyful shouting;
Then they said among the nations,
"The Lord has done great things for them."
3 The Lord has done great things for us;
We are glad.
4 Restore our captivity, O Lord,
As the streams in the South.
5 Those who sow in tears shall reap with joyful shouting.
6 He who goes to and fro weeping, carrying his bag of seed,
Shall indeed come again with a shout of joy, bringing his sheaves with him.

[2] Thomas Carlyle, Scottish Philosopher, 1795-1881; exact location of quote unknown

2.3. In addition, the Psalms are about God and His relationship to His entire creation, in particular, His believing people. He is seen as a loving God and tenderhearted Father, a faithful God who keeps His promises. The Psalms reveal the hearts of those who follow Him, their faith and doubts, their victories and failures, and their hopes for the glorious future.

SECTION 2
Wisdom

Proverbs, Ecclesiastes, Song of Solomon (Songs).

Theme Statement: *"...hear the words of the wise."* (Proverbs 22:17)

THE KEYS IN SECTION TWO

Section 2: Wisdom

Keys to Proverbs—

   A Key Word: *Wisdom*

   The Key Verses (1:5–7; 3:5–6)

1:5 A wise man will hear and increase in learning, And a man of understanding will acquire wise counsel, 6 To understand a proverb and a figure, The words of the wise and their riddles. 7 The fear of the Lord is the beginning of knowledge; Fools despise wisdom and instruction.

3:5 Trust in the Lord with all your heart And do not lean on your own understanding. 6 In all your ways acknowledge Him, And He will make your paths straight.

   The Key Chapter (31)

   The Key People in Proverbs

Solomon-king of Israel asked for, received, great wisdom from God (1 Kings 4:20-34)

Agur-son of Jakeh (30:1)

Lemuel-king whose mother's teachings are included in chapter 31. Some identify this as Solomon; otherwise unknown.

Keys to Ecclesiastes—

   A Key Word: *Vanity*

The Key Verses (2:24; 12:13–14)

2:24 There is nothing better for a man than to eat and drink and tell himself that his labor is good. This also I have seen that it is from the hand of God.

12:13 The conclusion, when all has been heard, is: fear God and keep His commandments, because this applies to every person. 14 For God will bring every act to judgment, everything which is hidden, whether it is good or evil.

Key Chapter (12)

The Key Person in Ecclesiastes

Solomon-king of Israel asked for and received great wisdom from God. Became the wisest person ever born (1:1-14)

Keys to Song of Solomon—

A Key Word: *Beloved*

The Key Verses (7:10; 8:7)

7:10 "I am my beloved's, And his desire is for me.

8:7 Many waters cannot quench love, Nor will rivers overflow it; If a man were to give all the riches of his house for love, It would be utterly despised."

The Key Chapter—Since the whole book is a unity, there is no Key Chapter; rather, all eight beautifully depict the love of a married couple.

The Key People in Song of Solomon

King Solomon-identified as king in several verses; called "beloved"; type of the bridegroom

Shulamite woman-the (probably first) bride of King Solomon (1:1-8:13)

Daughters of Jerusalem-young women who encouraged their friend to go to King Solomon. (1:4; 2:14; 3:5, 11; 5:1, 8; 6:1; 8:4)

THREE

Wisdom From Proverbs

1. We continue our "travels" with **Section 2** of our study course. This section is entitled **WISDOM.**
2. In this section, we will include Proverbs, Ecclesiastes, and Song of Solomon. The book of Job, considered part of the Wisdom Books, was reviewed in Volume 1 for chronological purposes. The theme statement for these three books comes from Proverbs 22:17 *hear the words of the wise.* We will not attempt any specific time period for these books, similar to the previous Section 1. They are related to the general period we are considering.

A Basic Outline of Proverbs
SEVEN DIVISIONS

1. The Proverbs of Solomon, son of David 1-9
2. The Proverbs of Solomon 10-22a
3. The Words of the Wise 22b-24
4. The Proverbs of Solomon, transcribed by King Hezekiah 25-29
5. The Words of Agur 30
6. The Words of King Lemuel 31:1-9
7. The Christian Woman 31:10-31

Depth of Bible Words and Locations
Proverbs Key Word: *Wisdom*

Of course, the KEY WORD in Proverbs is *Wisdom*. The Hebrew word carries a meaning of "skill." It may be wisdom in a trade (Ezekiel 28:4, 5), ability (Exodus 31:6), or even war (Isaiah 10:13). However, the most common wisdom would be in daily living—what we do when it is aligned with His Word is wisdom. It is an ability to judge correctly and follow the best course of action, based on knowledge and understanding of His Word.

The greatest reward that comes from wisdom is the fear and knowledge of God (Proverbs 2:5). Wisdom then is vitally connected with knowing God and having a proper relationship with Him. The biblical concept of wisdom is quite different from the classical view of wisdom, which is sought through philosophy and man's rational thought to determine the mysteries of existence and the universe.

The first principle of biblical wisdom is that man should humble himself before God in reverence and worship, obedient to His commands. The source of real wisdom is God who by it, numbered the clouds (Job 38:37), founded the earth (Proverbs 3:19), and made the world (Jeremiah 10:12).

How do we receive wisdom? (Proverbs 2:6)
How does wisdom help us? (Proverbs 2:7, 8)
What else do we have if we have wisdom first? (Proverbs 2:9)

> *Jesus in Proverbs and Ecclesiastes...He is your Wisdom. Trust His Word for every step of your life's journey.*

2.1. The Wisdom Literature deal with the great issues of life: Where we LIVE. Both sides of life are explored. Blessings...and...troubling times. Everyone has some suffering...that's life. The Scriptures include a believer's reaction to difficult times.
2.1.1. These books are concerned with the practical ethics, including God-likeness, integrity, morality, and character.
2.1.2. The meaning of life and love.
2.1.3. This indeed is a rich section of our journey.
2.2. In these books, we hear the very carefully presented thoughts and teachings of those who were called *"the wise men of Israel."*
2.2.1. They were not priests,
2.2.2. They were not prophets,
2.2.3. They had no part in the Temple work,
2.2.4. They conducted no formal schools for teaching.
2.2.5. They worked in the streets and homes, one-on-one, teaching the truth, showing the truth and real living...real life.
2.3. From these men grew a treasury of truth referred to as "Wisdom Literature."
2.3.1. Wisdom in Hebrew is not what other societies thought it to be. To many, including the Greek, it was a philosophy dealing with human reason. However, to the Hebrew, it was revealed truth.
2.3.2. So the Jews had no philosophers; the Greeks had no prophets.

Proverbs

2.3.3. The Hebrew wise man presented truth with the simple assurance of what was seen, rather than what he thought. He presented what he saw and what was revealed...as truth.
3   Our travels bring us to the book of Proverbs, perhaps read more than any Old Testament book, other than Psalms.
3.1. The Jews thought of Proverbs as The outer Court
3.2. Ecclesiastes as the Holy Place
3.3. Song of Solomon as the Holy of Holies.
3.4. To the Hebrews, the proverb had a broad meaning. It meant a likeness, comparison, or symbolic saying such as Jeremiah 31:20 and Ezekiel 18:2.
  3.4.1. Because there are 31 chapters, for years I took one-a-day for my health! I always knew that on August 15 I had a great word of wisdom, Proverbs 15. When the calendar read December 10, I knew Proverbs 10 was for me.
  3.4.2. Proverbs is a collection of Hebrew wisdom, most of it written by Solomon. He is associated with the Book of Proverbs from the very first verse. He was no doubt influenced by the Psalms-writing of his father, David.
  3.4.3. Actually, Solomon has left us more Scripture than any other Old Testament writer except Moses. Certainly, his strengths were not on the battlefield but in the realm of the mind: planning, negotiation, and organization.
    3.4.3.1. Solomon greatly expanded the Kingdom of Israel.
    3.4.3.2. He constructed the Temple.
    3.4.3.3. He built a palace.
    3.4.3.4. He placed strategic cities, many have been located by archeologists.
3.5. The book of Proverbs did not become its final form until at least the reign of Hezekiah.[1]
  3.5.1. We conclude that it would have been finalized during or after King Hezekiah's time, around 700 BCE
  3.5.2. 1 Kings 4:32 informs us of 3,000 proverbs and more than 1,000 songs penned by Solomon, so we do not have them all. There is a book named *Wisdom of Solomon* in the Apocrypha books, quite similar to Proverbs. It has many more of Solomon's proverbs; however, the book was not accepted into the canon of Scripture. Understand that we can be quite confident knowing we have exactly what God wanted us to have!

---

[1] Proverbs 25:1 *These also are proverbs of Solomon which the men of Hezekiah, king of Judah, transcribed.*

3.5.2.1. Solomon, by direction of the Holy Spirit, collected many wise sayings from many nations. Ecclesiastes 12:9-10 reads *In addition to being a wise man, the Preacher also taught the people knowledge; and he pondered, searched out and arranged many proverbs. 10 The Preacher sought to find delightful words and to write words of truth correctly.*

3.6. A proverb, to the Hebrews, meant "a likeness, a comparison, or symbolic saying."

3.6.1. For example Jeremiah 31:29 and Ezekiel 18:2 is each a proverb: *The fathers have eaten sour grapes, And the children's teeth are set on edge.*

3.6.2. There are seven subtitles dividing Proverbs by content. It is the outline we will briefly overview.

3.7. Each of the seven sections includes a specific type of Proverb:

3.7.1. The **first Section** consists of the first nine cps beginning with the subtitle *The proverbs of Solomon the son of David, king of Israel:*

3.7.1.1. These serve as a long introduction to the book, centered on the moral truth we should apply to life. The section begins the advice to the young person while still at home; the dangers he faces and suggesting wisdom as a guide.

3.7.2. Chapter 10 begins the **second Section**, with the words *The proverbs of Solomon*, and includes the next twelve and one-half cps. These 375 proverbs seem to be a large collection without any particular organization. We generally expect proverbs to concern a specific subject to be grouped as one; however, this Section has subjects interspersed throughout.

3.7.2.1. This is considered the central part of the book and is individual proverbs in couplet form, generally based on contrast.[1]

3.7.3. **Section three** begins with Proverbs 22:17 *Incline your ear and hear the words of the wise,*[2]

3.7.3.1. This brief section takes us through cp 24. Advice is given on many topics including the fear and awesome reverence of God.

3.7.3.2. They are in the form of a statement of a single idea, each being an individual proverb. They seem to be instructions, not in the short

---

[1] A few examples would include cp 16:1 *The plans of the heart belong to man, But the answer of the tongue is from the Lord.*
15:16 *Better is a little with the fear of the Lord Than great treasure and turmoil with it.*
15:28 *The heart of the righteous ponders how to answer, But the mouth of the wicked pours out evil things.*
Those are all couplets.

[2] It is interesting to note, Proverbs 22:17-24:22 is almost identical to a book discovered in Egypt, written about 600 BCE.

Proverbs

couplet form, but rather extending the subject for four, five, or even six more lines.[1]

3.7.4. **Section four** includes cps 25-29. This section begins *These also are proverbs of Solomon which the men of Hezekiah, king of Judah, transcribed.*

    3.7.4.1. This is another collection of Solomon's wisdom, but quite different from his other proverbs. This section was composed by Solomon, but copied and included later by Judah's king Hezekiah.

    3.7.4.2. Where he used the two line couplets before, now he extends his sayings in some cases to nine or ten verses.

    3.7.4.3. There seems to be an attempt to group this section into subjects. For example, the first seven verses of cp 26 deal with fools; another section verses 18-28 centers around a deceiving flatterer.

    3.7.4.4. He seems also to deal more with the practical topics rather than a spiritual or religious side. 28:19 reads *He who tills his land will have plenty of food, But he who follows empty pursuits will have poverty in plenty.* Practical matters of life.

3.7.5. **Section five** is chapter 30 with a heading that states The *words of Agur the son of Jakeh, the oracle.*[2]

    3.7.5.1. The form in this section is rather peculiar. It actually begins with four verses of a skeptic's unbelief of God, and immediately followed by a rebuke of his attitude as a result of the light of revelation and prayer! Wow. Maybe we should read this one.

> Proverbs 30:2-6 *Surely I am more stupid than any man,*
> *And I do not have the understanding of a man. 3 Neither have I learned wisdom,*
> *Nor do I have the knowledge of the Holy One. 4 Who has ascended into heaven and descended?*
> *Who has gathered the wind in His fists? Who has wrapped the waters in His garment? Who has established all the ends of the earth? What is His name or His son's name? Surely you know!*
> And then the rebuke: *5 Every word of God is tested; He is a shield to those who take refuge in Him.*
> *6 Do not add to His words Or He will reprove you, and you will be proved a liar.*

---

[1] For example: Proverbs 22:24 *Do not associate with a man given to anger; Or go with a hot-tempered man,*
25 Or you will learn his ways And find a snare for yourself.
Also 23:4 *Do not weary yourself to gain wealth, Cease from your consideration of it.*
5 When you set your eyes on it, it is gone. For wealth certainly makes itself wings Like an eagle that flies toward the heavens.

[2] Agur here, and then Lemuel who begins the next section, both were non-Hebrew authors. Isn't that interesting? Very little is known about them. Agur seems to be coming to a faith in God in a foreign land. Nothing is known about his father, Jakeh.

3.7.5.2. Quite a proverb, a real lesson for each of us.
3.7.5.3. Most of what follows in this section are called "foursomes" — groups of four things which are alike and which throw light on each other.
3.7.5.3.1. Four kinds of evil men vv. 11-14
3.7.5.3.2. Four greedy things vv. 15-16
3.7.5.3.3. Four mysterious things vv. 18-19
3.7.5.3.4. Four unbearable things vv. 21-23
3.7.5.3.5. Four wise little animals vv. 24-28
3.7.5.3.6. And four stately things vv. 29-31.
3.7.6. **Section six** consists of the first nine verses of cp 31 entitled *The words of King Lemuel, the oracle which his mother taught him...*
3.7.6.1. You know, let's be honest, we have to wonder how God decided what was to be in His word! Why detailed genealogies or numberings of the Israelites? Why Song of Solomon which we will consider next. And why some of these Proverbs? Anyone think that way? Let's just always accept that we have exactly what God wanted us to have! Trust in His sovereignty.
3.7.6.2. He decided what He wanted for us
3.7.6.3. Each word is for our benefit
3.7.6.4. Every Word is breathed by Him
3.7.6.5. Each person was important to Him
3.7.6.6. He preserved exactly what we are to have today.
3.7.6.7. This short section six is to champion the cause of the helpless.[1] Also warnings against sensuality and wine drinking.
3.7.7. The **seventh and final section** has no title but clearly, is set off from the rest. What a great section! The single subject centers on the praise of a moral woman. Used many times during a Christian woman's funeral.
3.7.7.1. It is also written in the unusual method, an acrostic poem, twenty-two verses beginning with each successive letter of the Hebrew alphabet. THIS IS A REAL LADY described using the entire Hebrew alphabet![2]
3.7.8. There are many teachings in this book of Proverbs. They sweep the whole horizon of practical, everyday life, touching on about every facet of human existence.
3.7.8.1. There are teachings **about God**
3.7.8.1.1. The power behind creation and nature

---

[1] *Open your mouth, judge righteously, And defend the rights of the afflicted and needy.*
[2] Forgive me for a personal reference...I've said it to God many times...my wife truly is referred to in this Proverb. Of course, many of you ladies are here also! A great section for every young girl to read.

Proverbs

- 3.7.8.1.2. His rulership is certain
- 3.7.8.1.3. He hates evil
- 3.7.8.1.4. He is the champion of those in need. Let's read some specifics:[1]
- 3.7.8.2. There are teachings **about man**
- 3.7.8.2.1. Great insights into the nature of man, which help US today.[2]
- 3.7.8.3. There are teachings, **about education and religion.**
- 3.7.8.3.1. Every man
- 3.7.8.3.2. Every woman
- 3.7.8.3.3. And every child needs growth, needs education. We all need training.[3]
- 3.7.9. Of course, the many great proverbs concerning the **Words of Our Mouth,** see the following Expanded Help Paper, using some of the Proverb Scriptures.

EXPANDED HELP PAPER
The Words of Our Mouth According to Proverbs

Proverbs 4:24

Put away from you a deceitful mouth

And put devious speech far from you.

Proverbs 6:2

If you have been snared with the words of your mouth,

Have been caught with the words of your mouth,

Proverbs 8:6-7

"Listen, for I will speak noble things;

And the opening of my lips will reveal right things.

7 "For my mouth will utter truth;

And wickedness is an abomination to my lips.

Proverbs 10:11

---

[1] 5:21 *For the ways of a man are before the eyes of the Lord, And He watches all his paths.*
3:19 *The Lord by wisdom founded the earth, By understanding He established the heavens.*
21:1 *The king's heart is like channels of water in the hand of the Lord; He turns it wherever He wishes.*
[2] 21:2 *Every man's way is right in his own eyes, But the Lord weighs the hearts.*
17:22 *A joyful heart is good medicine, But a broken spirit dries up the bones.*
[3] 14:8 *The wisdom of the sensible is to understand his way, But the foolishness of fools is deceit.*
14:6 *A scoffer seeks wisdom and finds none, But knowledge is easy to one who has understanding.*
22:6 *Train up a child in the way he should go, Even when he is old he will not depart from it.*
29:15 *The rod and reproof give wisdom, But a child who gets his own way brings shame to his mother.*

The mouth of the righteous is a fountain of life,
Proverbs 10:19
When there are many words, transgression is unavoidable,
But he who restrains his lips is wise.
Proverbs 10:20
The tongue of the righteous is as choice silver,
Proverbs 12:18
There is one who speaks rashly like the thrusts of a sword,
But the tongue of the wise brings healing.
Proverbs 12:13-14
An evil man is ensnared by the transgression of his lips,
But the righteous will escape from trouble.
14 A man will be satisfied with good by the fruit of his words, And the deeds of a man's hands will return to him.
Proverbs 13:2
From the fruit of a man's mouth he enjoys good,
Proverbs 15:4
A soothing tongue is a tree of life,
But perversion in it crushes the spirit.
Proverbs 15:26
But pleasant words are pure.
Proverbs 16:21
The wise in heart will be called understanding,
And sweetness of speech increases persuasiveness.
Proverbs 16:24
Pleasant words are a honeycomb,
Sweet to the soul and healing to the bones.
Proverbs 18:21
Death and life are in the power of the tongue,
And those who love it will eat its fruit.
Proverbs 21:23
He who guards his mouth and his tongue,
Guards his soul from troubles.

Proverbs

3.7.10. There are many other miscellaneous teachings about the entire scope of life.
    3.7.10.1. Proverbs 12:4 *An excellent wife is the crown of her husband, But she who shames him is like rottenness in his bones.*
    3.7.10.2. Proverbs 16:32 *He who is slow to anger is better than the mighty, And he who rules his spirit, than he who captures a city.*
    3.7.10.3. Proverbs 19:15 *Laziness casts into a deep sleep, And an idle man will suffer hunger*
    3.7.10.4. Proverbs 23:22 *Listen to your father who begot you, And do not despise your mother when she is old.*
    3.7.10.5. We see here, domestic relation
    3.7.10.6. Hard work contrasted with laziness
    3.7.10.7. Inner control more important than physical strength
    3.7.10.8. Old age is a time of honor and satisfaction for the believer.
    3.7.10.9. I have also included this summary of John MacArthur's list of a **Man's Relationship.** [1]

I. **Man's Relationship to God**
    A. His Trust Prov. 22:19
    B. His Humility Prov. 3:34
    C. His Fear of God Prov. 1:7
    D. His Righteousness Prov. 10:25
    E. His Sin Prov. 28:13
    F. His Obedience Prov. 6:23
    G. Facing Reward Prov. 12:28
    H. Facing Tests Prov. 17:3
    I. Facing Blessing Prov. 10:22
    J. Facing Death Prov. 15:11

II. **Man's Relationship to Himself**
    A. His Character Prov. 20:11
    B. His Wisdom Prov. 1:5
    C. His Foolishness Prov. 26:10, 11
    D. His Speech Prov. 18:21
    E. His Self Control Prov. 6:9–11
    F. His Kindness Prov. 3:3
    G. His Wealth Prov. 11:4
    H. His Pride Prov. 27:1
    I. His Anger Prov. 29:11

---

[1] MacArthur, John: *The MacArthur Bible Handbook*. Nashville, Tenn. : Thomas Nelson Publishers, 2003, S. 163

                J. His Laziness Prov. 13:4
      III. **Man's Relationship to Others**
                A. His Love Prov. 8:17
                B. His Friends Prov. 17:17
                C. His Enemies Prov. 19:27
                D. His Truthfulness Prov. 23:23
                E. His Gossip Prov. 20:19
                F. As a Father Prov. 20:7; 31:2–9
                G. As a Mother Prov. 31:10–31
                H. As Children Prov. 3:1–3
                I. In Educating Children Prov. 4:1–4
                J. In Disciplining Children Prov. 22:6

4   Another thought in closing Proverbs. An interesting thought on a view of Proverbs, which shows a possible continuity and design. It could be that of the journey of a young man confronting the dangers of youth and suggesting wisdom as his guide. It progresses with his life as the book continues:

4.1. A child at home
4.2. Advice while at home
4.3. Facing the world with going forth from the home
4.4. Refusing the "strange woman"
4.5. Learning about business affairs
4.6. Deciding which school to attend
4.7. Principles' of life
4.8. Graduation
4.9. A Wife

FOUR

Wisdom From Ecclesiastes and Song of Solomon

1   The next book is Ecclesiastes.
1.1. The name "Ecclesiastes" rarely was used in history. It was thought to mean "congregation" or "community," even "assembly." Eventually, it just became the well-known Greek word "ecclesia"…of course applied to the New Testament Church. We know the Church is the "called out ones," the "ecclesia." Down thru the years, a few other names were used for the book:
  1.1.1.   "The Meaning of Life"
  1.1.2.   "The Natural Man"
  1.1.3.   "The Philosophy of self-quest," probably an attempt to give an overview of what the book was.

A Basic Outline of Ecclesiastes
1. Solomon's Investigation, 1:12-6:9
2. Solomon's Conclusions, 6:10-12:8
3. Solomon's Advice, 12:9-14

Depth of Bible Words and Locations
Ecclesiastes Key Word: *Vanity*

Vanity, used 37 times, means "vapor" or "breath." One's warm breath vanishing in a cool day. And with this word, the writer of Ecclesiastes describes
        Wealth
        Honor
        Fame, etc

Jeremiah used the same word to denounce idolatry (18:15).
Job used it for the length of life (7:16).
Solomon uses it much more than any other Old Testament writer.

> *Jesus in Proverbs and Ecclesiastes...He is your Wisdom. Trust His Word for every step of life's journey.*

1.2 It is certainly one of the most puzzling books of the Old Testament. A friend of mine said he spent an entire summer in his Sunday school class teaching Ecclesiastes. I cannot imagine!

1.3 The likely author was Solomon because of the reading of the opening line and other references:

    1.3.1 *The words of the Preacher, the son of David, king in Jerusalem*

    1.3.2 Verse 12 states *I, the Preacher, have been king over Israel in Jerusal*em

    1.3.3 Then 2:9 *Then I became great and increased more than all who preceded me in Jerusalem*

    1.3.4 These Scriptures, along with several other verses in cp 2, make it clear, we are talking about Solomon.[1]

1.4 With that said, we must mention that various authorities suggest other authors:

    1.4.1 David

    1.4.2 Isaiah

    1.4.3 Hezekiah

    1.4.4 Some unknown writer during the Babylonian captivity.

    1.4.5 Generally, it is understood that Solomon is giving an interpretation of life through his elderly eyes, probably written about 930 BCE, and directed to the next generation of youth—an encouragement to live by the wisdom of God.

1.5 What *is* the message of Ecclesiastes?

    1.5.1 I believe it is the attempt of a man to look at life, perhaps even answer the question "Is there any meaning *to* life?" It is an attempt to solve the riddle of existence. If one understands the truth of existence, then each day is a gift from God. Each day is one day of existence and the day is precious, a part of an abundant life. It is a record of people's arguments, not God's. The problem that faced Solomon was how he could find happiness apart from God. He sought it:

        1.5.1.1 In fame

        1.5.1.2 in science

        1.5.1.3 in territory expansion

        1.5.1.4 in philosophy

        1.5.1.5 in drink

---

[1] As a reminder, It is thought that Solomon wrote:
Song of Solomon when he was a young man,
Proverbs in his middle years, and *Ecclesiastes* during older years.

Ecclesiastes and Song of Solomon

1.5.1.6 in building
1.5.1.7 in possessions
1.5.1.8 in music
1.5.1.9 in religion/ritualism
1.5.1.10 in wealth
1.5.1.11 in morality/reputation.
1.5.2 The author had seven philosophies of life, each one is meaningless:
1.5.2.1 Nothing in life except monotonous repetition.
1.5.2.2 The pursuit of pleasure is the chief goal in life.
1.5.2.3 No one gets out of life alive so live for the moment.
1.5.2.4 Live in the business world even though it consists of envy, the competition of climbing the ladder of success, and oppression.
1.5.2.5 "Trying" to live a good life and being a "good" person.
1.5.2.6 Riches only produce dissatisfaction.
1.5.2.7 Indifference to all events of life. Everything leads to the same in the end.
1.5.3 I like to keep in mind some unique observations about this book:
1.5.3.1 It is the only book in the Bible that reflects a human, rather than a divine point of view.
1.5.3.2 The book is filled with error! Yes, there is error in the Bible! And yet….it is indeed inspired truth. Examples of error help to direct God's people into Truth.
1.5.3.3 Inspiration does not guarantee truth. It merely guarantees the accuracy of a particular situation. God may say something is truth; man may see it as untruth.
1.5.3.4 Satan's statements may be in error. God records them because the errors are truth stated.
1.5.4 The author is a thinker. Thinking through life's experiences as to the meaning: He is not bitter but rather expresses some cynicism. Solomon squandered God's blessings and he writes to later generations—do not do the same as I did!
1.5.4.1 He starts out in verse 2 *Vanity of vanities, says the Preacher, Vanity of vanities! All is vanity.*
1.5.4.2 Wow! What a beginning. Most of us read that and just stop, not wanting to go through the rest of the book. He states his conviction that there is nothing permanent or lasting in life!
1.5.4.3 Solomon goes through these cycles of meaningless life, on and on exploring the spheres of life, some of it just not even true, expressing that cynicism.
1.5.4.3.1 What it *this*?
1.5.4.3.2 How about *that*?

1.5.4.3.3 He says at one point religion is full of shams.
1.5.4.3.4 But even in the cycles of vanity, he lists some proverbs for one to gain satisfaction from life.[1]
1.5.5 His final advice in cp 12 is very deep and moving—one of the most beautiful poems in the Bible.
1.5.5.1 A shift in viewpoint comes. His conclusion is that everything is vanity, apart from God.

Read these 6 verses:
Don't let the excitement of youth cause you to forget your Creator. Honor him in your youth before you grow old and say, "Life is not pleasant anymore." 2 Remember him before the light of the sun, moon, and stars is dim to your old eyes, and rain clouds continually darken your sky. 3 Remember him before your legs—the guards of your house—start to tremble; and before your shoulders—the strong men—stoop. Remember him before your teeth—your few remaining servants—stop grinding; and before your eyes—the women looking through the windows—see dimly. 4 Remember him before the door to life's opportunities is closed and the sound of work fades. Now you rise at the first chirping of the birds, but then all their sounds will grow faint. 5 Remember him before you become fearful of falling and worry about danger in the streets; before your hair turns white like an almond tree in bloom, and you drag along without energy like a dying grasshopper, and the caperberry no longer inspires sexual desire. Remember him before you near the grave, your everlasting home, when the mourners will weep at your funeral. 6 Yes, remember your Creator now while you are young, before the silver cord of life snaps and the golden bowl is broken. Don't wait until the water jar is smashed at the spring and the pulley is broken at the well. 7 For then the dust will return to the earth, and the spirit will return to God who gave it. (NLT)

2   The final book in this section of Wisdom; The Song of Solomon.

A Basic Outline of Song of Solomon
1. Falling in Love 1:1-3:5
2. United in Love 3:6-5:1
3. Struggling in Love 5:2-7:10
4. Growing in Love 7:14-8:14

Depth of Bible Words and Locations
Song of Solomon Key Word: *Beloved*
Found in—1:14; 2:8; 4:16; 5:1, 6:10; 6:1; 8:14—it is a Hebrew word in Hebrew poetry used for a male loved one, (also Isaiah 5:1). The writer of the Song of Solomon uses this word thirty-two times.

---

[1] 7:1 *A good name is better than a good ointment*
7:7 *bribe corrupts the heart.*
7:8 *Patience of spirit is better than haughtiness of spirit*
10:8 *He who digs a pit may fall into it*
10:14 *the fool multiplies words*

Ecclesiastes and Song of Solomon

Jesus in Song of Solomon...He is our Lover and Bridegroom

2.2 In Volume One of this work, the author wrote about both the Greek Septuagint and the Latin Vulgate, certainly two of the most important documents we have in existence. Each one was translated from the Hebrew into these other languages.

2.3 In both of them, they use the title "Song of Songs"; and that is the Hebrew title taken from the first two Hebrew words of the book. The words actually mean "Music that honors the Lord."

2.4 Our English "Song of Solomon" amplified on that to include the name of the King, from verse one: Solomon's Song of Songs.

2.5 Clearly, the title is meant to be dynamic!

  2.5.1 It's like "King of Kings"

  2.5.2 "Holy of Holies"

  2.5.3 "Lord of Lords"

  2.5.4 Here we have "Song of Songs."

2.6 One of the smallest books in the Old Testament, just 117 verses.

2.7 I love the colorful and descriptive language used. There are many descriptive words throughout this book: I suggest you sit back, close your eyes; listen to someone read these words from this small book, or just meditate on them as you read them. Some of them have been passed down almost as "sayings":

Tents of Kedar		1:5
Curtains of Solomon		1:5
My filly (and he meant a young female horse! Right!)		1:9
Spikenard and myrrh	Oil and perfume	1:12,13
Dove's eyes		1:15
Rose of Sharon		2:1
Lily of the valley		2:1
Apple		2:3
Cakes of raisons		2:5
Gazelles		2:7
Does	Female deer	2:7
Stag	Male deer	2:9
Dove		2:14
Frankincense	Spice	3:6
Fragrant powders		3:6
Couch		3:7
Lebanon and Mt Gilead		3:9;5:15
Tower of David		4:4

Spices		4:10
Saffron	A crocus stem	4:14
Calamus	Wild grass	4:14
Cinnamon		4:14
Aloes		4:14
Beryl	A stone	5:14
Sapphires		5:14
The dance of the double camp	Two groups in dance	6:13
Pools of water		7:4
Gate		7:4
Tower		7:4
Mount Carmel		7:5

2.8 Song of Solomon could be outlined in several ways; it really depends on your interpretation (we will review each of the interpretations later).

2.9 This book departs from the other Wisdom Literature;

   2.9.1 **Job** (which we included in Volume One for chronological reasoning) is the intense life and death struggle of a man to keep his faith in the midst of tragedies

   2.9.2 **Proverbs** has its teachings in almost every area of life

   2.9.3 **Ecclesiastes** is the cynic, discussing life's difficulties, what is life all about?

   2.9.4 Following these is a *single thought* in the 117 verses of **Song of Solomon.** The joy of life and one single emotion, love. Real, authentic, human love. The single manifestation of the joy of life.[1]

2.10 Any one of us who has read Song of Solomon, or has heard it taught, has come out of it with what they think the interpretation is.

   2.10.1 I have read several individual scholar's works on the book and even they do not agree on a single interpretation. I have a very old survey book which was used in an Old Testament Survey class years ago, (authored by Purkiser)[2] I have enjoyed it through the years, and that book has a different interpretation from most other's I've read. So believe me, I am not about to offer you the absolute interpretation.

   2.10.2 However, I will give you the various interpretations, which scholars list as the possibilities and then share my personal opinion. I do not know of any of the writers who just list a single interpretation (other than that survey book I learned from years ago). The interpretations fall into four categories:

---

[1] Solomon's name appears seven times and he's the probable author during his early life. His kingship is mentioned five times.

[2] Purkiser, Demaray, Metz, Stuneck, *Exploring The Old Testament,* Beacon Hill Press, Kansas City, Mo., 1955

2.10.2.1 (#1) Fictional
2.10.2.2 (#2) Historical
2.10.2.3 (#3) Allegorical
2.10.2.4 I add a (#4), that combines #2 & #3.
2.11 We get a little heavy here...stay with me. There is no other of the sixty-six books in our Bible, on which more commentaries have been written and more diversities of opinion expressed.
- 2.11.1 Delitzsch, an old German commentary author said: *"no other book of scripture has been so abused."*
- 2.11.2 But it is vital that we understand that no one can accept the Song of Solomon as a book of Scripture, without accepting its authority as canonical. God preserved what we have as thirty-nine Old Testament books in the canon, not thirty-eight. In addition, because of that statement, you and I as individuals have to form some theory of interpretation, which will justify this book.
- 2.11.3 No other book or any single scripture can be accepted because it is *only* a great piece of literature. No other of the sixty-six books of Scripture was placed in the Canon only because it was great literature.

2.12 Here are the interpretations of the Song of Solomon:
- 2.12.1 The **First** interpretation that some hold, is a **FICTIONAL** interpretation.
  - 2.12.1.1 This interpretation states, "it's a nice story," using Solomon and his marriage to a beautiful girl from the country, but with no truth at all. It's a fictional story used for good reading. Throw in a familiar name to make it interesting—but all fiction.
  - 2.12.1.2 However, in fact, the book indeed gives us every indication that the story did happen.
- 2.12.2 **Second**, many hold to the **HISTORICAL** interpretation. Similar to the first, only the story is true—Solomon's actual romance with this woman.
  - 2.12.2.1 A courtship, a marriage, and the beauty of love in marriage.
  - 2.12.2.2 It pictures the wonderful lovemaking in a marriage. Only when sexuality was viewed in a wrong way, did the interpretation become allegorical (which we will look at as a third view).
  - 2.12.2.3 Part of God's creation is pleasures and desires...so it is reasonable that He would provide a guide for a husband and wife. This view holds that the true-life love story of Solomon is God's endorsement of marital love. This view has many merits and must be considered at least a part of our interpretation.
- 2.12.3 Then a **Third** view: **ALLEGORICAL** interpretation, using symbols of spiritual meaning. This is the oldest of all the interpretations and has many thoughts included under its umbrella.

2.12.3.1 Many take the story and equate it to a symbol or type in one way or another. Abusive extremes are taken by some to the extent of making every item in the story, a mystical, fictional, or purely figurative component.

2.12.3.2 One group believes the hair of the bride represents a mass of people converted to Christianity! However, I do not conclude that He has that weird method of thinking! It is not wise to *entirely* use this method. Scripture must interpret Scripture.

2.12.3.3 However, *one* part of the belief holds validity. The early historian Josephus believed this was an allegory of the love of Jehovah for Israel, and later Origen taught the story as Christ's love for His Church. Certainly, some of the allegorical interpretation is acceptable.

2.12.4 Finally, I will add my own interpretation. I utilize the truth of both the HISTORICAL and the ALLEGORICAL...I do not have any name for it. Perhaps **REALISTIC VIEW**

2.12.4.1 Many scriptures indeed have double meanings...many passages proved true in history, and then will be fulfilled a second time. Double prophecy is found in many Old Testament passages.

2.12.4.2 This view would state that the true story of Solomon and perhaps his first wife is also a type of Christ and His extreme love for His Church.

2.12.4.3 This is really what Jewish tradition teaches.

2.12.4.4 They always held that Song of Solomon pictured Jehovah's love for Israel as well as the individual believer.

2.12.4.5 The "plot" centers on King Solomon's love for a humble maiden.

2.12.4.6 Courtship (1:1–3:5) leads to marriage (3:6–5:1) and then to the joys and trials of married love (5:2–8:14).

2.12.4.7 Indeed the book is a beautiful presentation of the love of husband and wife, for the Jews accepted sexuality as a precious gift from God, a holy expression of true commitment in marriage.

2.12.4.8 In addition, The Song of Solomon is an expression of the love relationship of the believer and the Savior. Christ calls us away from the trivial things of life that we might enjoy a deeper communion with Him. This communion is not without difficulties and disciplines, but it leads to a happier and holier life.

2.13 I hope you have drawn your conclusion about this unusual and many times-misunderstood book. We do not want any of His word to go unaccepted. I would suggest you also read Psalms 45 along with Song of Solomon.

2.14 In summary, The Wisdom Literature made up of the three books we reviewed, (along with Job, covered in Volume One), formed an important section of writing among the Jews. Wisdom was their attempt to solve problems, which each of them faced in their lifetime. The wise men were a distinct group of teachers who passed on the accumulated knowledge of the nation. As teachers, they were considered as important as prophets and priests.

SECTION 3
The Northern Kingdom: Israel

1 Kings 12-22, 2 Kings 1-17, 2 Chronicles 10-31, Jonah, Amos, Hosea.
The period from 975 to 721 BCE

Theme Statement: *"Ephraim is joined to idols"* (Hosea 4:17)

THE KEYS IN SECTION THREE

Section 3: The Northern Kingdom: Israel

Keys to First Kings—

A Key Word: Baal

The Key Verses (9:4–5; 11:11)

4 As for you, if you will walk before Me as your father David walked, in integrity of heart and uprightness, doing according to all that I have commanded you and will keep My statutes and My ordinances, 5 then I will establish the throne of your kingdom over Israel forever, just as I promised to your father David, saying, 'You shall not lack a man on the throne of Israel.'

11 So the Lord said to Solomon, "Because you have done this, and you have not kept My covenant and My statutes, which I have commanded you, I will surely tear the kingdom from you, and will give it to your servant."

The Key Chapter (12)

The Key People in 1 Kings

David—king of Israel; chose his son Solomon to be the next king (1–2:10); also see information for Key People in 1 Samuel (Volume One Section 6).

Solomon—third king of Israel; son of David and Bathsheba; builder of the first temple; God granted him his choice to become the wisest man ever born (1:10–11:43)

Rehoboam—son of Solomon; succeeded him as the fourth king of Israel; his evil actions led to the division of Israel into two kingdoms; later became king of the southern kingdom of Judah (11:43–12:24; 14:21–31)

Jeroboam—evil king of the northern ten tribes of Israel; erected idols and appointed non-Levitical priests (11:24–14:20).

Keys to Second Kings—

A Key Word: High Places

The Key Verses (17:22–23; 23:27)

22 The sons of Israel walked in all the sins of Jeroboam which he did; they did not depart from them 23 until the Lord removed Israel from His sight, as He spoke through all His servants the prophets. So Israel was carried away into exile from their own land to Assyria until this day.

27 The Lord said, "I will remove Judah also from My sight, as I have removed Israel. And I will cast off Jerusalem, this city which I have chosen, and the temple of which I said, 'My name shall be there.'"

The Key Chapter (25)

The **Key People** in 2 Kings

Elijah—a prophet of Israel; faced Ahab and Jezebel; raised a dead boy; called fire from heaven; never physically died; was carried directly to heaven in a chariot of fire (1:3–2:11; 10:10, 17)

Elisha—prophet trained under Elijah; close companion, became Elijah's successor; many similarities in ministry; asked for twice the anointing; saw Elijah taken to heaven (2:1–9:3; 13:14–21).

The woman from Shunem—the woman visited by Elijah in her home; brought her son back to life (4:8–37; 8:1–6)

Naaman—a Syrian warrior who suffered from leprosy; healed by Elisha (5:1–27)

Jezebel—evil queen of Israel; Baal worship introduced; attempted to prevent Israel from worshiping God; eventually killed and eaten by dogs (9:7–37)

Jehu—anointed king of Israel; used by God to punish Ahab's family (9:1–10:36; 15:12)

Keys in Section Three

Joash—king of Judah, saved from death as a child; followed evil advice of younger friends, ultimately assassinated by his own officials (11:1–12:21)

Hezekiah—king of Judah who remained faithful to God (16:20–20:21)

Keys to 2 Chronicles (Keys to 1 Chronicles are in, Section 4) —

A Key Word: *Passover*

The Key Verses (7:14; 16:9)

14 *and My people who are called by My name humble themselves and pray and seek My face and turn from their wicked ways, then I will hear from heaven, will forgive their sin and will heal their land.*

9 *"For the eyes of the Lord move to and fro throughout the earth that He may strongly support those whose heart is completely His. You have acted foolishly in this. Indeed, from now on you will surely have wars."*

The Key Chapter (34)

The Key People in 2 Chronicles

Solomon—a king of Israel and builder of the first temple (1:1–9:31)

Queen of Sheba—heard of Solomon's great reputation; visited him seeking information about his success (9:1–12; see Matthew 12:42)

Rehoboam—evil son of Solomon who became a king of Israel; soon divided the kingdom and later led the southern kingdom of Judah (9:31–13:7)

Asa—king of Judah; used very corrupt methods to accomplish God's purposes (14:1–16:14)

Jehoshaphat—son of Asa, followed him as king of Judah (17:1–22:9)

Jehoram—wicked son of Jehoshaphat who succeeded him as king of Judah; promoted idol worship and killed his six brothers (21:1–20)

Uzziah—(also called Azariah) succeeded his father, Amaziah, as king of Judah; mostly followed God, but prideful (26:1–23)

Ahaz—succeeded his father, Jotham, as king of Judah; continued Baal and other types of worship; sacrificed his own children (27:9–29:19)

Hezekiah—succeeded his father, Ahaz, as king of Judah; restored the temple (28:27–32:33)

Manasseh—succeeded his father, Hezekiah, as king of Judah; did evil in the sight of the Lord but repented later in his reign (32:33–33:20)

Josiah—succeeded his father, Amon, as king of Judah; followed the Lord; found the Book of the Law while restoring the temple; took the Book to the people. Brought revival/reforms (33:25–35:27)

Keys to Jonah—

A Key Word: *Prepared*

The Key Verses (2:8–9; 4:2)

8 "*Those who regard vain idols forsake their faithfulness,* 9 *But I will sacrifice to You with the voice of thanksgiving. That which I have vowed I will pay. Salvation is from the Lord.*"

2 *He prayed to the Lord and said, "Please Lord, was not this what I said while I was still in my own country? Therefore in order to forestall this I fled to Tarshish, for I knew that You are a gracious and compassionate God, slow to anger and abundant in loving-kindness, and one who relents concerning calamity.*

The Key Chapter (3)

Keys in Section Three

The Key People in Jonah

Jonah-an evangelist/missionary to Nineveh; swallowed by a large fish in order to bring his repentance. Reluctantly obeyed God (1:1-9)

The crew of the ship avoided killing him, opted for throwing him overboard in order to stop the storm (1:5-16)

Keys to Amos—

A Key Word: *Seek*

The Key Verses (3:1–2; 8:11–12)

1 Hear this word which the Lord has spoken against you, sons of Israel, against the entire family which He brought up from the land of Egypt: 2 "You only have I chosen among all the families of the earth; Therefore I will punish you for all your iniquities."

8:11 "Behold, days are coming," declares the Lord God, "When I will send a famine on the land, Not a famine for bread or a thirst for water, but rather for hearing the words of the Lord. 12 People will stagger from sea to sea And from the north even to the east; They will go to and fro to seek the word of the Lord, but they will not find it.

The Key Chapter (9)

The Key People in Amos

Amos-prophet from Judah warned Israel of God's judgment (1:1-9:15)

Amaziah-king of Judah, the southern kingdom; son of King Joash (7:10-17)

Jeroboam II-king of Israel following his father, King Jehoash (7:7-13)

Keys to Hosea—

A Key Word: *Stumble*

The Key Verses (4:1; 11:7–9)

1 Listen to the word of the Lord, O sons of Israel, For the Lord has a case against the inhabitants of the land, because there is no faithfulness or kindness or knowledge of God in the land.

7 So My people are bent on turning from Me. Though they call them to the One on high, None at all exalts Him. 8 How can I give you up, O Ephraim? How can I surrender you, O Israel? How can I make you like Admah? How can I treat you like Zeboiim? My heart is turned over within Me, All My compassions are kindled. 9 I will not execute My fierce anger; I will not destroy Ephraim again. For I am God and not man, the Holy One in your midst, And I will not come in wrath.

The Key Chapter (4)

The Key People in Hosea

Hosea-prophet to the ten tribes of the northern kingdom of Israel. His marriage was a picture of God's relationship to the kingdom (1:1-14:9)

Gomer-a prostitute or "strange woman" who became Hosea's wife. (1:3-9)

Jezreel, Lo-Ruhamah, and Lo-Ammi-the children of Hosea and Gomer whose names depicted God's relationship with Israel (1:3-2:1)

Approximate Dates of Key Events in Section 3	
975 BCE	The northern and southern kingdoms divide/Jeroboam's reign
967-935	Tilglath-Pileser in Assyria
918-897	Ahab reigns in Israel
914-	Elijah's ministry
899-	Elisha's ministry
884	Jehu anointed king by Elisha
826	Jeroboam II begins his reign in Israel
785	Jeroboam's reign in Israel ends
770	Approximate time of Jonah
755	Hosea begins to prophesy

Keys in Section Three

755	Amos delivers his prophecies
745	The Assyrian Empire strengthened under Tiglath-Pileser/push westward
730-720	Hoshea, last king of Israel
720	Hosea's ministry comes to an end
721	Israel is conquered by the Assyrians; taken to Assyria

FIVE

The Kings of Israel

1. **W**e continue our journey into **Section 3**, entitled **THE NORTHERN KINGDOM: ISRAEL.** We had a break in the historical sections, which we began in Volume One. Next, we return to the historical period in the Scriptures.
1.1. These next four sections (3-4-5-6) will cover different portions of both books of Kings, both books of Chronicles and several individual prophet's books. I will list the Scripture references as we arrive at each section. Section 3 will include 1 Kings cps 12-22, 2 Kings cps 1-17, 2 Chronicles cps 10-31, Jonah, Amos, and Hosea. These are the Scriptures that detail the Northern Kingdom
1.2. The Theme statement for Section 3 is a "sad" one: It comes from Hosea 4:17 *Ephraim is joined to idols.* The time period covered is approximately 250 years, 975 to 721 BCE.

> **Depth of Bible Words and Locations**
> *Ephraim*
> Following the division of the Promised Land into two separate nations, the Northern Kingdom (Israel), was also referred to as Ephraim.
>
> Joseph's younger son was named Ephraim (fruitful). He was born after Joseph became prime minister of Egypt (Gen 41:45-52). Jacob placed his right hand upon Ephraim and prayed for him, saying he would become the ancestor of a multitude of peoples. The descendants of Joseph's two sons would be considered two of the tribes. The tribe of Ephraim was located north of Jerusalem and north of the tribe of Benjamin. Shiloh was located in this territory.

1.3. See the next Extended Help Paper **The Six Related Books.**

The Kings of Israel

1.3.1. Though the years, I have found these last sections of our *Travel*, to be the most interesting of study.
    1.3.1.1. The division of Solomon's empire
    1.3.1.2. The prophets that God raises up; Elijah, Elisha, and of course Isaiah and Jeremiah
    1.3.1.3. The captivity of the ten Northern Tribes (Israel), followed years later by the captivity of the two Southern tribes (Judah)
    1.3.1.4. In addition, the wonderful calling back to Jerusalem to rebuild the walls, the city, and the temple. It is really an exciting period.

EXPANDED HELP PAPER
The Six Related Books

Now, put your thinking caps on...this IS a study course. Here we go... in order to help us in understanding this period of time.

The six books, 1 and 2 Samuel, 1 and 2 Kings, and 1 and 2 Chronicles are related directly to each other. Together, these six books are the recordings of the history of God's chosen people.

1 and 2 Kings were originally a single book called "Kings" in the Hebrew text, named from the very first verse which begins *"King David..."* When we studied 1 and 2 Samuel in Volume One, we noted that those two books were a single volume called "Samuel."

The important and widely used Greek Septuagint and the later Latin Vulgate both divided Kings into two books, probably because of the immense length. There was no ideal place to make the division; it was pretty much divided half-way.

The Vulgate further defined these six books. The Vulgate used the names 1 and 2 Kings for what we have as 1 and 2 Samuel. They then named what we have as 1 and 2 Kings, as 3 and 4 Kings, to keep them in their continuous history.

So, their books of 1st, 2nd, 3rd and 4th Kings, which we have as 1 and 2 Samuel and 1 and 2 Kings, were the complete history of Judah and Israel's Kingdoms. Are you with me so far?

I think it was clearer to have those earlier names. You would immediately realize their relationship and continuity.

Then we add to this study, 1 and 2 Chronicles—a similar pattern was used. Originally they were a single book in the Hebrew text, named "The annals (or events) of the days." It became the name Chronicles when the Hebrew was translated into the Latin in approximately 400 CE.

Those original books of Samuel and Kings were a history of both Israel and Judah both in their united state and also after they were divided. The Annals (our two books of Chronicles) only reviews the line of David, emphasizing only the kingdom of Judah.

Now, concerning the authors of Kings and Chronicles, similar to the books called Samuel, not a great amount of detail is known. Most likely Kings was authored by some unnamed prophet who lived with Israel in Babylon and wrote the history of the nation. Whoever the author was, it was written during the period of 561 and 450 BCE.

It is believed that the author of Chronicles was Ezra the priest known as "The Chronicler." It was probably written a little later, around 450 BCE. We will look more at Ezra in the final Section of our study. The author used many non-Biblical sources to pen the books (refer to the list in Volume One). This does not change the fact that God inspired the Books and made sure that the sources used were accurate.

Refer below to the Outlines and Key Words of Kings and Chronicles. The Key people in each of these books are listed at the beginning of this Section. The Keys in 1 and 2 Samuel are in Volume One, Section 6. In addition, you can refer to **Chronology of Old Testament History** in the Appendix, which lists the Kings and Prophets, who are a part of the next few sections.

A Basic Outline of 1 and 2 Kings
1. God's Kingdom United: The Reign of Solomon, I Kings 1-11
2. God's Kingdom Divided: The Kings of Israel and Judah, 1 Kings 12-2 Kings 17
3. God's Kingdom Surviving: The Kings of Judah, 2 Kings 18-25

Depth of Bible Words and Locations
1 Kings Key Word: *Baal*

Found in 1 Kings: 16:31; 18:19, 21, 26, 40; 22:53. *Baal* The word has the literal meaning of "master." Baal was considered as the "son" of the god EL or "father bull" and the fertility goddess Asherah, who is mentioned in 2 Kings 21:7. Baal was the leader of all the Canaanites' gods. Terrible rituals were linked with this worship including prostitution and infant sacrifice. Several times God's people were punished for their worship of Baal and Asherah (Judges 2:11–15; Jeremiah 19:4–6).

Depth of Bible Words and Locations
2 Kings Key Word: *High Places*

The Kings of Israel

Found in 2 Kings: 12:3; 14:4; 15:4; 23:8, 15, 20. This refers to a sacred area located on high ground such as a hill or ridge. There was nothing wrong with this in the early days of worship before the temple was built (1 Kings. 3:2–4). At a later time, the Israelites started worshiping pagan gods at these sacred sites. Because of that, this term *high places* in the Old Testament became associated with Israel's religious rebellion and apostasy (1 Kings. 14:23; Psalms 78:58; Jeremiah 19:5).

A Basic Outline of 1 and 2 Chronicles
1. A Selected Genealogical History of Israel, 1 Chronicles 1-9
2. Israel's United Kingdom under **Saul**, 1 Chronicles 10; **David** 11-29; **Solomon**, 2 Chronicles 1-9
3. Judah's Monarchy in the Divided Kingdom, 2 Chronicles 10-36:21
4. Judah's Release From Their Seventy-year Captivity, 2 Chronicles 36:22, 23

Depth of Bible Words and Locations
1 Chronicles Key Word: *Sons*
Found in 1 Chronicles 1:43; 3:12; 4:25; 5:14; 9:4; 11:22; 26:28. This word has the literal meaning of "to build." The Hebrews considered their children to be "builders" of the future generations. The word may refer to a direct son or to a future descendant. (1 Kings 2:1; 1 Chronicles 7:14). Benjamin in the Old Testament means "Son of my Right Hand." In the plural, *ben* can be translated as "children" regardless of gender (see Exodus 12:37—"children of Israel"). Even God used this term to describe His relationship with Israel: *"Israel is My son, My firstborn"* (Exodus 4:22).

Depth of Bible Words and Locations
2 Chronicles Key Word: *Passover*
Found in 2 Chronicles 30:1, 15; 35:1, 9, 11, 13, 18, 19. This word has a literal meaning of "to pass" or "to leap over." An important word to consider, the Passover celebration commemorated the day God spared the firstborn children of the Israelites from the death plague brought on Egypt. The Lord "passed over" those who sprinkled the blood from the Passover lamb on their doorposts (Exodus 12). It was the first of the three annual Hebrew festivals at which all the men must appear at the sanctuary (Exodus 13:3-10). Passover, as specified in the Law of Moses, reminds the Israelites of God's great mercy on them (Leviticus 23:5–8; Numbers 28:16–25; Deuteronomy 16:1–8). The Passover meal is a type of Christ, our "Passover Lamb," whose blood rescues us from death.

TRAVEL THROUGH THE OLD TESTAMENT

> *Jesus in Kings and Chronicles...He is our reigning King!*

2   Following Solomon's death, (reviewed at the end of Section 6 in Volume One), division of the Israelites' kingdom took place.

  2.1. The story of the present Section (3) is related in 1 and 2 Kings and deals alternately with Israel and the ten tribes which make up the Northern Kingdom, and Judah and the two tribes which make up the Southern Kingdom.

  2.2. In addition, much of 2 Chronicles deals with Judah, while some of the parallel events in both kingdoms are mentioned.

  2.3. These next four books in the Bible refer to Israel and Judah. Make sure you understand this kingdom division:

    2.3.1. The Hebrews comprise a total of twelve tribes. Two of those tribes, Judah and Benjamin will comprise a Southern Kingdom: JUDAH

    2.3.2. The other ten tribes comprise a Northern Kingdom: ISRAEL.

    2.3.3. Each had its separate leadership, and its own capital city; also, God sent Prophets to EACH of them.

    2.3.4. It is much easier to understand Old Testament history with this in view.

  2.4. Here is a diagram to assist in keeping these six books clear:

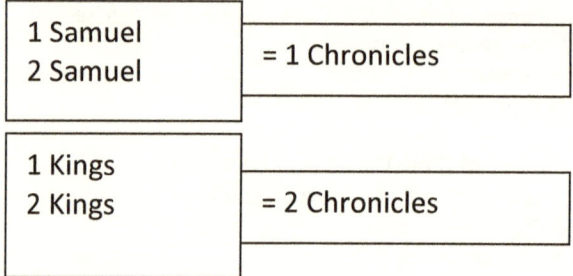

  2.5. Now back to the "division" of the United Kingdom following the death of Solomon. Upon his death and the accession of his son Rehoboam, the twelve tribes of Israel, divided into two separate nations.[1]

---

[1] What was the Northern Kingdom called? How many tribes formed it?
How about the Southern Kingdom, what was it called? Which ones made up the Southern Kingdom?

2.6. Let's go further...WHY did they divide? Let me list four possible reasons for division.
  2.6.1. #1 **Jealousy** between the tribes
    2.6.1.1. The tribes of Judah and Ephraim were in conflict. King David and King Solomon (both from the tribe of Judah) elevated the Judah tribe to great leadership.
    2.6.1.2. At the same time, Ephraim, the largest of the twelve tribes, had always claimed the highest position in the tribes. Later the Northern Kingdom was even referred to as Ephraim, as in this Section's theme verse from Hosea 4:17 *Ephraim is joined to idols*.
    2.6.1.3. Following Saul's death (the first King of the united twelve tribes), ten Northern tribes, recognized a man named Ishbosheth as King for the next seven years during the same period David was King of his own tribe of Judah. So a constant state of jealousy contributed greatly, to a divided nation.
  2.6.2. Then #2, **communication was difficult.** The ten Northern tribes, rather than making the long journey over the mountains to worship in unity in Jerusalem, on many occasions held their own separate gatherings, which caused division. All tribes were to worship in unity in Jerusalem even though it meant a long journey over the mountains.
  2.6.3. #3, **idolatry** entered in during Solomon's reign.[1] It is during his reign that pagan worship worked its way in and weakened all the tribes. Worship of one true God, Yahweh, had kept them united in their beginning. However, eventually, idolatry divided the Northern Tribes from Jerusalem.
  2.6.4. #4, Solomon's **extravagance** added to the division. He had to build more and more, greater and greater. Therefore, the taxes kept going up to pay for the expansion. The North did not like to be taxed for great buildings in Jerusalem, where they seldom visited.
    2.6.4.1. High taxes have destroyed many nations. Is any nation exempt from this?
2.7. Another theory suggests the Northern and Southern "peoples" were actually different groups, exiting Egypt at different times, eventually

---

Keep it clear!
Note that the Northern Kingdom was also referred to as Samaria (its capital city) and Ephraim (its dominant tribe). (answers; Israel, 10; Judah, Judah and Benjamin)

[1] Keep in mind what period we are in. Samuel, a Prophet—anointed Saul as 1st King—David is King of only one tribe, Judah for seven years—Then Solomon was the King who had it all!

settling in the same territory. This author locates little conclusive evidence of separate peoples.

2.8. In either theory, the Northern Kingdom, (What was it called?)[1]; was formed. NOTE: During these next few studies, the Chronology of Old Testament History, printed in the Appendix, will help you as we look at the kings. Skip down in that chart, review and follow the kings of the two nations.

   2.8.1. Israel had natural advantages:
- 2.8.1.1. Three times as much territory
- 2.8.1.2. Twice the population
- 2.8.1.3. Most of the fertile land
- 2.8.1.4. A location ideal for worldwide commercial trade because most of the main routes went through their territory.

   2.8.2. Israel had these advantages over the smaller Judah and seemed to be the chosen land!

   2.8.3. An interesting synopsis of the Northern Tribes:
- 2.8.3.1. Moral DECADENCE began with Solomon;
- 2.8.3.2. Which led to the DIVISION of the Kingdom;
- 2.8.3.3. Which led to the DETERIORATION of Israel;
- 2.8.3.4. And ended with their early DEPORTATION.

   2.8.4. The first king of the ten tribes, Jeroboam (referred to as Jeroboam I) was chosen by God. If he would have accepted that calling and remained true to God, *he* might have even been the spiritual leader to follow David and reunite the two nations. However, he was not true to God's direction. They seem to fall into the same cycle that the Judges had experienced.

The Kings of Israel (Ten Northern Tribes)

King	Date
1 Jeroboam I	975-954 BCE
2 Nadab	954-953
3 Baasha	953-930
4 Elah	930-929
5 Zimri	929
6 Tibni	929-924
7 Omri	929-917
8 Ahab	918-897
9 Ahaziah	898-897

---

[1] Israel

The Kings of Israel

10 Jehoram (Joram)	897-884
11 Jehu	884-857
12 Jehoahaz	857-840
13 Jehoash	840-826
14 Jeroboam II	826-785
15 Zachariah	784-773
16 Shallum	772
17 Menahem	772-762
18 Pekahiah	761-760
19 Pekah	759-739
20 Hoshea	730-720

2.8.4.1. Jeroboam was afraid to allow his ten Northern Tribes to make the journey to worship in Jerusalem, the capital of Rehoboam's Southern Kingdom as well as God's designated center for worship. Therefore, he made two golden calves for his people to worship on *high places*.

2.8.4.2. Jeroboam was unfaithful and caused the entire Northern Kingdom to fall in disgrace.

2.8.4.3. For twenty-two years, Israel fought against the Southern Kingdom; a war we might think of as a civil war, with friend against friend.

2.8.5. Jeroboam's son Nadab followed his dad's reign, but only for a short time before he was murdered (along with his entire family) by Baasha who ruled for the following twenty-four years. The war with Judah continued at various times through the entire period. Asa defeated Nadab, ending his reign.

2.8.6. Spiritually, there followed an even darker era for Israel under Omri and his son Ahab.

2.8.6.1. Omri was a strong political ruler and was respected by many of Israel's neighbors.

2.8.6.2. He built the capital city of Samaria.

2.8.6.3. His conquest of Moab is described on a record discovered in 1868 CE.[1]

2.8.6.4. During their reigns, which lasted from 929 through 897 BCE, Omri, and his son Ahab, established

---

[1] A Prussian missionary discovered the famous Moabite Stone in 1868. Written on it were these words: *Omri, king of Israel, oppressed Moab many days, because Chemosh, the god of Moab, was angry with his land...Omri took possession of Medeba, and dwelt there all his days, and half the days of his son, forty years.*

strong foreign alliances for the Northern Kingdom. Ahab, in particular, was shrewd and brave, defeating the Syrian army.

2.8.6.5. In general, he maintained a friendly relationship with the Phoenicians (through his marriage to Jezebel). He battled with Assyria and Judah.

2.8.6.6. However spiritually, total idolatry was demanded ...no worship of Jehovah was allowed! Isn't that sad! Part of God's people not allowed to worship Him! Ahab married Jezebel, forcing the national religion of Baalism.

EXPANDED HELP PAPER
Jezebel

Jezebel is introduced in 1 Kings 16:31 in the listing of the evils of her husband's reign. Probably Ahab's marriage to her sealed an alliance between Israel and Tyre just as the powers of Syria were threatening the coastal states.

Jezebel induced her weak husband not only to introduce the worship of her native idols but eventually to become himself a worshipper of them, Jezebel was able to cut off the worship of God by killing the prophets of Yahweh (1 Kings 18:4,13). She is the first great instigator of persecution against the saints of God. At the same time, she was able to maintain the prophets of Baal. Notice her father's name: Eth**baal;** taught his daughter very well! He ought to be proud!

The New Testament was the first to say, "This is [a] Jezebel." She literally stamped her name on history as the representative of all that is *designing, crafty, malicious, revengeful, and cruel.*

2.8.6.7. The Scriptures make it clear that Ahab was the most wicked of the northern kings.[1]

2.8.6.8. Jezebel continued her influence over the Northern Kingdom for the thirteen years following the death of Ahab, in spite of Ahab's two sons, Ahaziah and Jehoram who officially reigned.

2.8.7. We continue with Jehu who reigns for twelve years. He rushes on his chariot to Tirzah to take over the kingdom and rid Israel of the

---

[1] 1 Kings 16:33 *Ahab also made the Asherah. Thus Ahab did more to provoke the Lord God of Israel than all the kings of Israel who were before him.*

house of Ahab. We might agree that he starts positive---he destroys Ahab's house (THAT WAS GOOD); he puts down the worship of Baal (THAT WAS GOOD)—he just murders them all!

    2.8.7.1.   Jehu made little attempt to remove idolatry. The idolatrous shrines at Bethel and Dan were continued in greater scale.

Depth of Bible Words and Locations
Shechem

Located west of the Jordan River near Samaria, an important city, an ancient fortified city in central Palestine, long before the Israelites occupied Canaan. It was first mentioned in the Bible in connection with Abraham's journey into the land of Canaan. When Abraham eventually came to Shechem, the Lord appeared to him and announced this was the land He would give to Abraham's descendants.

After the Israelites conquered Canaan under the leadership of Joshua, an altar was built at Shechem. The significance of Shechem in Israel's history continued into the period of the Divided Kingdom. Rehoboam, the successor to King Solomon, went to Shechem to be crowned king over all Israel (1 Kings 12:1). Here, at this same place, the ten tribes renounced the house of David and transferred their allegiance to Jeroboam (ver. 16), under whom Shechem became the capital of his kingdom. Eventually, Samaria became the permanent political capital of the Northern Kingdom, but Shechem retained its religious importance. We note also that it apparently still was a sanctuary for the worship of God in Hosea's time.

Depth of Bible Words and Locations
Tirzah

Became the capital city of the northern kingdom, located a few miles northeast of *Shechem*. During Tirzah's glory days, Song of Solomon was written. It was the capital of the northern kingdom for forty years while Baasha and his son Elah were in rule. Then a short rule of Zimri ended as Omri, the army general, seized the country. A scared Zimri burned down the citadel while inside it, (a 3' tall area of burned debris has been located). It was re-built for a short period while the permanent capital was being constructed in Samaria. Song of Solomon mentions *Tirzah* as one of the two great cities of Israel. The location seems to be forgotten after the fall of the Northern Kingdom.

Samaria

Built as a political capital of the Northern Kingdom about 880 BCE by Omri, the sixth king of Israel (1 Kings 16:24). Samaria occupied a 300-foot high hill about 42 miles north of Jerusalem.

Because of its hilltop location, Samaria could be defended easily. Several kings ruled from there, including Omri, Ahab, and Jehu.

During this period, it was the seat of idolatry (Isaiah 9:9; Jeremiah 23:13; Ezekiel 16:46-55; Amos 6:1; Micah 1:1). Ahab, Omri's son, built a temple to Baal here.

Archeologists have discovered that at the time of Ahab, the city may have been 20 acres in extent, enclosed by an outer wall 20 to 30 feet thick, with a more narrow inner stone wall about 5 feet thick. A two-story palace was constructed at the higher western end of the hill around some courtyards. In one of these courtyards, a pool about 17 by 33 feet has been discovered. This may have been the pool where the blood of Ahab was washed from his chariot after he was killed in a battle against the Syrians. Samaria finally fell to the Assyrians, in 722-21 BCE.

2.8.8. A gradual increase in prosperity was gained during the reign of the next three kings, Jehoahaz, Jehoash, and Jeroboam II.

    2.8.8.1. In particular, under Jeroboam II's reign; the territory is expanded, however, the morals decayed more and more. However, this period became by far the most prosperous since the time of Solomon.

    2.8.8.2. During the 40 years of his reign, no invasion by a foreign power occurred and he is credited with extending the boundaries of Israel from Moab an area mentioned in 2 Kings 14:25 (probably near Mt. Hermon).

2.8.9. Then for thirty-two years following Jeroboam Jr., five of the last six kings of Israel were murdered.

    2.8.9.1. Zechariah, one of many in the Old Testament with this name meaning *"remembered of Jehovah."* Son of Jeroboam II, the last of the Jehu dynasty. Slain by Shallum (2 Kings 14:29; 15:10).

    2.8.9.2. Shallum, son of Jabesh (2 Kings 15:10)

    2.8.9.3. Menahem, murdered Shallum, to take the throne

    2.8.9.4. Pekahiah, son of Menahem

    2.8.9.5. Pekah, killed Pekahiah to take the throne

The Kings of Israel

2.8.10. Hoshea became the last king of the Northern Kingdom. This period of thirty-two years sounds like a repeat of the cycles during the Judges. I do not see any progress at all. More like deterioration.

2.8.11. The nation of Assyria turns against Israel. Amos (3:11; 5:27) and Hosea (1:4-6; 3:4; 9:3) prophesied the doom. The downfall of the Northern Kingdom began as Tiglath-pileser III (called Pul) invaded and controlled most of the territory in 735 BCE.

    2.8.11.1. Shalmaneser V in 728 BCE and Sargon II in 721 BCE completed the annihilation of the Northern Kingdom; Israel became a part of the Assyrian Empire.

    2.8.11.2. Sargon's great castle was excavated in 1845 CE. In 1847 CE the historic Nineveh of the Bible was located. In Sargon's castle were his reports on his campaigns in Palestine and his capture of Samaria in Israel.

SIX

The Prophets to Israel

1. During this period Elijah, Elisha, and three other prophets direct their comments to the Northern Kingdom.
    1.1. First, let us learn about the characteristics of Old Testament prophets.[1]
        1.1.1. Too many times in modern days, we describe a prophet with words like "predict" or "forecast," however that's a *small part* of their office. The primary message was "FORTHtelling" rather than "FOREtelling."
        1.1.2. They were spiritual leaders, like priests, but the prophet depended on a direct call of God, the priest did not. This set the prophet apart, and people seemed to recognize that call. They were men of prayer and seemingly pure moral character.
        1.1.3. These prophets banded together in "schools" for common instruction. Sort of like an association having its own seminars. No doubt, the contemporaries at different periods had met one another in these schools. The Scriptures record the *sons of the prophets* were young members of these schools mentored by the older prophets.[2]
    1.2. So first, we meet Elijah "the Tishbite," a prototype of John the Baptist. He had quite a life. His ministry fell chiefly in the time of Ahab and Jezebel. I love his life and admire the many lessons from it. Let's travel briefly with this great prophet:

---

[1] The word "prophet" comes from a word meaning "one who speaks on behalf of another." He makes a "public declaration."

[2] In my studying this, I concluded there were those who stood in the *office* of Prophet, and others who were not IN the office, but who exercised the *gift* of prophecy in their ministry.

The Prophets to Israel: Elijah & Elisha

1.2.1. He comes on the scene like a flash; 1 Kings 17:1 records it like this *Now Elijah.*[1] J. Oswald Sanders likened him to a meteor that *"flashed across the inky blackness of Israel's spiritual night."*

1.2.2. He comes *and* goes, quickly. God's punishment to Israel came through Elijah because of the idolatry that was allowed.

1.2.3. Elijah appeared in front of Ahab with a message for the king that was unsettling. He announced that no rain would come until he (Elijah) called it back. His departure was similar to his arrival—sudden.

1.2.4. God wants to teach Elijah a lesson. So beside a brook at Cherith where God provides a "heavenly diner" with bread every morning, a sandwich every night and cool water all day long, Elijah grows. This was Elijah's advanced training. God took him there—probably to mature him, to get him ready for what was to come.

    1.2.4.1. I can imagine Elijah watched each morning, as the stream had less and less flow of water, until one morning, the stream stopped. Wet sand, then dryness. The Scriptures tell us he went and **lived** by the brook. Maybe he planned to stay a long time. However, dryness came. Elijah was not to live by a fresh brook of water.

    1.2.4.2. Brooks dry up in our life, be ready to go on.

1.2.5. Then the meeting at Zarephath.

    1.2.5.1. At Zarephath, Elijah, no longer *"Elijah the Tishbite,"* rather now called *"Elijah man of God,"* tells a woman to go and mix all the oil and flour she has because "I'm hungry," and stays in her upper room many days with plenty to eat for all.

    1.2.5.2. Then with only a few words (a lesson for us perhaps?), he takes the widow's dead son into his arms and doing what was never heard of before (he did not learn this from anyone else), raised a young dead boy, to life. Truly now, Elijah *is a man of God*.

    1.2.5.3. I am reminded of the great ministry of the gentle Smith Wigglesworth, the "apostle of faith." Raising the dead was only one amazing facet of the ministry of Smith Wigglesworth[2]

---

[1] Elijah is described in 2 Kings 1:8 *"He was a hairy man with a leather girdle bound about his loins."* In manner of dress, as in other characteristics, he was the prototype of the New Testament prophet, John the Baptist.

[2] The Wigglesworth Family, *The Complete Collection of His Life Teachings,* Wilmington Group Publishers, Fort Lauderdale FL, 1996

TRAVEL THROUGH THE OLD TESTAMENT

Prophets to Israel and Judah

Joel	Judah	835 BCE
Isaiah	Judah	742-680
Micah	Israel and Judah	750-697
Jeremiah	Judah	627-586
Zephaniah	Judah	640-622
Habakkuk	Judah	612-598
Amos	Israel	760-753
Hosea	Israel	755-722
Ezekiel	In exile, Babylonia	594-571
Daniel	In exile, Babylonia	606-535
Haggai	Post exile in Jerusalem	520
Zechariah	Post exile in Jerusalem	520-480
Malachi	Post exile in Jerusalem	432-424

1.2.6. Three years following the "school at the brook," God sent Elijah back to face Ahab (Elijah was now ready). God sends him back to where he started. I love the words of Ahab *when Ahab saw Elijah, Ahab said to him, "is this you, you troubler of Israel?"* (1 Kings 28:17)

    1.2.6.1. Don't you love this? How would you like to be called "troubler of your city?"; "troubler of your office," or maybe "troubler of your church!" (Stand up for what's right). I guess if birds feed you every day, you speak to flour and oil and eat all the cakes you want, raise a dead child or two...You would be called SOMETHING...I know it would be trouble to the devil!

    1.2.6.2. I know of a minister who when his wife received a healing, became a "troubler" of both his church and entire denomination. He was removed because of what God did. Oh let us become "troublers" for God. We are to live "all the Word," which may make us "troublers."[1]

Depth of Bible Words and Locations
The Cave of Elijah

It is located near on the west side of the modern Israeli city of Haifa. In ancient times, what is now called the Cave of Elijah the Prophet was a place where believers practiced the cult of the pagan god Ba'al. The Cave of Elijah is a large natural cavern in a sloping rocky outcrop at the foot of Mount Carmel, 131 feet above the sea. Its limestone walls were carved in ancient times to suit its cultic purposes and smoothed by countless

---

[1] You *do* understand what I refer to here! You stand for God and His plan for His Kingdom way of living, while others slip in to a world system. You become their "troubler."

The Prophets to Israel: Elijah & Elisha

hands in the centuries since then, enlarging it to its current size, so that its floor is about 28.5 by 47.5 feet, and the ceiling is about 15–16 feet high

Depth of Bible Words and Locations
"Troubler `akar (aw-kar')

In Hebrew, it is a noun referring to "snake, or to bring calamity." Ahab in referring to Elijah left little doubt of his hatred for him. To him, Elijah was behind all the trouble in the land....drought, famine, disease, death. Elijah was trouble to the enemy. Ahab called Elijah a "trouble-bringer."

Also translated as "troublemaker," "destroyer," or "one who brings disaster."

We read in Joshua 7:25 Joshua said, "Why have you troubled us? The Lord will trouble you this day."

1.2.7. Elijah gathers an audience.[1]

    1.2.7.1. He challenged the king to a contest between God and Baal on Mount Carmel. Two sacrifices were to be offered, one by Elijah and one by the followers of Baal. The god which sent fire to consume his sacrifice was to be recognized as the true God.

    1.2.7.2. Elijah waits until all the false prophets "cried out" to their gods, Elijah even says "cry a little harder, maybe your god has gone into the bathroom"...and says "now soak this altar that I have prepared (I'm not going to touch the altar you served your idols on) and watch what MY God will do!"

    1.2.7.3. And the fire...comes!

1.2.7.3.1. God's fire always consumes evil, and always commands good.

1.2.7.3.2. His fire always protects His own children who are close to it. God's fire surrounds the natural fire.

1.2.7.3.3. It burns in a furnace, but never even scorches His children who are standing IN it.

1.2.7.3.4. Isaiah will later say, *"the fires will not harm you."* [2]

---

[1] 1 Kings 18:19 *"Now then send and gather to me all Israel at Mount Carmel, together with 450 prophets of Baal and 400 prophets of the Asherah, who eat at Jezebel's table."*

[2] Isaiah 43:2 *When you walk through the fire, you will not be scorched, Nor will the flame burn you.* I have always associated the fire with the worst tribulation in life. That fire that attempts to burn your life, will not defeat your faith in Him.

1.2.7.4. The fire of God consumed the sacrifice of Elijah, dried up the water, and melted the very stones of the altar! Any doubt who is God?

1.2.8. Then later, Elijah "man of God," tells Ahab, *get ready, for rain is coming* (1 Kings 17:1). They were experiencing a long three-year dry period.

    1.2.8.1. Can't you see it in that clear sky! Our God *calls into being that which does not exist.* (Romans 4:17)

    1.2.8.2. And when it starts "pourin' Ahab starts fearin' and Elijah starts runnin'!" A seventeen-mile race between a scared man in a chariot and a faith man on wings...no contest. (The faith man will always win). What a hero of the Bible!

1.3. Next, comes the prophet Elisha—the greatest miracle worker in the Old Testament— a type of the Messiah. As with the review of Elijah, we will only review the brief highlights of Elisha's life.[1]

    1.3.1. God gave Elijah a chosen companion in his later years, Elisha. From the moment that Elijah cast his mantle upon a young Elisha plowing out in a field, Elisha "sticks to Elijah like glue," perhaps for years, we do not know. In the last scene of Elijah's life, he is taken to heaven in a whirlwind with a chariot and horses of fire. His mantle fell on Elisha.

    1.3.2. We know that Elijah taught him well. God had commanded by the Lord at Sinai to anoint Elisha as his successor (1 Kings 19:15-17). Elisha requested a double portion of Elijah's spirit...what a request.[2]

    1.3.3. The reforms and later prosperity of Jehu, Jehoash, and Jeroboam II were a direct result of the religious and political leadership of Elisha. Elisha's ministry covered that entire period of approximately sixty years.

    1.3.4. Elisha's personality was attractive, and along with his life of miracles, stands out as a type of Christ:

        1.3.4.1. Most of his miracles were works of mercy and some of them very much resembled the miracles recorded in the Gospels.

        1.3.4.2. He sweetens a spring of salty waters

---

[1] Remember *Elijah* was a type of John the Baptist, now *Elisha* follows, and is a type of Messiah. Elijah is referred to several times in the New Testament. He appeared at the transfiguration of Jesus as one the representatives of the prophetic order (Matthew 17:3).

[2] 2 Kings 2:9 *And Elisha said, "Please, let a double portion of your spirit be upon me."*

2 Kings 2:15 *the sons of the prophets who were at Jericho opposite him saw him, they said, "The spirit of Elijah rests on Elisha"*

The Prophets to Israel: Jonah

       1.3.4.3.   Multiplies the loaves of bread
       1.3.4.4.   Multiplies a widow's oil, (like Elijah did)
       1.3.4.5.   Raises a son from the dead, (like Elijah did)
       1.3.4.6.   And heals an official of leprosy
       1.3.4.7.   He uses the golden rule on the Syrian troops sent to capture him
       1.3.4.8.   Then uses some very stern acts, similar to when Christ met the scribes.

   1.3.5.   The ministry of Elisha was a remarkable fulfillment of a double portion of Elijah's spirit (2 Kings 5:10-14). He attained a spiritual stature above most other prophets of that day.

       1.3.5.1.   The rabbis' point out that eight miracles came by the hand of Elijah, and sixteen by the hand of Elisha.

2.1. Also at this time, Jonah, followed by the contemporaries, Amos and Hosea were prophets to Israel.

2.1.1. The book of Jonah, unlike other prophets, relates a single episode in Jonah's life. We could consider it as a short story.

       2.1.1.1.   The author is never mentioned; tradition says it was Jonah writing in the third person. His name meant, "dove"; which was a symbol of "silliness"; We find it in Hosea 7:11 *So Ephraim has become like a silly dove, without sense.*

       2.1.1.2.   Jonah relates his own story and then makes his final statement about coming to terms with the will of God. Not a lot is known about him other than what is in this book. He IS mentioned one other time in the Old Testament, 2 Kings 14:25, which locates his "ministry of encouragement" to the Northern Kingdom during the time of King Jeroboam II which establishes the time of the book at about 790 BCE. The book portrays Jonah in a negative light, but in fact, he tried to uplift Israel.

       2.1.1.3.   Many do not take this book seriously, even calling it a "fable." But do not allow that thinking to cause you to miss the true message of this flesh and blood man. (I'll say more concerning this at the close of Jonah).

A Basic Outline of Jonah

1. Running From God, Cp 1
2. Submitting to God, Cp 2
3. Following God, Cp 3
4. Angry with God, Cp 4

Depth of Bible Words and Locations
Jonah Key Word: *Prepared*

Found in 1:17; 6-8. The word means "to count" or "to assign." Psalms 147:4 praises God for knowing the number of stars and counting each one. In Jonah, it carries the meaning of "appointing" or "ordaining" and shows God's intervention in natural events to bring about His will. God "appoints" a fish. He "assigns" a small worm to teach Jonah about His mercy.

Jesus in Jonah...He is your deliverer.

2.1.2. The book of Jonah is four short chapters describing an event where God directs the prophet to go and preach to a wicked city—Nineveh. Jonah is unwilling, goes to Joppa, and takes a ship heading for Spain, the opposite direction from Nineveh. Do you think that maybe he was running from the assignment?

2.1.3. When you run from God, a boat is always available to move you away from Him.

Depth of Bible Words and Places
Nineveh

Located near the Tigris River in Mesopotamia, 200 miles east of Haran. Nineveh is first mentioned in the Bible in Genesis 10:11, which states that Nimrod, a mighty hunter before the Lord, came from the land of Shinar (Babylonia) to Assyria and there built Nineveh. A huge city, taking three days to walk from one side to the other. 2 Kings 19:36 simply states that Sennacherib after his aborted attack on Jerusalem (19:35) returned to Nineveh, where he had made his capital. Two contemporary prophets, Zephaniah (2:13-15) and Nahum, told of the fall of Nineveh (612 BCE). Nineveh became "*a desolation, a dry waste like a desert,*" and passed into oblivion for 2,500 years.

There is archeological evidence that the site of Nineveh was occupied as early as 5000 BCE (which would demand an early date for creation).

2.1.4. Jonah was a citizen of a small village near Nazareth in Galilee. He was credited with having predicted the successful conquests by Jeroboam II.

2.1.5. After God directs Jonah to go and preach to the wicked city of Nineveh, we read he is unwilling because of fear that the Ninevites will repent and be forgiven. He does not want that because Assyria was an enemy.

The Prophets to Israel: Jonah

2.1.6. Jonah knows what God is like; gracious, compassionate, full of love...which is why he did not want to go to Nineveh. He wanted the *destruction* of his enemy—God would *love* them!

2.1.7. As you may remember from a Sunday School lesson when you were a child, after being thrown overboard, God sends "a great fish" (most of us call it a whale, which may or may not be true), to give Jonah a place of rescue but more so, a place of repentance.

    2.1.7.1. In the fish's belly, he prays to God and promises to repent. His situation simulates death, the belly of Sheol.

Depth of Bible Words and Locations
Sheol

Found in Ps 9:17; 2 Sam 22:6; Isa 5:14; Jonah 2:2. One of five distinct areas of departments under the earth. They are Tartaros, Paradise, Sheol/Hades, Bottomless Pit, and Gehenna. Sheol (Heb, OT) /Hades (Greek, NT) is a place of the unrighteous until after the Millennium. We refer to it as Hell and is a literal place, one of the departments under the earth. It is referred to in the New Testament in Acts 2:27; Luke 10:15; Rev 1:18 etc.

Some scholars prefer to translate Hades as "grave." Job's description of Sheol as a place of darkness, dust, worms, and decay may refer to "grave." In many places, such as Prov 15:11 and 27:20, and Ps 9:17 would demand "hell" because of context.

    2.1.7.2. After three days, God repeats His mission call to Jonah, who has now been "spit-up" onto an island. It seems like the great fish got a stomachache from God! Jonah quickly responds "yes sir" to the second call. He holds a revival in Nineveh and a city repents!

    2.1.7.3. Interesting, Jonah, who did not want God to be compassionate to the undeserving Assyrians in Nineveh, recognized that God's undeserved compassion had been given to himself (2:9). Following the Nineveh revival, Jonah runs away and prays that he may die.

    2.1.7.4. The message of Jonah remains to this day: God loves every human on earth! Regardless of race, color, or lifestyle. He loves you...mankind may not love fellow man...however, God loves every single one.

2.1.7.5. THAT I believe is why Jesus has not come back to take His Church home! God can not accept the possibility that even one person would perish.[1]

2.1.7.6. Jesus refers to the story of Jonah being historically accurate, in two scriptures.[2] Nowhere do we find evidence of Jonah's experience being a parable or allegory. He was a real person (2 Kings 14:25), the places referred to are real historical locations, and the Jews have always regarded the story as historical.

2.1.7.7. I was asked years ago, "Pastor, do you believe Jonah was really swallowed by a whale?" (*Yes! And if the Bible said Jonah swallowed the whale, I'd believe that too)!*

2.2. Next is Amos ("burdened" or "burden-bearer") a native of Tekoa in Judah, a few miles south of Jerusalem. Amos gets his assignment from God, but unlike Jonah, he immediately agrees with God and speaks judgment on Israel's neighbors. He was to prophesy against Samaria and Bethel, two important cities of the Northern Kingdom. Wickedness ran rampant there.

2.2.1. Amos is probably the most familiar of all the twelve minor prophets. It's a book of justice. Amos, the writer of the book, was a sheep breeder in Judah, just south of Bethlehem; he was not a hired shepherd, rather he was the owner of one or more flocks.

2.2.2. He had a message for Israel and it was delivered during the time of Uzziah king of Judah (south) and Jeroboam king of Israel (north). Again, that pinpoints the date. He spoke to Israel for a short time, probably in 755 BCE. The earthquake of verse 1:1 has been verified by archaeologists who found destruction dated to this period.

2.2.3. Amos' message was delivered close to the end of Israel because Jeroboam II died three years after Amos appeared. The Assyrians came a few years after this. He closes chapter 9 with a promise of restoration.

A Basic Outline of Amos
1. Messages of Judgment Against Several Nations, Cps 1-2
2. Messages Against Israel, Cps 3-6
3. Visions, Cps 7-9

---

[1] 2 Peter 3:9 *not wishing for any to perish but for all to come to repentance.*
[2] Matthew 12:39-40 reads *no sign will be given to it but the sign of Johan the prophet; 40 for just as JONAH WAS THREE DAYS AND THREE NIGHTS IN THE BELLY OF THE SEA MONSTER..* Jesus also referred to this in Luke 11:29.

The Prophets to Israel: Amos

Depth of Bible Words and Locations
Amos Key Word: *Seek*

Found in 5:4. It means just about what you would think, "to inquire" or "to ask." It carries the thought of going to someone and seeking an answer. You can see this same word in Ezra 6:21, Psalms 119:10 and Isaiah 34:16.

Jesus in Amos...He is your Burden Bearer. Cast your burden on Him!

2.2.4. Amos was deeply religious and was passionately against the injustice and immortality, which he found in the cities of the Northern Kingdom. In describing God's call to him (Amos 7: 14-15), he says *I am not a prophet, nor am I the son of a prophet; for I am a herdsman and a grower of sycamore figs.* 15 "*But the Lord took me from following the flock...*" So this book was not written by a trained prophet. He was an ordinary person.

2.2.5. Amos was a humble man but possessed a deep insight into politics and religious morality. He stood up for the poor who were being oppressed by the rich and ruling classes.

2.2.6. These three prophets (Jonah, Amos, and Hosea) were contemporaries, along with Isaiah, who we will visit in the Southern Kingdom later. From Amos and then Hosea, we get quite a picture of the conditions that existed in Israel during this time.

2.2.7. Very prosperous, in fact, an upper class literally *lived for their riches*.
    2.2.7.1.   Palaces furnished with ivory,
    2.2.7.2.   Winter and summer homes.[1]
    2.2.7.3.   They seemed to have an *outward* religion; they worshiped at Bethel and Gilgal, with many singing of Psalms.

---

[1] 3:15 reads "*I will also smite the winter house together with the summer house;*
The houses of ivory will also perish
And the great houses will come to an end"
4:1 tells about their hearts:
Who oppress the poor, who crush the needy,
And 5:11
Therefore because you impose heavy rent on the poor
And exact a tribute of grain from them,
Though you have built houses of well-hewn stone,
Yet you will not live in them;

2.2.7.4. But, *inwardly* they were insincere. No spiritual substance where it counted.
2.2.7.5. We see drunkenness
2.2.7.6. Dishonesty
2.2.7.7. The rich oppressing the poor
2.2.7.8. Even an opposition to the truly religious people.
2.2.7.9. We see highway robberies
2.2.7.10. Adultery, murders
2.2.7.11. In addition, of course...idolatry (2:6-8; 3:9-10).

2.2.8. Amos states in cps 1-2 that God's judgment is about to fall on many nations. Note the judgments on Damascus, Gaza, Tyre, Edom, Ammon, Moab, Judah, *and Israel*. These judgments make it clear that the Lord demands justice of any nation.

2.2.8.1. His last announcement was to the Northern Kingdom, which God was to judge for corruption and *lack of good hearts*.

2.2.8.2. Cps 3-6 form the main emphasis in the book. Three sermons concerning Israel's wickedness; in spite of the favor, which God had shown them, they were guiltier than the Gentile nations around them. In spite of all the warnings received, they had not returned to the Lord. The prophet's message is quite clear from verses 5:4, 6 *Seek Me that you may live.* Verse 5:14 repeats the simple message of morality, *Seek good and not evil, that you may live.*

2.2.8.3. They pretended to "worship," but their lives were filled with immortality. (5:21-24)

2.2.8.4. A lesson for us today. Do not settle for only "the appearance" of good. Goodness, in itself, will not assure you of a heavenly home. Only receiving Christ into one's heart will be the assurance of a home with Him.

2.2.8.5. Amos includes a series of five visions of God's approaching judgment (cps 7-9), each telling of doom coming upon Israel. His intercession withholds the locusts and devouring fire; other judgments take place.

2.2.8.5.1. The first two (locusts and intense heat) follow a pattern; Amos sees a woe to come, intercedes for Israel, and wins a reprieve. God delayed His judgment.

2.2.8.5.2. The third vision was God measuring Israel, found to be "out of plumb" and in danger of collapsing.

2.2.8.5.3.   The vision, which opens cp 8, is similar to Jeremiah's basket of figs (Jer 24:1-3). Israel is pictured as "ripe fruit" come to fullness and about to spoil. Darkness is approaching in verse 8:9.

2.2.8.5.4.   The fifth vision (9:1-10) Amos saw the Lord standing by the altar in His sanctuary, ready to destroy all the worshipers for living a sinful lifestyle. This foreshadows the return of Christ and the eventual judgment.

2.2.8.6.   The final cp ends with a promise of salvation and a returning remnant of Israel. The verses are so positive that a defining contrast is evident.

2.3. Then we conclude Section 3 of this volume, with **Hosea** (meaning *help* or *salvation*).

2.3.1. Hosea was a countryman of the Northern Kingdom, unlike Amos a citizen of Judah. Hosea was the only prophet native to the North. He implied that Israel "should have known better." Therefore, Hosea shows a strong compassion for the people of his land. He was quite able to understand God's love for his people. He was a contemporary of both Amos and Isaiah. He was inspired by God with a word to both the northern and southern kingdoms.

A Basic Outline of Hosea
1. An Unfaithful Wife, And A Faithful Husband, Cps 1-3
2. An Unfaithful Israel, And A Faithful God, Cps 4-14

Depth of Bible Words and Locations
Hosea Key Word: *Stumble*

Found in 4:5; 5:5. It literally means, "to totter, to trip and fall." It was generally used to describe the Hebrews spiritual life. Isaiah used it (40:30) to warn those who rely on their own strength would fall. Then again in Isaiah 63:13 he says those who are led by the Lord will NOT stumble. Also see 1 Samuel 2:4. Hosea wrote the book during this same period of Jonah and Amos; actually, his career spanned the last six kings of Israel—longer than the others. He probably knew a lot more than what we glean from his book.

> *Jesus in Hosea...He is your Redeemer! Your redemption is a completed act. Accept it! Thank Him for it.*

2.3.2. The book begins with a difficult and humiliating lesson to any man, a lesson that would emphasize the prophet's message.

2.3.3. The Lord tells Hosea to get married and announces his wife will not be faithful!

2.3.4. How would you like that? *("John, I want you to get married, and by-the-way, she's going to step out on you!")*.

2.3.5. Hosea marries a woman of questionable morals, named Gomer, and they have three children; their names tell the story quite clearly. 1. God will cause the northern kingdom to cease;[1] 2. He will no longer show love to them, His patience was over;[2] 3. He states openly *"You are not my people and I will not be your God."*[3] In spite of Israel's sin, God would find a way to restore them to sonship; Christ will come and unite all twelve tribes in one nation under one savior. We realize throughout this story, that Gomer is a symbol of Israel, and God tells her He will bring judgment upon her.

2.3.6. Then as God said, Gomer (Israel) deserts Hosea and becomes a common prostitute, eventually a slave. We understand that the fruit of her activity is the instrument of her redemption.[4] Ashamed of what has happened, and a lesson deeply learned, she cries out in Hos 2:7 *Then she will say, 'I will go back to my first husband, For it was better for me then than now!'*

2.3.7. A picture of the future millennial kingdom concludes the chapter. The earth will be set free from the curse. The land will overflow with corn, wine, and oil. The desert will blossom as the rose. The redeemed of Israel (along with those already taken to heaven), will live in prosperity and joy.[5]

2.3.8. In the small chapter three, again in the symbol of the relationship of Hosea to his wife, we view the ways of God with earthly people. Israel pictured as a harlot in earlier verses, now is an adulteress. Now she follows after strangers/foreigners instead of her husband.

---

[1] Hos 1:8...*Name him Jezreel; for yet a little while, and I will punish the house of Jehu for the bloodshed of Jezreel, and I will put an end to the kingdom of the house of Israel.*

[2] Hos 1:6 *"Name her Lo-ruhamah, for I will no longer have compassion on the house of Israel, that I would ever forgive them."*

[3] Hos 1:8b-9 *she conceived and gave birth to a son. 9 And the Lord said, "Name him Lo-ammi, for you are not My people and I am not your God."*

[4] Jer 2:19 *"Your own wickedness will correct you, And your apostasies will reprove you"*;

[5] Hos 2:19 *"I will betroth you to Me forever;*
Yes, I will betroth you to Me in righteousness and in justice,
In lovingkindness and in compassion,"
20 And I will betroth you to Me in faithfulness.
Then you will know the Lord. 22
And the earth will respond to the grain, to the new wine and to the oil,
23" I will also have compassion on her who had not obtained compassion,
And I will say to those who were not My people,
'You are My people!'
And they will say, 'You are my God!'"

The Lord tells Hosea in 3:1 *love a woman who is loved by her husband, yet an adulteress;* buy her back!

2.3.9. What a picture of love. Gomer is now striped of clothing in front of gawkers as bidding begins. Finally, the gavel falls, Hosea has brought back his wife! He rushes to her, putting clothing back on her, placing his protective arm around her as he escorts her home.

    2.3.9.1.1. It is here we hear these prophetic words of Hos 3:4 *For the sons of Israel will remain for many days without king or prince, without sacrifice or sacred pillar and without ephod or household idols. 5 Afterward the sons of Israel will return and seek the Lord their God and David their king; and they will come trembling to the Lord and to His goodness in the last days.*

    2.3.9.1.2. The *many days* run throughout the present day until the fullness of the Gentiles shall be completed.

2.3.10. That story serves as a picture of God's love for Israel. We never learn the end of Hosea and Gomer's story. It is a true story with a message of importance. The experience of Hosea's love for an unfaithful wife is a typology of God's love for an idolatrous people. It explains God's agony over Israel's unfaithfulness to their covenant relationship. Hosea, after the tragedy of his own marriage, reports on God's divorce case against Israel.

2.3.11. The story cries forth of grace to the underserved and exemplifies that grace, not merely *unmerited* favor, but it is favor in spite of *merited* judgment.

2.3.12. Hosea did not have to die for Gomer his wife; however, the experience allows us insight into God's love in Jesus Christ who loved us to the point of death.

2.3.13. Several years ago, my friend experienced his wife moving away and living a "free, open life style." Months into this, he found her in an evil place, told her he loved her and accepted her back into his home. During the remainder of their life, they seemingly loved one another, and he remained faithful to minister and teach the Word. As I think of this, I realize that only God could give such a rich love. Do you limit forgiveness?

2.4. Chapter 4 begins the second section of the book. Hosea records a series of messages to the Northern cities, whose knowledge and trust in God, had departed.[1] Their sins, thus far, had not been

---

[1] Hos 4:6 My people are destroyed for lack of knowledge.
Because you have rejected knowledge,
I also will reject you from being My priest.
Since you have forgotten the law of your God,

judged. Because Hosea was a citizen of the Northern Kingdom, his ministry was one of love for the people. He was able to express to them the love of God in unforgettable terms. His first warning was a catalog of sins, then a pleading with them to return to the God who loves them.[1]

2.5. The remaining chapters may have been writings at various intervals in Hosea's life, or as some scholars have suggested, a part of a single discourse continuing from chapter 4. The additional chastisement is similar, being addressed to Israel, but also at times including Judah.[2] I point out only a few key verses.

2.5.1. The first verses of chapter six are a momentary reference for the time when a remnant returns to God during the Tribulation and the following years of the Millennium. Revival and blessing along with daily growth in the knowledge of God rake place.

2.5.2. Chapter 7 details the *leaven* that for a considerable time was present.

Depth of Bible Words and Locations
Leaven

Throughout Scripture, the word always refers to some form of evil. False doctrine (Matt 16:11) are compared to yeast (leaven), because like yeast once fermentation begins, eventual permeation of the entire substance takes place. During the Passover week, no leaven was allowed in the house.

2.5.3. This was the constant state of Israel, Hos 7:8 *Ephraim mixes himself with the nations;* foreigners, strangers were allowed in, mixing their unbelief and gods with what should have remained a holy people. This was Ephraim's first and most disastrous mistake, keeping them from God's blessings until a remnant returned from Babylonia. Note how Hosea uses "Ephraim" to refer to the Northern Kingdom, no doubt because of the strength of that tribe.

2.5.4. Hos 7:10 *Though the pride of Israel testifies against him, Yet they have not returned to the Lord their God...12 I will chastise them....*

2.5.5. Sin always finds one out, judgment must come.

I also will forget your children.

[1] Hosea 4:1-2 *1 Hear the word of the Lord, O people of Israel! The Lord has brought charges against you, saying:"There is no faithfulness, no kindness, no knowledge of God in your land. 2 You make vows and break them; you kill and steal and commit adultery. There is violence everywhere—one murder after another.* (NLT)

[2] Hos 5:5 *Judah also has stumbled with them.*

2.5.6. Chapter eight warns a deluded people of their impending scattering among the nations, Hos 8:8 *Israel is swallowed up; They are now among the nations Like a vessel in which no one delights.* This verse describes their history for over two thousand years. They were driven out of their land and divided, a vessel in which God could take no delight. They would individually exist with no help from any nation, including Assyria who they turned to.

2.5.7. Chapter 10 compares Israel to an empty vine. Her empty heart[1] has no place for faith. The vine is similar to the crimson cord we have previously discussed. They both travel through Scripture, woven between its pages with significantly connected theology. Verse 10:6 shows the shadow of Assyria's "lurking."

    2.5.7.1. We may note that from Palms 80: 8 "Thou hast brought a vine out of Egypt..." to the *true vine* of John 15 we decipher the picture of an empty vine of Israel and Judah set aside by judgment with the True Vine who will never be replaced.

    2.5.7.2. Hos 10:8 *the sin of Israel, will be destroyed;*

2.5.8. Chapter eleven begins *When Israel was a youth I loved him, And out of Egypt I called My son.* Several times, Hosea references are to Egypt (see Ex 19-24).

    2.5.8.1. We note that God had in view, His own Son, Jesus Christ when the prophet uttered those words.[2] Once Israel was free from Egypt, she could never return there (v. 5). However, spiritually she did, and now judgment had to come.

    2.5.8.2. Chapters twelve and thirteen are a new section of prophecy (which actually began in 11:12). God exposes the moral decay of Israel and included Judah in His words.[3] Israel states in 12:8 *Surely I have become rich, I have found wealth for myself.* The pride reminds me of a friend, who even though had made a confession of Christ as Lord, forgot Him when the prosperity came. He commented, "One thing I will say, God did not give me this wealth, I earned it all."

    2.5.8.3. Israel had left her first love. Sin now prevailed in every class of society (v.2). A ray of grace shines in v. 14

---

[1] Hos 10:2 Their heart is faithless;
[2] Matt 2:14 *So Joseph got up and took the Child and His mother while it was still night, and left for Egypt. 15 He remained there until the death of Herod. This was to fulfill what had been spoken by the Lord through the prophet: "OUT OF EGYPT I CALLED MY SON."*
[3] Hos 12:2 *The Lord also has a dispute with Judah,*

> *Shall I ransom them from the power of Sheol? Shall I redeem them from death?*

2.5.8.4. This verse is the possible last hope for Israel and each person on earth. They answer is "Yes, but only if you turn from your evil ways and accept my grace through Jesus Christ."

2.5.8.5. The terrible extent of judgment they must undergo is stated in the final two verses of chapter 13.

2.5.9. The book ends with one of the most touching statements in Scripture. The final chapter of the book of Hosea looks beyond punishment to a better future. Return to the LORD your God. Come with your words before him and ask for forgiveness. No one can bring about redemption except God. The final words about His people...make wise use of the light you receive.[1]

2.6. Then, **Assyria** became the destroyer of Israel. Two invasions take place over a period of three years, taking most of Israel's land. Sargon the king of Assyria penned in his own written records that he captured 27,290 Israelites.

2.6.1. Interesting, this written description of that invasion was found in Assyrian records:

> The Assyrian invaders swept over Syria, northern Israel, Edom, and Moab in a deluge of death. Over 500 cities perished or paid tribute. Captives by the thousands were carried away to Assyria. The Assyrian monarch knew no mercy: *"His captains alive on stakes I hung them and exhibited them to his land."* The treasures of many lands were taken to Assyria to decorate the palaces of the king of Assyria and the mighty temples of his gods.

2.7. The Northern Kingdom, which fell in 721 BCE, existed 210 years and had twenty evil kings. Not all of the people were taken captive, some migrated to the South. Few, if any, of the people, returned from that Assyrian Captivity. The ten tribes, some say disappeared from history; however, that is not the case. We will not take the time to detail it here, but you may refer to the earlier Expanded Help Paper **The Terms "Israel" and "Judah,"** which will offer additional information on this.

---

[1] Hosea 14:9 *Whoever is wise, let him understand these things; Whoever is discerning, let him know them. For the ways of the Lord are right, And the righteous will walk in them,*

When you learn something from God: NEVER leave it behind; walk as He shows you the way.

2.8. In spite of many warnings through the prophets along with several judgments that manifested upon them, the kings continued in idolatry and the people failed to turn to God.
2.9. A sparse, mixed population grew in the old territory of Israel, made of people from the surrounding nations, a people who became the ancestors of the New Testament Samarians. Some Israelites migrated to the northwest. Not much of an ending for the nation, called Israel.

SECTION 4
THE SOUTHERN KINGDOM: JUDAH BEGINS

1 Kings 12:1-2 Kings 16:20; 2 Chronicles 10:1-28:27, Joel. The period from *c.* 975 to 721 BCE

Theme Statement: *"What shall I do with you, O Judah? For your loyalty is like a morning cloud*
And like the dew which goes away early."
(Hosea 6:4)

THE KEYS IN SECTION FOUR

Section 4: The Southern Kingdom: Judah Begins

Keep in mind, Sections Three and Four, include scriptures from the same books. The Keys and Outlines are repeated here for clarity.

Keys to First Kings—

A Key Word: *Baal*

The Key Verses (9:4–5; 11:11)

4 As for you, if you will walk before Me as your father David walked, in integrity of heart and uprightness, doing according to all that I have commanded you and will keep My statutes and My ordinances, 5 then I will establish the throne of your kingdom over Israel forever, just as I promised to your father David, saying, 'You shall not lack a man on the throne of Israel.'

11 So the Lord said to Solomon, "Because you have done this, and you have not kept My covenant and My statutes, which I have commanded you, I will surely tear the kingdom from you, and will give it to your servant."

The Key Chapter (12)

The Key People in 1 Kings

David—king of Israel; chose his son Solomon to be the next king (1–2:10); also see information for Key People in 1 Samuel (Section 6, Volume 1)

Solomon—third king of Israel; son of David and Bathsheba; builder of the first temple; God granted him his choice to become the wisest man ever born (1:10–11:43)

Rehoboam—son of Solomon; succeeded him as the fourth king of a united Israel; his evil actions led to the division of Israel into two kingdoms; later became king of the southern kingdom of Judah (11:43–12:24; 14:21–31)

Jeroboam—evil king of the northern ten tribes of Israel; erected idols and appointed non-Levitical priests (11:24–14:20).

Keys to Second Kings—

A Key Word: *High Places*

The Key Verses (17:22–23; 23:27)

22 The sons of Israel walked in all the sins of Jeroboam which he did; they did not depart from them 23 until the Lord removed Israel from His sight, as He spoke through all His servants the prophets. So Israel was carried away into exile from their own land to Assyria until this day.

27 The Lord said, "I will remove Judah also from My sight, as I have removed Israel. And I will cast off Jerusalem, this city which I have chosen, and the temple of which I said, 'My name shall be there.'"

The Key Chapter (25)

The Key People in 2 Kings

Elijah—a prophet of Israel; faced Ahab and Jezebel; raised a dead boy; called fire from heaven; never physically died; was carried directly to heaven in a chariot of fire (1:3–2:11; 10:10, 17)

Elisha—prophet trained under Elijah; close companion, became Elijah's successor; many similarities in ministry; asked for twice the anointing; saw Elijah taken to heaven (2:1–9:3; 13:14–21).

The woman from Shunem—the woman visited by Elijah in her home; brought her son back to life (4:8–37; 8:1–6)

Naaman—a Syrian warrior who suffered from leprosy; healed by Elisha (5:1–27)

Jezebel—evil queen of Israel; Baal worship introduced; attempted to prevent Israel from worshiping God; eventually killed and eaten by dogs (9:7–37)

Jehu—anointed king of Israel; used by God to punish Ahab's family (9:1–10:36; 15:12)

Joash—king of Judah, saved from death as a child; followed evil advice of younger friends, ultimately assassinated by his own officials (11:1–12:21)

Hezekiah—king of Judah who remained faithful to God (16:20–20:21)

Keys to First Chronicles—

A Key Word: *Sons*

The Key Verses (17:11–14; 29:11)

11 "When your days are fulfilled that you must go to be with your fathers, that I will set up one of your descendants after you, who will be of your sons; and I will establish his kingdom. 12 "He shall build for Me a house, and I will establish his throne forever. 13 "I will be his father and he shall be My son; and I will not take My lovingkindness away from him, as I took it from him who was before you. 14 "But I will settle him in My house and in My kingdom forever, and his throne shall be established forever."

11 Yours, O Lord, is the greatness and the power and the glory and the victory and the majesty, indeed everything that is in the heavens and the earth; Yours is the dominion, O Lord, and You exalt Yourself as head over all.

Key Chapter (17)

The Key People in 1 Chronicles

David—king of Israel and ancestor of Jesus Christ; described by God as "a man after My own heart" (2:8–29:30; see Acts 13:22) See Key People info. From 1 Samuel and 1 Kings.

The mighty men—a special group of soldiers who were dedicated to fighting for King David (11:10–28:1)

Nathan—a prophet and advisor to David; told Solomon of God's will for him to build the great first temple (17:1–15)

Solomon—David's son who became the third king of Israel (3:5–29:28)

Keys to Second Chronicles—

A Key Word: *Passover*

The Key Verses (7:14; 16:9)

14 *and My people who are called by My name humble themselves and pray and seek My face and turn from their wicked ways, then I will hear from heaven, will forgive their sin and will heal their land.*

9 *"For the eyes of the Lord move to and fro throughout the earth that He may strongly support those whose heart is completely His. You have acted foolishly in this. Indeed, from now on you will surely have wars."*

The Key Chapter (34)

The Key People in 2 Chronicles

Solomon—a king of Israel and builder of the first temple (1:1–9:31)

Queen of Sheba—heard of Solomon's great reputation; visited him seeking information about his success (9:1–12; see Matthew 12:42)

Rehoboam—evil son of Solomon who became king of Israel; soon divided the kingdom and later led the southern kingdom of Judah (9:31–13:7)

Asa—king of Judah; used very corrupt methods to accomplish God's purposes (14:1–16:14)

Jehoshaphat—son of Asa, followed him as king of Judah (17:1–22:9)

Jehoram—wicked son of Jehoshaphat who succeeded him as king of Judah; promoted idol worship and killed his six brothers (21:1–20)

Uzziah—(also called Azariah) succeeded his father, Amaziah, as king of Judah; mostly followed God, but prideful (26:1–23)

Ahaz—succeeded his father, Jotham, as king of Judah; continued Baal and other types of worship; sacrificed his own children (27:9–29:19)

Hezekiah—succeeded his father, Ahaz, as king of Judah; restored the temple; (28:27–32:33)

Manasseh—succeeded his father, Hezekiah, as king of Judah; did evil in the sight of the Lord but repented later in his reign (32:33–33:20)

Josiah—succeeded his father, Amon, as king of Judah; followed the Lord; found the Book of the Law while restoring the temple; took the Book to the people. Brought revival/reforms (33:25–35:27)

Keys to Joel—

A Key Word: *Spirit*

The Key Verses (2:11, 28–29)

11 The Lord utters His voice before His army; Surely His camp is very great, for strong is he who carries out His word. The day of the Lord is indeed great and very awesome, and who can endure it?

28 It will come about after this That I will pour out My Spirit on all mankind; and your sons and daughters will prophesy, your old men will dream dreams, your young men will see visions. 29 "Even on the male and female servants I will pour out My Spirit in those days."

The Key Chapter (2)

The Key People in Joel

Joel—prophet to the people of Judah during the reign of Joash (1:1–3:21)

The people of Judah—the southern kingdom punished for their sins by a locust plague (1:2; 2:1; 3:1–2, 19–21)

\	Approximate Dates of Key Events in Section 4
975BCE	The northern and southern kingdoms divide
955	Asa king of Judah
898	Jehoram becomes king in Judah
879	Joash becomes king of Judah
810	Azariah (Uzziah) becomes king in Judah
758	Jotham co-reigns in Judah with the leprous Uzziah
750	Isaiah/Micah begin to prophesy in Judah
742	Ahaz begins his reign in Judah
734	Israel and Syria was against Judah
732	Damascus falls to the Assyrians
726	Hezekiah becomes king of Judah
721	The Northern Kingdom is taken captive by the Assyrians
701	Assyria lays siege against Jerusalem in the south

SEVEN

Judah begins

1. We begin Section 4, **THE SOUTHERN KINGDOM: JUDAH BEGINS**.
   - 1.1. We'll review the Southern Kindom of Judah over the next three sections of our journey. *Both* the history of Israel and Judah are noted in these sections.
     - 1.1.1. In Section 4 we will cover the same 250 years, which we covered in Section 3. Section 4 concerns the Southern Kingdom. Specifically, in this Section, we will cover 1 Kings 12 through 2 Kings 16, 2 Chronicles 10-27, and Joel.
     - 1.1.2. I again point out that the events we review in Judah were happening during the same period as the events we reviewed in Section 3 which covered Israel. Our theme for this section is from Hosea 6:4: *What shall I do with you, O Judah? For your loyalty is like a morning cloud And like the dew which goes away early*. Not a very encouraging summary for any nation.
   - 1.2. We discovered in Section 3 that the Northern Kingdom of Israel had all the advantages to be a spiritual and commercial giant. However, the Southern Kingdom of Judah existed an additional 140 years following the capture of Israel. We will look at those additional years in the next Section.
   - 1.3. Judah had twenty rulers, a single dynasty,[1] and all but one (Queen Athaliah) are in the line of David. The seed-line to Jesus Christ went through Judah.

---

[1] A reminder: Israel, the Northern Kingdom, had *twenty* rulers from *nine* dynasties.

The Kings of Judah (Two Southern Tribes)

King	Date
1 Rehoboam	975-959 BCE
2 Abijam (Abijah)	958-955
3 Asa*	955-914
4 Jehoshaphat*	914-889
5 Joram (Jehoram)	898-884
6 Ahaziah	884
7 Athaliah**	884-878
8 Jehoash (Joash)*	879-839
9 Amaziah*	839-811
10 Uzziah (Azariah)*	810-758
11 Jotham*	758-742
12 Ahaziah	742-726
13 Hezekiah*	726-697
14 Manasseh	697-642
15 Amon	642-640
16 Josiah*	640-609
17 Jehoahaz (Shallum)	609-
18 Jehoiakim (Eliakim)	607-596
19 Jehoiachin (Jeconiah)	597
20 Zedekiah (Mattania)	597-586

*"positive" kings   **only female ruler of Judah

1.4. A short comparison of kings (see the Kings of Israel in Section 3) reveals that all the kings of Israel were idolaters. Jehoahaz turned to God only in times of great distress. However, among Judah's kings were many who started out well, of whom it might be said that "as long as he sought the LORD, God make him to prosper" (2 Chron 26:5). With most of them, however, failure came eventually to mar their testimony and bring sorrow and troubles.

Depth of Bible Words and Locations
Judah

One of the sons of Jacob and Leah. Also the descendants of Judah, later becoming the tribe of Judah. When the division of the nation took place, the two tribes of Judah and Benjamin took the name Judah referring to the Southern Kingdom. These were the Jews.

1.5. For clarification, 1 and 2 Kings concerns *both* the Northern (Israel) and the Southern (Judah) Kingdoms, first reviewing one, and then mentioning the events in the other, during the same 250-year period. So both Sections 3 and 4 of our course draw from the same Old Testament books.

    1.5.1. For Judah, as with Israel, this was a period of spiritual decline. Only a few periods of revival interrupt the decline.

Judah Begins: The Kings

1.5.2. Most of 2 Chronicles covers only the events in Judah and emphasizes the period when a priesthood and worship in the Temple were maintained which did not happen in Israel. This is perhaps the main reason Judah was allowed to exist 140 years longer than Israel.

1.5.3. Refer to the following simplified method to use in identifying these six books. It is repeated here for clarification.

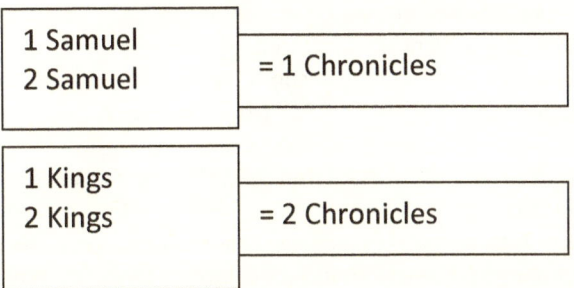

1.5.4. It is believed Ezra wrote Chronicles. The final verses of 2 Chronicles and beginning verses of Ezra are almost identical.

1.5.5. Ezra was a priest and scribe. Ezra mentions fifteen different books, outside the canon, which he draws his history from. (See list in Vol One, Cp FIFTEEN). A couple of other scriptures that mention other writings are 1 Kings 11:41 & 2 Chronicles 16:11. Review the chart included in this work which lists many Scriptures referring to other books utilized in Scripture. None of them made it into the cannon but were valuable history for Ezra. Archeologists have found fragments of many books dating back to that period.

1.5.6. There are also other writings in existence, which give us information about different periods of history. Archeologists found one tablet in 1993 CE,[1] mentioning David and his family line, the first historical verification of King David's existence.

1.5.7. The first eighty years of Judah's history was a cycle of a declining spiritual life followed by revival.

1.5.8. Only four kings ruled during the first eighty years. The four were descendants of David and Solomon, but as we will see, quite unlike them. Note that during this same period, ten kings ruled in Israel.

---

[1] Called the Dan Stele, now viewable in the Israel Museum. It reads "House of David"

1.6. The four kings, Rehoboam, Abijah, Asa, and Jehoshaphat, formed the foundation of the Southern Kingdom of Judah. We highlight the era of those four kings.
- 1.6.1. After Solomon's death in 975 BCE, his son, Rehoboam, became king with little opposition. We are not told of any other sons of Solomon, however, we do know of two daughters mentioned in 1 Kings 4:11, 15.
    - 1.6.1.1. Rehoboam grew up in luxury (the son of a king, surrounded by a "kingly" atmosphere). However, he did not seem to absorb much of the wisdom of his dad. His attitude at the beginning of his rule is far from the early humility of Solomon.
    - 1.6.1.2. He ruled with absoluteness, believing the people did not have any rights. Representatives of the tribes demanded relief from high taxation in exchange for their loyalty. However, after considering their demands, he turned from his father's counselors to the advice of his young friends.[1] Not a very wise leader!
    - 1.6.1.3. Rehoboam barely escaped with his life from the revolution which followed.
    - 1.6.1.4. Soon he gathered an army in an attempt to force the ten tribes of the North to come under his rule. For three years, he fortified his border towns and his capital in Jerusalem.
    - 1.6.1.5. He ruled a total of seventeen years with a marked increase in establishing idolatry. Many of the Levites and other Godly families moved from the Northern Kingdom to Jerusalem so they could continue the required worship. Nevertheless, this was not enough to overcome the idolatry.
    - 1.6.1.6. Think about this: The grandson of David, leading God's nation into idol worship!
    - 1.6.1.7. Of course, this made Judah weak. Within five years into his rule, Egypt invaded and advanced all the way into the temple stealing much of Solomon's treasuries. Shishak was the king of Egypt who invaded Jerusalem (2 Chron 12:9). Shishak has

---

[1] *2 Chronicles 10:8-11 and (Rehoboam) consulted with the young men who grew up with him and served him. 9 So he said to them, "What counsel do you give that we may answer this people, who have spoken to me, saying, 'Lighten the yoke which your father put on us'?" 10 The young men who grew up with him spoke to him, saying, "Thus you shall say to the people who spoke to you, saying, 'Your father made our yoke heavy, but you make it lighter for us.' Thus you shall say to them, 'My little finger is thicker than my father's loins! 11 'Whereas my father loaded you with a heavy yoke, I will add to your yoke; my father disciplined you with whips, but I will discipline you with scorpions.'"*

possibly been identified as Shoshenq 1 according to discovered Egyptian records. His invasion was aimed at strengthening the new kingdom of Israel.[1]

1.6.1.8. Solomon's magnificent kingdom took a plunge. Ten of the twelve tribes rebelled and formed the Northern Kingdom called Israel.

1.6.1.9. Back in Egypt, the king pictured the victory on *his* great temple walls, which Archeologists have discovered. Egypt's real goal was to weaken Judah so that Israel and Judah would balance each other in world affairs. As a result, Israel and Judah would not be in the way of expansion for Egypt. This changed when Egypt fell into Babylonian hands.

1.6.2. Following Rehoboam, his son, Abijah, ruled for three years. Before his death in 959 BCE, Rehoboam seems to have been grooming Abijah to be his successor (2 Chronicles 11:21-22). Abijah continues the idolatry with the worship of Asherah, a goddess of immortality which was extremely offensive to God. He also was the king when a full-scale war broke out between Judah and Israel. This was a civil war between "God's" people.

1.6.2.1. For the first eighteen years of the two separate nations, various skirmishes took place. These were in the form of guerrilla strikes (1 Kings 15:6). However, Abijah gathered an army of some 400,000 and inflicted a massacre on the northern army of 800,000. Although Abijah was an idolater, the Judeans cried out to God for help.

1.6.2.2. This victory helped prepare the way for a revival of Judah's faith, which came during the reign of Abijah's son, Asa.

1.6.3. King Asa began his forty-one-year rule in 955 BCE, at a very young age. His grandfather, Rehoboam, the first king of Judah, passed away only three years earlier at the age of fifty-eight. During Asa's rule in Judah, seven kings followed each other in the north (Israel).

1.6.3.1. For ten years, peace prevailed between North and South. The Northern Kingdom had been left weakened by the civil war and Egypt was slowly deteriorating. All this contributed

---

[1] Jeroboam, the first king of Israel had fled Solomon and found refuge with Sheshonk in Egypt. Sheshonk felt it was best to have Solomon's empire divided in two halves, thus cancelling each other out in the site of world power.

towards relative peace. A religious revival was now underway and to some extent, idolatry was being driven away.[1]

1.6.3.2. During these first ten years of young Asa's rule, he burned the idol shrines and the people were urged to serve God and keep the Law. The ugly practices required in the worship of Asherah and Baal were driven from the land. This was all positive and led to religious reformation.

Depth of Bible Words and Locations
Asherah

(A'sherah) A fertility goddess, the mother of Baal, whose worship was concentrated in Syria and Canaan.

According to ancient mythology, Asherah, the mother goddess, was the wife of El and mother of seventy gods, of whom Baal was the most famous.

The Asherah existed in both the Southern and Northern Kingdoms of Israel. Jezebel of Tyre apparently installed Asherah worship in the north when she married King Ahab. Like so much else in Canaanite religion, the name and worship of Asherah were borrowed from Assyria. Her "image" is mentioned in the Old Testament (1 Kings 15:13 II Kings 21:7; 2 Chronicles 15:16), as well as her "prophets" (2 Kings 18:19) and the vessels used in her service (2 Kings 23:4).

1.6.3.3. After years of attempts to correct morals and spiritual live, peace came to an abrupt halt. Military invasion came from Ethiopia and Libya along with some assistance from a weakened Egypt. Asa's prayer before the battle is one of the most faith-filled in the Old Testament:

2 Chronicles 14:11-13. *Then Asa called to the Lord his God and said, "Lord, there is no one besides You to help in the battle between the powerful and those who have no strength; so help us, O Lord our God, for we trust in You, and in Your name have come against this multitude. O Lord, You are our God; let not man prevail against You."* And note, when he prays in faith, what happens? Verse 12 *So the Lord*

---

[1] 1 Kings 15:14 *But the high places were not taken away; nevertheless the heart of Asa was wholly devoted to the Lord all his days.* So he made only a partial attempt at revival. He left the HIGH PLACES of idol worship, alone. He should have torn those down also. We looked at the KEY WORD in 2 Kings "High Places." This was the downfall time and again; make reforms, but leave these High Places, which became locations to worship pagan gods.

routed the Ethiopians before Asa and before Judah, and the Ethiopians fled.

- 1.6.3.4. Asa's army was outnumbered more than two to one (sound familiar to Abijah's battle?). However, this is no obstacle for God; He intervenes and defeats the larger force in the valley of Zephathah.
- 1.6.3.5. So victory came and Asa gathered the people for worship at the request of the prophet Azariah, son of Oded. Asa renewed the ancient covenant with God, destroying idol worship in the land.
- 1.6.3.6. But, again following the sad cycle that we've seen so many times, one sin after another in Asa's life leads to him dying of disease, recorded in 2 Chronicles 16:12 *In the thirty-ninth year of his reign Asa became diseased in his feet. His disease was severe, yet even in his disease he did not seek the Lord, but the physicians.*
- 1.6.3.7. We see in Asa's life that a good start does not guarantee a victorious finish. A life for God must be maintained until death to experience final victory.
- 1.6.4. The son of Asa was Jehoshaphat and was a rare bright light in Judah's long history. His twenty-five years of reign saw revival and end to the war with Israel. His rule started in 914 BCE and was a co-rule with his father during his 2 years of severe illness.
- 1.6.4.1. His first task was to restore a pure religion to Judah. He carried the available Scriptures (possibly the Torah, and Law) throughout Judah teaching it to the people. You would think that the four kings we are reviewing would once and forever realize how simple it was to serve God and reap His blessings!
- 1.6.4.2. Then Jehoshaphat makes serious mistakes.[1]
- 1.6.4.2.1. #1 He thought he could unite the two kingdoms by the marriage of his son to the daughter of Ahab and Jezebel, king and queen on the Northern Kingdom (we will review that marriage later).
- 1.6.4.2.2. #2 He made a military agreement with Ahab (2 Chronicles 18:1) of the Northern Kingdom. Together they led the armies into battle against the Syrians; a battle they lost and in which Ahab was killed.
- 1.6.4.2.3. #3 He also attempted to make a major trade agreement with the Northern Kingdom, which also failed to unite the two nations.

---

[1] 2 Chronicles 18:1-2 *Now Jehoshaphat had great riches and honor; and he allied himself by marriage with Ahab.*

1.6.4.3. Jehoshaphat continued his works of religious reformation and other reforms. His formation of judges throughout the nation, sort of a court of appeals, was the possible forerunner of the Sanhedrin of Christ's time.

1.6.4.4. #The time of peace was interrupted by an invasion of Moabites and Ammonites from east of the Jordan River. The people, after seeking God, received His assurance of victory.[1]

1.6.5. The final words at Jehoshaphat's death at the age of sixty summarize a good attempt to do right.[2]

1.7. The next difficult period of fifty years is a direct result of the unholy alliance, which was made with Ahab. Judah is ruled during these fifty years by three kings and a wicked queen.

1.7.1. First, Jehoram (also known as Joram), an unhappy son of Jehoshaphat married the daughter (Athaliah) of Ahab and Jezebel. This is the marriage mentioned above, as one of the mistakes of his father. 2 Kings 8:17-19 *He was thirty-two years old when he became king, and he reigned eight years in Jerusalem. 18 He walked in the way of the kings of Israel, just as the house of Ahab had done, for the daughter of Ahab became his wife; and he did evil in the sight of the Lord.*

1.7.1.1. His eight years of reign began by murdering his six brothers and some princes who might have been a threat to his supremacy. The throne was really ruled by the daughter of Jezebel and wife of Jehoram. Athaliah forced Judah to turn from God to worship Baal (2 Chronicles 21:11).

1.7.1.2. She had shrines erected throughout the land to escalate this worship of Baal, which resulted in national weakness. Many of the territories of Judah began to revolt. We read a clear summary in 2 Chronicles 21:19-20.[3]

1.7.1.3. This is the time when Elijah (Prophet to the Northern Kingdom), sent a letter to Jehoram denouncing the idolatry.

---

[1] 2 Chron 20:15 *the battle is not yours but God's.*

[2] 2 Chronicles 20:32-33 *He walked in the way of his father Asa and did not depart from it, doing right in the sight of the Lord. 33 The high places, however, were not removed; the people had not yet directed their hearts to the God of their fathers.*

[3] *Now it came about in the course of time, at the end of two years, that his bowels came out because of his sickness and he died in great pain. And his people made no fire for him like the fire for his fathers. 20 He was thirty-two years old when he became king, and he reigned in Jerusalem eight years; and he departed with no one's regret, and they buried him in the city of David, but not in the tombs of the kings.*

However, the influence of Jehoram's wife was so strong that Elijah's message went unheeded.

1.7.1.4. Because of continued decline by Judah, Edom denounced and revolted against them. Next, the Philistines and Arabians invaded Judah from the south and west.

1.7.1.5. We read that Jehoram lived a short, sinful life and died a lonely death. His bones were separated from the burial of past kings because of unworthiness.

1.7.2. Jehoram's son Ahaziah, grandson of Jezebel, reigned only one year, 884 BCE. His rule was controlled by the evil mother who forced her leadership into becoming queen. Ahaz continued the agreement of peace with Israel where his uncle was king (same name, a different man, Jehoram).[1]

1.7.2.1. It was during this time in the North that Jehu, (a future king of Israel) set out to bring judgment on the evil King Ahab. He believed he was appointed by God to destroy Ahab and his house. Eventually, he killed Jehoram, King of Israel, along with his mother Jezebel, and the entire Ahab house. He then killed Ahaziah, King of Judah.

1.7.3. This daughter of Ahab and Jezebel (Athaliah) became queen of Judah. We mentioned her as the real power during eight years of her husband, Jehoram's rule and the one-year rule of her son, Ahaziah. She was nasty!

1.7.3.1. She murders all of her grandchildren except Joash. Joash, (also known at times as Jehoash), was saved by his aunt Jehoshabeath and was hid in the temple while his vicious grandmother ruled Judah. Hid in secret for the six years of Athaliah's reign, he was passed off as a grandson of the high priest.

1.7.3.2. Athaliah probably was concerned that one of Ahaziah's sons would become king following his death, so she removed them.

1.7.3.3. Again, we mention, Satan tried every angle to destroy the "seed." Joash was the only remaining son in the line that led to that seed, The Messiah. Kill Joash and there would be no seed to strike Satan's seed (at least that was Satan's hope).

---

[1] 2 Chronicles 22:3 *He also walked in the ways of the house of Ahab, for his mother was his counselor to do wickedly.*

TRAVEL THROUGH THE OLD TESTAMENT

Depth of Bible Words and Locations
Baal

We have not talked much about *Baal*, (which is also **A KEY WORD** in 1 Kings). We mentioned this idol several times. We will see it again.

Baal was a pagan god of storms and fertility and had a strong influence on the Hebrews.

Saul, Jonathan, and even David had sons with the name Baal in it.

Jeremiah reports that altars of incense were burned to Baal in Jerusalem (Jeremiah 11:13). We know the worship of Baal goes back to Moses' time in Numbers. Babylonia called their god, Bel identical to Baal. We came across Baal-Zebub in 2 Kings.

Almost the entire Middle East worshiped Baal because of his (supposedly) powerful forces, which they believed.

The name means "owner" or "master," even translated "husband" in some cases. We've seen Baal associated with the goddess of fertility, Ashtaroth. Judges 2:13 reads *So they forsook the Lord and served Baal and the Ashtaroth*. The following of Baal involved prostitution and infant sacrifice. And to think, God's people time and again turned to Baal!

> 1.7.4. Joash became king when the high priest Jehoiada revealed him when he was seven years old, and proclaimed him as the rightful king. The high priest initiated an elaborate plan to rid Judah of its unworthy ruler. On the specific Sabbath, Jehoiada anointed Joash in front of the people. The Queen? The people took her out and killed her!
>
> 1.7.4.1. This action returned a descendant of David to the throne of Judah.
>
> 1.7.4.2. Joash reigned for forty years beginning in 835 BCE. His reign neatly fits into two periods.
>
> 1.7.4.3. As mentioned, the early years were under the influence of the high priest Jehoiada who mentored and encouraged Joash to make spiritual changes in the nation. God's people made a covenant, but as we will see, "people break covenants." God's covenants are eternal. He never breaks a promise.
>
> 1.7.4.4. Refer to the next Expanded Help Paper, **Four Covenants**, which we see in the Old Testament. They were "fixed"; they were sure.

EXPANDED HELP PAPER

Judah Begins: The Kings

Four Covenants

The Noah Covenant

The rainbow that appears after a rain shower is a sign of God's promise (covenant/agreement) to never again destroy the earth by flood.

Because of the violence on earth, God determined to save a righteous man, Noah and his family and make a covenant with them.

The Bible says Noah walked with God in the midst of all kinds of evil. His obedience to God is recorded five times in this story, (Genesis 6:22; 7:5, 9, 16; 8:17).

Noah followed God's instructions in building a large ark, which saved him and his family in the cleansing waters of a flood. Noah and his family (God's people) could then start a new generation. Indeed, God's covenant promised that until the end of the earth, there would be seasons of planting and harvest and day and night. It also included a promise to uphold the rhythms of the earth in order to sustain human life, even though humans had rebelled against their Creator.

Today all of us, Noah's descends, should remember God's mercy to us when we see the beauty of the rainbow.

The Abraham Covenant

God's covenant with Abraham began with the unconditional promise in Genesis 12:2 *And I will make you a great nation, And I will bless you.* God promised He would multiply Abram's descendants and give them a land of promise, Canaan (13:14-17). I love this: He swore by Himself that He would do it! (22:15-18). Nothing is surer than His Word.

As with all covenants, God made demands. He commanded Abram and Sarai to leave their home and family in Ur, and go to a new land (12:1). He commanded them to be a blessing to others (12:2), to walk before Him and be blameless (17:1), and to circumcise the males in their household as a sign of the covenant (17:10). God asked for obedience, and Abram withstood the test of believing and obeying (15:6; 22:1-19).

The Moses Covenant

At a mountain called Mt. Sinai, for the first time, God made a covenant with the entire nation of Israel (Exodus cps 19-24).

In this covenant, God first reminded the Israelites of who He was and how He had acted on their behalf. He was their Savior (19:4). And if they made a covenant with Him, He promised to make the Israelites *My own possession* (Exodus 19:5). He would pay special attention to them and make them *a kingdom of priests and a holy nation.* God demanded of them that they would become holy or separated from all other nations. By that separation, they were to be the means by which the other nations would learn of the living God. This nation of priests would lead others to a correct worship of the true God (Psalms 117).

In this covenant, God promised to instruct the Israelites on how they should live (cp 20). As a people who had a relationship with the living God, the Israelites had to act a certain way, His Way. His Law would instruct them on this way of life. He loved them so much He taught them how to live in His Kingdom, now being established on earth.

The New Covenant
Jeremiah is the only Old Testament prophet who speaks of the New Covenant, (which Jesus authored in Matthew 26:28). In reading "new" in the New Covenant, one might be tempted to think of the former covenant, the Moses Covenant, as something that was incorrect. The Law of Moses was never designed as a means to obtain salvation. Instead, forgiveness of sins has always been God's gracious gift to those who have humbled themselves before Him in faith (Genesis 15:16; Micah 6:6-8). The Law was God's way of showing the journey, which believers should follow. In actuality, Israel did not follow that Law which pointed to life. The Israelites continually broke that covenant. God had demands to be met; however time and again through priests and prophets, they would repent and then fall away from Him. Idols many times replaced God. The hearts of the people remained unchanged. Only God Himself could change hearts and minds—thus, a New Covenant was needed.

Think of what the Israelites must have thought considering this New Covenant, announced by Jeremiah. The old covenant had come from the very hand of God, written as His glory streamed from His finger, cutting out words on a tablet of stone. The New Covenant would be His glory burning in a new heart, which would lead to the changed life! Also, now they would have a "helper" to guide them to the covenant (Jeremiah 31:34). No priest or prophet would be needed to stand between a human and God! That Spirit would teach the people the knowledge of God, a knowledge that would be evidence by faith, obedience, and devotion to a personal Lord.

1.7.4.5. Always keep in mind; God is still a covenant maker. If a believer will find a Word of God to stand on, follow it, and do it, God covenants with him/her to do what He says.

1.7.4.6. Joash repaired the temple through gifts of the people. Temple worship was reestablished because of that influence from the High Priest. You remember that Joash's grandmother Queen Athaliah had set up idol worship, and as a result, the temple had deteriorated. As long as the high priest lived, the sacrifices required for worship were observed.

1.7.4.7. Things changed in Joash's later years of rule. Jehoiada the High Priest died at the age of 139, and it becomes quite evident that Joash had little spiritual foundation of his own. He soon allows Baal worship back into the temple! He even has the high priest's son, Zechariah, killed.[1]

1.7.4.8. And because of Joash's weakness, Jerusalem is invaded by Syrians within a year and the temple treasuries took away. Joash's own servants killed him in his bed.

1.7.4.9. The king's body was buried in Jerusalem, but not in the burial place of the kings who ruled before him. His death brings to close the second cycle of the decline of Judah. Its death is soon to come.

1.8. Now keep in mind that we are looking at this "common" 250-year period of the Northern and Southern Kingdoms.

1.8.1. We have reviewed four kings of the Southern Kingdom, during eighty years.

1.8.2. They were followed by three kings and a queen during the next fifty-two years.

1.8.3. Below is a list of kings from both the Northern and Southern Kingdoms (combined from the earlier two lists.)

The Kings of Judah (Two Southern Tribes) and
The Kings of Israel (Ten Northern Tribes)

Judah		Israel	
1 Rehoboam	975-959 BCE	1 Jeroboam	975-954 BCE
2 Abijam (Abijah)	958-955		
3 Asa*	955-914	2 Nadab	954-953
		3 Baasha	953-930
		4 Elah	930-929
		5 Zimri	929
		6 Tibni	929-924

---

[1] 2 Chronicles 24:20-22 *Then the Spirit of God came on Zechariah the son of Jehoiada the priest; and he stood above the people and said to them, "Thus God has said, ' Why do you transgress the commandments of the Lord and do not prosper? Because you have forsaken the Lord, He has also forsaken you."' 21 So they conspired against him and at the command of the king they stoned him to death in the court of the house of the Lord. 22 Thus Joash the king did not remember the kindness which his father Jehoiada had shown him, but he murdered his son. And as he died he said, "May the Lord see and avenge!"*

			7 Omri	929-917
			8 Ahab	918-897
4 Jehoshaphat*	914-889			
			9 Ahaziah	898-897
			10 Jehoram (Joram)	897-884
5 Joram (Jehoram)	898-884			
6 Ahaziah	884		11 Jehu	884-857
7 Athaliah**	884-878			
8 Jehoash (Joash)*	879-839			
			12 Jehoahaz	857-840
9 Amaziah*	839-811		13 Jehoash	840-826
10 Uzziah (Azariah)*	810-758		14 Jeroboam II	826-785
			15 Zachariah	784-773
			16 Shallum	772
11 Jotham*	758-742		17 Menahem	772-762
12 Ahaziah	742-726		18 Pekahiah	761-760
			19 Pekah	759-739
13 Hezekiah*	726-697		20 Hoshea	730-720
14 Manasseh	697-642			
15 Amon	642-640			
16 Josiah*	640-609			
17 Jehoahaz (Shallum)	609-608			
18 Jehoiakim (Eliakim)	607-596			
19 Jehoiachin (Jeconiah)	597			
20 Zedekiah (Mattania)	597-586			

2   It is generally accepted that a prophet named Joel ministers at this time.
  2.1. We begin with two difficult issues surrounding the book of Joel. (1) What is the historical period, and (2) Who is the author?
    2.1.1. Concerning the first difficulty, many theories have been suggested, placing the book at any time from the ninth to the second centuries BCE. This book, along with Obadiah, which we'll review in Section 6, seems to be the only two Old Testament books having this difficulty. Specific dating can only be speculative. Even though the message of the book is not hindered by an uncertain date, we will attempt to identify the date as precisely as the evidence allows. This identification must be made from whatever internal evidence the book might offer.

Judah Begins: Joel

2.1.1.1. Most scholars settle on one of three dates for the book. An *early date* proposed by some scholars (including this author) includes the period during the reign of Joash (879-839 BCE). A young Joash became king at the age of seven (2 Kings 11:21) and was trained under the high priest Jehoiada. The style of writing is close to the style of other early prophets, Amos, Micah, and Isaiah, allowing for the credibility of the early date. The placement in the Hebrew canon, between Hosea and Amos who we know, are early pre-exilic prophets, help to date the book. Joel in mentioning several enemies, Philistia, Egypt, and Edom, may indicate a time prior to the Assyrian and Babylonian threats, which he would have mentioned. If this is the correct period, Joel was a contemporary with and probably knew Elijah and Elisha, which made him the first of the writing prophets.

2.1.1.2. A second proposed date would include invasions by Assyria (722-702) and Babylon (588-586).

2.1.1.3. A third proposed date, *a later date,* is a post-exilic date after the exiles returned to Jerusalem and rebuilt the walls and temple. Several reasons are offered for this date. Judah's government was under the control of the Persians who directed the priests in Judah, for there was no king. Joel directed his book to the elders rather than to the king.[1] There is no mention of the invading armies of Assyria (709 BCE), Babylon (588 BCE) or any other. In addition, the frequent references (if they are indeed references to other prophet's writings) would place Joel as one of the later prophets. In addition, there is no mention of Baal worship, which would have been present during the earlier date. This proposal places the book of Joel during the period after 516 BCE.

2.1.1.4. We will recognize that Joel prophesied during or slightly after the period of King Joash (879-839). As we will see, Joel, the first of the writing prophets, looks down through the centuries and sees the Day of the Lord. We note that prophecy may be in many parts, have many applications, and is not limited to local events. Several of the prophets would speak to a local situation and then move out into the future events of Tribulation and Millennium.

2.1.2. The second difficulty centers on the author of the book. Joel, like Jonah, limits his identification. The book is named after the

---

[1] Joel 1:2 *Hear this, O elders*

writer, the prophet Joel, a common Old Testament name—the name meaning "the Lord is God." In Hebrew, it is the name *Yo el*, "el" always meaning God. Little is known about him other than 1:1 *"Joel the son of Pethuel."* He was not a son of Samuel mentioned in 1 Samuel 8:1-2, for Samuel's sons' character, was the opposite of Joel's. His father's name means "vision" or "wisdom of God." We are not even aware of his tribe.

2.1.3. The author of Joel refers to Zion and the ministry of the temple, indicating he was a prophet to Judah and Jerusalem. Like all true prophets, Joel was commissioned to call the people back to the worship of the true God; Joel wanted the people of Judah to understand what God was saying to them through the plague and the drought. He uses the destruction of the locusts and blends that event into the future threat out of the northern army, the Day of the Lord.

2.1.4. Joel was the one to announce "The Day of the Lord." He applied it to two events: The destruction by the locusts (during his day), and the future threat of the northern army, the Day of the Lord, the judgment that the Lord would send on the whole world. Joel has the amazing insight given by the wisdom of God as he blends the two events together.

A Basic Outline of Joel
1. Devastation of Judah (historical), Cp 1
2. Destroyers From The North (transitional), Cp 2:1-17
3. Restoration By God, Cp 2:18-3:21

Depth of Bible Words and Locations
Joel Key Word: *Spirit*

Found in Joel, we read in 2:28. The basic word in Hebrew signifies breath, "to breathe" or "to blow." Actually, the word could be associated with an evil spirit or the Spirit of God, (1 Samuel 16:14-16; Psalms 51:11).

Jesus in Joel...He is the baptism with the Holy Ghost and Fire.

---

3   Joel begins his writing by addressing four groups of citizens and delivers the thoughts from the Lord. *Hear this* he states in v.1.

3.1. He addressed the old men first, asking them if they had ever experienced or even heard of devastation such as this. He tells them to pass this experience on to their children. He also addresses the drunkards, the farmers, and the priests, all who would be affected by the destruction from swarms that resemble a nation of mighty warriors (which will naturally blend into the further description in chapter two).

    3.1.1. Joel describes a black cloud over the land, an invasion of locusts and a famine, which followed.[1] Every green thing is stripped bare.[2] The prophet seeks to use the calamity under which the people were then suffering to enlighten them as to their own spiritual state. He interprets this as God's judgment upon the people because of their sin. In that situation, the people are urged to turn to the Lord.

    3.1.2. The four-fold description of locusts (v. 4) probably conveys the idea of successive swarms of locusts invading the land, each swarm destroying what the others had left behind. A judgment from God because of their refusal to follow His will.

    3.1.3. The desolate description of the land is stated later in vv. 10-12.

3.1.3.1.	Ruined fields, grain destroyed
3.1.3.2.	Wheat and barley gone
3.1.3.3.	Vines dried up
3.1.3.4.	Fig trees gone
3.1.3.5.	Fruit dried up
3.1.3.6.	Trees destroyed

    3.1.4. Joel, using the event of his day as an example, calls upon the elders and all of the inhabitants of the land to sanctify a feast and cry unto the Lord.[3]

    3.1.5. The words of v. 15 perhaps could be the theme of the entire book of Joel, *For the day of the Lord is near.* See The Day of The Lord below.

3.2. In chapter two, we are ushered into the events of that (future) Day of the Lord.[4] The Day will come after the church has been taken into heaven, that God will again call Israel His nation. We note in verse 2:13 the very heart of prophecy:

---

[1] Joel 1:2 Has anything like this happened in your days
Or in your fathers' days?

[2] Joel 1:4 *What the gnawing locust has left, the swarming locust has eaten;
And what the swarming locust has left, the creeping locust has eaten;
And what the creeping locust has left, the stripping locust has eaten.*

[3] Joel 1:14 *Consecrate a fast, Proclaim a solemn assembly; Gather the elders And all the inhabitants of the land To the house of the Lord your God, And cry out to the Lord.*

[4] Joel 2:11 *The day of the Lord is indeed great and very awesome, And who can endure it?*

And rend your heart and not your garments. Now return to the Lord your God, For He is gracious and compassionate, Slow to anger, abounding in lovingkindness And relenting of evil.

- 3.2.1. Twice in chapter two, we read of the trumpet (v. 1, 15), each with a different emphasis. First, a trumpet sounds *an alarm*, informing the people of the events which will soon take place. The people will pass through dark days of Tribulation. An enemy will sweep over the land leaving it a desolate wilderness. An enemy like mighty horses running to battle,[1] they will seem to leap from mountains, leaving in flames all that is behind. They are an organized army, not breaking ranks, pressing on in power, nothing able to stop them.
    - 3.2.1.1. Even then, the LORD invites them (v. 12) to *"Return to Me with all your heart, And with fasting, weeping and mourning; And rend your heart and not your garments."* Outward acts are not what God demands; rather He desires a *heart* towards Him.
- 3.2.2. The second trumpet is recorded in v. 15. Not an alarm of what is to come, rather *blow a trumpet* of assembly. Again, a fast is called—the people must fast and cry out to God[2]
    - 3.2.2.1. They will repent, and God promises not only to remove the invading army but also to restore what has been destroyed.[3] The invasion of locusts was used as a picture of the great army, which will invade Israel in the last days. Had there been a turning to God in Joel's day, the immediate invasion would have been turned away.
- 3.3. Then Joel looks into the future and sees a worse coming judgment when God will destroy His enemies, followed by joy for His faithful ones.
    - 3.3.1. Five times Joel refers to the **Day of the Lord,** usually referring to an end time when God's holiness and power are shown to all.

EXPANDED HELP PAPER
The Day of the Lord

---

[1] Joel 2:4 *Their appearance is like the appearance of horses; And like war horses, so they run.*
[2] Joel 2:15 *Consecrate a fast, proclaim a solemn assembly,*
[3] Joel 2:19-20 *"Behold, I am going to send you grain, new wine and oil, And you will be satisfied in full with them; And I will never again make you a reproach among the nations. 20 "But I will remove the northern army far from you, And I will drive it into a parched and desolate land*

Judah Begins: Joel

One of the central themes of the Book of Joel is "the day of the Lord" (1:15; 2:1). This language describes a period of time in which God "comes down" in a dramatic way to bring wrath and judgment on the wicked *and* blessings *and* salvation to the righteous. God is Lord of time. Technically, there is no period that is not "the day of the Lord" in a general sense. But at times God enters the space-time arena to assert in bold, dramatic ways that He is in control.

The day of the Lord is a major theme of Old Testament prophecy. Thirteen of the sixteen prophets address this subject. The concept of the day of the Lord probably originated with the conquest of Canaan—a conquest which was in fact the Lord's war (see Deut. 1:30; 3:22; Josh 5:13–15; 6:2); that is, a day of judgment for the wicked Canaanites (see Lev. 18:25; Deut 9:4, 5).

The day of the Lord is not an *isolated* phenomenon or a *single event* in human history. Periods in Israel's early history and latter history, the coming of Jesus, and His second advent are all called "the day of the Lord" in Scripture. The predictions of a coming day of the Lord can be fulfilled in a number of different events. The invasion of locusts in the historic events of the life of Joel was the day of the Lord (cp. 2). In addition, the day of wrath and deliverance that soon fell on Judah in the Babylonian invasion was also the day of the Lord.

While most references speak of *future events*, and this author prefers to examine the subject in this manner, four biblical texts describe the day of the Lord in terms of *past judgments* (see Is 22:1–14; Jer 46:2–12; Lam 1:1–2:22; Ezek 13:1–9). These texts reflect circumstances of military defeat, tragedy, and judgment. Such events may have stimulated the development of the prophetic concept of a future "day" or time of judgment for the disobedient Israel and all of the nations (see Joel 1:15; Is 13:6, 9; Zeph 1:14–18).

However, the day of the Lord is not just a day of wrath and judgment on the disobedient. In some contexts, it *also* includes deliverance and restoration for the righteous, and indeed this author refers The Day in his summary below (and separate detailed manuscript. The day of the Lord speaks not only of future judgment, but also of future hope, prosperity, and blessing (see Is. 4:2–6; Hos 2:18–23; Amos 9:11–15; Mic 4:6–8). Joel reveals that this day is to be heralded by heavenly phenomena (2:30, 31) which will bring sudden darkness and gloom on the earth (2:2). It will be a day of divine destruction (1:15 on the nations that have persecuted Israel (3:12–14) and on the rebellious and disobedient of Israel (Amos 5:18–20). Yet it will also be a time of deliverance and unprecedented blessing for God's people (2:32; 3:16, 18–21; 1 Thess 5:2–5), a direct reference to a "catching away" of believers.

With that summary, note that the author has an extensive manuscript on "The Day of the Lord." A few additional statements will outline the main points. (1) As we approach the final days and **final** Day of the Lord, we should expect greater insight into the time of the rapture, the tribulation, including the days of

Daniel's 70th week. His people will be informed by revelation knowledge of those times (2) Daniel's vision of the final seven years of God's plan for all Gentiles will include (chronologically), the first six seals of events brought about by anti-Christ upon all people, the rapture of His Church following the six seals when the righteous are taken away, the final "Day of the Lord" beginning with the seventh seal, bringing God's wrath on mankind including Israel and the nations, and the trumpets and bowls upon all the remaining unrighteous. (3) Seventy-five days of mourning and cleansing of the new Jerusalem Temple. (4) Eternal Kingdom age.

3.3.2. It is interesting, even though Joel is only three chapters long, it is referenced twenty-three times in the New Testament, many of them in John's Revelation.

3.3.3. The message in Joel is timeless; it can be repeated and applied in any age. Because of the described invasions, the only hope is the power of the Spirit of God. Let's read the wonderful prophecy beginning in 2:28.

28 "It will come about after this
That I will pour out My Spirit on all mankind;
And your sons and daughters will prophesy,
Your old men will dream dreams,
Your young men will see visions.
29 "Even on the male and female servants
I will pour out My Spirit in those days.
30 "I will display wonders in the sky and on the earth,
Blood, fire and columns of smoke.
31 "The sun will be turned into darkness
And the moon into blood
Before the great and awesome day of the Lord comes.

3.3.4. The Holy Spirit made His presence heard and felt on the day of Pentecost and shortly after, recorded in Acts. The Spirit of God would be the power of both the Jew and the Gentile. Also, notice the Holy Spirit says *after this*. Not all of this prophecy will be fulfilled until after the people of Israel are restored to the blessings of God in their land. Only then will His Spirit be poured out upon *all mankind*. Before that time, the wonderful vv. 30-32 will take place. Salvation is extended to all Gentiles who had never heard the message of grace during the current period. What a wonderful God of grace.

3.3.5. Joel balances the locusts and invasion from the north, with the words of hope in his last words. Joy will come! The Spirit of God

Judah Begins: The Kings

would be poured out upon all flesh in a new way. Joel carries us all the way to a future Pentecost and beyond; Peter in his sermon on the Day of Pentecost says:[1]

3.3.6. The nations will be called to war (chapter three). This is the call to the ultimate judgment of the enemies of Israel, who are the enemies of God. The surrounding nations form in unity against the Lord. Joel records a call for God to bring down an army from heaven to battle the enemies. They all assemble in *the valley of Jehoshaphat*. It is there that the Son will sit in judgment of the sins against Israel. Two enemies of Israel, Egypt, and Edom are pointed out and will become *waste* and a *desolate wilderness*.

3.3.7. The final words of Joel record the blessings in the millennial kingdom.
- 3.3.7.1. Mountains dripping with sweet wind
- 3.3.7.2. Hills flowing with milk
- 3.3.7.3. Brooks will flow with water
- 3.3.7.4. A spring from the house of the LORD

3.3.8. Joel 3:21 *For the Lord dwells in Zion.*

4 Now we look at the four kings over the last seventy years of the common 250-year period.

4.1. Amaziah, Joash's son rules the next thirty years, 839-811 BCE. We mentioned Joash had been assassinated in his bed, so his son experienced a considerable time in unrest. His first act was to invade Edom. This was a mistake for he eventually worships the gods of the Edomites.

4.1.1. Edom had revolted against Judah when Jehoram was king, fifty years earlier. However, now God was with Amaziah and directs them to a victory; 10,000 enemy soldiers killed in battle, 10,000 more taken and forced to live in one city, Petra, also called Sela in the Bible.

Depth of Bible Words and Locations
Edom

A nation located southeast of the Dead Sea.

Edom was important because it controlled the trade routes. Edom was strongly involved in the economy of that entire area. The Edomites ancestry is traced back to Esau the brother of Jacob. Remember those twins? Edom descended from Esau; Judah descended from Jacob.

---

[1] Acts 2:16-17 *but this is what was spoken of through the prophet Joel: 17 'AND IT SHALL BE IN THE LAST DAYS,' God says, 'THAT I WILL POUR FORTH OF MY SPIRIT ON ALL MANKIND'*

Many times Edom took advantage of a hatred relationship and assisted other nations in attacking Israel and Judah.

4.1.2. Amaziah returned to Judah, bringing back the idols of the pagan nation of Edom.

4.1.3. Of all things to do next, Amaziah developed Judah's military strength and goes to war against the Northern Kingdom, Israel. They were at peace at the time. The king in Israel, who we reviewed in the previous Section, was Jehoash. Jehoash defeats Amaziah, tares down part of the wall around Jerusalem and plunders the Temple. An uprising took place, Amaziah flees to Lachish and hides there for several years; eventually is assassinated.

4.1.4. Soon after he ran, the people made his son Uzziah (called Azariah in Kings 14) King in 810 BCE. He was sixteen years of age.

4.1.4.1. Uzziah's long reign was the second longest of any of the kings of Judah or Israel. It seems that the Northern Kingdom had control over Judah for around twelve years of Uzziah's rule.

4.1.4.2. Then follows, a good period for Judah—and we know why—2 Chronicles 26:4-5.[1]

4.1.4.3. Much of the credit for these good years is given to a priest or prophet named Zechariah (not the son of Jehoiada; he is only mentioned here). Nor is this the Zechariah who wrote an Old Testament book. THAT Zechariah will minister later, in 522 BCE. There are thirty-one Zechariahs mentioned in the *Bible*. *This one in the book we are reviewing had an understanding through the vision of God.*

4.1.4.4. Uzziah the king, "turned Judah around." At the age of 16, he re-established Judah who had fallen under Israel for a period after the battle with Amaziah, which we mentioned.

4.1.4.5. This became one of the highest points of prosperity ever attained for Judah. Uzziah fortified the walls, which had partially been torn down, and built strong towers for defense. He also built some towers in the surrounding desert areas,

---

[1] *He did right in the sight of the Lord according to all that his father Amaziah had done. 5 He continued to seek God in the days of Zechariah, who had understanding through the vision of God; and as long as he sought the Lord, God prospered him.* What great advice, really a verse for us to stand on today.

Judah Begins: The Kings

which have been discovered by archeologists and have been dated to Uzziah's time.[1]

4.1.4.6. His public works programs, construction of a harbor at Eloth, and capture of Philistine and Arab communities all contributed to a positive, new kingdom. Wells were dug along with the raising of cattle, encouraged in the lowlands. Vineyards were expanded to the hillsides.

4.1.4.7. In 1958 CE, traces of several Judean farms equipped with irrigation systems and fortifications were located and have been dated back to Uzziah's time.

4.1.4.8. However...as Ronald Reagan said on several occations, *"There you go again."*[2]

4.1.4.9. 2 Chronicles 26:16-17 *But when he became strong, his heart was so proud that he acted corruptly, and he was unfaithful to the Lord his God, for he entered the temple of the Lord to burn incense on the altar of incense.*

4.1.4.10. Uzziah, lifted up with pride, entered the temple, and placed himself in the office of priest, which was forbidden. As a result, he is struck with leprosy, which separates him from his own office.

4.1.4.11. All of his authority is shifted over to his son, Jotham.

4.1.4.12. It is at this time we have mention of the prophet Isaiah, whom we will cover in the next section. Isaiah witnessed this reign of Uzziah but says little of those fifty-two years in his book; only that it was in the year that Uzziah died that he had his great vision. Isaiah 6:1 reads In *the year of King Uzziah's death I saw the Lord sitting on a throne, lofty and exalted, with the train of His robe filling the temple.*

4.1.5. Jotham's reign overlaps with Uzziah because of the leprosy—an overlap of approximately ten years. Jotham's rule lasts a total of sixteen years; he dies at the age of forty-one. Interesting...[3]

4.1.5.1. Jotham seems to have done a reasonable job ...continuing the worship of the Lord in Jerusalem. He seems to have learned a lesson from dad...he avoids any priestly duties.

---

[1] 2 Chronicles 26:15 *In Jerusalem he made engines of war invented by skillful men to be on the towers and on the corners for the purpose of shooting arrows and great stones.*

[2] **"There you go again"** was a phrase spoken during the 1980 presidential election debate by Governor Ronald Reagon to his opponent, Jimmy Carter. He use the same quote in a few debates over the years. "There you go again" emerged as a single defining phrase of the 1980 presidential election.

[3] In 1941 CE, his signet ring was found, with a date in the 8th century and with Jotham's name on it.

He also fortified the surrounding area and won a campaign against the Amorites.

4.1.5.2. The reason for Jotham's success is stated in 2 Chronicles 27:6.[1]

4.1.6. Jotham's son was Ahaz, the last of this cycle of kings. He ruled for the next fourteen years. Ahaz, right from the beginning at age twenty-six, was an idolater. He is listed as one of the kings paying tribute to Tiglath-pileser of Assyria from the Temple funds. Isaiah went to him telling him not to pay but rather trust God.

4.1.6.1. Isn't it tragic, how a boy can be raised in a good environment, exposed to good examples from dad and grandpa, then turns to idol worship!

4.1.6.2. Ahaz casts images of Baal and falls to a place of offering one of his own sons as a human sacrifice. This is where Isaiah's ministry comes on strong, telling Ahaz to call on the Lord and stop asking for the help of foreigners.

4.1.6.3. But Ahaz gathers the remaining treasures of the temple and gives them to the Assyrian emperor. Ahaz, while visiting the emperor in Damascus sees a beautiful pagan altar, copies it, and places it in the temple of God, in place of the brazen altar which God set in place. This was his greatest sin!

4.1.6.4. As a result of idolatry, Syria, and Israel from the north, the Edomites from the east, and the Philistines from the west invaded Judah.

4.1.6.5. A sad ending to this period of 250 years of side-by-side history of Judah and Israel.

4.1.7. Only a few years of revival, under Hezekiah's reign, which we will review next, extended Judah's existence beyond that of Israel.

---

[1] *So Jotham became mighty because he ordered his ways before the Lord his God.*

SECTION 5
A GOLDEN AGE OF PROPHECY

2 Kings 15-20, 2 Chronicles 26-32, Isaiah, Micah. The period from 740 to 697 BCE.

Theme Statement: *"...the word of the Lord which He had spoken through His servants the prophets."* (2 Kings 24:2)

THE KEYS IN SECTION FIVE

Section 5: The Southern Kingdom: A Golden Age of Prophecy

Keys to Isaiah—

A Key Word: *Salvation*

The Key Verses (9:6–7; 53:6)

   6 *For a child will be born to us, a son will be given to us; And the government will rest on His shoulders; And His name will be called Wonderful Counselor, Mighty God, Eternal Father, Prince of Peace. 7 There will be no end to the increase of His government or of peace, on the throne of David and over his kingdom, to establish it and to uphold it with justice and righteousness from then on and forevermore. The zeal of the Lord of hosts will accomplish this.*

   6 *All of us like sheep have gone astray, each of us has turned to his own way; but the Lord has caused the iniquity of us all to fall on Him.*

Key Chapter (53)

The Key People in Isaiah

Isaiah—prophet who ministered throughout the reigns of four kings of Judah; gave both a message of judgment and hope (1–66)

Shear-Jashub—Isaiah's son; name means "a remnant shall return," denoting God's promised faithfulness to His people (7:3; 8:18; 10:21)

Maher-Shalal-Hash-Baz—Isaiah's son; name means "hasting to the spoil, hurrying to the prey," denoting God's coming punishment (8:1, 3, 18)

Keys to Micah—

A Key Word: *Compassion*

The Key Verses (6:8; 7:18)

8 He has told you, O man, what is good; and what does the Lord require of you but to do justice, to love kindness, and to walk humbly with your God?

18 Who is a God like You, who pardons iniquity and passes over the rebellious act of the remnant of His possession? He does not retain His anger forever, because He delights in unchanging love

The Key Chapters (6–7)

The Key People in Micah

The people of Israel—the northern kingdom, which was about to fall into Assyrian captivity (1:2–7:20)

Approximate Dates of Key Events in Section 5	
750 BCE	Isaiah, Micah
721	The Northern Kingdom is taken captive by the Assyrians
709	Assyria lays siege against Jerusalem in the south

EIGHT

Isaiah and Micah

1. **W**e travel to **Section 5** of our journey, entitled **A GOLDEN AGE OF PROPHECY,** still concerning The Southern Kingdom of Judah.
    1.1. Specifically, we'll look at 2 Kings cps 15-20; 2 Chronicles cps 26-32, and the books of Isaiah and Micah. The time period will cover 740 to 697 BCE. We will use as a Theme Statement: 2 Kings 24:2 *"the word of the Lord which He had spoken through His servants the prophets."*
    1.2. This period of Isaiah and Micah truly can be called *"A Golden Age of Prophecy."* Rich with God's Words, both with immediate relevance to Judah, and eternal relevance to all believers.
        1.2.1. Isaiah and Micah ministered in the Southern Kingdom while Amos and Hosea (we reviewed them in Section 3), ministered in the North. The kings in the south during the time of Isaiah and Micah, were Uzziah, Jotham, and Ahaz of whom we looked at in the previous Chapter SEVEN...and then Hezekiah whom we'll begin with in this section.
    1.3. Five years before the fall of the Northern Kingdom to Assyria, Hezekiah became king of Judah. I'll repeat what I wrote earlier: *Hezekiah's reforms caused an extension to Judah's very existence.*
        1.3.1. For the first time, the royal seal of King Hezekiah in the Scriptures was found in an archaeological excavation in 2013 CE. The stamped clay seal, also known as a bulla, was discovered at the foot of the southern wall of the Temple Mount in Jerusalem. The "Ophel treasure" excavations, called "a once-in-a-lifetime discovery" was led by Dr. Eilat Mazar.

Isaiah and Micah

1.3.2. Of all the Old Testament kings of both the North and the South, Hezekiah had the highest rating from heaven. He proved to be the most faithful to God of all the kings since David's time.

    1.3.2.1. He tore down the high places of idol worship...read 2 Kings 18:5-6[1]

    1.3.2.2. Trace the great reforms by scanning chapter 18 in 2 Kings

    1.3.2.3. Religious revival took place

    1.3.2.4. A cleansing and repairing of the temple, much of it at the urging of Isaiah

    1.3.2.5. The re-instated Passover after many years of neglect[2]

    1.3.2.6. He was a REFORMER![3]

    1.3.2.7. However, the outstanding event during his reign...was a negative one. In his 14th year of office, Assyria invaded Judah under Sennacherib, 709 BCE. The details of this invasion are recorded in 1 Kings 18:13-19:37, 2 Chronicles 32:1-26, and Isaiah 36-37.

    1.3.2.8. Sennacherib's own chronicle of what happened was located by archeologists, protected in a cylinder, Sennacherib's Prism, for all these years. Also, Sennacherib decorated his palace at Nineveh with reliefs of his successful siege of Judahite Lachish, recorded in 2 Chron. 32:9. The relief is accompanied by the text: "Sennacherib, the mighty king, king of the country of Assyria, sitting on the throne of judgment, before (or at the entrance of) the city of Lachish."

1.3.2.8.1. King Sennacherib of Assyria instructed his scribes to record his victories on a massive clay prism mentioned above. The prism tells of Sennacherib's siege against Jerusalem in 709 BCE, during the reign of Hezekiah. The narrative says following the siege: "Hezekiah himself I

---

[1] *5 He trusted in the Lord, the God of Israel; so that after him there was none like him among all the kings of Judah, nor among those who were before him. 6 For he clung to the Lord; he did not depart from following Him, but kept His commandments, which the Lord had commanded Moses.* What a great testimony!

[2] 2 Chronicles 29:35-36 records it this way: *Thus the service of the house of the Lord was established again. 36 Then Hezekiah and all the people rejoiced over what God had prepared for the people, because the thing came about suddenly.*

[3] 2 Kings 20:20 *Now the rest of the acts of Hezekiah and all his might, and how he made the pool and the conduit and brought water into the city, are they not written in the Book of the Chronicles of the Kings of Judah? 21 So Hezekiah slept with his fathers, and Manasseh his son became king in his place.*

shut up like a caged bird in Jerusalem, his royal city. I erected fortifications against him and blocked the exits from the gate of his city…"

1.3.2.9. Twenty years after the Northern Kingdom fell, according to Sennacherib's own words; he came into Judah with a great army and captured forty-six cities, taking 200,000 captives. Now his eyes were on the prize—Jerusalem. It appeared that nothing could stop him.

1.3.2.10. Hezekiah offered a tribute to Sennacherib in the form of gold, to "buy him out." He even stripped the gold plating off the doors and pillars in and around the Temple. However, that didn't satisfy Sennacherib. Greed always demands more! Its hunger is never satisfied. Sennacherib broke his promise and planned to lay siege to Jerusalem. Hezekiah rebuilt the wall around the city, added a second wall farther out, and increased the production of weapons and shields.[1] Sennacherib sent a letter of demand to Hezekiah. Surrender!

Depth of Bible Words and Locations
Greed (or covetousness)

The characteristic word for "greed" or "covetousness" in the Old Testament is *betsa,* which means "unjust gain" or "to have an inordinate desire for what belongs to someone else." It is consistently denounced in the Bible, from the Ten Commandments (Exodus 20:17; Deuteronomy 5:21) and throughout the Bible:

Achan, the Israelite whose greed cost his nation a battle
Ecclesiastes blasts the emptiness of greed and materialism and exhorts the reader to "remember now thy Creator …"
The sad story of **Gehazi's greed** serves as a contrast to the principled behavior of his master Elisha.
The first "woe" uttered by **Isaiah,** is against covetousness and greed. Isaiah encouraged the Jews to put away greed (56:9–11),
Nehemiah is quick to address the spirit of greed when it rose
Micah also is known as the champion of the oppressed. He condemns wealthy landowners for taking the land, attacks dishonest merchants for charging excessive interest rates, and even the priests and prophets who seemed to be caught up in the tidal wave of greed and dishonesty that swept his country.

---

[1] 2 Chronicles 32:5

Isaiah and Micah

1.3.2.11. Hezekiah needed a solution to the problem the terrified inhabitants had in Jerusalem. His solution was ingenious. He blocked up the natural springs outside the city to ensure that the Assyrians would not benefit from having such a significant source of unlimited water supply nearby.[1] He then redirected a spring into Jerusalem by means of a tunnel underneath the city.[2]

Depth of Bible Words and Locations
Hezekiah's Tunnel

Hezekiah's Tunnel, discovered in 1880 CE was dug through solid rock from the Pool of Siloam to Jerusalem in order to ensure a supply of water for the city in anticipation of an Assyrian attack. It was cut through 1,750 feet of solid rock, with workers starting on opposite sides of the city and meeting in the middle, following an "S" shape. Had it followed a straight line, the length would have been 1,070 feet or 40% shorter.

The tunnel remains today and funnels water into the Pool of Siloam. Visitors from around the world visit the tunnel and view the markings on its walls.

Depth of Bible Words and Locations
Lachish

Lachish is generally regarded as the second most important city in the southern kingdom of Judah. Sennacherib invaded here, during his 701 BCE battle with Judah. More than 1,000 iron arrowheads were found in the ramp as well as a chain for catching the battering rams. The city was surrounded by two walls including a lower retaining wall.

1.3.2.12. Hezekiah cries out to God—he spreads the letter he received from Sennacherib, which demanded a total surrendering of Judah, out on the floor.

1.3.2.13. Isaiah, who had already been preaching for some forty years and had great prestige because he mentored the young Hezekiah, steps forth and assured Hezekiah that if he would stand up to Sennacherib, God would defend *His* city of Jerusalem.[3] Note that God has never failed to honor the declaration of faith uttered by His follower.

---

[1] Ibid, vv 3,4
[2] 2 Kings 20:20; 2 Chronicles 32:30
[3] 2 Kings 19:35 *Then it happened that night that the angel of the Lord went out and struck 185,000 in the camp of the Assyrians; and when men rose early in the morning, behold, all of them were dead.*

1.3.2.14. Sennacherib withdrew in shame back to the capital city of Nineveh, and never again returned to Jerusalem. This marks the turning point of his empire. He died a violent death, assassinated by his two sons. Assyria, in a state of decline, is crushed in 612 BCE by Babylon under Nebuchadnezzar, and a new world ruler ascended.

1.3.3. We have a picture of the social climate during Isaiah's ministry. Several examples will verify this.

1.3.3.1. There was a distrust between people
1.3.3.2. Different factions arose
1.3.3.3. The rich taking advantage of the poor
1.3.3.4. Many priests teaching for money
1.3.3.5. Judges were accepting bribes
1.3.3.6. Hezekiah had made many great reforms, but still, the social community needed an "inner" reform.

1.3.4. Both Isaiah and Micah ministered in this climate.

2. Let's review the book of Isaiah

2.1. The book is named after its author, Isaiah, which means *"The Lord is Salvation,"* quite similar to the names Joshua, Elijah, Elisha, and Jesus. Each of those names includes God in the meaning.

2.2. The authorship of Isaiah has been a source of controversy. It can be clearly divided into two distinct historical periods, suggesting each half is written by different authors. Some scholars assign only the first thirty-nine chapters to Isaiah referring to First Isaiah (1-39) and Second Isaiah (40-66).

2.2.1. However, the author of this volume holds that many scholars overlook the characteristic of God that speaks future events to His Prophets. Regardless of authorship, the reason for the book of Isaiah is to see the Lord through the events recorded.

2.3. Many Scholars note that, of all the prophets, Isaiah easily stands out as the greatest. He has such a great influence on all generations. Karl Delitzsch called Isaiah the "Universal prophet."

2.3.1. He spoke to Judah during the critical years of Assyrian expansion.

2.3.2. Isaiah is quoted in the New Testament more than any other Old Testament prophet—over 65 times and alluded to over 250 times. He is mentioned *by name* over 20 times. Refer to the following two tables, **Fulfilled Prophecies** and **Future Kingdom**.

Isaiah

2.3.3. The book of Isaiah...is filled...with Christ! The 53rd chapter is referred to as "The Mount Everest" of Old Testament prophecy, picturing Christ on the Cross—700 years in advance.

2.3.4. This book of Isaiah is like a miniature Bible. Thirty-nine chapters of judgment upon immorality and rejection, followed by twenty-seven chapters of hope; the Messiah is coming as a Savior to bear a cross and to wear a crown.

A Basic Outline of Isaiah
1. Judah and Jerusalem Under the Monarchy, Cps 1-39
2. Exile In Babylon (an interim period), Cps 40-55
3. Prophecies of Israel's Glorious Future, (back in Jerusalem), Cps 56-66

Depth of Bible Words and Locations
Isaiah Key Word: *Salvation*

Found in Isaiah 12:2 *"Behold, God is my salvation, I will trust and not be afraid; For the Lord God is my strength and song, And He has become my salvation."*

Isaiah 25:9 *And it will be said in that day, "Behold, this is our God for whom we have waited that He might save us. This is the Lord for whom we have waited; Let us rejoice and be glad in His salvation."*

Isaiah 49:6 He says, *"It is too small a thing that You should be My Servant To raise up the tribes of Jacob and to restore the preserved ones of Israel. I will also make You a light of the nations. So that My salvation may reach to the end of the earth."* There are many other references in Isaiah of this same word, salvation.

This great word describes deliverance from distress as a result of victory. It's God's work on your behalf, carrying a meaning of the deliverance of a single individual...YOU...ME.

Then, always realize, this word is much, much more than a new birth. This word includes—deliverance from the power of sin, including forgiveness as well as wholeness for the whole personality.

In the Old Testament, the word salvation sometimes refers to deliverance from danger (Jeremiah 15:20), deliverance of the weak from an oppressor (Psalms 35:9-10), the healing of sickness (Isaiah 38:20), and deliverance from guilt and its consequences.

All this is in salvation.

Jesus in Isaiah...He's the Prince of Peace.

2.3.5. I am sure we could study this great book for several months. In my personal library, I have the classic three-volume set of commentaries by Edward Young, on Isaiah. However, our travels will not *detail* the entire sixty-six chapters of Isaiah.

2.4. First, feast on these wonderful words from Isaiah's writings to get a "feel" for its greatness:

    2.4.1. *1:18 "Come now, and let us reason together," Says the Lord, "Though your sins are as scarlet, They will be as white as snow; Though they are red like crimson, They will be like wool..."*

    2.4.2. *4:2-3 In that day the Branch of the Lord will be beautiful and glorious, and the fruit of the earth will be the pride and the adornment of the survivors of Israel.*

    2.4.3. *7:14-15 "Therefore the Lord Himself will give you a sign: Behold, a virgin will be with child and bear a son, and she will call His name Immanuel."*

    2.4.4. *12:5 Praise the Lord in song, for He has done excellent things; Let this be known throughout the earth.*

    2.4.5. *25:1 O Lord, You are my God; I will exalt You, I will give thanks to Your name;*

    2.4.6. *30:18 Therefore the Lord longs to be gracious to you, And therefore He waits on high to have compassion on you.*

    2.4.7. *32:1 Behold, a king will reign righteously*

    2.4.8. *40:5 Then the glory of the Lord will be revealed, And all flesh will see it together; 42:10 Sing to the Lord a new song, Sing His praise from the end of the earth!*

    2.4.9. *53:5 But He was pierced through for our transgressions, He was crushed for our iniquities;*

    2.4.10. *55:6 Seek the Lord while He may be found; Call upon Him while He is near.*

    2.4.11. *59:1 Behold, the Lord's hand is not so short That it cannot save; Nor is His ear so dull That it cannot hear.*

    2.4.12. *60:1 "Arise, shine; for your light has come, And the glory of the Lord has risen upon you."*

    2.4.13. *66:15 For behold, the Lord will come in fire And His chariots like the whirlwind, To render His anger with fury, And His rebuke with flames of fire.*

2.5. This entire Section 5 and the following Section 6 include "repeat information"—we're dealing with history. This is the historical period of Isaiah's life and how it intertwines with several kings and nations. So I find in order to understand Judah during this period, some repetition is beneficial.

    2.5.1. Isaiah was a gifted preacher, using illustrations and making use of language to emphasize his message, (Judah is the vineyard in

2.5.2. chapter five). His poetry is comparable to the best ever composed. He was married and had at least two children, and lived in Jerusalem. The very names given these sons were a message to Judah and Jerusalem (Isaiah 8:3); Shear-jashub, "a remnant shall return" and Maher-shalal-hash-baz, "he hastened to the prey."

2.5.3. Isaiah ministered near Jerusalem for at least fifty years as a prophet to Judah in approximately 742 to 680 BCE. The northern kingdom had already been destroyed. Four kings, Uzziah, Jotham, Ahaz, and Hezekiah reigned during his ministry (refer to **Chronology of Old Testament History** in Appendix).

2.5.4. Isaiah was called to be a counselor to God's nation—and he willingly responded with joy while knowing his ministry would be filled with rejection.

2.5.5. He was a man with a mission, called to warn the people of their rush into disaster. Isaiah received a glimpse of God's glorious throne so even though he knew his message was of judgment. He also saw the coming of the Lord to comfort and bless His people!

Fulfilled Prophecies from Isaiah[1]

The Prophecy	The Fulfillment
The Messiah...	*Jesus Christ...*
will be born of a virgin (Is. 7:14).	was born of a virgin named Mary (Luke 1:26–31).
will have a Galilean ministry (Is. 9:1, 2).	ministered in Galilee of the Gentiles (Matt. 4:13–16).
will be an heir to the throne of David (Is. 9:7).	was given the throne of His father David (Luke 1:32, 33).
will have His way prepared (Is. 40:3–5).	was announced by John the Baptist (John 1:19–28).
will be spat on and struck (Is. 50:6).	was spat on and beaten (Matt. 26:67).
will be exalted (Is. 52:13).	was highly exalted by God and the people (Phil. 2:9, 10).
will be disfigured by suffering (Is. 52:14; 53:2).	was scourged by the soldiers who gave Him a crown of thorns (Mark 15:15–19).
will make a blood atonement (Is. 53:5).	shed His blood to atone for our sins (1 Pet. 1:2).

---

[1]MacArthur, John: *The MacArthur Bible Handbook*. Nashville, Tenn. : Thomas Nelson Publishers, 2003, S. 189

will be widely rejected (Is. 53:1, 3).	was not accepted by many (John 12:37, 38).
will bear our sins and sorrows (Is. 53:4, 5).	died because of our sins (Rom. 4:25; 1 Pet. 2:24, 25).
will be our substitute (Is. 53:6, 8).	died in our place (Rom. 5:6, 8; 2 Cor. 5:21).
will voluntarily accept our guilt and punishment (Is. 53:7, 8).	was silent about our sin (Mark 15:4, 5; John 10:11; 19:30).
will be buried in a rich man's tomb (Is. 53:9).	was buried in the tomb of Joseph, a rich man from Arimathea (Matt. 27:57–60; John 19:38–42).
will save us who believe in Him (Is. 53:10, 11).	provided salvation for all who believe (John 3:16; Acts 16:31).
will die with transgressors (Is. 53:12).	was numbered with the transgressors (Mark 15:27, 28; Luke 22:37).
will heal the brokenhearted (Is. 61:1, 2).	healed the brokenhearted (Luke 4:18, 19).

Isaiah's Description of Israel's Future Kingdom[1]

Description	Isaiah passages
1. The Lord will restore the faithful remnant of Israel to the Land to inhabit the kingdom at its beginning	1:9, 25–27; 3:10; 4:3; 6:13; 8:10; 9:1; 10:20, 22, 25, 27; 11:11, 12, 16; 14:1, 2; 14:22, 26; 26:1–4; 27:12; 28:5; 35:9; 37:4, 31, 32; 40:2, 3; 41:9; 43:5, 6; 46:3, 4; 49:5, 8; 49:12, 22; 51:11; 54:7–10; 55:12; 57:13, 18; 60:4, 9; 61:1–4, 7; 65:8–10; 66:8, 9, 19
2. As the Lord defeats Israel's enemies, He will provide protection for His people.	4:5, 6; 9:1, 4; 12:1–6; 13:4; 14:2; 21:9; 26:4, 5; 27:1–4; 30:30, 31; 32:2; 33:16, 22; 35:4; 49:8, 9; 49:17, 18; 52:6; 54:9, 10; 55:10, 11; 58:12; 60:10, 12, 18; 62:9; 66:16
3. In her kingdom, Israel will enjoy great prosperity of many kinds.	26:15, 19; 27:2, 13; 29:18–20; 22:22, 23; 30:20; 32:3; 32:15–20; 33:6, 24; 35:3, 5, 6, 8–10; 40:11; 42:6, 7, 16; 43:5, 6, 8, 10, 21; 44:5, 14; 46:13; 48:6; 49:10; 52:9; 54:2, 3; 55:1, 12; 58:9, 14; 60:5, 16, 21; 61:4, 6–10; 62:5; 65:13–15, 18, 24; 66:21, 22
4. The city of Jerusalem will rise to world preeminence in the kingdom.	2:2–4; 18:7; 25:6; 40:5, 9; 49:19–21; 60:1–5, 13–15, 17; 62:3, 4
5. Israel will be the center of world attention in the kingdom.	23:18; 54:1–3; 55:5; 56:6–8; 60:5–9; 66:18–21

---

[1]*Ibid* p. 186

6. Israel's mission in the kingdom will be to glorify the Lord.	60:21; 61:3
7. Gentiles in the kingdom will receive blessing through the channel of faithful Israel.	11:10; 19:18, 24, 25; 42:6; 45:22, 23; 49:6; 51:5; 56:3, 6–8; 60:3, 7, 8; 61:5; 66:19
8. Worldwide peace will prevail in the kingdom under the rule of the Prince of Peace.	2:4; 9:5, 6; 11:10; 19:23; 26:12; 32:18; 54:14; 57:19; 66:12
9. Moral and spiritual conditions in the kingdom will reach their highest plane since the Fall of Adam.	27:6; 28:6, 17; 32:16; 42:7; 44:3; 45:8; 51:4; 61:11; 65:21, 22
10. Governmental leadership in the kingdom will be superlative with the Messiah heading it up.	9:6, 7; 11:2, 3; 16:5; 24:23; 25:3; 32:1; 32:5; 33:22; 42:1, 4; 43:15; 52:13; 53:12; 55:3–5
11. Humans will enjoy long life in the kingdom.	65:20, 22
12. Knowledge of the Lord will be universal in the kingdom.	11:9; 19:21; 33:13; 40:5; 41:20; 45:6, 14; 49:26; 52:10, 13, 15; 54:13; 66:23
13. The world of nature will enjoy a great renewal in the kingdom.	12:3; 30:23–26; 32:15; 35:1–4, 6, 7; 41:18, 19; 43:19, 20; 44:3, 23; 55:1, 2, 13; 58:10, 11
14. "Wild" animals will be tame in the kingdom.	11:6–9; 35:9; 65:25
15. Sorrow and mourning will not exist in the kingdom.	25:8; 60:20
16. An eternal kingdom, as a part of God's new creation, will follow the millennial kingdom.	24:23; 51:6; 51:16; 54:11, 12; 60:11, 19; 65:17

2.5.6. Isaiah's general pattern was a shifting back and forth between events of his own time and the future. Keep this in mind as you read his book. He describes a current event and suddenly turns to a future event.

    2.5.6.1. A good example is cps 11 and 12. He predicts the overthrow of Assyria and then jumps to a wonderful future event, a world without war, ruled by a righteous Branch of David (Isaiah first mentioned *The Branch,* the future

Messiah, in cp 4, verses 2-6), one of the most glorious pictures of the world to come in all Scripture.

2.5.6.2. He mentions this again in cp 25 as he moves quickly from the judgments of nations to an age of new heavens and new earth. You may also be happy to read of a future feast of rich foods for all! Quickly he then again returns to his current time concerning Moab.

2.5.7. He seems to have come from a family of some rank because he had access to the king—some believe he was a cousin of King Hezekiah, The Reformer. 2 Chronicles 32:32[1] probably refers to a separate biography of Hezekiah authored by Isaiah. (Also, see another reference in 2 Chronicles 26:22 to a book he wrote which we no longer have).

2.5.8. In addition, he was well educated as evidenced by his advanced vocabulary and knowledge of world history. It has been said he knew more about world kingdoms than any other man living did. His vocabulary is called brilliant, filled with imagery. Many liken him to the great Greek orators.

2.6. Much of this book of Isaiah uses poetry intertwined with prophecy. To understanding this:

2.6.1. The Hebrew used a technique called "parallelism" in their poetry, which we talked about in Section 1. We see an example of parallelism at the beginning of Isaiah:

2.6.1.1. Cp 1:3 *"An ox knows its owner, And a donkey its master's manger, But Israel does not know, My people do not understand."* Both the ox and the donkey know the objects they depend on are the owner as well as what the master provides, a crib. Then the verse contrasts this with the behavior of the Israelites. Israel does not know "its owner" even though they are God's people; they do not consider God's crib or His provision. So Isaiah is using a well-known language technique of the Hebrew.

2.6.2. And then Prophetic Poetry uses colorful images that point to further meaning…Isaiah is the master of this. For example:

2.6.2.1. Isaiah 42:15 says *"I will lay waste the mountains and hills And wither all their vegetation; I will make the rivers*

---

[1] 2 Chronicles 32:32 *Now the rest of the acts of Hezekiah and his deeds of devotion, behold, they are written in the vision of Isaiah the prophet, the son of Amoz, in the Book of the Kings of Judah and Israel.*

into coastlands And dry up the ponds. The mountains and hills are all types of physical and spiritual obstacles in the way of the exiles' return to Jerusalem...but the Lord promises to "dry up" those obstacles so they could return.

    2.6.2.2. Similar to that is Isaiah 41:18 *"I will open rivers on the bare heights And springs in the midst of the valleys; I will make the wilderness a pool of water And the dry land fountains of water.* The Lord promises to the exiles He will "open rivers" and make "dry land springs of water" just like He had provided water from a rock in Exodus 17.

2.7. The early chapters of his book deal with the future glory of God's nation. God's people will be the center of world civilization in an eternity of peace.

    2.7.1. Cps 2-5 seem to be one prophecy looking at a future time of God's dealing with Israel (all 12 tribes). He is not talking about the last days of the church in these cps. The church will have been removed.

    2.7.2. The brief cp 4 shows the conditions of the Babylonia captivity and also the conditions during the great tribulation.

    2.7.3. Cp 5 includes one of the most beautiful songs ever written, "The Vineyard" (vv 1-7, the house of Israel). Perhaps the people who ignored his sermons would listen to his song. The cp also lists six sins, which bring judgment to Israel.

        2.7.3.1. Covetousness (vv 8-10)
        2.7.3.2. Drunkenness (vv 11-17)
        2.7.3.3. Carelessness (vv 18-19)
        2.7.3.4. Deception (v 20)
        2.7.3.5. Pride (v 21)
        2.7.3.6. Injustice (vv 22-25)

    2.7.4. He has a wonderful encounter with Christ in chapter six. To be in chronological order, the chapter actually belongs at the beginning of Isaiah.[1]

2.8. The next few chapters in Isaiah include a series of prophetic messages against Judah's enemies.

    2.8.1. The defeat of the Assyrian army is recorded three times in the Bible: Isaiah 36-37, 2 Kings 18-19, and 2 Chronicles 32.

---

[1] Isaiah 6:1-3 *In the year of King Uzziah's death I saw the Lord sitting on a throne, lofty and exalted, with the train of His robe filling the temple. 2 Seraphim stood above Him, each having six wings: with two he covered his face, and with two he covered his feet, and with two he flew. 3 And one called out to another and said, "Holy, Holy, Holy, is the Lord of hosts,*
The whole earth is full of His glory."

2.8.2. In one night, the army was destroyed by divine intervention. Several times, Isaiah (and other prophets) referred to the event.

2.8.3. He begins with Babylon in chapter 13, a *future* enemy who would destroy Judah. He tells of the fall of Babylon 100 years before becoming a world power! The Medes, an unknown people in Isaiah's time were named by him (vv 17-19) as the future destroyer's of Babylon. Amazing!

2.8.4. Then Assyria and Philistia in cp 14. Assyria was a strong empire during Isaiah's time. They had been expanding during the previous 150 years, conquering Israel and Samaria. The origin of Satan is also mentioned in this chapter.

2.8.5. The sudden destruction of Moab in chapter 15

Depth of Bible Words and Locations
Moab

Descendants of Lot (Moab was a son by incest), thus a nation related to the Jews. Located along the eastern border of the Dead Sea, 35 miles long, and 25 miles wide. To the south and west was Edom. To the north was Ammon.

The Moabites were enemies of Israel. Arabs invaded Moab following the fall of the Assyrian Empire. Eventually, Moab became a Roman province. Prophecies about Moab are in Jeremiah 48, Amos 2, and Zephaniah 2.

2.8.6. Syria and the Northern Kingdom in cp 17. The city of Damascus, perhaps the world's oldest city, has never been made a *"fallen ruin"* or "ruinous heap" of v 1. Therefore, it *will* happen in the future.

2.8.7. A land beyond Ethiopia, in chapter 18, Cush, probably located in Africa near the Nile River.

2.8.8. Egypt in chapter 19, who at the time of Isaiah's death, fell under Assyrian advances. Many Jews had located to Egypt after the Babylonian Exile. In fact, The Septuagint was produced in Alexandria. The idolatry in Egypt was as strong as that of Babylonia, in fact, it was the source of it! Ezekiel tells us every idol will disappear from Egypt.

2.8.9. Then back to Babylon, this time with her allies in cp 21. Her future capture by Cyrus is mentioned. Edom (Dumah) and Arabia are included.

2.8.10. Even Jerusalem is included in Isaiah's words, with her unbelieving leaders in cp 22.

2.8.11. Many of these prophecies were fulfilled in Isaiah's time, verifying that he was indeed a great and trusted prophet.

Isaiah

2.8.12. Isaiah's final message to Israel's enemies is in cp 23. This one concerning Tyre, a city of importance in commercial activity. The destruction of Tyre, which was fulfilled, affected the trade and wealth of Egypt, who depended on this coastal city. Tyre will again be a commercial center in the last days.
    2.8.12.1. He said Sennacherib's attack against Jerusalem would fail, it failed.
    2.8.12.2. He said the Lord would heal Hezekiah's deadly illness—He healed him.
    2.8.12.3. In addition, long before Cyrus the king of Persia even appeared on the scene (he was not even known), Isaiah *named* him as Judah's deliverer from captivity in Babylon and as we will see, happened.

2.8.13. All of these perfect, exact thoughts could only have come from God.

2.8.14. One of the grandest chapters in the Bible is Isaiah 35. A poem pictures the last days when the redeemed, after long-suffering, will shine forth with the radiance of God's Glory. The curse of sin is gone in cp 35 as a renewed earth of the millennium is pictured.

2.8.15. Then back to the terrifying days of the Assyrian invasion of Jerusalem by King Sennacherib is told in cps 36-37. This is where Assyria demands the surrender of Jerusalem. Read the wonderful miracle of 37:36! *Then the angel of the Lord went out and struck 185,000 in the camp of the Assyrians; and when men arose early in the morning, behold, all of these were dead.*

2.9. Isaiah is also known as the "evangelical prophet" speaking much about the grace of God in the last 27 chapters. The coming Saviour comes to the forefront in cps 40-66.

    2.9.1. Isaiah states the identical words *In that day* forty-three times in his book, forty-two of them in the last twenty-one cps.[1]

    2.9.2. The verses of chapter 40:3-5 are quoted in all four Gospels; the arrival of Christ! The woes and burdens of the first cps are lifted, now there is a burden-bearer! The clear prophecies of Christ (see Fulfilled Prophecies From Isaiah) fulfilled in the life of Jesus the Messiah provide proof that the Bible is the divinely inspired Word of God.

---

[1] *Isa 27:1 In that day the Lord will punish Leviathan the fleeing serpent, With His fierce and great and mighty sword, Even Leviathan the twisted serpent; And He will kill the dragon who lives in the sea. 2 In that day, "A vineyard of wine, sing of it!*

2.9.3. Chapters 44-45 are the prediction of Israel's return from Exile under Cyrus, (150 years before it happened!) Isaiah again mentions his name before his birth! This was not added by some later historian as some suggest (see my earlier comments concerning 2 Isaiah authorship). The promise of the Holy Spirit is in verse 43, corresponding to Joel's promise in his cp 2.

2.9.4. Chapters 46-48 tell the story of Babylon, almost as a continuation of cps 13 and 14. For the third time, we see the decline of Babylon (cps 13, 14, and 21). God says to Babylon in 47:1 *"come down."* He brought Babylon *down*.

2.9.5. Perhaps the best-loved chapter in the entire Bible is Isaiah 53, the Suffering Savior, mentioned some 750 years before the actual crucifixion of Jesus. These details could only have been given by the Holy Spirit. This cp, along with Psalms 22, gives us a detailed description of Christ's crucifixion; found nowhere else in the Scriptures.

2.9.6. He pictures a restored kingdom in cps 56-61.
- 2.9.6.1. Proper observance of the Sabbath
- 2.9.6.2. Fasting which God answers
- 2.9.6.3. Turning from iniquities
- 2.9.6.4. Glory of the Lord will rise
- 2.9.6.5. All nations will visit Jerusalem
- 2.9.6.6. Sorrows turned to joy

2.9.7. The Church of Christ is commanded to go forth and witness, in Cp 60. The darkness of the world is to be dispersed by the light of Christ and His followers will grow into a mighty nation (60:1-3, 22).

2.9.8. Cp 65 shows us that at the end of the Millennium, changes will be made in the earth.

2.10. Concerning Isaiah's death, according to tradition, he hid in a hollow tree to escape Manasseh. The king's soldiers, knowing he was in that tree, sawed it in half. Thus *he* was sawed in half! There is a reference in the New Testament (Hebrews 11), which refers to the heroes of faith who were sawed in two, perhaps a reference which included Isaiah.[1]

3. During this same period, we note the events and ministry recorded by Micah.

3.1. The title, like Isaiah, is named for the prophet who wrote it. He was commissioned to speak these words to the people. Micah means, "Who is like the Lord?" Little is known about Micah beyond the first verse.

---

[1] Heb 11:37 *They were stoned, they were sawn in two,*

Micah

3.1.1. His ministry and the events in the book of Micah take place about 722 BCE, just prior to the fall of the Northern Kingdom to Assyria. Jeremiah 26:18 places him in Jerusalem during the reign of Hezekiah and notes his prophecy that Jerusalem would become a heap of ruins. Primarily Micah preached to the Southern Kingdom with a few messages directed to the north. Jesus quoted Micah 7:6 in Matthew 10:35. Quite interesting, Assyria was the immediate threat to Judah, but Micah by the direction of the Holy Spirit, tells them that Babylonia would conquer them: *4:10 Writhe and labor to give birth, Daughter of Zion, Like a woman in childbirth; For now you will go out of the city, Dwell in the field, And go to Babylon. There you will be rescued; There the LORD will redeem you From the hand of your enemies.*

3.1.2. This was difficult, if not impossible, for anyone to believe at the time—Babylonia did not become a power until much later.

A Basic Outline of Micah
1. Judgment of the Leaders and the People, Cps 1-3
2. Restoration (Prophecies of Christ), Cps 4-5
3. Repentance (What Does the Lord Demand of Us?), Cps 6-7

A KEY WORD in Micah is found at the end of Micah
Compassion

We read in 7:19 *He will again have compassion on us; He will tread our iniquities under foot. Yes, You will cast all their sins Into the depths of the sea.* The Hebrew word means, "to love from the womb." Several times it's also translated *mercy*. Isaiah 14:1 uses the same word, and the AMP and NKJV both translate it *mercy*.

We know this word expresses the deepest of emotion; "from the womb." God loves His people with a deep compassion that is beyond expression. The Lord expressed this same love to Moses when it's recorded Exodus 34:6 *Then the Lord passed by in front of him and proclaimed, "The Lord, the Lord God, compassionate and gracious, slow to anger, and abounding in loving-kindness and truth; 7 Who keeps loving-kindness for thousands, who forgives iniquity..."*

Jesus in Micah...He is the Majesty and Glory of God!

3.2. Micah was a country preacher, ministering in his hometown of Moresheth, about twenty miles south of Jerusalem near the old Philistine stronghold of Lachish. During this period, Isaiah was preaching in Jerusalem and Hosea in the north. It is likely the three Prophets knew each other, possibly even ministering together.

- 3.2.1. Micah and Isaiah were alike in many respects, although Micah was younger. Micah's interests were with the common people and with the individual while, Isaiah's interests were in matters that concerned the nation. Micah in chapter 3 has criticism of the rulers and leaders for their injustices. The prophets of the time are criticized as losing their vision of the divine and God will turn a deaf ear when they cry out for help.
- 3.2.2. Chapter 4 changes the mood. The Torah will be found and become guidance towards the path of God.
- 3.2.3. Glance at the similarity in writing of the second verse of each book.[1] Also in comparing Micah 4:1-5 with Isaiah 2:2-4, the similarities of the two men is evident. One may have quoted from the other. Note the identical familiar words: *Then they will hammer their swords into plowshares And their spears into pruning hooks*.
- 3.2.4. Much like Isaiah's style, more than once Micah shifts from his present day to a future day. In cp 4 *"and it will come about in the last days"* he mentions a warless, peaceful world (similar to Isaiah cp 2) and then shifts in the later verses to his own troubled time. The Babylonia captivity will take place!
- 3.2.5. Also, chapter 5 moves from a future coming of Christ in Bethlehem, back to the exile in his own time, and even further backward to the Assyrian's siege of Jerusalem. Keep in mind the two books of Isaiah and Micah, are not chronological in all events. 5:1 recalls the siege of Jerusalem described with dread by Jeremiah and Ezekiel.
- 3.2.6. A well-known passage in Micah 5:2, *But as for you, Bethlehem Ephrathah, Too little to be among the clans of Judah, From you One will go forth for Me to be ruler in Israel. His goings forth are from long ago, From the days of eternity.*
- 3.2.7. This was well known to the Jews who thought the Messiah would certainly be born in the metro-city of Jerusalem with bands playing and a victory parade!

---

[1] Mic 1:2 *Hear, O peoples, all of you; Listen, O earth and all it contains, And let the Lord God be a witness against you,*
Isa 1:2 *Listen, O heavens, and hear, O earth;*
For the Lord speaks,

Micah

- 3.2.7.1. This verse caused wise men to search for Christ in the little town of Bethlehem. It is the only Scripture that locates His birth.
- 3.2.7.2. Much of the emphasis of his ministry, recorded in cps 3-5, concerns a chastisement to the leaders.
- 3.2.8. The priests were responsible for the terrible state of the nation. Bribery, cheating, and covetousness were destroying the nation. Micah tells of judgment upon Judah and the destruction of Jerusalem and its Temple. Babylon will take you captive! But Micah then looks beyond captivity to a time of return to the city. He describes in detail God's love and mercy. Micah's message is one of "hope."
    - 3.2.8.1. God will reign!
    - 3.2.8.2. Christ will return!
    - 3.2.8.3. Peace on earth!
    - 3.2.8.4. Israel will be re-gathered from the nations!
- 3.2.9. Then the great question and answer in cp 6. The people turned to various ways to please God—v6 with *what shall I come to the LORD And bow myself before the God on high? Shall I come to Him with burnt offerings, With yearling calves? 7 Does the LORD take delight in thousands of rams, In ten thousand rivers of oil? Shall I present my firstborn for my rebellious acts, The fruit of my body for the sin of my soul?*
- 3.2.10. But God replies in this wonderful v8 by reminding them of the many things He has done for them; *He has told you, O man, what is good; And what does the LORD require of you But to do justice, to love kindness, And to walk humbly with your God?*
- 3.2.11. Chapter 7 continues the images of the lack of character. The unreliability of human beings is the cause for mis-trust in God.
- 3.2.12. Verse 7:7 is another mood shift. He offers the people an encouragement of deliverance, placing them into God's care. Verse 7:8 is a gem for all of us. *Though I fall I will rise; Though I dwell in darkness, the Lord is a light for me.* No matter what we face in life, whatever the difficulty, or "rut" we are in, God is always there, listening.
- 3.3. His final encouragement is also for each one of us, Mic 7:14 *Shepherd Your people,* 15 *will show you miracles,* and 19 *He will again have compassion on us*

SECTION 6
JUDAH FALLS

Kings 21-25, 2 Chronicles 33-36, Nahum, Zephaniah, Jeremiah, Habakkuk, Obadiah, and Lamentations. The period from 697 to 586 BCE

Theme Statement: *"Have you completely rejected Judah?"* (Jeremiah 14:19)

THE KEYS IN SECTION SIX

Section 6 The Southern Kingdom: Judah Falls

Keys to Zephaniah—

A Key Word: *Humble*

The Key Verses (1:14–15; 2:3)

   14 Near is the great day of the Lord, near and coming very quickly; listen, the day of the Lord! In it the warrior cries out bitterly. 15 A day of wrath is that day, a day of trouble and distress, a day of destruction and desolation, a day of darkness and gloom, a day of clouds and thick darkness.

   3 Seek the Lord, all you humble of the earth who have carried out His ordinances; seek righteousness, seek humility. Perhaps you will be hidden in the day of the Lord's anger.

The Key Chapter (3)

The Key People in Zephaniah

Zephaniah—prophet who warned Judah of coming judgment and future hope (1:1–3:20)

The People of Judah—led by King Josiah to repent but eventually fell into Babylonian captivity (1:6–11; 2:2–20)
The Edomites—the nation originating from Esau, despised and judged by God (vv 1–16)

Keys to Nahum—

A Key Word: *Jealous*

The Key Verses (1:7–8; 3:5–7)

7 The Lord is good, a stronghold in the day of trouble, and He knows those who take refuge in Him. 8 But with an overflowing flood He will make a complete end of its site, and will pursue His enemies into darkness.

5 "Behold, I am against you," declares the Lord of hosts";And I will lift up your skirts over your face, and show to the nations your nakedness and to the kingdoms your disgrace. 6 "I will throw filth on you and make you vile, and set you up as a spectacle. 7 "And it will come about that all who see you will shrink from you and say, 'Nineveh is devastated! Who will grieve for her?' Where will I seek comforters for you?"

The Key Chapter (1)

The Key People in Nahum

The people of Nineveh—Assyrians who returned to evil and were destined for destruction (2:1–3:19)

Keys to Jeremiah—

A Key Word: *Heal*

The Key Verses (7:23–24; 8:11–12

23 "But this is what I commanded them, saying, 'Obey My voice, and I will be your God, and you will be My people; and you will walk in all the way which I command you, that it may be well with you.' " 24 Yet they did not obey or incline their ear, but walked in their own counsels and in the stubbornness of their evil heart, and went backward and not forward.

11 "They heal the brokenness of the daughter of My people superficially ,saying, 'Peace, peace,' but there is no peace. 12 Were they ashamed because of the abomination they had done? They certainly were not ashamed, and they did

Keys In Section Six

not know how to blush; therefore they shall fall among those who fall; at the time of their punishment they shall be brought down," says the Lord.

The Key Chapter (31)—

The Key People in Jeremiah

Jeremiah—priest and prophet in the Southern Kingdom of Judah

King Josiah—sixteenth king of the Southern Kingdom of Judah; attempted to follow God (1:1–3; 22:11, 18)

King Jehoahaz—evil son of Josiah and seventeenth king of the Southern Kingdom of Judah (22:9–11)

King Jehoiakim—evil son of Josiah and eighteenth king of the Southern Kingdom of Judah (22:18–23; 25:1–38; 26:1–24; 27:1–11; 35:1–19; 36:1–32)

King Jehoiachin—evil son of Jehoiakim and nineteenth king of the Southern Kingdom of Judah (13:18–27; 22:24–30)

King Zedekiah—evil uncle of Jehoiachin and twentieth king of the Southern Kingdom of Judah (21:1–14; 24:8–10; 27:12–22; 32:1–5; 34:1–22; 37:1–21; 38:1–28; 51:59–64)

Baruch—served as Jeremiah's scribe (32:12–16; 36:4–32; 43:3–45:4)
Ebed-Melech—Ethiopian palace official who feared God and helped Jeremiah (38:7–39:16)

King Nebuchadnezzar—greatest king of Babylon; led the people of Judah into captivity (21–52)

The Rechabites—obedient descendants of Jonadab; contrasted to the disobedient people of Israel (35:1–19)

Keys to Habakkuk—

A Key Word: *Faith*

Key Verses (2:4; 3:17–19)

4 "Behold, as for the proud one, his soul is not right within him; but the righteous will live by his faith."

17 Though the fig tree should not blossom and there be no fruit on the vines, though the yield of the olive should fail and the fields produce no food, though the flock should be cut off from the fold and there be no cattle in the stalls, 18 Yet I will exult in the Lord, I will rejoice in the God of my salvation. 19 The Lord God is my strength, and He has made my feet like hinds' feet, and makes me walk on my high places. for the choir director, on my stringed instruments.

Key Chapter (3)

The Key People in Habakkuk

Habakkuk—the last prophet sent to Judah before its fall into Babylonian captivity (1:1–3:19)

The Chaldeans—Babylonians raised up by God to punish Judah (1:6–11; 2:2–20)

Keys to Obadiah—

A Key Word: *Pride*

The Key Verses (10, 21)

10 Because of violence to your brother Jacob, You will be covered with shame, and you will be cut off forever.

21 The deliverers will ascend Mount Zion to judge the mountain of Esau, and the kingdom will be the Lord's.

Keys In Section Six

The Key People in Obadiah

The Edomites—the nation originating from Esau, despised and judged by God (v. 1-16

Keys to Lamentations

A Key Word: *Weeps*

The Key Verses (2:5–6; 3:22–23)

5 *The Lord has become like an enemy. He has swallowed up Israel; He has swallowed up all its palaces, He has destroyed its strongholds and multiplied in the daughter of Judah mourning and moaning. 6 And He has violently treated His tabernacle like a garden booth; He has destroyed His appointed meeting place. The Lord has caused to be forgotten the appointed feast and sabbath in Zion, and He has despised king and priest in the indignation of His anger.*

22 The Lord's lovingkindnesses indeed never cease, for His compassions never fail. 23 They are new every morning; Great is Your faithfulness.

The Key Chapter (3)

The Key People in Lamentations

Jeremiah—prophet of Judah; mourned the destruction of Jerusalem (1:1–5:22)

People of Jerusalem—people judged by God because of their great sins (1:1–5:22)

Approximate Dates of Key Events in Section 6	
697-642 BCE	Manasseh
689-681	Sennacherib, king of Assyria
670	Egypt conquered by Assyria; culmination of power
663-654	Assyria occupies Egypt's capital
630-622	Nahum's ministry
640.	Josiah becomes king of Judah
640	Zephaniah's ministry begins
626-605	Nabopolassar king of Babylon

TRAVEL THROUGH THE OLD TESTAMENT

626	Jeremiah is called to prophesy
622	Revival in Jerusalem under Josiah
612	Assyria falls to the Babylonians and Medes
612	Habakkuk's ministry
610	Jehoahaz's short reign begins in Judah
607	Jehoiakim's reign begins in Judah
607	Some Judeans are taken captive to Babylon, including Daniel
605	Nebuchadnezzar's reign begins in Babylon, defeated Assyria and Egypt
603	Daniel interprets the king's dream
598	Jehoiachin becomes king in Judah
598	Ezekiel is deported to Babylon along with Jehoiachin
597	Zedekiah becomes Judah's last king
594-521	Ezekiel's prophetic ministry
588	Zedekiah rebels against Babylonia
586	Jerusalem falls to Nebuchadnezzar/Babylonians; temple destroyed
585	Jeremiah is taken to Egypt

NINE

Judah In Decline

1. As we continue our travel through this Old Testament study course, we are still concerned with The Southern Kingdom.
1.1. We will cover a large number of Scriptures, 2 Kings 21-25, 2 Chronicles 33-36, Zephaniah, Nahum, Jeremiah, Habakkuk, Obadiah, and Lamentations. We are reviewing the final 110 years of Judah, from the death of King Hezekiah 697 BCE to the destruction of Jerusalem in 586 BCE.
1.2. The Theme Statement is a question asked in Jeremiah 14:19 *"Have You completely rejected Judah?"* Judah declines!
1.3. The story of these last years is told in both 2 Kings and 2 Chronicles with slight variations. Some of the details are added from the prophecies of Jeremiah, Ezekiel, and Daniel. The very graphic picture of conditions following Jerusalem's fall is given in Lamentations.
1.4. When Hezekiah *The Reformer* died, Judah lost its independence. The day of Judah being in control of her own destiny, with any resemblance of leadership, the day of her trusting in God in one form or another was gone. She was a pawn in the hands of Assyria, followed by Egypt, and finally Babylonia, for the 100+ years of this period.
1.5. Remember Sennacherib? Sennacherib was the leader of Assyria who destroyed Babylon in 689 BCE. He attacked Jerusalem and demanded, by letter, the total surrender of Judah. His journal was located and recounts the eyewitness attack. He was killed by his sons in 681.
1.6. For the next few years after Sennacherib, his son Esarhaddon *rebuilt* Babylon and molded the Assyrian Empire into the master of a huge territory. This Empire held dominion over Palestine during this

period. This great, but cruel empire covered the whole of the Fertile Crescent, with only Jerusalem and Judah saved from its complete control by a miraculous defeat of the threatening army (2 Kings 19).

    1.6.1.   The Assyrian Empire did not last for a long period. During the next thirty years, they relaxed under several kings (Shamash-shumukin, Kandalanu, Sin-shumu-lisher and Sinsharishku). Very little emphasis was placed on military power.

    1.6.2.   The Medes had an alliance with a rebuilt Babylonia, and together this powerful confederacy moved to invade Assyria. In 614 BCE, the Assyrian capital city of Nineveh was captured by Nabopolassar, father of Nebuchadnezzar, and king of Babylon.

    1.6.3.   The struggle actually dragged on for several years, similar to many wars, and allowed Egypt to again gain a foothold over Judah. In 606 BCE the leader of the Babylonian military, Nebuchadnezzar (not yet emperor), smashed Assyria and Egypt. A new revived world power resulted, The Babylonian Empire.

Depth of Bible Words and Locations
Chaldea

A name used for the nation of Babylon. The *Chaldeans* defeated the Assyrians in late seventh century BCE and elevated Babylonia to its greatest power.

    1.6.4.   Nebuchadnezzar, the emperor in 604 BCE, began to stretch outward and ruled all of the previous Assyrian Empire, which had captured Israel and Egypt.

    1.6.5.   Babylon was made into a magnificent city, full of beauty and wealth. This was the condition while Judah was in captivity during the period that covered seventy yrs, 606-536 BCE.

Depth of Bible Words and Places
Babylon

The incredible splendors of the city, including its "hanging gardens," its famous Ishtar Gate, ziggurat, and temples, were defended behind a vast system of fortifications.

    The wall was about eleven miles long and eighty-five feet thick and was protected by a moat filled with water from the Euphrates. Actually, the wall was double: the outer wall was twenty-five feet thick and the inner one twenty-three feet thick with an intervening space filled with rubble.

Judah in Decline

Watchtowers stood sixty-five feet apart on the walls. Eight or nine gates pierced the wall. The population of greater Babylon (the walled city and its suburbs) in Nebuchadnezzar's day has been estimated at about a half million. Hebrew accounts represent the city as great in size, beauty, and strength.

The "hanging gardens," which to the Greeks were one of the Seven Wonders of the World, are described as the hanging gardens of Nebuchadnezzar, rising in terraces, which supported full-grown trees. Recent archeological discoveries have shed new light on its location and construction. An ingenious method of *raising* the irrigation to each of the levels was found. How well the words of Daniel 4:30 fit this ambitious builder: *"Is this not Babylon the great, which I myself have built as a royal residence by the might of my power and for the glory of my majesty?"*

1.7. We return to Judah
- 1.7.1. These last 110 years of Judah's history are pitiful. Wicked rulers nearby led them into a state of apostasy. They really became easy prey for invaders. A nation without God is a weak and lonely people. Judah was in the lowest state in their entire history. Read 2 Chronicles chapter 33[1]
- 1.7.2. Just prior to this period, King Hezekiah, *The Reformer* had taken some positive steps, but the period quickly descended to a dark state as Manasseh became king. In fact, it is recorded that as a result, *it came upon Judah, to remove them from His sight because of the sins of Manasseh, according to all that he had done* (2 Kings 24:3-4). Manasseh received his earthly judgment from the Assyrians, *Therefore the Lord brought the commanders of the army of the king of Assyria against them, and they captured Manasseh with hooks, bound him with bronze chains, and took him to Babylon* (2 Chron 33:11-12).
- 1.7.3. The death of King Hezekiah in 697 BCE marks an important turning point in Judah's history.
- 1.7.4. The idolaters surrounding this young twelve-year-old. erected altars to Baal and brought back the worship of other

---

[1] 33:5 *For he built altars for all the host of heaven in the two courts of the house of the Lord. 6 He made his sons pass through the fire in the valley of Ben-hinnom; and he practiced witchcraft, used divination, practiced sorcery and dealt with mediums and spiritists. He did much evil in the sight of the Lord, provoking Him to anger.*
9 thus Manasseh misled Judah and the inhabitants of Jerusalem to do more evil than the nations whom the Lord destroyed before the sons of Israel.

gods. In addition, following his grandfather's paying tributes of great wealth to the Assyrians, Judah became a puppet state.

1.7.5. A sad state of God's Promised Land!

1.7.6. King Manasseh, who followed his father's (Hezekiah) rule, fell into total idolatry, even naming his own son after the Egyptian god Amon. He rebuilt the idols his father had destroyed and burned his own children on an altar! He became the worst, most wicked ruler of all Judah's kings.

1.7.7. Josephus in writing about this period said, *"Manasseh persecuted and killed the prophets of the Lord."* Refer to the information on Josephus below. He is an important source for Bible history.

EXPANDED HELP PAPER
Flavius Josephus

Flavius Josephus was born the son of a priest in Jerusalem shortly after the crucifixion of Jesus Christ in 37 CE and died in Rome early in the 2nd century (not known precisely). He was well educated and rose to a respected position in the Jewish community.

At the age of nineteen, Josephus joined the Pharisees. When he was twenty-six (63 CE) he traveled to Rome and successfully called for the release of some fellow priests who had been sent there to be tried by Nero. As a result, he strongly opposed the Jewish revolt against Rome in 66 CE, fearing the results for his nation.

By 67 CE he was imprisoned in Rome; however, he gained the favor of Vespasian who had invaded Jerusalem, later becoming emperor in 69. Now free, he returned to Jerusalem with Titus, Vespasian's son, and future emperor, where he served the Roman commander as interpreter and mediator. He believed the Roman forces would achieve military victory, so he attempted to convince the Jews holding Jerusalem to surrender in order to save the city. They refused. However, in 70 CE, the city fell to the Romans and was demolished.

Because Jerusalem was in ruins, Josephus returned to Rome with Titus, earning a pension from Rome and gaining the rights of a Roman citizen. He accepted the emperor's family name, Flavius and began his writing. He is the author of the most significant extra-biblical writings we have. The works of Josephus render him one of the most valuable authorities for the student of New Testament times. However, his works, which included the Old Testament, are also of significance. He is very reliable as a historian and deserving of careful study for the serious reader.

Judah in Decline

His writings, which we have in their entirety, include (1) His first work, *The Wars of the Jews* written approximately 79 CE to give a general history of the wars from the time of the Maccabees to the Great War with Rome, which resulted in the final demise of the nation of Israel. It includes the period from Antiochus Epiphanes (175 BCE) to occurrences in Galilee in 167 CE, the course of the war until the capturing and destruction of Jerusalem by Titus, and the fall of Masada in 73.

(2) Josephus' other major work *The Antiquities of the Jews* was published some twenty years later. It is the longest of his works. This work is a history of the Jewish nation, from the creation story to the War of 66 CE in Josephus' own time. This work included 20 books and showed that the Jews preceded the Greeks in antiquity. It uses the Septuagint (the Hebrew Scriptures translated into Greek) as well as several writings of Greek and Roman historians and contains many details of importance to any student of the Bible.

(3) His autobiography, *The Life of Flavius Josephus*, was an appendix to *The Antiquities*. In this work, Josephus defended himself and his war record against other works of historians. We have Josephus at his worst here. He gives the wrong impression concerning the part he played during the great crisis. (4) A formal discourse was also written, originally entitled *Concerning the High Antiquity of the Jews,* is a most unusual work. Josephus approaches as an enthusiastic writer, rather than a historical reporter. Later it was called *Against Apion.* Josephus visits Apion and contrasts the Jewish faith with the Greek beliefs.

1.7.8. 2 Kings 21:16 records it this way.[1] It was because of Manasseh that God found it necessary to remove Judah out of His sight (2 Kings 24:3-4).

    1.7.8.1. Manasseh is the king who is believed to have had the prophet Isaiah "sawed asunder." Jeremiah records *Your sword has devoured your prophets Like a destroying lion.* (2:30)

    1.7.8.2. Little if any was heard from prophets during this period of fifty years. Almost a prequel to the 400 years of silence between the Old and New Testaments, the period between BCE and CE (or the more familiar B.C. and A.D.) when nothing was heard from any prophet. What Manasseh did was

---

[1] *Moreover, Manasseh shed very much innocent blood until he had filled Jerusalem from one end to another;*

shameful. Satan has never stopped his attempt at destroying the Word of God. He is a destroyer!

1.7.8.3. This fifty-five-year reign of Manasseh (697-642 BCE) decided the fate of Judah. Idolatry was so embedded in Judah it became impossible for a good king like Josiah who followed, or a great prophet like Jeremiah, to bring a people back to God.[1]

1.7.9. Next, a young king, Josiah comes on the scene at age eight. Again, a great attempt is made to bring the people to God. We find some interesting persons connected to his reign:

1.7.9.1. Hilkiah the priest
1.7.9.2. Shaphan the scribe
1.7.9.3. And Huldah the prophetess
1.7.9.4. Which tell us of the good influence that surrounded Josiah. In addition, because of this influence, we read in 2 Chronicles 34:3.[2]
1.7.9.5. At sixteen years old, Josiah seeks God. He sets out to re-establish the Temple. This first Temple in Jerusalem was now 300 years old!
1.7.9.6. By this time, it had been literally stripped of anything of value. Even the walls and pillars had been stripped of gold. This was the glorious Temple of Solomon, which a visiting Queen said is more than could even be imagined.
1.7.9.7. During Josiah's reconstruction program, some workers found a volume of the law. We do not know if it was part or all of the Law (Torah, Pentateuch). One source holds that Josiah's discovery was a work, which eventually became the final composition included in the Pentateuch, Deuteronomy.[3]

---

[1] 2 Kings 24:3-5 reads *Surely at the command of the Lord it came upon Judah, to remove them from His sight because of the sins of Manasseh, according to all that he had done, 4 and also for the innocent blood which he shed, for he filled Jerusalem with innocent blood; and the Lord would not forgive.*
What power—evil brings!
[2] *For in the eighth year of his reign while he was still a youth, he began to seek the God of his father David;*
[3] Carmody, John, *Exploring the Hebrew Bible*, Prentice-Hall, Inc. Englewood Cliffs, New Jersey, 1988, pg 18

Judah in Decline

1.7.9.8. Neither do we know how a valuable scroll had been lost. Perhaps it was hidden in order to preserve it?

1.7.9.9. What a joy for Josiah to read the law for the first time.

1.7.9.10. The prophetess Huldah confirms and declares this is the Word of God in 2 Chronicles 34:22-28 *...written in the book which they have read in the presence of the king of Judah*

Depth of Bible Words and Locations
Huldah

Huldah a prophetess lived during critical years in Judah's history. She foretells the destruction of Jerusalem, 2 Kings 22:14–20; 2 Chronicles 34:22–28. The name "Huldah" (Weasel) is derived from the Hebrew root *cheled,* which means, "to glide swiftly." Perhaps Huldah's name reflects her quickness of mind and her ability to swiftly and rightly discern the things of God.

Clearly, Huldah had established a reputation as God's spokes-person. We are even more impressed when we realize that the prophet Habakkuk, whose book is part of the Old Testament, was living at this time. Yet Huldah was clearly the king's first choice when seeking to know God's will.

Huldah had a word from God for the young king Josiah. God would indeed bring calamity on His sinning people. But because Josiah's heart was tender and he had responded when he heard God's Word, judgment would not fall during his reign.

Huldah experienced no conflict between the roles of prophetess and wife. Huldah's husband did not feel threatened by the fact that his wife had an important ministry.

1.7.9.11. Josiah finds just how far Judah had fallen from God's promised blessings. It is at this time that Jeremiah helps to bring about revival (see Chapter TEN).

1.7.9.12. However, things do not continue as King Josiah and the prophets Huldah and Jeremiah believed.

1.7.9.13. Egypt, led by Egyptian pharaoh Necho II (610-595 BCE) marches into the land and joins forces with Assyria at Carchemish. They confront Babylonia and Josiah with the intention of protecting the Egyptian Kingdom. Megiddo is quite a historical place. We of course immediately connect Megiddo with the end-time battle of Armageddon. However, it was also connected with much of ancient history. See the Expanded Help Paper **End Time Events** (in Chapter TWELVE).

1.7.9.14. There is no absolute clarity on how Josiah died. We read in 2 Chronicles 35[1] that Josiah was gravely wounded at Megiddo while leading a military strike against Necho who ruled In Egypt. In addition, two other sources, the first-century CE Jewish historian Josephus and the apocryphal First Book of Esdras, also refer to the fatal consequences of a battle.

1.7.9.15. However, the account found In the Second Book of Kings 23 makes no mention of a battle. *Pharaoh Neco king of Egypt went up to the king of Assyria to the river Euphrates. And King Josiah went to meet him, and when Pharaoh Neco saw him he killed him at Megiddo.*

1.7.9.16. This version of the story has led some scholars to question whether Josiah ever led his troops into battle against Necho. Scholars suggest perhaps Josiah approached his Egyptian counterpart on peaceful terms whereupon he was seized and subsequently killed either by Necho or by individuals acting on the pharaoh's orders

1.7.9.17. This author would accept that King Josiah is killed on that battlefield at Megiddo—the last great king of Judah--has fallen! The last, sad days of the kingdom are at hand. Judah declines!

EXPANDED HELP PAPER
What is Armageddon?

During the past fifty or more years, various writings have emerged attempting to understand *Armageddon*. This is but another writing on this oft-misunderstood term. The attempt is to explain the meaning in simple language.

---

[1] 2 Chron 35:23 *The archers shot King Josiah, and the king said to his servants, "Take me away, for I am badly wounded." 24... where he died and was buried in the tombs of his fathers.*

Judah in Decline

The English term *Armageddon* comes from two Hebrew words, *Har* and *Megiddo*. *Har* means "hill" and *Megiddo* roughly means "a place of troops." The city of Megiddo was located at a very critical junction in Palestine. A valley is located just south and east of Megiddo called Valley of Megiddo. Perhaps there have been more wars fought in that area than any other spot on earth. For example:

One of the earliest battles involved an Egyptian Pharaoh we have mentioned (chart of Pharaohs in Volume 1, Chapter TEN), Thutmose III called "the Napoleon of Egypt," oppressor of God's people. He defied all his advisors and marched his army single file through a narrow pass and so surprised the Canaanites—they ran!

It was here that Deborah and Barak sang a song of praise to God (Judges 5) thanking Him for literally sweeping away the Canaanite army by swollen waters.

Gideon defeated the Midianites (Judges 7) in this valley or plane of Meggido. It also was here that the deaths of King Saul and King Josiah happened.

The Assyrian Empire made it the capital of an entire province in 740 BCE, because of its strategic location.

And of course, another powerful leader figures prominently in this location sometime in the future; for it's here that Satan will gather armies to make a final attack near Jerusalem in a futile attempt to usurp God.

Armies heading north or south used this location, really a hill. This was the most traveled trade route in those days making it a vital junction for all travel in the known world. The town of Megiddo overlooked the Valley of Jezreel and controlled the narrow pass leading from Egypt and Mesopotamia and from Phoenician cities to Jerusalem. In an article by the Israel Ministry of Foreign Affairs in 2000 CE, he remarks "Megiddo is mentioned many times in Egyptian royal inscriptions from the 15th to the 13th centuries BCE. They attest to the city's importance as the center of Egyptian administration in Canaan as a logistical base on the road north." It is little wonder why so much is written concerning the term *Armageddon*, with widely differing conclusions, some of them false.

Revelation chapter 16 tells the true story surrounding *Armageddon*. Let us set the records straight by using His Word to do so. Revelation 16 informs us that God will dry up the mighty Euphrates River so that the "the great armies of the East" can walk across it, verse 12 *The sixth angel poured out his bowl on the great river, the Euphrates; and its water was dried up, so that the way would be prepared for the kings from the east.*

They will head directly to the Valley of Jezreel and on to the hill of Megiddo. At the same time, the "king of the North" (Daniel 11:40) will have gathered his forces south of Megiddo. He is located there because of a sudden attack on the king of the South. This king of the North will have great "Beast power" and be composed of a confederation of nations in the European vicinity. (It should be noted that as of 2008 CE, the Lisbon Treaty has been presented to twenty-seven European Union member states asking for ratification of this "constitution." The Los Angeles Times on Jun 14, 2008, reported, "This treaty will turn the EU into a super state"). The king of the South likely will be a confederation of Islamic states and its leader.

Dan 11:40-45 *"At the end time the king of the South will collide with him, and the king of the North will storm against him with chariots, with horsemen and with many ships; and he will enter countries, overflow them and pass through.*
41 "He will also enter the Beautiful Land, and many countries will fall; but these will be rescued out of his hand: Edom, Moab and the foremost of the sons of Ammon.
42 "Then he will stretch out his hand against other countries, and the land of Egypt will not escape.
43 "But he will gain control over the hidden treasures of gold and silver and over all the precious things of Egypt; and Libyans Ethiopians will follow at his heels.
44 "But rumors from the East and from the North will disturb him, and he will go forth with great wrath to destroy and annihilate many.
45 "He will pitch the tents of his royal pavilion between the seas and the beautiful Holy Mountain; yet he will come to his end, and no one will help him."

The final battle does NOT take place in this location! Read carefully Revelation 16:16 *And they gathered them together to the place which in Hebrew is called Har-Magedon.* Notice *gathered.* Just before this verse, in verse 14 we read *for they are spirits of demons, performing signs, which go out to the kings of the whole world, to gather them together for the war of the great day of God, the Almighty.* Lying spirits persuade the kings of the earth to move down to Jerusalem in the "Har-Megiddo" where they gather. In Zechariah 14 we read *For I will gather all the nations against Jerusalem to battle.*

Christ will war on all these kings and destroy them and their armies. *Now this will be the plague with which the LORD will strike all the peoples who have gone to war against Jerusalem; their flesh will rot while they stand on their feet, and their eyes will rot in their sockets, and their tongue will rot in their mouth.* (Zechariah 14:12)

Judah in Decline

Armageddon is the gathering or staging place where the kingdoms of armies are motivated to go *up* (located on a hill) to Jerusalem for the battle of the great "day of God."

1.7.10. Following a short three-month reign of Josiah's son (Jehoahaz), he was taken away into Egypt by the Egyptian king Necho, where he died. King Necho placed Eliakim on the throne of Judah, the last actual king of Judah, who ruled eleven years. Necho changed his name to Jehoiakim.

    1.7.10.1. Jehoiakim, another son of Josiah, served as vassal, first of Egypt, then of Babylonia, for the eleven years. We see quickly, all the gains of his father Josiah were lost. An even greater period of religious abuse takes place (if that were possible). He served the king of Babylon for three years and then revolted.

    1.7.10.2. It was a sad day when Jehoiakim was placed in power. He was proud and selfish, weighing the people down with taxes demanded by Egypt (2 Kings 23:35).

    1.7.10.3. We have seen this during our entire journey through the Old Testament, idolatry begins, followed by leaders ushering in reform, resulting in a turning back to God, then followed again by idolatry. Sad!

1.7.11. Jeremiah's forty years of prophecy, which we reviewed, took place during the same forty years of Judah's final existence. According to him, idolatry was at its strength.[1]

1.8. We're also told that during this final, sad period, a prophet named Uriah was condemned and killed for prophesying against the wickedness of the king (Jeremiah 26:20-23).

    1.8.1. Judah's fate at this time was tied directly into what was happening in Assyria, Babylonia, and Egypt. First, it was Assyria, and then Babylonia who marched into Jerusalem

---

[1] Jeremiah 2:8 *"The priests did not say, 'Where is the Lord?' And those who handle the law did not know Me; The rulers also transgressed against Me, And the prophets prophesied by Baal And walked after things that did not profit.* 11 *"Has a nation changed gods When they were not gods? But My people have changed their glory For that which does not profit.* 13 *"For My people have committed two evils: They have forsaken Me, The fountain of living waters, To hew for themselves cisterns, Broken cisterns That can hold no water."*

and took the valuables back to Babylon during the time Jehoiakim was in rule.

1.8.2. This also was the time Daniel and other young men were taken to Babylon in what is called the *first* captivity, 606 BCE.

1.8.3. This rebellion of King Jehoiakim against Nebuchadnezzar eventually stirred Nebuchadnezzar who was off fighting in other parts of the world. Jehoiakim's son Jehoiachin reigned after only three months. Nebuchadnezzar stormed the gates of Jerusalem during those three months, capturing Jehoiachin, his family, and many of the elite, taking them to Babylon. Jehoiachin lived with his family in the palace of Nebuchadnezzar in Babylon.

1.8.4. Nebuchadnezzar marched into Jerusalem, taking 10,000 leading citizens to Babylon (including Ezekiel) in what was the *second* captivity. Daniel and Ezekiel were approximately the same age. Only the poor and weak were left behind.

1.9. Then almost a repeat of Jehoiakim's reign takes place. Zedekiah, a caretaker or governor, another son of Josiah, ruled Judah for eleven years. It's recorded in 2 Chronicles 36[1]

1.9.1. Zedekiah, like Jehoiakim, rebelled against Nebuchadnezzar. He was captured as he ran away, and taken to Babylon where his two sons were killed in front of him. He was blinded and sent to prison for the rest of his life.

1.9.2. In 586 BCE Jerusalem and the Temple were all plundered and destroyed by Nebuchadnezzar in a determination to bring an end to the kingdom of Judah. Jerusalem's population decreased remarkably, but the rural areas show rather little change in population throughout this period. In fact, the effects of the exile on the Judean peasantry seem minor. This was the *third* and final invasion of Jerusalem by Nebuchadnezzar.

1.9.3. The removal of the elite meant the end of national temple worship and other elements of centralization. However, we cannot assume that all priests went into exile, only their connections with the temple were severed. After 586, Jeremiah was forced to go to Egypt with others who were fleeing from the invasions. He continued to deliver

---

[1] 2 Chronicles 36:12 *He did evil in the sight of the Lord his God; he did not humble himself before Jeremiah the prophet who spoke for the Lord.*

Judah in Decline

messages to those in Egypt. The walls of Jerusalem were broken down and would remain a rubble heap for the next seventy years. The Southern Kingdom's decline was complete!

TEN

Judah Falls

1. The history of God's people moves towards captivity. Therefore, we turn to the books of Jeremiah (we mentioned some of his messages previously) and his contemporaries[1]--each book named after its author. We will review them chronologically.
2. All twelve of Jacob's sons, the twelve Tribes of Israel, were represented in this captivity. Additional detail concerning the on-going Tribes is offered in this volume (see Chapter ELEVEN).
    - 2.1.1. The fall of Judah, with the destruction of Jerusalem and the Temple in 586 BCE, was a terrible blow to the people. From a *material* standpoint, it was devastating.
    - 2.1.2. From a *spiritual* viewpoint, perhaps we can see God's work in these events. Hebrew nationalism was ending, but what we could call "the religious movement" of this period in history, was just beginning.
    - 2.1.3. The cycle of 750 years had its "ups and downs" in the Hebrews serving God. From Judges to Solomon to Kings, over and over again. Maybe these last few years are what it would take to establish a solid foothold for a spiritual people.
    - 2.1.4. The recent teaching in Judah was perhaps awakening a nation. God was using His prophets to plant a seed of revelation.
    - 2.1.5. Jeremiah and Ezekiel were teaching something new. *An individual responsibility for sin; a need for heart-cleansing.*[2]
    - 2.1.6. Zephaniah with his view of God's judgments.
    - 2.1.7. In addition, Habakkuk had a new insight into faith.

---

[1] Nahum, Zephaniah, Habakkuk, and Obadiah.
[2] Jeremiah said it like this in 31:33 *"But this is the covenant which I will make with the house of Israel after those days," declares the Lord, "I will put My law within them and on their heart I will write it..."*

Judah Falls: Nahum

    2.1.8.   All of this revelation was building a new understanding for the people.
3 We look next at Jeremiah and four contemporaries. His ministry continued for fifty years. Chronologically, these five books (with Lamentations the sixth book in this period) would list as Nahum, Zephaniah, Jeremiah, Habakkuk, Obadiah, and Lamentations.
  3.1. **Nahum,** (meaning comfort) was from the small village of Elkosh in southwest Judah. Nahum prophesied from Jerusalem shortly after Sennacherib laid siege to the city. The only mention of Nahum in the entire Old Testament is 1:1. His short book is written in the form of poetry with powerful, vivid messages.
  3.1.1. We know nothing about the prophet other than what we are told in verse 1:1.

A Basic Outline of Nahum
Concerning Nineveh

1. Destruction Declared, Cp 1
2. Destruction Detailed, Cp 2
3. Destruction Deserved, Cp 3

Jesus in Nahum...He is the All Powerful One.

Depth of Bible Words and Locations
Nahum Key Word: *Jealous*

Found in 1:1. It is a word meaning "to be eager" or even "to be furious." It's even one of God's names in Exodus 34:14. Usually, the word is associated with idol worship. God is Jealous when it comes to His people. He is creator and redeemer, furious and eager, for His people. He will tolerate no rival.

  3.1.2.   His prophecy is concerning Nineveh (1:1), the capital of the Assyrian Empire. God's divine intervention during the siege saved the city from destruction by killing 185,000 Assyrians. However, Assyria's 300-year rule as a world empire was ending, and Nahum's message of doom is quite clear. Nineveh was not only to be destroyed—it would never be restored.
  3.1.3.   120 years earlier, Jonah extended Nineveh's existence by his revival there. Nahum serves as a sequel to Jonah, both concerning Nineveh, and together forming a continuous story. The repentance under Jonah delayed its destruction for over one hundred years.

3.1.4. His words were given around 630 BCE just before Josiah's reign of reformation, which we have noted began while Manasseh and Amon were ruling. Their reigns were full of cruelty and idolatry. As mentioned, Amon was named after an Egyptian god. Verse 3:8 refers to the fall of Thebes, 663 BCE, and the fall of Nineveh, 612.

3.1.5. Nahum wrote three cps on predicting the fall of Nineveh, the capital of Assyria. He begins by saying *"This is about you Nineveh."* Note 2:13 *Behold, I am against you.*

    3.1.5.1. Vv 1:3-5 state the majesty of God and His right to judge. Nahum's messianic picture of peace is quite memorable, 1:15 *Behold, on the mountains the feet of him who brings good news, Who announces peace!*

    3.1.5.2. His description of Nineveh's destruction in cp 2 is a prophecy with great detail:

3.1.5.2.1. Mighty men and warriors
3.1.5.2.2. Rattling of the wheel, speeding chariots
3.1.5.2.3. Horsemen charging
3.1.5.2.4. Flashing swords
3.1.5.2.5. Mass of corpses
3.1.5.2.6. Falling walls
3.1.5.2.7. Plunder the riches
3.1.5.2.8. Moaning women
3.1.5.2.9. Running scared
3.1.5.2.10. Hearts melting, knees knocking

3.1.6. During the excavation of Nineveh, (buried since 612 BCE), the discovery of many written tablets, has allowed better translations in our day, including the NIV.

    3.1.6.1. In addition, many passages tell of His anger against Assyria's treatment of other nations. He devoted thoughts to the destruction of Nineveh and of her calamity, which no one would pity.[1] Her shed blood, lies, and plunder (3:1) establishes the justice for its fall.

---

[1] 1:14 *The Lord has issued a command concerning you: " Your name will no longer be perpetuated. I will prepare your grave, For you are contemptible."*
2:13 *"Behold, I am against you," declares the Lord of hosts.*
3:1 *completely full of lies and pillage*
3:5 *And show to the nations your nakedness And to the kingdoms your disgrace.*
3:7 *And it will come about that all who see you Will shrink from you and say, 'Nineveh is devastated!*
3:19 *There is no relief for your breakdown, Your wound is incurable. All who hear about you Will clap their hands over you.*

Judah Falls: Zephaniah

- 3.1.7. Nahum's contemporary, Zephaniah also predicted the destruction of Nineveh.
- 3.2. **Zephaniah** (which means "hidden of the Lord"), prophesied at this time, during the reign of King Josiah. He begins his ministry a few years after Nahum's prophecy.
  - 3.2.1. He both knew and told of Nineveh's coming destruction, which happened in 612 BCE. He speaks as a representative of the remnant of faith, those few who remain true to God and His Word through the time of trouble coming upon the earth.

A Basic Outline of Zephaniah
1. Judgments Promised, Cps 1-2
2. Salvation Promised, Cp 3

Depth of Bible Words and Locations
Zephaniah Key Word: *Humble*

Found in 2:3 and 3:12. The Hebrew word may be translated "meek." It means "to be bowed down" or "to be afflicted." Sometimes it refers to the oppressed but also signifies the strength of character in enduring suffering without resentment. This is a character, which is rooted in God.

Jesus in Zephaniah...He is Savior.

- 3.2.2. We know considerable details concerning his background. He was a descendant of the good king Hezekiah who ruled for twenty-nine years preceding the evil reigns of Manasseh and Amon. The first verse traces Zephaniah's lineage back four generations, which reveals he was the *only* prophet of royal descent. We are quite certain that Zephaniah shared in the great work of King Josiah and the prophet Jeremiah in preaching reform and revival.
- 3.2.3. Zephaniah solves any dating problem in the first verse *"in the days of Josiah son of Amos, king of Judah."* Josiah reigned from 640-609 BCE, placing Zephaniah very close to 630.
- 3.2.4. He starts out in v. 2 with this statement: *"I will completely remove all things From the face of the earth,"* declares the Lord. A shocking word from God that comes like a tornado! The next few verses detail God's thoughts of "removing all things."

3.2.5. Zephaniah's prophecy is aimed at the coming judgment upon Judah and Jerusalem.[1]

3.2.6. He too, along with Joel earlier, speaks of *the great day of the Lord*. That day will fall upon all (including Jews) who refuse to follow God. The day of the Lord will be terrible 1:7-18)

    3.2.6.1. Soldiers will cry

    3.2.6.2. Troubles, destruction, desolation, and distress

    3.2.6.3. Walk around like they are blind

    3.2.6.4. Rich people will not be able to buy security

    3.2.6.5. Destruction will be everywhere.

3.2.7. Interesting, in cp 2 he records this coming judgment will not just only on Nineveh (Assyria) but will extend to all the nations of the earth. Mentioned are:

    3.2.7.1. Gaza

    3.2.7.2. Ashkelon

    3.2.7.3. Ashdod

    3.2.7.4. Ekron

    3.2.7.5. Philistines and nations of the seacoast

    3.2.7.6. Moab

    3.2.7.7. Ethiopia

    3.2.7.8. Assyria

3.2.8. Chapter 3 applies to Jerusalem, called the *tyrannical city!*

    3.2.8.1. Her leaders, judges, prophets, and priests all fail their responsibilities. However, we then see an assembly with pure lips calling on the name of the Lord in verses 3:9-14. Note verse 15 in which the statement is made that God is Israel's King.

3.2.9. He offers an invitation

    3.2.9.1. First to those in Jerusalem, verse 2:3 *Seek the Lord, All you humble of the earth Who have carried out His ordinances; Seek righteousness, seek humility. Perhaps you will be hidden In the day of the Lord's anger.*

    3.2.9.2. Then, second, to the remnant that remained faithful, verses 3:14-15 *Shout for joy, O daughter of Zion! Shout in triumph, O Israel! Rejoice and exult with all your heart, O daughter of Jerusalem! 15 The Lord has taken*

---

[1] Read the prophecy in cp 1:14 *Near is the great day of the Lord, Near and coming very quickly; Listen, the day of the Lord! In it the warrior cries out bitterly. 15 A day of wrath is that day, A day of trouble and distress, A day of destruction and desolation, A day of darkness and gloom, A day of clouds and thick darkness*
And this very pointed prophecy goes on thru v 18.

away His judgments against you, He has cleared away your enemies. The King of Israel, the Lord, is in your midst; You will fear disaster no more.

3.2.10. Twice he mentions the return from captivity (2:7; 3:20) when he would "purify their lips." After the return from Babylon, never again did they allow idol worship in their nation.

3.3. Jeremiah is the most colorful figure of them all, perhaps because we know more about him than any other Old Testament prophet.

3.3.1. His book abounds in biographical material. Many of the other prophets are introduced with very little background, in some cases only their name. Jeremiah, during his forty years of ministry, never saw any success. Jeremiah was called to be a prophet before he was born.[1]

A Basic Outline of Jeremiah
1. The Call of Jeremiah, Cp 1
2. The Prophecies to Judah and Jerusalem, Cps 2-45
3. The Prophecies to the Nations, Cps 46-51
4. The Fall of Jerusalem, Cp 52

Depth of Bible Words and Locations
Jeremiah Key Word: *Heal*

Found in 3:22, 6:14, 8:11, 15:18. It literally means the work of a physician. Generally the idea of restoring to normal. God is praised for His healing:
Disease (Psalms 103:3)
Brokenhearted (Psalms 147:3)
The soul (Psalms 30:2; 107:20)

Jesus in Jeremiah...He is the Righteous Branch

3.3.2. Jeremiah's calling by God was when he was only a child. Verse 1:6 *Then said I, Ah, Lord God! Behold, I cannot speak, for I am only a youth.*

3.3.3. However, he invests forty years doing everything he could to bring the people back to God.

3.3.4. He witnessed the disintegration of the Davidic kingdom and the destruction of Solomon's temple, which had been the pride and glory of Israel for almost four centuries. He lived through the final, difficult times of Jerusalem, which we reviewed.

---

[1] The name Jeremiah means "The Lord Exalts" or "The Lord Establishes."

This city was the last territory left of David and Solomon's empire. Jeremiah wanted the citizens to escape the doom that was to come.

3.3.5. He was God's final cry to Jerusalem! *If you will repent—God will deliver you.*

3.3.6. He belonged to an upper class, similar to Isaiah, and had the respect of kings and officials. He was educated and very familiar with the history of his nation. He was the son of a priest, Hilkiah, who perhaps was the one who found the Book of the Law (2 Kings 22:8).

3.3.7. During his era, the three empires were in a struggle for supremacy.

    3.3.7.1. The world ruler in the north, Assyria, was growing weak during this period.

    3.3.7.2. Babylon in the southern Euphrates valley was growing strong.

    3.3.7.3. Egypt, who was a great world power in earlier years, now again was having thoughts of expansion.

3.3.8. Jeremiah experienced Babylon winning this three-empire struggle. Babylon's rule was for 70 years, the same 70 years of Judah's captivity.

3.3.9. Zephaniah and Habakkuk helped Jeremiah in Jerusalem.

3.3.10. We mention his closest friend, a scribe named Baruch. Baruch assisted Jeremiah in ministry. Baruch recorded Jeremiah's words and had custody over the prophet's writings. He also compiled his messages.[1]

3.3.11. Now, understand that Jeremiah's book, like some others we have reviewed is not chronological, so let me help you understand some things about chronology in Scripture.

    3.3.11.1. Close to the time of exile, Jeremiah was commanded to write down the messages, which he had orally delivered (30:2). *Thus says the Lord, the God of Israel, 'Write all the words which I have spoken to you in a book.* He requested Baruch to write them down.

    3.3.11.2. Then King Jehoiakim destroyed that scroll (36:23) *the king cut it with a scribe's knife and threw it*

---

[1] Jeremiah 36:4 *Then Jeremiah called Baruch the son of Neriah, and Baruch wrote on a scroll at the dictation of Jeremiah all the words of the Lord which He had spoken to him.*
Jeremiah 45:1 *This is the message which Jeremiah the prophet spoke to Baruch the son of Neriah, when he had written down these words in a book at Jeremiah's dictation*

Judah Falls: Jeremiah

into the fire that was in the brazier, until all the scroll was consumed.

EXPANDED HELP PAPER
The Indestructible Bible

The Bible has proven it is indestructible. The fact that the text of the Bible has survived throughout history is a wonderful testimony to the preserving power of God. The Scriptures have survived time, persecution, and criticism.

Satan does not question the importance and authority of the Bible. He has attempted to destroy it throughout history. Whether Romans in New Testament times, barbarians of the dark ages, Spanish Inquisitors in the Middle Ages, French radicals in the eighteenth century, Nazis in World War II, Soviet Communists or Chinese revolutionaries, all have tried to destroy the Bible. It is not unusual throughout history to read of gigantic fires where Bibles were burned.

Note with me its indestructibility: The first book of the Bible was composed some thirty-five hundred years ago; the last was completed nearly two thousand years ago. The original manuscripts were all written on perishable materials and have since disappeared. The thousands of copies we possess, however, accurately represent the originals. We investigated this in a paper printed in Volume 1 of this study course.

We also note the Bible has survived the persecution of its adherents. Consider the following examples of the tenacity of the followers of the Bible in preserving its text in the midst of persecution.

The mad tyrant Antiochus Epiphanes in 167 BCE decreed, "The books of the law (i.e. Jewish scripture) that they found they tore to pieces and burned with fire. Anyone found possessing the book of the covenant, or anyone who adhered to the law was condemned to death."

Note, in 303 CE, the Roman emperor Diocletian wrote an imperial letter ordering the destruction of all churches, the burning of all Scriptures, and the loss of civil liberties by all professing Christians. That did not stop the spread of Christianity or the proclamation of God's revelation in the Bible. Constantine, the Roman emperor who succeeded Diocletian, converted to Christianity and eventually ordered Eusebius to make fifty copies of the Scriptures, to be produced by the best scribes and at government expense.

TRAVEL THROUGH THE OLD TESTAMENT

Time passes, but the Bible remains a dramatic testimony to the keeping power of God for his revelation. Rulers come and go. The Bible remains. Critics come and go. The Bible remains.[1]

With the rise of Islam in the seventh century, the Bible has been consistently outlawed in strict Moslem countries. To this very day, distribution of Bibles is strictly forbidden in Moslem countries. Countless Christians have lost their lives for attempting to distribute the Bible and/or share its teachings to receptive Moslems.

In the year 1199 CE, Pope Innocent the First ordered that all French Bibles were to be burned and that people were forbidden to read it. In the year 1234 CE, Pope Gregory IX again ordered all people to surrender their Bibles for burning. In Spain, Ferdinand and Isabella, the very ones that sent Columbus out to find the new world, ordered the Bible to be turned in, and destroyed; and there are many other examples where people tried to destroy the Bible—and yet, it has survived!

In 1530, Henry VIII gave orders that all English Bibles were to be destroyed. People caught distributing the Tyndale Bible in England were burned at the stake. This attempt to destroy Tyndale's Bible was very successful, as only two copies have survived.

Voltaire, the noted French infidel who died in 1778, said that within one hundred years from his time, Christianity would be swept from existence and passed into history. But what has happened? Voltaire has passed into history, while the circulation of the Bible continues to increase in almost all parts of the world, carrying blessing wherever it goes. For example, the English Cathedral in Zanzibar is built on the site of the Old Slave Market, and the Communion Table stands on the very spot where the whipping-post once stood! The world abounds with such instances.[2]

There is a historical irony about the Voltaire matter. Fifty years after his death, the Geneva Bible Society used Voltaire's house and printing press to print hundreds of Bibles. Further, over two hundred years after Voltaire's death, Christianity is still not extinct!

In spite of persecution, perversion, criticism, abuse, and time, the Bible has survived virtually intact. An anvil has worn out many hammers. There is no ancient document, which has the manuscript support that even approximates that of the New Testament. The Scriptures are unique in the quantity, quality, and antiquity of their manuscripts. Many have sought to ban and destroy the Bible, but their efforts have been futile. The Bible is by far the most popular book in the world. Portions have been

---

[1] McDowell, Josh, *Josh McDowell's Handbook on Apologetics*, electronic ed., Nashville, Thomas Nelson, 1997
[2] Collett, Sidney, *All About the Bile*, Old Tappan, N.J., Revell, p. 63

translated into over one thousand seven hundred languages, and it has been copied and circulated more extensively than any other literature. Recent archaeological, historical, and linguistic evidence have refuted destructive critical theories in favor of the trustworthiness of Scripture.[1]

Then we add to our study, in Jeremiah, *God's Word was "destroyed," early in the sixth century* BCE (Jer Cps 11–26). The king should have been copying the Law for his self and heeding its message. Instead, he destroyed what Jeremiah had spoken and Baruch had written. King Jehoiakim dearly paid for his arrogance. You can try to destroy the Bible, but you will fail.

However, God's Word indeed is preserved (27–32). The king and his family are gone and would be forgotten were it not for the Book he tried to destroy! God's Word will endure: "Forever, O LORD, Your word is settled in heaven" (Psalms 119:89).

Jehoiakim listened as the scroll was read aloud; he did not appreciate this Word and tossed it into the fire. Read it in Jeremiah 36:23. Jehoiakim did not repent, later to be defeated by the Babylonians and dragged away in chains. He died in captivity. A lesson for all: "He who would attempt to destroy God's Word puts himself in great danger."

> *"The deathless Book has survived three great dangers: the negligence of its friends; the false systems built upon it; the warfare of those who have hated it."* Isaac Taylor

In the past 100 years, Communist governments have attempted to discredit the Bible and to prevent its circulation in their countries. They have used both educational and legal measures.

Educationally, people have been taught that the Bible is a superstitious fairy tale book to be rejected by enlightened communist minds. Legally, many people have been arrested and imprisoned for attempting to smuggle Bibles into Communist countries.

The Bible will stand, even if all else were destroyed! Luke 21:33 makes it clear: *Heaven and earth will pass away, but My words will not pass away.*

3.3.12. God commanded Jeremiah to write a new scroll. And he wrote down, first the contents of the original scroll, in the order that God had given it to him.

---

[1] Wilkinson, Bruce; Boa, Kenneth: Talk Thru the Bible, Nashville

3.3.12.1. Then He added other materials, perhaps some new details, in order to supplement those earlier messages. In addition, other additions could only have been added at a later location in the scroll, not inserted.[1]

3.3.12.2. In addition, since it was a later time in his life, Jeremiah added messages he received after the original materials, which had to do with those previous subjects. So he added the information to the scroll *as it was unrolled* or as individual "sheets" were added.

3.3.12.3. As other messages were received after the new scroll was written, they were *added* to the scroll as they were given. (He did not have an "insert" key to go back and place an earlier event). In this way, earlier events appear later in the scroll.

3.3.12.4. Then Chapters 45-52 were special supplements added to the scroll, perhaps by later authors (see JEDP theory). Therefore, the book had all this information, not always in chronological arraignment.

3.3.13. I hope that this insight will help clear up the method of writing in ancient days.

3.3.14. We know much about Jeremiah's ministry years, which were from King Josiah's reign, 628 BCE to beyond Judah's fall in 586, making him a contemporary of Daniel, Nahum, Zephaniah, Habakkuk, and probably Obadiah and Ezekiel.

3.3.15. His first eighteen years of ministry were side-by-side with young King Josiah; both of them worked to bring Judah back to worshipping God. Jeremiah's remaining years following Josiah were still in the courts during the reigns of Josiah's two evil sons, Jehoiakim and Zedekiah who we reviewed. Therefore, Jeremiah had both the good and the bad to deal with.

3.3.16. He suffered much during the reigns of those two sons. False prophets stood against him and cursed him.

3.3.17. The approaching armies of Babylon are mentioned in chapter four, while the actual later destruction of Jerusalem is reported in chapter six. Jeremiah, returning to his own time, appeals to the people to repent, in chapter seven. Babylon is also the theme in cps 39, 50-52.

3.3.18. He was arrested, beaten, and put in stocks by a priest. After being released he prophesied that all the followers of that

---

[1] I know I have personally delivered a teaching, then lost the notes. Later in re-creating the teaching, additional information was added to make it better or more complete. Then even later, I would add an additional "word" with a notation *"insert here."*

Judah Falls: Jeremiah

priest would be exiled. Jeremiah in looking at that experience curses the day he was born, vv. 20:14-18.[1]

3.3.19. The wonderful passage of Jeremiah 31 could be read as New Testament! The very essence of New Testament religion.[2]

3.3.20. Jeremiah is a great book. Even though he was in the mist of gloom, he gives some of the most glorious prophecies of Christ in all the Old Testament.

3.3.21. In vv. 3:15-17, Jeremiah saw a gospel age in which Jew and Gentile would have an equal share in the Kingdom, with individual responsibilities.

3.3.22. Later, in the New Testament, Paul is given the full revelation of this "mystery," which reveals a single, unified body of believers. Any person has the invitation to become a part of His body.

3.3.23. He explains why he is unmarried in these chapters. Disaster is coming because of the people's sins. It was better to remain single during that time.

3.3.24. Read the first eight verses of cp 23; these true shepherds are promised, who will gather the flock and feed it, followed by the rule of the Righteous Branch.

3.3.25. Cps 30-33 Jeremiah was in prison and talks of a righteous one coming from David's house to rule them.

3.3.26. His theme in cp 32 is *hope*. A truly rich book.

3.3.27. Notice Jeremiah used symbols to gain attention to his message:

    3.3.27.1. A belt (cp 13)
    3.3.27.2. Potter's clay (cp 18)

---

[1] Here's a couple of those verses:
14 *Cursed be the day when I was born;*
Let the day not be blessed when my mother bore me!
15 *Cursed be the man who brought the news*
To my father, saying,
"A baby boy has been born to you!"
And made him very happy.

[2] Jeremiah 31:31 *"Behold, days are coming," declares the Lord, "when I will make a new covenant with the house of Israel and with the house of Judah, 32 not like the covenant which I made with their fathers in the day I took them by the hand to bring them out of the land of Egypt, My covenant which they broke, although I was a husband to them," declares the Lord. 33 "But this is the covenant which I will make with the house of Israel after those days," declares the Lord, "I will put My law within them and on their heart I will write it; and I will be their God, and they shall be My people. 34 "They will not teach again, each man his neighbor and each man his brother, saying, 'Know the Lord,' for they will all know Me, from the least of them to the greatest of them," declares the Lord, "for I will forgive their iniquity, and their sin I will remember no more."*

   3.3.27.3. Clay jar (cp 19); a shattered city was coming
   3.3.27.4. Figs (cp 24)
   3.3.27.5. Yoke of straps (cp 27)
   3.3.27.6. Field (cp 32)
3.3.28. In cp 34, Jeremiah mentions the city of Lachish. It is mentioned by Jeremiah as being overrun by Babylonia. In the ruins, located in 1935 CE, twenty-one letters written during the siege were found. These letters were written from an outpost to the captain who defended Lachish.

3.3.29. This period is so interesting I had to chart the events to understand them.

Jeremiah's Time

King of Judah	Dates	Events of the Period
Manasseh	697-642 BCE	Jeremiah born
Amon	642-640	The short reign of Manasseh's son.
Josiah	640-609	A great reformer; Jeremiah's call, assists Josiah; Babylonia rises in power; Assyria declines.
Jehoahaz	609	Reigned 3 months, taken to Egypt.
Jehoiakim	609-597	A vassal of Egypt while Egypt dominated Jerusalem; Rise of Nebuchadnezzar; Jeremiah arrested, threatened, beaten, etc.
Jehoiachin	598	Reigned 3 months, taken to Babylon.
Zedekiah	597-587	A weak king. Jeremiah placed in confinement; suffering is at a climax in prison; Jerusalem invaded.
Gedealiah made governor		Governor assassinated; Jeremiah and his scribe taken to Egypt

  3.3.30. Note, Jeremiah's Trials
   3.3.30.1. Death threats (11:18-23
   3.3.30.2. Isolation (15:15-21)
   3.3.30.3. Placed in stocks (20:1-18)
   3.3.30.4. Arrested (26:7-24)
   3.3.30.5. Challenged (28:10-16)
   3.3.30.6. Falsely arrested, placed in a dungeon (37:11-16)
   3.3.30.7. Starvation, released, restricted to courtyard (37:17-21, 38:5)
   3.3.30.8. Imprisoned in a miry cistern (38:6-9)
   3.3.30.9. Released into courtyard (38:10-28)
   3.3.30.10. Carried away in chains, finally released (39:11-40:4)

Judah Falls: Habakkuk

3.3.30.11. Rejection (42:1-43:4)

3.3.31. The defeat of Egypt at Carchemish is mentioned in Jeremiah chapter 46, in the middle of Jeremiah's life. The actual prophecy is mentioned in 43:8-13 and then continued in 46:13-26. (Remember, the method that the scroll was written?)

3.3.32. Moab is mentioned in chapter 48. Moab helped Nebuchadnezzar invade Judah. Moab is told that Yahweh is going to punish it so that it will never recover. Later Nebuchadnezzar destroyed much of Moab. The length of this chapter concerning the woes that will be suffered suggest the satisfaction of the writer contemplating the downfall of this bitter foe.

3.3.33. Chapter 49 states the messages against the Ammonites, Edomites, Damascus, Kedar Hazor, and Elam.

    3.3.33.1. The words against Edom reflect the message of Obadiah 1-9. The Edomites consistently clashed with the Jews. Esau is referenced as an ancestor of the Edomites.

    3.3.33.2. The judgments against Damascus, Kedar, Hazor, and Elam are mentioned in the remainder of chapter 49. Amos prophesied against the people of Damascus because of their cruelty (1:3-5). The people of Kedar were descendants of Ishmael, Abraham's son by Hagar (Gen 25:13). Elam, located east of Babylon (Iran), would be restored following God's judgment.

    3.3.33.3. In chapter 50, Babylon is scheduled for destruction. Babylon fell to Persia in 539 BCE. Note the parallel between Assyria and Babylon, both nations later conquered. The coming destruction of Babylon is justified by the comparison to Sodom and Gomorrah.

    3.3.33.4. Chapter 51 continues the long message against Babylon using a variety of figures for an illustrative explanation.

3.4. The book of Habakkuk is in the form of a question concerning the conditions while King Jehoiakim reigned. The captivity was starting in 608 BCE, so he prophesies after the fall of Nineveh in 612.[1] He is the only Habakkuk in Scripture.

A Basic Outline of Habakkuk #1
1. Habakkuk's Questions, Cps 1-2

---

[1] Habakkuk identifies himself as a prophet, and as the author in both v1 and in his prayer in 3:1. He was probably a priest in the temple, while also being a prophet. He mentions *"Chief Musician"* in the close of the book indicating he may have been a musician in Jerusalem.

2. Habakkuk's Song, Cp 3

A Basic Outline of Habakkuk #2
By Three Prayers
1. A Prayer for God's Justice, 1:1-11
2. A Prayer Questioning God's Justice, 1:12-2:20
3. A Prayer for Mercy, Cp 3

Depth of Bible Words and Locations
Habakkuk Key Word: *Image*
Found in 2:18. It is a word meaning "to hew out stone" or "to cut or carve wood." You can see the word in Exodus 34:4. God prohibited this at Mt Sinai in Exodus 20:4. The Bible calls them worthless and anyone who worships them, shameful. Isaiah mentions the images several times.

> *Jesus in Habakkuk...He is the God of Glory and Greatness.*

3.4.1. Habakkuk, rather than a prophecy addressed to Israel, is a dialogue between the prophet and God. He seems to ask the question "Why?" He had the wisdom concerning what is "good," but could not reconcile it with what was happening around him.
    3.4.1.1. Why does God allow this awfulness?
    3.4.1.2. If He is all-powerful, why not interrupt and stop it? He struggles with the similar questions Job had.
    3.4.1.3. Such questions could be asked today. Why do the wicked prosper? We question the theodicy as much as Habakkuk did in his book, and ask, "How can a just God tolerate today's state of affairs and not act to deliver a believer from his suffering?"

3.4.2. King Jehoiakim heard of Nebuchadnezzar's return from Egypt on continued military march—first through Nineveh (612 BCE), the capital of Assyria; then through Haran and Carchemish—on his way to take Jerusalem. The King of Judah also watched as Daniel and others are taken to Babylon. Then he rebels against Babylon and tries to hold them off as Jerusalem is invaded.

3.4.3. Habakkuk begins with two complaints to God, and God answers them both. The answers seem to confuse the prophet, but in the end learned to trust God and to live by faith in God's way, regardless of the circumstances.
    3.4.3.1. The first four verses state Habakkuk's quandary. Habakkuk states *"your people are getting worse and worse!"* and God answers (verses 1:5-6—this

Judah Falls: Habakkuk

is not your problem!), *"I'll punish them by raising up the Babylonians against them."*

3.4.3.2. The verses 1:6-11 are a description of Babylon's power and might, which God is using for His purpose.

3.4.3.3. Then, second, Habakkuk questions (verses 1:12-2:1) the use of a people more wicked than the ones to be judged. He almost accepts God's method of judgment, however in v. 13 wavers. God responds (2:2-6—this is not your concern!) *as time goes on my judgment will be understood as the events develop. All wickedness will be punished.* God states the verse for all of us, His method, in verse 2:3 *For the vision is yet for the appointed time; It hastens toward the goal and it will not fail. Though it tarries, wait for it; For it will certainly come, it will not delay.*

3.4.4. The five woes of cp 2 also help explain. Good advice for us today.

3.4.4.1. Verse 6 *"Woe to him who increases what is not his —For how long —And makes himself rich with loans?"*

3.4.4.2. Verse 9 *"Woe to him who gets evil gain for his house To put his nest on high..."*

3.4.4.3. Verse 12 *"Woe to him who builds a city with bloodshed And founds a town with violence!"*

3.4.4.4. Verse 15 *"Woe to you who make your neighbors drink."*

3.4.4.5. Verse 19 *"Woe to him who says to a piece of wood, 'Awake!' To a mute stone, 'Arise!'"*

3.4.5. In contrast, we read in verse 2:4 the opposite attitude-- the New Testament revelation in the Old Testament. *But the righteous will live by his faith.*

3.4.6. This is the lesson of Habakkuk. No matter how dark the times are, God has the outcome in His hands. Trust, then wait.

3.4.7. We cannot help but interpret Habakkuk's recording with that of Job.

3.4.7.1. When injustice flourishes, most people stop seeing the thousands of small acts of fairness that keep life going in the family or on the job.

3.4.8. The final verses in cp 3 are among the finest expressions of faith to be found in the Bible.

Habakkuk 3:17 Though the fig tree should not blossom And there be no fruit on the vines, Though the yield of the olive should fail And the fields produce no food, Though the flock should be cut off from the fold And there be no cattle in the stalls, 18 Yet I will exult in the Lord, I will rejoice in the God of my salvation. 19 The Lord God is my strength, And He has made my feet like hinds' feet, And makes me walk on my high places. For the choir director, on my stringed instruments.

3.4.9. The book started with gloom, now closes with glory! We see in this book, the questions and gloom led to a prayer tower, which in turn led to trust and faith in following God. A good pattern for us today.

3.5. Then (another possible contemporary) of Jeremiah—Obadiah. The book of Obadiah is the shortest book in the Old Testament, just twenty-one verses. The exact date of the events is not known. However, it is believed he is referring to Nebuchadnezzar's march into Jerusalem about 585 BCE, and living through the final devastating Babylonian war on Judah during the reign of Zedekiah.

3.5.1. Obadiah was obscure, living in southern Judah, nothing known of his family. Probably not from any priestly line or any association with kings. Therefore, this creates a problem in the exact date of events.

A Basic Outline of Obadiah #1
1. Judgment on Edom, vv 1-18
2. Restoration of Israel, vv 19-21

A Basic Outline of Obadiah #2
1. Announcement of Doom, vv 1-9
2. Judgment of Doom, vv 15-16
3. Deliverance of Israel Promised, vv 17-21

Depth of Bible Words and Locations
Obadiah Key Word: *Pride*

Found in v. 3. The same word in Jeremiah 49:16 and Proverbs 11:2. It means, "To boil up."

This was the key characteristic of the nation of Edom. Jeremiah used the word as a synonym for Babylon. It insights rebellion toward God and brings shame and destruction.

Jesus in Obadiah...He is the Mighty One.

3.5.1.1. His book is a single thought centered around the destruction of Edom. Obadiah is like Ezekiel in stressing the pride of the nations that the Lord will bring

Judah Falls: Obadiah

        low. Edom took advantage of the war with Nebuchadnezzar.
- 3.5.1.2. They robbed and killed the fleeing Jews.
- 3.5.1.3. They tried to claim Judah as their own territory.
- 3.5.1.4. Worst of all, they spoke against God. Later, God destroyed Edom, contributing to the Jews' return to their land (1:17, 19, 21).

3.5.2. Some historians have placed Obadiah at an earlier date, around 850 BCE as a contemporary of Elijah. However, I do not conclude that as being logical.

3.5.3. Dates of books are many times based on the reference to a king in reign or a recognizable historical person. It makes for difficulty when no references are made.

3.5.4. Obadiah scolded the people of Edom because they were rejoicing over the end of Judah. But Obadiah says *you may feel secure Edom, but your pride will be your fall*. We quickly see that the sin of Edom in v3 was pride.[1]

Depth of Bible Words and Locations
Edom

Located south of the Dead Sea. The mountainous region with many homes cut into the sides. Obadiah refers to "who live in the clefts of the rocks" v3. Descendants of Esau considered "brothers" by Israel. Edom was under Assyrian domination and prospered from the mining of iron and copper under them until the fall of Jerusalem. They participated in the 586 BCE destruction of Jerusalem, eventually *disappearing* from history.

3.5.5. God had told Isaiah, years before, not to attack or even offend an Edomite. However, we are informed that Edom:
- 3.5.5.1. Refused Israel to pass through their territory on their way to the Promised Land.
- 3.5.5.2. Cried out *"tear down Jerusalem to its foundations"* (Psalms 137:7).

3.5.6. A list of God's reasons to destroy Edom are in vv 10-14, each coming from pride:
- 3.5.6.1. Violence

---

[1] V. 3 *"The arrogance of your heart has deceived you, You who live in the clefts of the rock, In the loftiness of your dwelling place, Who say in your heart, 'Who will bring me down to earth?' 15 "For the day of the Lord draws near on all the nations. As you have done, it will be done to you. Your dealings will return on your own head.*

3.5.6.2.		Joining with Israel's enemies
3.5.6.3.		Rejoicing over Israel's trouble
3.5.6.4.		Looting
3.5.6.5.		Betrayal of their brothers

3.5.7. Notice the eternal law of God in v 15 *For the day of the Lord draws near on all nations. As you have done, it will be done to you. Your dealings will return on your own head...*

3.5.8. Verse 18 foresees Israel in renewed prosperity. In the process, it will burn Edom like stubble.

3.5.9. Verse 21 concludes the short book by affirming that rule and salvation completely belong to the Lord of Israel.

3.5.10. A few Edomites continued to exist for four centuries, always as enemies of the Jews. They were absorbed by the Maccabeans. Later, an Edomite family, the Herods, were placed in charge of Judah but disappeared from history with the 70 CE destruction of Jerusalem.

Depth of Bible Words and Locations
Maccabeans

Following the return from exile in Babylon in the sixth century BCE until the death of Alexander the Great in 323 BCE, the Hebrews continued under the direction of the high priest. However, the generals of Alexander divided up the regions of his vast empire. By 198 BCE the Syrian King had added Palestine to his territory. The Hebrews were allowed to live by their law, the Torah. Syria was so pressed by Rome, that they seized the silver and gold in safe keeping in the Temple at Jerusalem. This was the beginning of the revolt by the Jews. In 167 BCE, a Jewish priest, Mattathias organized the uprising against the Syrians but died in 165. Two of his five sons, Simon and Judah led the revolt. Judah was given the name "Maccabee" meaning "hammerhead." The Maccabeans, led by Judah's skills and courage, gained control of their land in 164 BCE and restored the worship of God in a rededicated Temple (now celebrated as Hanukkah).

3.6. Lamentations follows Jeremiah in most Bibles. However, because we are reviewing them in approximate chronological order, we review it here. The author of Lamentations was anonymous in Hebrew Scriptures. However, through the years it became accepted as *Jeremiah's Lamentation* over the fall of Jerusalem.

3.6.1. The title according to the Hebrews, as we have seen in other books, came from the first word. They just called it "Now"; that's it! The name "Lamentations" came later from the general content. We know that Lamentations was written during or soon after the destruction of Jerusalem in 586 BCE. It was mid-July when the city fell and mid-August when the temple was burned. Jeremiah likely saw the destruction of walls, towers, homes, and the Temple. He wrote while it was fresh in his mind before he was taken to Egypt in 583 BCE.

3.6.2. There are many passages in Lamentations that have almost the same language as in Jeremiah.[1] The last chapter of Jeremiah could be read as an introduction to Lamentations.

A Basic Outline of Lamentations
A Series of Laments

1. Jerusalem's Devastation, Cp 1
2. The Lord's Anger, Cp 2
3. Jeremiah's Grief, Cp 3
4. God's Grief, Cp 4
5. The Remnants' Prayers, Cp 5

Depth of Bible Words and Locations
Lamentations Key Word: *Weeps*

It expresses emotions—from grief to happiness. It certainly is in this area of "Laments." Of course, in this book, it is associated with a wailing over the destruction of Jerusalem and their sins. However, in Genesis 29:11 it's weeping with joy. Ruth 1:9 weeps over the departure. I like Ezra 3:12 a weeping with joy over the rebuilt temple.

Jesus in Lamentations...He is our Unfailing Compassion.

3.6.3. The construction of the book is perhaps the most unusual of any book in the Bible.[2] It is written in the rhythm of a funeral dirge. It laments the downfall of Jerusalem in the form of five metaphors; each one in a chapter, characterized by a single word.

    3.6.3.1.   1. Widow
    3.6.3.2.   2. Daughter

---

[1] The Greek translation from the original Hebrew includes a notation to the effect that Jeremiah said these lamentations as he sat on the hillside overlooking the destroyed city. Jeremiah's overwhelming heart of sorrow is expressed more vividly than by any other person in the Scriptures.

[2] There are twenty-two letters in the Hebrew alphabet, beginning with *aleph*, the equivalent of our *a* and ending with *tau* the equivalent of our *t*. (The letter z is near the middle of the Hebrew alphabet). The poetic style called "acrostic" has the first letter of lines, when read vertically, reading as a word or in Lamentations case, the entire alphabet.

3.6.3.3. 3. Man
3.6.3.4. 4. Gold
3.6.3.5. 5. Women

3.6.4. A good outline or pattern for remembering Lamentations. Then also, four of the five cps are written as an acrostic, perhaps to aid in memorization. Each of the five chapters revolves around twenty-two verses. Chapters 1, 2, and 4 have twenty-two verses corresponding to the twenty-two letters of the Hebrew alphabet, and in sequence. Chapter 3 has three sets of those twenty-two letters in sequence. And then chapter 5 has twenty-two verses, even though they're not in the acrostic pattern

3.6.5. I mentioned each chapter is a lament.[1]

3.6.6. Chapter 3, the high point of the book, has a Psalms with unparalleled beauty.

> vv. 3:22-26 *The Lord's lovingkindnesses indeed never cease,*
> *For His compassions never fail.*
> *23 They are new every morning;*
> *Great is Your faithfulness.*
> *24 "The Lord is my portion," says my soul,*
> *"Therefore I have hope in Him."*
> *25 The Lord is good to those who wait for Him,*
> *To the person who seeks Him.*
> *26 It is good that he waits silently*
> *For the salvation of the Lord.*

3.6.7. The sufferings of the invasion are on Jeremiah's mind in chapter 4.
    3.6.7.1. Starving children
    3.6.7.2. The awful behavior of mothers

3.7. Let's note here that Zephaniah, Habakkuk, and Lamentations chronologically follow each other and concern the fall of Jerusalem.[2]

Zephaniah	**Habakkuk**	**Lamentations**
Decades before the fall of Jerusalem (640 B.C.)	Just before the fall of Jerusalem (612)	Just after the fall of Jerusalem (586)

---

[1] A lament is a song or poem expressing grief, regret, or mourning. Many times a cry of sorrow and grief; other times it was to regret strongly; *"I deplore this hostile action."*
[2] Wilkinson, Bruce; Boa, Kenneth: *Talk Thru the Bible.* Nashville : T. Nelson, 1983, S. 280

Judah Falls: Lamentations

God will judge	God, when will you judge?	God has judged
Preview of trouble	Promise of trouble	Presence of trouble
Declaration	Dialogue	Dirge
Day of the Lord	Dominion of the Lord	Destruction of the Lord
God is in your midst (see 3:15, 17)	God is your strength (see 3:19)	God is your portion (see 3:24)

SECTION 7
Captivity

2 Kings 25, 2 Chronicles 36, Isaiah 39, Jeremiah 25, 29, Daniel, Ezekiel, Psalms 137. The period from 605 to 586 BCE.

Theme Statement: *"This whole land will be a desolation and a horror, and these nations will serve the king of Babylon seventy years."*
Jer 25:11

THE KEYS TO SECTION SEVEN

Section 7: Captivity

Keys to Daniel—

A Key Word: *Vision*

The Key Verses (2:20–22; 2:44)

20 Daniel said, "Let the name of God be blessed forever and ever, for wisdom and power belong to Him. 21 "It is He who changes the times and the epochs; He removes kings and establishes kings; He gives wisdom to wise men and knowledge to men of understanding. 22 "It is He who reveals the profound and hidden things; He knows what is in the darkness, and the light dwells with Him."

44 "In the days of those kings the God of heaven will set up a kingdom which will never be destroyed, and that kingdom will not be left for another people; it will crush and put an end to all these kingdoms, but it will itself endure forever."

The Key Chapter (9)

The Key People in Daniel

Daniel—also called Belteshazzar; later became a royal advisor (1:1–12:13)

Nebuchadnezzar—the greatest king of Babylon; went temporarily insane for not acknowledging God's sovereign position (1:1–4:37)

Shadrach—also called Hananiah; exiled Jew placed in leadership in Babylon; saved by God from the "fiery furnace" (1:7; 2:49; 3:8–30)

Meshach—also called Mishael; exiled Jew placed in leadership in Babylon; saved by God from the "fiery furnace" (1:7; 2:49; 3:8–30)

Abed-Nego—also called Azariah; exiled Jew placed in leadership in Babylon; saved by God from the "fiery furnace" (1:7; 2:49; 3:8–30)

Belshazzar—successor of Nebuchadnezzar as king of Babylon; also used Daniel as an interpreter (5:1–30)

Darius—Persian successor of Belshazzar as ruler of Babylon; his advisors tricked him into sending Daniel to the lions' den (5:31–6:28)

Keys to Ezekiel—

A Key Word: *Son of Man*

The Key Verses (36:24–26; 36:33–35)

24 "For I will take you from the nations, gather you from all the lands and bring you into your own land. 25 "Then I will sprinkle clean water on you, and you will be clean; I will cleanse you from all your filthiness and from all your idols. 26 "Moreover, I will give you a new heart and put a new spirit within you; and I will remove the heart of stone from your flesh and give you a heart of flesh."

33 Thus says the Lord God, "On the day that I cleanse you from all your iniquities, I will cause the cities to be inhabited, and the waste places will be rebuilt. 34 "The desolate land will be cultivated instead of being a desolation in the sight of everyone who passes by. 35 "They will say, 'This desolate land has become like the garden of Eden; and the waste, desolate and ruined cities are fortified and inhabited."

The Key Chapter (37)

The Key People in Ezekiel

Ezekiel—prophet to the people of Israel in Babylonian captivity (1:1–48:35)

Israel's leaders—led the people of Israel into idolatry (7:26–8:12; 9:5, 6; 11; 14:1–3; 20:1–3; 22:23–29)

Ezekiel's wife—unnamed woman whose death symbolized the future destruction of Israel's beloved temple (24:15–27)

Keys In Section Seven

Nebuchadnezzar—king of Babylon used by God to conquer Tyre, Egypt, and Judah (26:7–14; 29:17–30:10)

Approximate Dates of Key Events in Sections 7 & 8	
586 BCE	The Babylonians take Judah captive
585	Jeremiah and others were taken to Egypt
560	Daniel's three friends survive the fiery furnace
559-530	Cyrus reigns in Persia
550	Belshazzar assumes the throne in Babylon; Daniel's visions
539	Cyrus of Persia conquers Babylon/Belshazzar's kingdom
537	The return of the Jews to Judea begins
536-534	The temple rebuilding begins then stops
522-486	Darius I reigns in Persia
520	Haggai and Zechariah begin to prophesy/the temple rebuilding resumes
516	The temple is completed
486-465	Ahasuerus (Xerxes I) reigns in Persia. Events of Esther
465-424	Artaxerxes Longimanus reigns in Persia
467	Ezra leads a group of returnees
440-425	Malachi's ministry
454	Nehemiah leads a group of returnees
453	Jerusalem's wall is reconstructed
442	Nehemiah returns to Jerusalem (last datable event in O.T.)

ELEVEN

Babylonia and Persia

1 The next two Sections of our course are concerned with the final period in Old Testament Biblical History. CAPTIVITY AND RESTORATION. During this study/survey of the Old Testament, we have traveled from:
1.1. The Creation of a world
1.2. The Four Great Patriarchs
1.3. Moses and Joshua
1.4. Judges
1.5. Kings
1.6. The early Prophets
1.7. We next include a few scriptures in 2 Kings 25 (vv. 27-30, King Jehoiachin), 2 Chronicles 36 (vv, 22-23, Cyrus), and Psalms 37.
    1.7.1. Also, the prophecies in Isaiah 39 (the exile), and Jeremiah 25 (the seventy years) & 29 (the exile).
    1.7.2. Daniel and Ezekiel
    1.7.3. A lot of scripture in this period. Note again, *our travel through the Old Testament has NOT been entirely in the order of the Books of the Bible. Rather we viewed them in their individual time period.*
1.8. In these two Sections, we will cover a period from just prior to the destruction of Jerusalem in 605 BCE to the end of the Old Testament period, approximately 400 BCE. The theme of Section 7 is from Jer 25:11 *This whole land will be a desolation and a horror, and these nations will serve the king of Babylon seventy years.*
1.9. First I want to review two of the terms we've used in various ways throughout this journey. I mentioned in the preceding Section that all twelve Tribes were represented when Judah was taken to Babylonia.

1.9.1.   Some refer to ten of the tribes as being *lost* forever. Refer to the following Expanded Help Paper on the terms "Israel" and "Judah."

1.9.2.   At times these two names were interchangeable, other times they had a separate identity. So it's appropriate to review some thoughts here, including the terms Jews, and Israelites. It's easy to refer to all of them as being identical.

EXPANDED HELP PAPER
"Israel" and "Judah"

Let's clarify these. We have used the names Israelites, Jews, and Hebrews, even Judah in describing God's people. Loosely, we can interchange these names, but let us be clear about some specifics. Generally, we have been using *Israel*.

Today most of the world identifies the name Israel with the Jews. Most assume the Jews are the sole remaining descendants of the ancient nation of Israel.

Many say, "There are ten lost Tribes known only to God and later to be found by Him." The scriptures used to conclude this, are misread.

Consider some facts here. The ten tribes, which became the Northern Kingdom and called Israel, were never called Jews. The Jews are descendants of two tribes, which comprised the Southern Kingdom called Judah; the tribes of Judah and Benjamin, and a part of the priestly tribe of Levi. The name Jew was derived from this kingdom of Judah.

Those northern ten tribes already were an independent nation by the time the name Jew first appears in the Bible. I like what we are told in 2 Kings 16:5-6:

5 Then Rezin king of Syria and Pekah son of Remaliah king of Israel (the ten Tribes) came up to Jerusalem to wage war; they besieged Ahaz, but could not conquer him.
6 At that time, Rezin king of Syria got back Elath [in Edom] for Syria and drove the Jews (the two Tribes) from [it].

Before any captivity took place, many from the northern tribes joined in with David's line. When Jeroboam led ten tribes in forming Israel, many from those tribes rebelled from the separation and remained loyal to the House of David. This was the territory of two tribes, but not only the people *from* the two. In God's eyes, all twelve tribes were represented in Judah. The return of the three groups from Babylon, following the Babylonian captivity of Judah, represented the entire nation, not two tribes of the south. So the Jews were separate from the other Tribes of Israel, but all twelve tribes were represented in Judah. Slightly confusing, but entirely understandable.

Are all Israelites Jews? NO. The people of the Southern Kingdom and its descendants are all Israelites, but not all Israelites are Jews. (Read this again). All twelve tribes are descendants of Jacob, also named Israel, so all twelve tribes can be called Israelites. However, again, the term Jew is accurate only for the tribes of Judah. The Jews retained their identity and many returned to their land after seventy years of exile. Israel lost its identity during their captivity. Many things that identified them disappeared from history.

Jesus confirmed that when He referred to the entire *house of Israel* in Matt 10:5-7 *These twelve Jesus sent out after instructing them: "Do not go in the way of the Gentiles, and do not enter any city of the Samaritans; 6 but rather go to the lost sheep of the house of Israel. 7 "And as you go, preach, saying, 'The kingdom of heaven is at hand.'*

Also, it is clear from James 1:1 that all twelve tribes are represented in Israel: *James, a bond-servant of God and of the Lord Jesus Christ, To the twelve tribes who are dispersed abroad*

And also in Acts 26:7-8 *the promise to which our twelve tribes hope to attain, as they earnestly serve God night and day. And for this hope, O King, I am being accused by Jews.*

God preserved all twelve tribes, Amos 9:8 *"Behold, the eyes of the Lord God are on the sinful kingdom, And I will destroy it from the face of the earth; Nevertheless, I will not totally destroy the house of Jacob," Declares the Lord.*

Many of the ten tribes, already far from their homeland eventually migrated northwest and intermarried with Europeans. 1 Kings 14:15 *For the Lord will strike Israel, as a reed is shaken in the water; and He will uproot Israel from this good land which He gave to their fathers, and will scatter them beyond the Euphrates River...*

Isaiah 49:12 also tells us *"Behold, these will come from afar; And lo, these will come from the north and from the west, and these from the land of Sinim."*

We also use *Hebrews* many times.

We also have the name *Palestine* with the people *Palestinians*.

1.10. Now, the Captivity.
    1.10.1. The *captivity* part of this story is largely understood from Ezekiel and Daniel. Those two books along with many non-Biblical sources of other literature and archeological finds will help

Babylonia and Persia

us follow this period. The *restoration* history will come from several of the prophets, along with Esther.

1.10.2. To understand these empires in historical order for us, consider this list:

1.10.2.1. In the earliest period of our journey, the empires at the time were Egypt and a large group of people called Hittites. Then remember Assyria became the world player around 700 BCE when she took Egypt and aligned with the Medes empire.

1.10.2.2. Assyria was conquered and an even larger empire resulted—Babylonia.

1.10.2.3. Following Babylonia, again all the territory was conquered, this time by the confederacy of Medes and Persians, eventually all coming under the Persian Empire around 560 BCE.

1.10.2.4. If we were to go a little further in history, the empires of Greece and Rome became the empires of importance.

1.10.3. We again look at the history of two great powers; the people of Judah were subject to Babylonia followed by Persia during this period of exile. These two powers ruled the Middle East for 300 years, so we must understand what was happening to Judah by reviewing these two peoples/nations.

EXPANDED HELP PAPER
Babylon/Babylonians
Persia/Persians

Many references to Babylon, Babylonians, Persia, and Persians are cited in this volume. Because of their important place in the history of Israel, extensive detail is offered concerning the nations, following this brief summary.

The destruction of Jerusalem (587 BCE) resulted in the removal of certain Jerusalemites to Babylonian territory, but within two generations (530 BCE) the Persian Empire defeated Babylonia and offered opportunities for some of the exiles' children and grandchildren to migrate to the Jerusalem area. This group intermingled with other groups and continued in a post-exilic community under Persian rule for about two centuries until Persia's defeat in 333 BCE. The term "Yehud" was the Persian name for the area that included Jerusalem. It distinguished

Jerusalem from "Judah" of the pre-exilic period. The importance of this period requires close examination.

The remnant of people who returned to Jerusalem from Babylon were a different people from the pre-exilic period. Persia kept a close scrutiny over all its provinces. Several views concerning the reconstruction in Jerusalem have been suggested.

Julius Wellhausen[1] suggests the people wanted to be different from the way of life and self-governance that had transpired earlier, which led to a path of disaster. Their memories of past experiences haunted them, leading them a separation of religion and government. The government part was under the strong hand of Persia. Wellhausen's attitude toward Judaism as a whole was extremely negative. His theological statements should be taken with great hesitancy while his historical reconstructions should not be rejected.[2]

Other conclusions were suggested, by Martin Noth, Vehezkel Kaumann, and in recent years, Paul D. Hanson. Those suggested possible reconstructions included a strong priestly influence, which could not be enforced because of Persian structure, a strong dependence upon the cult system of idolatry from historical practice, and inner groups fighting for power in Jerusalem.

1.10.4.   First, Babylonia. At a battle in 605BCE, Nebuchadnezzar broke the Kingdom of Assyria at the Battle of Carchemish and then became the ruler of this large, expanded, territory.
    1.10.4.1.   Nebuchadnezzar's rule of forty-three years is considered one of the most illustrious in history.
    1.10.4.2.   Daniel gives us a glimpse of the great city of Babylon. He lived there for seventy-five years and could certainly describe it. He tells us that one day while Nebuchadnezzar was walking on the roof of the palace *The king reflected and said, 'Is this not Babylon the great, which I myself have built as a royal residence by the might of my power and for the glory of my majesty'* (Daniel 4:30-31). No pride or ego there!
    1.10.4.3.   Archeologists in early 1900 CE discovered six columns of writings describing the beauty of Babylon. Double walls, a splendid palace, and a huge network of

---

[1] Julius Wellhausen, *Prolegomena to the History of Ancient Israel* (New York: Meridian Books, 1957
[2] Jon L. Berquist, *Judaism in Persia's Shadow*, Fortress Press, Minneapolis, 1995, p. 6

Babylonia and Persia

canals and temples made it one of the great cities of the world. The Tower of Babel, now a massive mound of destruction, is located just outside the city. Discovered brickwork of Babel corresponds with the bricklaying technique described in Genesis 11:3-4.

1.10.4.4. Babylon *was* Nebuchadnezzar, and when he died in 561 BCE, his empire began to rapidly decline. Soon Cyrus captured Babylon as a result of the weak reigns of Nebuchadnezzar's son Belshazzar followed by the rule of two other relatives.

1.10.4.5. Nebuchadnezzar captured Jerusalem and destroyed the Temple.

1.10.4.6. The last of the Babylonian Kings was Nabopolassar, founder of the new empire, the Chaldean dynasty, 626-605

1.10.4.7. Then Awil-Marduk called Evil-Merodach in the Old Testament, who released King Jehoiachin of Judah *c.* 562-560 BCE and later was murdered by Nergal-shar-usur.

1.10.4.8. Nergal-shar-usur, or Neriglissar, killed his brother-in-law Evil-Merodach, 560-556 BCE.

1.10.4.9. Aramaean Nabonidus, last king of the Chaldean dynasty of Babylon, died of a mysterious God-initiated disease, 556-539 BCE.

1.10.5. The new world-empire of Persia was ruled by Cyrus of Persia 559-530 BCE, Cambyses 530-522, Darius the Great 522-486, and Xerxes I 486-465 (see below).

1.10.6. Daniel describes Babylon's fall in his 5th chapter. Also, a written chronicle was located in Babylon, later describing three important events.

1.10.6.1. A sudden attack on the city by Cyrus (of Persia)

1.10.6.2. The death of Belshazzar, son of Nebuchadnezzar following a banquet

1.10.6.3. The capture of the city, "without a battle." [1]

1.10.7. The Persians along with the Medes became rulers of this huge territory, under Cyrus. They were one empire/with two territories, not two separate empires. The Medes (under King Astyages) were overtaken and defeated by the King's own

---

[1] Daniel 5:28 concludes the matter when it's recorded *your kingdom has been divided and given over to the Medes and Persians.* This is what was determined by God, before even thought to be possible.

grandson, Cyrus. An added list of the rulers of this new empire follows, beginning with the order of Persian emperors (also see the table in chapter THIRTEEN):

    1.10.7.1.   Cyrus the Great (559–530 BCE),
    1.10.7.2.   Cambyses (530–522),
    1.10.7.3.   Darius (522–486),
    1.10.7.4.   Ahasuerus, also known as Xerxes I (486–465)
    1.10.7.5.   Artaxerxes Longimanus (465–423),
    1.10.7.6.   Xerxes II (423)
    1.10.7.7.   Darius II (423-404)
    1.10.7.8.   Artaxerxes II (404-359)
    1.10.7.9.   Artaxerxes III (359-338)

1.10.8.   Note that the return to Jerusalem and reconstruction was interrupted during the reign of Cyrus, resumed, and completed during the time of Darius.

1.10.9.   Under Cyrus, some important changes were made, some of which are recorded in the book of Ezra. The first verse introduces Cyrus *And in the first year of Cyrus king of Persia, that the word of Jehovah by the mouth of Jeremiah might be accomplished, Jehovah stirred up the spirit of Cyrus king of Persia.*

1.10.10.   Isaiah mentions Cyrus by name centuries before he was born. Josephus said that Cyrus himself was influenced by reading about himself in Isaiah 45! Although a pagan who did not know or worship God (Isaiah 45:4), the Lord said of Cyrus,

> "He is My shepherd,
> And he shall perform all My pleasure,
> Saying to Jerusalem, 'You shall be built,'
> And to the temple, 'Your foundation shall be laid.' "
> (Isaiah 44:28)

1.10.11.   Cyrus was one of the great figures of world history.

    1.10.11.1.   He was the founder of the Persian Empire, thus ending the Jewish captivity. He united the Medes and the Persians. But there were still two powerful rivals remaining: Babylon and Egypt. Before a march against Egypt could be made, Cyrus had to conquer Babylon. He defeated the entire might of the Babylonians in 539 BCE. He built the greatest world empire that had existed up to his time. Constructed a capital and palace complex at Pasargadae. Cyrus reached his goal of building an empire even greater than Babylon.

Babylonia and Persia

1.10.11.2. This is the ruler whom God prophesied would free His people Israel from Babylonian captivity (Isaiah 44:28; 45:1–14). Cyrus, a non-Israelite king, is called God's anointed, a term elsewhere only used for Israelite leaders. Cyrus' belief included the permission to allow conquered peoples to return to their homeland, and financing the project. Concerning the Israelites, he encouraged them to rebuild their worship center. He returned the religious items taken from their temple, asking only that those he returned to their homelands pray for him and his empire.

1.10.11.3. God used him to continue His plan for His people. A new policy was begun, as Cyrus decided to become a friend to all the peoples who had been captured by the Babylonians. In his second year of reign, by decree, he allowed all people to return to their homelands (although remained in Persia).

1.10.11.4. Assyria, followed by Babylonia, had treated their captives as prisoners and slaves. The period of Persia reverses that bondage. (Of course, we know this was all in God's plan to bring His people back to a Promised Land; he uses Cyrus and later Darius for that purpose).

1.10.11.5. Ezra tells us Cyrus favored the Jews and gave them great aid. This was the historical act that brought about individual and religious freedom. So we should have high regards for Cyrus, who almost certainly became a believer in God.

1.10.11.6. Cyrus died in 530 BCE and was succeeded by Cambyses (530–522) who invaded and conquered Egypt. Resistance to his rule kept Cambyses in Egypt almost until his death. Cambyses had no son to inherit his kingdom, so Darius, a distant relative of Cambyses, rose to the throne by quelling a revolution.

1.10.11.7. Cyrus reigned for ten years until his death, followed by his son Cambyses' rule for seven years. Cambyses lacked his father's gift for governing.

An Approximate Time-line of this Period

536 BCE	The decree of Cyrus to rebuild the temple
536	Zerubbabel's expedition to Jerusalem
536	Foundation of the temple laid
535	Work on the temple halted

TRAVEL THOUGH THE OLD TESTAMENT

520	Ministry of Haggai and Zechariah
520	Decree of Darius to resume work on the temple.
516	Temple completed.
486	Reign of Ahasuerus (Xerxes) begins.
478	Esther crowned queen.
465	Reign of Artaxerxes Longimanus begins.
454	Nehemiah arrives in Jerusalem.

1.10.12. Darius The Great, a cousin of Cambyses, began his lengthy rule in 522 and broadens the Persian Empire to extend the borders to Greece and India. This is the man who Ezra says gave aid in the rebuilding of the Temple (6:1-12). Darius ("he that informs himself") [duh-RI-uhs], was actually the name of four different Persian kings.

    1.10.12.1. 539 BCE, Darius the *Mede,* the king who put Daniel in the lions' den (Daniel 6).

    1.10.12.2. 522-485 Darius the Great, who authorized completion of the temple as ordered by Cyrus (Ezra 5:6; Haggai 1:1; Zechariah 1:1).

    1.10.12.3. 424-404 Darius II mentioned only in Nehemiah 12:22. The son of Artaxerxes I and father of Cyrus the Younger.

    1.10.12.4. 336-330 Darius III. Unsuccessful invasion of Macedonians. He fled and was murdered.

    1.10.12.5. Darius the Great demonstrates his importance in God's sovereign scheme by issuing a decree that ensures the completion of the Temple project. In his early, difficult years, he had to deal with the temple in Jerusalem. Builders had laid the foundation of the temple, but no further work had been done (Ezra 4:5). The Jews concentrated on building homes and reestablishing their lives in the desolate land.

    1.10.12.6. About eighteen years later, the prophets Haggai and Zechariah began challenging the people to resume rebuilding. They were helped by a letter from King Darius, who sent word to the local governor, commanding him to give all available support to the Jews to help them with their task.

    1.10.12.7. At his death in 486 BCE, Darius I controlled a larger and stronger empire than he had inherited. Darius improved the government of the empire with many military and economic measures. But his new taxes were

Babylonia and Persia

to cause the empire's downfall. Following his death, his son Xerxes was made king.

1.10.12.8. Persia attempted to conquer all of Greece by force and rule the world. However, the military battles in 492 and then 490 BCE were unsuccessful. The defeat in the Battle of Marathon in 490 sent the Persian's home. Darius died in preparation for a third invasion. These three battles are known as the Greco-Persian Wars, also the Persian Wars.

1.10.12.9. Darius's son Xerxes (as Ahasuerus), mentioned in the story of Esther, also attempts to defeat the Greeks, in the final of the wars but is turned back in 480 BCE at the Battle of Salamis. Persia never defeated Greece. Of course, Greece began its rise to power, later defeating the Persian Empire. Ironic.

1.10.13. The last emperor of Persia mentioned in the Old Testament (Artaxerxes Longimanus) is the ruler who allowed Ezra to lead many Jews back to Palestine and was a friend with Nehemiah and allowed the rebuilding of the walls of Jerusalem. Another man who God used in His plan.

1.10.13.1. After his father, Xerxes was murdered in his bedroom in 465 BCE, his younger son, Artaxerxes (Longimanus) took over a weakened Persian Empire. Ezra and Nehemiah were officials at his court.

1.10.13.2. This is the king, who The Samaritans had sent a letter to and then ordered an immediate halt of all wall-building activities in Jerusalem. However, later in 458 BCE, another group of exiles was sent by Artaxerxes, with additional monies and valuables to enhance the temple worship.

1.10.13.3. King Artaxerxes sent Nehemiah, his influential cupbearer, and a Jew, to serve as governor of the restored city of Jerusalem. The walls were quickly completed. It is unclear how Nehemiah became King Artaxerxes' cupbearer, but the fact that Esther was the king's stepmother may have inclined the king to consider a Jew for such a trusted position.

1.10.13.4. We conclude that God definitely used the Persian Empire in His purpose.

2   With this history lesson in mind, we turn to the Captivity of Judah in the following chapter.

TWELVE

Daniel and Ezekiel

A Basic Outline of Daniel
1. Daniel's Background, Cp 1
2. Visions of Worldly Powers, Cps 2-7
3. Visions of Israel's Future, Cps 8-12

Depth of Bible Words and Locations
A Key Word in Daniel: *Vision*
Found in 8:1, 13; 15:26. It means, "to see" (Isaiah 1:1 uses the same word). It is associated with a revelation from God, in Daniel's case revelation accompanied by symbols that required an interpretation by an angel. His ministry was entirely in Babylon, at least 70 years from 604-536 BCE.

As we mentioned, several prophets lived at this same time; Ezekiel, Habakkuk, Jeremiah, and Zephaniah.

Jesus in Daniel...He's the 4th Man in your fiery furnace of life

---

1.1. During the period when the Jews were captive in Babylonia, preachers still ministered to them. God never deserted His plan for a chosen people. We now look at their ministry during this period.

1.2. The first captives were taken in 604 BCE. Included in that first group were Daniel (about fifteen years old), Hananiah, Mishael, and Azariah. These boys are the boys who are later given Babylonian names.
    1.2.1.   Daniel is named Belteshazzar
    1.2.2.   Hananiah; Shadrach
    1.2.3.   Mishael; Meshach
    1.2.4.   Azariah; Abednego

1.3. The book of Daniel was named after the prophet who received these revelations. He is named the author in 8:15, 27, 9:2 and several other verses. Some call it the "apocalypse of the Old Testament." Nine of the twelve chapters relate to dreams or visions.

Daniel

1.3.1. The story of these four young boys is told in the first six chapters of Daniel. They were all of noble birth; Nebuchadnezzar chose them for special training, for his own personal benefit.[1]

1.3.2. It would be like going into the capital city of a nation, into its best schools, and stealing its best students. Remove the best young men from a nation, the nation is weakened.

1.3.3. These four determined to live by the Law of God while in Babylon. They made such progress in their learning that they soon surpassed all other companions in wisdom and gained favor with Nebuchadnezzar. Nebuchadnezzar underestimated these men's faith in their God. He had gods too, but to risk his life for them! Not.

1.3.4. Satan still has that problem. What great character each of these young men possessed.[2]

1.3.5. Daniel possessed a rare gift, similar to young Joseph in Genesis; the gift of interpreting dreams. By stepping out in that gift, it brought him to a place of honor in the very nation that took him captive.

1.3.6. In addition to the early visions, a number of remarkable experiences are recorded in these early cps of the book:

    1.3.6.1. Cp 3 Deliverance from a furnace of fire[3]

    1.3.6.2. Cp 5 Handwriting on a wall at Belshazzar's feast[4]

    1.3.6.3. Cp 6 Deliverance from a lion's den.[5]

---

[1] Daniel 1:3-4 Then *the king ordered Ashpenaz, the chief of his officials, to bring in some of the sons of Israel, including some of the royal family and of the nobles, 4 youths in whom was no defect, who were good-looking, showing intelligence in every branch of wisdom, endowed with understanding and discerning knowledge, and who had ability for serving in the king's court; and he ordered him to teach them the literature and language of the Chaldeans.*

[2] Daniel 1:8a *But Daniel made up his mind that he would not defile himself*

[3] Daniel 3:21 *Then these men were tied up in their trousers, their coats, their caps and their other clothes, and were cast into the midst of the furnace of blazing fire.*
Daniel 3:27 *king's high officials gathered around and saw in regard to these men that the fire had no effect on the bodies of these men nor was the hair of their head singed, nor were their trousers damaged, nor had the smell of fire even come upon them.*

[4] Daniel 5:26-28 *This is the interpretation of the message:God has numbered your kingdom and put an end to it. 27 ...you have been weighed on the scales and found deficient. 28 "...your kingdom has been divided and given over to the Medes and Persians."*

[5] Daniel 6:19-22 *Then the king arose at dawn, at the break of day, and went in haste to the lions' den. 20 When he had come near the den to Daniel, he cried out with a troubled voice. The king spoke and said to Daniel, "Daniel, servant of the living God, has your God, whom you constantly serve, been able to deliver you from the lions?" 21 Then Daniel spoke to the king, "O king, live forever! 22 "My God sent His angel and shut the lions' mouths and they have not harmed me..."*

- 1.3.6.4. The message found in all of this is "God never fails those who stand strong and remain firm and fixed in Him." *The angel of the Lord encamps around those who fear Him, And rescues them.* (Psalms 34:7).
- 1.4. Daniel is unusual, being the only Old Testament prophet who did not preach to Jews.
  - 1.4.1. He was trained as a statesman, and remained so dedicated to God, that he was given a special gift of understanding and interpreting dreams.
  - 1.4.2. His prophecies saw the future, not only to the time of Christ but to the end of the world. We call this "apocalyptic." The book of Daniel in the Old Testament stands with Revelation in the New Testament.

EXPANDED HELP PAPER
Apocalypsis

"Apocalypsis" is a Greek word meaning "revelation," "hidden." or "concealed." It's a special type of literature that arose among Jews--it reveals mysteries.

These writings were not named apocalyptic for several hundred years after the Old Testament prophets' times. There were many books classified apocalyptic in ancient days. Most of them never made it to the "canon" of scripture, which is our Bible.

Some of the names of those books are *Book of Jubilees, I and II Enoch,* and *War Scroll.*

Of course, we are looking at God's Word. The earliest apocalypse book we have is Daniel, and all the other similar books were written were in imitation of it.

- 1.5. We first, must understand Daniel's first prophecy (Nebuchadnezzar's dream) in cp 2, in order to understand the last six chapters of the book. Once we understand the first prophecy, the four later visions can better be understood, for they are all related. It is important because Jesus used chapter two for all His comments in His Olivet Discourse concerning a yet future Kingdom. (Matthew 24).
  - 1.5.1. In Nebuchadnezzar's dream and its interpretation (which he did not remember, and was greatly disturbed)[1], he sees

---

[1] Daniel tells him, recorded in 2:31-32: *You, O King, were looking and behold, there was a single great statue; that statue, which was large and of extraordinary splendor, was standing in front of you, and its appearance was awesome.*

Daniel

this HUGE image. It's a man, with a head of gold, breast of silver, a belly and thighs of brass, legs of iron, and feet and toes of iron (weaker than iron because the toes are a mixture with clay).

1.5.2. As the king looked at the strange man-image, a stone is formed and smashes the image. The image is shattered into pieces and blown away by a wind. That stone grows larger and larger, becoming a mountain filling the earth.

1.5.3. Daniel interprets the dream because of his prayer to God. He had great faith in His living God. He simply presented his case to God, and God revealed Nebuchadnezzar's dream to Daniel. Daniel was given the entire history of the Gentile world in the interpretation. He says to Nebuchadnezzar, "You're the head of gold." Babylonia was the empire in existence at the time and Nebuchadnezzar was the leader on top, the head; mighty, seemingly indestructible—solid as gold!

1.5.4. The other three parts of the image represent the next three Gentile empires, which would come in the future, each inferior to the preceding one; silver, brass, and iron—each weaker as to its endurance when compared to gold. In this

1.5.5. History has allowed us to understand the three empires which followed Babylonia:

    1.5.5.1. **Medo-Persia**[1], which we have reviewed, and will see more of in this volume.

    1.5.5.2. **Greece**, the brass belly and thighs, under Alexander the Great following the period of the Old Testament and before the New Testament

    1.5.5.3. The third, **Rome**, legs and toes of baked clay and iron.

1.5.6. The Gentile world would be ruled from Daniel's time to the coming of Christ, by these four empires.

1.5.7. Notice the statement concerning *four* kingdoms— not five or six. The Roman Empire would be in existence in some form during the final days. Rome is alive in Europe today in the nations of Italy, France, Great Britain, Germany, and Spain—each a part of the old Roman Empire. Her laws and language live on. It is in revival today and the Anti-Christ will rule it one day.

1.5.8. The stone is Christ, setting up the Kingdom of God, establishing His Body, the Church, which would be established, in

---

[1] Daniel 5:28 *Your kingdom has been divided and given over to the Medes and Persians*

the last days of the fourth empire. The Church is very much alive. Christ and His Body will surely smash all other kingdoms/empires.[1]

1.5.9. Isaiah identified this kingdom as water, which would cover the entire earth.[2]

1.6. Now, with that understanding, we continue with the book of Daniel. Notice in the following table, the similarity between Nebuchadnezzar's *dream* and Daniel's *first vision*. Chapter 7 expands this history lesson using different images. Note:

The Fulfilled Prophecies in Daniel 2, 7, and 8

	Babylon (606-538 BCE)	Medo-Persia (538-331 BCE)	Greece (331-146 BCE)	Rome (146 BCE-476 CE)
Daniel 2:31-45 Dream, 603 BCE	Head of Gold 2:32, 37-38	Breast, arms of silver 2:32, 39	Belly, thighs of Brass 2:32, 39	Legs of iron Feet of iron and clay 2:33, 40-41
Daniel 7 Vision: Four beasts, 553 BCE	Lion 7:4	Bear 7:5	Leopard 7:6	Strong Beast 7:7, 11, 19, 23
Daniel 8 Vision: Ram and goat, 551 BCE		Ram 8:3-4, 20	Goat with one horn 8:5-8, 21 Four horns 8:8, 22 Little horn 8:9-14	

1.6.1. Daniel was much older as Scriptures recorded his continuing story. It was the first year of the rule of Nebuchadnezzar's son, Belshazzar, which places the period at 539 BCE near the end of the "head of gold."

1.6.2. Daniel, seventy years old in this *first vision*, sees four beasts come up out of the sea.[3] Again, they represent the entire Gentile world in four world empires.

Depth of Bible Words and Locations
Beast

---

[1] Daniel 2:44-45 *"In the days of those kings the God of heaven will set up a kingdom which will never be destroyed, and that kingdom will not be left for another people; it will crush and put an end to all these kingdoms, but it will itself endure forever.*

[2] Isaiah 11:9 *For the earth will be full of the knowledge of the Lord As the waters cover the sea.*

[3] Daniel 7:3-4 *And four great beasts were coming up from the sea, different from one another.*

Daniel

This word *beast* misleads us. We immediately relate it to some incredible creature from the black lagoon! Noah had used this word to describe all the animals he gathered. He referred to "clean and unclean, beasts." So let us not get the wrong idea here.

Most of our more recent translations use "animal" for the translation. The translation is sometimes "[wild] animal."

The translation "beast" is used in apocalyptic literature simple to represent the enemies of God and His people

Daniel says, *"These four great beasts are four great kings, four world empires who shall arise out of the earth."*

1.6.2.1. The first, a **lion**, (7:4) represents Babylon, the empire of Daniel's time (the gold head of the *dream* he had earlier, recorded in 2:31). The *eagle's wings* suggest a swift conquest; *wings...plucked* and the rest of the verse probably refers to the insanity and recovery of Nebuchadnezzar

1.6.2.2. Then the **bear** (7:5) is Medo-Persia the second empire, (breast and arms of silver of the previous dream). The *three ribs in its mouth* are the three sections of the Babylonian Empire, which the Medes and Persians conquered, united as Persia.[1]

1.6.2.3. The **leopard** (7:6) is Greece the third empire, (belly and thighs of brass of the previous dream). Its four wings of a bird symbolize the rapid expansion, the quick movement by Alexander who within thirteen years marched east to India and southwest to Egypt. The four heads are the division of the empire to four of Alexander's generals after his early death.[2] (All of which is proven by later history).

1.6.2.4. Then much attention is given to the **fourth beast** (7:7) the legs of iron, and toes of clay and iron mixed of the previous dream) described as *dreadful and terrible, exceedingly strong, with huge iron teeth.*

1.6.3. We have seen the other three animals in our zoos, we are familiar with these somewhat common animals; lion, bear, and leopard. However, this final kingdom will be the worst of all.

---

[1] They took Babylon in the east, Egypt in the south, and the Lydian kingdom in Asia Minor; All were backed by Cyrus to expand the Medo-Persian empire.

[2] Cassander took Macedonia; Lysimachas took Asia-Minor; Seleacus took Syria; Ptolemy took Egypt

This is the Roman Empire, which followed the Grecian Empire, described as *different from all the former beasts.*

    1.6.3.1.   In this vision, we can conclude certainly that because the first three were fulfilled, so too will be the final part. This one (Rome), would rule (which it did)—then stop its rule (which history records)—and after an *unknown* period of time, be revived (in the area of the old Roman empire) in a form that would have *ten horns,* (ten kings or nations) and a *little horn,* the future ruler, the Antichrist. *And a mouth uttering great boasts.*

    1.6.3.2.   The world in our day has been taken captive by the *system* of the fourth beast. The system we call "freedom" will usher in the rapture of Christ and bring forth a period of tribulation.

1.6.4.   Each of those four empires has a time of grandeur, loses it, and becomes savage. The image carries us all the way to a final judgment. Let's read it beginning in Daniel 7:9 (see below).

    1.6.4.1.   Note that Daniel 2:4-7 through 7:28 was written in Arabic the business /commerce language of his location. The reason for the change in language would suggest he wanted it to be read by those who did not speak Hebrew. Daniel had been chosen for a three-year education program to learn the language and extensive literature he was exposed to in Babylonia.

> 9 "I kept looking
> Until thrones were set up,
> And the Ancient of Days took His seat;
> His vesture was like white snow
> And the hair of His head like pure wool.
> His throne was ablaze with flames,
> Its wheels were a burning fire.
> 10 "A river of fire was flowing
> And coming out from before Him;
> Thousands upon thousands were attending Him,
> And myriads upon myriads were standing before Him;
> The court sat,
> And the books were opened.
> 13 "I kept looking in the night visions,
> And behold, with the clouds of heaven
> One like a Son of Man was coming,
> And He came up to the Ancient of Days
> And was presented before Him.
> 14 "And to Him was given dominion,

*Glory and a kingdom,
That all the peoples, nations and men of every language
Might serve Him.
His dominion is an everlasting dominion
Which will not pass away;
And His kingdom is one
Which will not be destroyed."*

1.7. Then a *second vision*, in chapter 8 came two years after the first vision. Daniel was exhausted from this vision and rested for several days. He did not understand the vision's meaning.

1.7.1. The ram having two horns was the kings of Media and Persia. The two-fold nation would follow Babylonia. The goat was Greece and a *prominent* king (Alexander the Great, a short rule), divided to four of his generals (v 8). The *small horn* (v 9) refers to Antiochus Epiphanies who set up an image in the temple and sacrificed a pig. It has been suggested that Antiochus Epiphanies is a type of the antichrist. However, the context seems to infer that entire episode took place in his era, including the 3 ½ years after the altar was removed by Antiochus.

2 Daniel 9 has been called *"the greatest chapter in the book,"* and one of the greatest in the Bible, by Dr. Philip Newel.

2.1. Daniel goes to the Lord, praying and fasting concerning the writings of Jeremiah, his contemporary. He was drawn to the seventy-year period of servitude and desolations of the city of Jerusalem and its temple. The seventy years, when ended, will usher in the promised restoration back to Jerusalem.

2.2. The angel Gabriel is sent to him, again with the vision. Angels are mentioned many times in the Bible.

Depth of Bible Words and Locations
***Angels*[1]**

Heavenly beings created by God before He created Adam and Eve. There worship God and are His messengers to men and women.

**EXPANDED HELP PAPER
Angels In the Old Testament**

---

[1] Article used from the author's work, *HELP FROM THE BIBLE... when you need it!*

TRAVEL THROUGH THE OLD TESTAMENT

This is an extended paper on the vital place of angels. While there is more information on Angels in the New Testament, we do find several scriptures concerning Angels in the Old Testament.

Angel carries the meaning of "a messenger" (or "to deliver a message"), sent whether by God or by man or by Satan.

The noun form, meaning one sent over a great distance, appears over 200 times in the Hebrew Old Testament. In historical books is also was used with the meaning of "messenger." We might use this same word when one performs the function of a diplomat or representative of a nation or king.

We know a lot about Angels from the Old Testament: Much of the following is taken from my earlier work *Help From the Bible…..When You Need It!*

Three ruling angels are named in the Old Testament.

(1) Gabriel. *And I heard the voice of a man between the banks of Ulai, and he called out and said, "Gabriel, give this man an understanding of the vision."* (Daniel 8:16);

(2) Michael. *AND AT that time [of the end] Michael shall arise, the great [angelic] prince who defends and has charge of your [Daniel's] people.* (Daniel 12:1, AMP);

The last two letters of the names of Gabriel and Michael -el, stand for "God." The name Gabriel means "strength of God," and Michael means "who is like God." The names of these two angels remind us that most angels are wonderful creatures who are close to the Lord and reflect His own desire to do us good.

(3) The third angel, the first one mentioned in the Bible, had a dark side, Lucifer *Then he showed me Joshua the high priest standing before the angel of the Lord, and Satan standing at his right hand to accuse him. 2 The Lord said to Satan, "The Lord rebuke you, Satan!"* (Zechariah 3:1-2)

There are Seraphim. *Seraphim stood above Him, each having six wings: with two he covered his face, and with two he covered his feet, and with two he flew.* (Isaiah 6:2-3)

There are Cherubim. *And out of the midst of it came the likeness of four living creatures [or cherubim]. And this was their appearance: they had the likeness of a man,* (Ezekiel 1:5, AMP)

They were Created by God

Nehemiah 9:6 *You alone are the Lord.*
You have made the heavens,
The heaven of heavens with all their host,
The earth and all that is on it,
The seas and all that is in them.
You give life to all of them
And the heavenly host bows down before You.

Psalms 148:2,5 *Praise Him, all His angels;*
Praise Him, all His hosts!
5 Let them praise the name of the Lord,
For He commanded and they were created.

Job 38:4-7 *"Where were you when I laid the foundation of the earth?*
Tell Me, if you have understanding,
5 Who set its measurements? Since you know.
Or who stretched the line on it?
6 "On what were its bases sunk?
Or who laid its cornerstone,
7 When the morning stars sang together
And all the sons of God shouted for joy?

They Follow God's Instructions

Psalms 103:20 *Bless the Lord, you His angels,*
Mighty in strength, who perform His word,
Obeying the voice of His word!

I Kings 19:5 *He lay down and slept under a juniper tree; and behold, there was an angel touching him, and he said to him, "Arise, eat....."*

Psalms 104:4 *He makes the winds His messengers,*
Flaming fire His ministers.

Daniel 8:16-17 *And I heard the voice of a man between the banks of Ulai, and he called out and said, "Gabriel, give this man an understanding of the vision." 17 So he came near to where I was standing, and when he came I was frightened and fell on my face; but he said to me, "Son of man, understand that the vision pertains to the time of the end."*

Many times in the Old Testament, they executed the judgments of God.

2 Samuel 24:16 *When the angel stretched out his hand toward Jerusalem to destroy it, the Lord relented from the calamity and said to the angel*

who destroyed the people, "It is enough! Now relax your hand!" And the angel of the Lord was by the threshing floor of Araunah the Jebusite.

2 Kings 19:35-36 Then it happened that night that the angel of the Lord went out and struck 185,000 in the camp of the Assyrians; and when men rose early in the morning, behold, all of them were dead.

Psalms 35:5-6 *Let them be like chaff before the wind,*
With the angel of the Lord driving them on.
6 Let their way be dark and slippery,
With the angel of the Lord pursuing them.

They offer praise to God

Job 38:7 *When the morning stars sang together And all the sons of God shouted for joy?*

Psalms 148:2 *Praise Him, all His angels;*
Praise Him, all His hosts!

Isaiah 6:3 *And one called out to another and said,*
"Holy, Holy, Holy, is the Lord of hosts,
The whole earth is full of His glory."

They watch over God's children

Psalms 34:7 *The angel of the Lord encamps around those who fear Him, And rescues them.*

Psalms 91:11-12 *For He will give His angels charge concerning you,*
To guard you in all your ways.
12 They will bear you up in their hands,
That you do not strike your foot against a stone.

Daniel 6:22-23 "My God sent His angel and shut the lions' mouths and they have not harmed me, inasmuch as I was found innocent before Him; and also toward you, O king, I have committed no crime."

They are intelligent

2 Samuel 14:20 *In order to change the appearance of things your servant Joab has done this thing. But my lord is wise, like the wisdom of the angel of God, to know all that is in the earth.*

They are mighty.

Psalms 103:20 *Bless the Lord, you His angels,*
Mighty in strength, who perform His word,
Obeying the voice of His word!

They are innumerable

> Job 25:3 *"Is there any number to His troops? And upon whom does His light not rise?*
>
> Deuteronomy 33:2 *He said, "The Lord came from Sinai, And dawned on them from Seir; He shone forth from Mount Paran, And He came from the midst of ten thousand holy ones;*
>
> 2 Kings 6:17-18 *Then Elisha prayed and said, "O Lord, I pray, open his eyes that he may see." And the Lord opened the servant's eyes and he saw; and behold, the mountain was full of horses and chariots of fire all around Elisha.*
>
> Daniel 7:10 *"A river of fire was flowing And coming out from before Him; Thousands upon thousands were attending Him, And myriads upon myriads were standing before Him;*

We find the phrases *"the angel of the Lord"* and *"the angel of God"* used interchangeably. It always is used in the singular form. The identification of this angel is almost certainly to be the pre-incarnate Christ.

> Genesis 31:11 *"Then the angel of God said to me in the dream, 'Jacob,' and I said, 'Here I am.' "*
>
> Daniel 6:22 *"My God sent His angel and shut the lions' mouths and they have not harmed me, inasmuch as I was found innocent before Him; and also toward you, O king, I have committed no crime."*
>
> Judges 13:6 *Then the woman came and told her husband, saying, "A man of God came to me and his appearance was like the appearance of the angel of God, very awesome. And I did not ask him where he came from, nor did he tell me his name."*

2.1. The vision of chapter 9 is referred to as "Seventy Weeks" representing the total time period remaining for the Jews. It helps us to understand the above interpretation of the entire Roman era, including the interrupted temporary period. Daniel is now 85 years old and he has been thinking and praying about Jeremiah's prophecy concerning the current seventy years of captivity of the Jews.

2.2. Let's clarify the "seventy weeks." I do not believe that even Daniel understood the vision.

2.2.1.	The angel reveals to Daniel that the seventy years in this vision, represent 70 *weeks* of years, not the seventy-year period that he was living in captivity. So the total number of weeks represented is calculated by multiplying 70x7 (7 days in each week)

Depth of Bible Words and Locations
Seven

The word translated "seven" means a unit of seven years. In the Hebrew, the "seventy sevens" prophecy is speaking of "seventy sevens" of years or a total span of 490 years.

2.2.2.	70x7=490 total years in this vision of chapter 9. This is 490 years of future designated history set into motion by the event mentioned (9:25). Nothing will change that fact.

2.2.3.	The Scriptures for consideration are Dan 9:24-27

24 "Seventy weeks have been decreed for your people and your holy city, to finish the transgression, to make an end of sin, to make atonement for iniquity, to bring in everlasting righteousness, to seal up vision and prophecy and to anoint the most holy place. 25 "So you are to know and discern that from the issuing of a decree to restore and rebuild Jerusalem until Messiah the Prince there will be seven weeks and sixty-two weeks; it will be built again, with plaza and moat, even in times of distress. 26 "Then after the sixty-two weeks the Messiah will be cut off and have nothing, and the people of the prince who is to come will destroy the city and the sanctuary. And its end will come with a flood; even to the end there will be war; desolations are determined. 27 "And he will make a firm covenant with the many for one week, but in the middle of the week he will put a stop to sacrifice and grain offering; and on the wing of abominations will come one who makes desolate, even until a complete destruction, one that is decreed, is poured out on the one who makes desolate."

2.2.4.	During these 490 years, God is dealing **with Israel, not the Gentiles.** To repeat, all 490 years concern Israel.

2.2.5.	Now, of these 490 years of dealing with Israel, we understand first, the explanation of 483 of them *from the issuing of a decree to restore and rebuild Jerusalem until Messiah the Prince* comes, would be 483 years

2.2.6.	So, what is the date by which the 483 years is determined? What is this decree? The books of Ezra and

Daniel

Nehemiah reveal four "decrees." Each has its advocates for "the date." The four possibilities from Ezra and Nehemiah are:

2.2.6.1. Ezra 1:1-6, 5:13-17. The decree of Cyrus in his first year (536 BC) to rebuild the temple.

2.2.6.2. Ezra 4:24, 6:1-12. The decree of Darius in his second year (519) to complete the temple.

2.2.6.3. Ezra 7:7-28. The decree of Artaxerxes in his seventh year to beautify the temple.

2.2.6.4. Neh 2:1-8, 13, 17. The decree of Artaxerxes in his twentieth year (454) *to build the city and its wall*.

2.2.6.5. One of these four must be identified as being the specific decree, which included **both** *to restore and rebuild Jerusalem* according to Scripture. Each of the first three decrees has only to do with the temple proper, nothing mentioned about the rebuilding of the city, the street, and its walls. The conditions of Daniel 9:25 are *only* met in the fourth decree. I note that C.I. Scofield's Study Bible originally favored this fourth decree.[1]

2.2.6.6. This author's conclusion which agrees with Scofield's[2] original statement is that from the time when the command was given to rebuild Jerusalem *and* the walls (given to Nehemiah in 454 BCE by King Artaxerxes)[3] to the crucifixion of the Messiah, was exactly 483 years.[4]

2.2.6.7. I would also note one other calculation, which has been offered. Another scholar, Sir Robert Anderson gave detailed calculations of the sixty-nine weeks (483 years), using leap years, errors in the calendar and the change from BCE to CE (B.C. to A.D.) and concluded

---

[1] *The Scofield Study Bible*, Oxford University Press, Inc, New York, 2004, p. 1136 (original information from 1909)

[2] Not all of Scofield's conclusions were correct. He is sited here as one of several, who, in his first notes, had this viewpoint.

[3] Nehemiah 2:5

[4] 454 BCE + 30 CE (less 1 for going from BCE to CE)=483 years

/calculated the sixty-nine weeks ended on the very day of Jesus entry into Jerusalem, five days before his death.

2.2.6.8. These 483 years are past history. Only one more week or 7-year period remains to be fulfilled. The final 7 years will be delayed until the reign of Anti–Christ. We do not know how many years are between the two periods. No one, not even Christ knows how long—only the Father knows.

2.2.7. In conclusion, we know these 483 years were fulfilled exactly as Daniel said they would be. We also know a seven-year period will still come which will complete *God's dealing with Israel*.

2.2.8. Heavy and powerful. Only direct revelation from God has allowed an understanding of His timetable.[1]

2.3. I love discovering, as I mentioned before, where Daniel was reading from Jeremiah, (chapters 25:11-12 and 29:10). He read where the people would return to Jerusalem after 70 years.[2] He realized what year it currently was: 538 BCE. So he prayed and fasted asking God to return His people. It is so amazing that God had *seventy* planned out for Daniel's understanding.

2.3.1. In the last chapter of Daniel, we are given another glimpse of the times of the end.[3]

---

[1] Further clarification:
1 week=7 years
70 weeks=490 years
The total of 70 weeks are mentioned consisting of three periods:
    7 weeks
    62 weeks
    1 week

We read in first about 69 of the 70 weeks in Daniel 9:25 *until Messiah the Prince there will be seven weeks and sixty-two weeks;*
7+62=69 weeks; 69 weeks x 7days in each week=483 years. So first he explains 483 of the 490 years.

[2] Daniel 9:2-3 *I, Daniel, observed in the books the number of the years which was revealed as the word of the Lord to Jeremiah the prophet for the completion of the desolations of Jerusalem, namely, seventy years.*

[3] Daniel 12:1-3 *Now at that time Michael, the great prince who stands guard over the sons of your people, will arise. And there will be a time of distress such as never occurred since there was a nation until that time; and at that time your people, everyone who is found written in the book, will be rescued. 2 "Many of those who sleep in the dust of the ground will awake, these to everlasting life, but the others to disgrace and everlasting contempt. 3 "Those who have insight will shine brightly like the brightness of the expanse of heaven, and those who lead the many to righteousness, like the stars forever and ever*

Ezekiel

2.3.1.1. In 536 BCE when Cyrus allowed anyone interested to return to Jerusalem, a much older Daniel had stayed behind. He was still in a place of authority after the Persians defeated the Babylonians.

2.4. We next review another prophet to the captives, Ezekiel. He arrived in Babylonia nine years after Daniel was taken there. He probably had been a student of the older Jeremiah, as their message was similar. He lived with his wife north of Babylon near the River Keber, a ship channel.

2.4.1. The period of time covers Ezekiel's ministry, which began when he was 30 yrs old, in 594 and extended for at least twenty-two years until 571. Nowhere else in scripture is he mentioned. His name means, "strengthened by God," which is true of his life. He and Daniel were the same age and contemporaries with Jeremiah.

A Basic Outline of Ezekiel
1. Ezekiel's Early Sermons Before Judah's Fall, Cps 1-24
2. Ezekiel's Messages Against the Nations, Cps 25-32
3. Ezekiel's Latter Sermons After the Fall, Cps 33-48

Depth of Bible Words and Locations
A Key Word in Ezekiel: *Son of Man*

A **KEY WORD** in Ezekiel was easy to pick. It is found in 2:1; 3:17; 12:18. Ezekiel uses this phrase *"son of man,"* over 90 times in referring to himself. He was chosen by God to be a spokesperson for God.

It simply means "human one." Only found two other times in the Old Testament. Daniel saw a heavenly being *"like the Son of Man"* (Daniel 7:13). Of course, Jesus later adopted the title "Son of Man," as He too was a living sign to all.

So Ezekiel was to be a living example, a representative of God to the captives.

Jesus in Ezekiel...He's the Messiah who reigns.

2.4.2. In the second of the three *returns*, in 598 BCE, 10,000 of Judah's statesmen, including Ezekiel, craftsmen, and soldiers, were taken captive into Babylonia. Ezekiel remained in Babylon almost thirty years. This was eleven years before Judah and Jerusalem were destroyed. As mentioned before, Ezekiel and Daniel were about the same age.

2.4.2.1. Ezekiel had been training to become a priest, serving in the Temple, like his father. Now, far from Jerusalem, his dreams and hopes of priesthood in Jerusalem's Temple, were shattered. His ministry began when God called him to prophesy to the people of the captivity five years after his own captivity began.

2.4.2.2. We view Ezekiel as a comforter and encourager to God's people—he was a priest as well as a prophet. The people seem to have had a false sense of hope of an early return to Israel. He also emphasized the *glory of God* with a future restoration. The words *glory of God* occurs twelve times in the first eleven chapters.

2.4.2.3. He lived at the same time as Daniel and Jeremiah.

2.4.2.4. When he was thirty (the meaning of verse 1:1), God called him to be a prophet, by a remarkable vision (see detailed description in later paragraphs). He saw God in all His glory, the all-seeing, all-knowing God. The description reminds me of Revelation 1:14. God appears as *the appearance of a man,* gives Ezekiel a scroll, and says *eat this scroll.* Whether figuratively or actual we do not know. Undoubtedly, it represents the Word and judgments upon the people. Ezekiel "eats," accepts the message, and commits to delivery. It is recorded *I ate it, and it was sweet as honey in my mouth.*

2.4.2.5. Against that dazzling brilliance, Ezekiel saw the blackness of sin in people's lives. That vision "colored" his entire ministry.

2.4.2.6. He uses the words *"they will know that I am"* twenty-six times and *"I the LORD",* twenty-five times.

2.4.2.7. Ezekiel's prophecies in Babylonia began several years before Jerusalem was destroyed, and continued after it was in ruins. He was in Babylon for almost 30 years; however, little is learned from Ezekiel about the conditions that existed there. He was more interested in describing to the exiles, the condition back in Judah.

2.4.2.8. He was an extraordinary man, a visionary, imaginative, who understood symbols and rituals. He was passionate, dedicated, and utterly obedient to God. He seems to be quite free to preach his message and under no persecution. He became a guiding light with a responsibility[1] to the people in the dark days of the Captivity.

2.4.2.9. His book was written in the first person and completely balanced by structure and orderliness. The fall of Jerusalem was used as the pivotal point, and his prophecies were precisely dated.

2.4.2.10. He was much more flamboyant than any other prophet, merging into "apocalyptic," which John borrows in his much later book of Revelation (95-98 CE).

2.4.2.11. As a preacher, a writer, a pastor, and a prophet of God, Ezekiel takes his place among the greatest men of the Old Testament.

2.4.3. Allow me to briefly describe his dramatic vision and calling in Chapter one. Chapters 1-24 contain sermons delivered before the fall of Jerusalem.

2.4.3.1. As Ezekiel looks out over the Babylonian land, he sees what appears to be an approaching storm out of the north with thunder and lightning.

2.4.3.2. Then he views four cherubim, angelic creatures standing wing-tip to wing-tip forming a square. Beside each of the 4-faced cherub is a whirling wheel full of eyes, probably terrifying at first view. In the hollow area, fire glows; above is the Lord of Glory in human form seated on a sapphire-like throne, and God is like a "fire" all around, the brightness of His Glory! This entire scene encircled by a rainbow.

Chapters	View
6-7	Judgment of Jerusalem; a remnant to be saved
8-10	His glory departs the Temple
11-13	The rulers left in Jerusalem
14	Vision of the Vine, Israel (Isaiah 5:7)
18-19	Individual responsibility
20-24	The final prophecies leading to Jerusalem's judgment; Babylon
25-28	Prophecies begin against the nations: Ammonites Moab Edom Philistines Tyre/Tarshish

---

[1] Ezekiel 3:17 *"Son of man, I have appointed you a watchman to the house of Israel; whenever you hear a word from My mouth, warn them from Me.*

2.4.4. Cps 29-32 reveals six visions that tell of Nebuchadnezzar's invasion of Egypt. He plundered Egypt in 570-568 BCE and Egypt never recovered.

2.4.5. Ezekiel's prophecy in cps 38 and 39 is perhaps the fullest view of future events that we have. They contribute greatly to the understanding of the events of the final days of history.

2.4.6. The names mentioned, Magog, Meshech, Tubal, and Gomer were all sons of Noah's son, Japheth.[1]

    2.4.6.1. Magog is the name of the people following Gog into war. The Hebrew "ma" could allow us to interpret this as "land of Gog," rather than people. Josephus locates Magog as an actual descendant of Japheth and located near the Black Sea.

    2.4.6.2. Meshech and Tubal seemingly are near modern day Turkey; Gomer is modern day Armenia. Some try to make Meshech and Tubal into Russia and/or Moscow, interesting but not proven.

    2.4.6.3. Their names were probably given to European peoples living in the Black Sea area, as far North as the known world existed at that time.

2.4.7. Ezekiel pictures an invasion by these people from the North, led by an unidentified Gog. Gog may represent the forces of evil; he may be the leader of those forces. They ally with many other armies from near and far

    2.4.7.1. Persia, today called Iran

    2.4.7.2. Ethiopia is south of Egypt

    2.4.7.3. Libya is North Africa.

2.4.8. See the next Expanded Help Paper, **A Basic Summary of End Time Events**.

2.4.9. Summing up, a chief prince, who is the enemy of God's people, will lead a coalition of nations against Jerusalem. This attack comes not just from the North but the four corners of the world. They gather in the valley we earlier mentioned. They join for the purpose of waging war on God's people—God demonstrates His awesome power of destruction quickly.

2.4.10. Cp 39 repeats the message and enlarges on it. Gog's army is so large that the weapons provide Israel with seven years of fuel. I cannot imagine that the weapons will be made of wood; all I know is that they indeed will provide plenty of fuel…God said it…it will happen!

---

[1] Noah's three sons were Ham, Shem, and Japheth.

Ezekiel

2.4.11. Ezekiel gives a horrifying picture of that final event. Then following that short war, Ezekiel envisions the new Temple, which God will dwell in, and be among His people; Ezekiel pictures the events in exact and precise order, agreeing with John's later choice of Gog and Magog followed by a new Temple.

EXPANDED HELP PAPER
A Basic Summary of End Time Events

(Also, refer to the Expanded Help Paper, The Day of the Lord, in Chapter SEVEN). In addition, the author has an extensive manuscript considering the entire End Time Events summarized below.

The next events in God's timetable will be the six seals of Revelation 6 followed by a "catching" or "snatching" away of all true believers, along with the bodies of all believers who have already died. The first four seals or events which take place during the first 3 ½ years, are the *beginning of sorrows,* and will reveal a leader who seemingly will step forth in a peace-negotiating place of world acceptance. Seals five and six are what we may refer to as the Great Tribulation which will take place at the mid-point of the seven-year period and end *much before* the end of the seventieth week (Daniel).

Mankind will initiate the first six seals and could be called "man's wrath" initiated through Antichrist. The seventh seal will open "God's wrath which will include the *trumpets and bowls.* The six seals are: (1) revealing of the Antichrist and his world religion, (2) war which brings about (3) famine and (4) pestilence, (5) martyr of a remnant of believers, and finally (6) the cosmic disturbance which *cuts short the Great Tribulation.* The seventh seal will open the *trumpets.* The body of Christ, the true Christ-serving believers, is removed following the sixth seal, on the very Day of the Lord (Luke 17:22-36), and prior to the Day of the Lord's Wrath (Trumpets and Bowls). The sign revealed in Matt 24:30 (Rev 6:12-13, *the sign of His coming)* is chaos, God's wrath, which will break out on earth at the opening of the seventh seal, following the rapture of the Church. We note that the word *wrath* in Revelation does not occur until verse 6:17, the Day of the Lord, informing us that the Lord's Wrath begins following the rapture. The word *wrath* is found eight times in Revelation—all eight times follow the opening of the seventh seal. **His** wrath *does not* include the first six seals.

For our continuing consideration, a man will already have stepped forth, out of the Western Democracies (see below), the "little horn" of Daniel two, and brokered a peace covenant with Israel. Many nations will follow him, in particular, a European Federation of nations, a revived empire from the old Roman Empire territory. Perhaps this group of European nations is taking shape today.

This man will break that covenant with Israel exactly 3 ½ years from when it is signed. He gathers a large army, marches into Israel, and captures the rebuilt Temple in Jerusalem (which he allows the Jews to build on the Temple of the Mount before or during the 3 ½ years).

He enters the Temple's Holy of Holies and sets himself up as a god! He reveals a six-symbol numbering system, which he demands of all people. Perhaps it will include a set of numbers related to six, such as an expanded SS# of six numbers-six-numbers-six-numbers. If groceries (or other needs) are to be purchased, the mark must be present on the head or hand, perhaps utilizing "chip" implants or other technology.

Immediately, a tribulation will come upon the entire earth, like nothing ever seen before, which this author believes will take place before the rapture.

The four confederacies converge on Jerusalem after the great-tribulation on earth. They gather in the Jezreel Valley and march towards their real goal: Jerusalem. Jesus Christ then comes to earth in the actual "second coming," *with* His body of believers (already taken away in the rapture), the real Church, destroying the four confederacies.

Following will be His 1,000-year rule of full peace on earth, never before experienced since the entry of evil in the garden. The author of discord, evil, death, and suffering is placed in a pit for the 1,000 years, no influence on any person on earth. (I enjoy reading that it only takes a single angel to take hold of him, casting him in that pit!).

What a glorious period it will be on earth. The confederacies of all nations will be aligned during the seven-year period. The following is a pretty clear alignment:

The confederation of **northern nations**, which will include Russia. Daniel 11:40 represents a group of northern nations led by Russia. It is quite possible this federation will include Iran and the nations of central Asia.

The confederation of **southern nations** Daniel 11:40 represents the group consisting perhaps of Egypt and Islamic nations of North Africa and the Middle East.

The confederation of **eastern kings** Daniel 11:44; Revelation 16:12 representing nations east of the Euphrates River, possibly China, Afghanistan, India, Pakistan, Japan, and Korea.

Ezekiel

The confederation of **western democracies**. Daniel 2:40-43 representing the old Roman Empire, perhaps now the European Federation of Nations. This is the 10-king led nations or territories, with one becoming the strong ruler we know as Antichrist. It also is possible that this will be the confederation that the United States will be joined with. Keep in mind that *all the nations of the earth* will gather against Israel in the final days; Zechariah 12:3; 14:2; Revelation 16:14.

At the end of the 1,000 years, Satan will be released from the pit "for a season." Again he gathers a following, since many will be born during the 1,000 years of peace, and each person must make a decision of who to follow. He again builds a strong army and tries to destroy Jerusalem and Christ's people. A battle takes place with Christ quickly putting an end to Satan and all who choose to stand with him. All who have not chosen Christ from all the ages will stand in front of God in heaven, pronounced guilty, and cast away into a lake of eternal fire. This is the Great White Throne Judgment. A new heaven and an earth renovated by fire are revealed as the eternal location of all the righteous!

2.4.12. Ezekiel also, in very clear style, presented the personal responsibility of an individual before God. As clear as any modern evangelist.[1]

2.4.13. He emphasizes a heart-cleansing, which really introduced a period of the Holy Spirit. Read this in cp 36 of Ezekiel.

2.4.14. Jeremiah had a similar passage in 31:31-34, noted below.[2]

---

[1] Ezekiel 36:25-28 "Then I will sprinkle clean water on you, and you will be clean; I will cleanse you from all your filthiness and from all your idols. 26 "Moreover, I will give you a new heart and put a new spirit within you; and I will remove the heart of stone from your flesh and give you a heart of flesh. 27 "I will put My Spirit within you and cause you to walk in My statutes, and you will be careful to observe My ordinances."

[2] Jeremiah 31:31-34 "Behold, days are coming," declares the Lord, "when I will make a new covenant with the house of Israel and with the house of Judah, 32 not like the covenant which I made with their fathers in the day I took them by the hand to bring them out of the land of Egypt, My covenant which they broke, although I was a husband to them," declares the Lord. 33 "But this is the covenant which I will make with the house of Israel after those days," declares the Lord, "I will put My law within them and on their heart I will write it; and I will be their God, and they shall be My people. 34 "They will not teach again, each man his neighbor and each man his brother, saying, 'Know the Lord,' for they will all know Me, from the least of them to the greatest of them," declares the Lord, "for I will forgive their iniquity, and their sin I will remember no more."

2.4.15. Of course, Ezekiel teaches in an unusual way, about the Holy Spirit revitalizing His people and eventually bringing about a restoration of His nation, which we've seen come to pass. That's the dry bones in cp 37.

2.4.16. The final eight cps of Ezekiel describe the glorious future Temple that will be the center of worship for a restored Israel. In the New Testament, Paul uses similar imagery in describing the true Church (Ephesians 2:19-22).

SECTION 8
Restoration and Rebuilding

Ezra, Esther, Nehemiah, Psalms 85, 102, 126,146-150, Haggai, Zechariah, Malachi. The period from 586 to 400 BCE.

Theme Statement: " the Lord brought back the captive ones of Zion." (Psalms 126:1

THE KEYS TO SECTION EIGHT

Section 8: Restoration and Rebuilding

Keys to Ezra—

A Key Word: *Jews*

The Key Verses (1:3; 7:10

   3 'Whoever there is among you of all His people, may his God be with him! Let him go up to Jerusalem which is in Judah and rebuild the house of the Lord, the God of Israel; He is the God who is in Jerusalem."

   10 For Ezra had set his heart to study the law of the Lord and to practice it, and to teach His statutes and ordinances in Israel.

The Key Chapter (6)

The Key People in Ezra

Ezra—scribe and teacher of God's Word who began religious reform among the people; led the second group of exiles from Babylon to Jerusalem (Ezra 7:1–10:16)

Cyrus—Persian king who conquered Babylon; assisted the return of the Israelite exiles to their homeland (Ezra 1:1–6:14)

Zerubbabel—led the first group of Israelite exiles from Babylon to Jerusalem; completed the rebuilding of the temple (Ezra 2:2–5:2)

Haggai—post-Exilic (after the Exile) prophet who encouraged Zerubbabel and the Israelite people to continue rebuilding the temple (Ezra 5:1–2; 6:14)

Zechariah—post-Exilic prophet who encouraged Zerubbabel and the Israelite people to continue rebuilding the temple (Ezra 5:1–2; 6:14)

Darius I—Persian king who supported the rebuilding of the temple by the Israelites (Ezra 4:5–6:14)

Artaxerxes—Persian king (Xerxes I) who allowed Ezra to return to Jerusalem (Ezra 7:1) and reinstitute temple worship and the teaching of the Law

Keys to Esther—

A Key Word: *Fasting*

The Key Verses (4:14; 8:17)

14 "*For if you remain silent at this time, relief and deliverance will arise for the Jews from another place and you and your father's house will perish. And who knows whether you have not attained royalty for such a time as this?*"

7 *In each and every province and in each and every city, wherever the king's commandment and his decree arrived, there was gladness and joy for the Jews, a feast and a holiday. And many among the peoples of the land became Jews, for the dread of the Jews had fallen on them.*

The Key Chapter (8)

The Key People in Esther

Esther—replaced Vashti as queen of Persia; saved the Jews against Haman's evil plot (2:7–9:32)

Mordecai—adopted and raised Esther; advisor to Esther as queen; later replaced Haman as second in command under King Xerxes (2:5–10:3)

King Xerxes I—king of Persia; married Esther and made her queen (1:1–10:3)

Haman—second in command under King Xerxes; plotted to kill the Jews (3:1–9:25)

Keys to Nehemiah—

A Key Word: *Awesome*

The Key Verses (6:15–16; 8:8)

15 So the wall was completed on the twenty-fifth of the month Elul, in fifty-two days. 16 When all our enemies heard of it, and all the nations surrounding us saw it, they lost their confidence; for they recognized that this work had been accomplished with the help of our God.

8 They read from the book, from the law of God, translating to give the sense so that they understood the reading.

The Key Chapter (9)

The Key People in Nehemiah

Nehemiah—influential cupbearer of the Persian king Artaxerxes; led the third group of exiles to Jerusalem to rebuild the city walls (1:1–13:31)

Ezra—led the second group of exiles to Jerusalem; worked with Nehemiah as Israel's priest and scribe (8:1–12:36)

Sanballat—governor of Samaria who attempted to discourage the people and thwart the rebuilding of Jerusalem's wall (2:10–13:28)

Tobiah—Ammonite official who mocked the rebuilding of the wall and discouraged the people (2:10–13:7)

Keys to Haggai—

A Key Word: *Signet Ring*

The Key Verses (1:7–8; 2:7–9)

Keys In Section Eight

7 Thus says the Lord of hosts, "Consider your ways! 8 "Go up to the mountains, bring wood and rebuild the temple, that I may be pleased with it and be glorified," says the Lord.

7 'I will shake all the nations; and they will come with the wealth of all nations, and I will fill this house with glory,' says the Lord of hosts. 8 'The silver is Mine and the gold is Mine,' declares the Lord of hosts. 9 'The latter glory of this house will be greater than the former,' says the Lord of hosts, 'and in this place I will give peace,' declares the Lord of hosts."

The Key Chapter (2)

The Key People in Haggai

Haggai—prophet of Judah after the return from the Babylonian exile; urged the people to rebuild the temple (1:3–2:23)

Zerubbabel—led the Jews out of Babylonian exile; stood as the symbolic representative of the line of David; called "the signet ring" (1:1–2:23)

Keys to Zechariah—

A Key Word: *Angel*

The Key Verses (8:3; 9:9)

3 "Thus says the Lord, 'I will return to Zion and will dwell in the midst of Jerusalem. Then Jerusalem will be called the City of Truth, and the mountain of the Lord of hosts will be called the Holy Mountain.'"

9 Rejoice greatly, O daughter of Zion! Shout in triumph, O daughter of Jerusalem! Behold, your king is coming to you; He is just and endowed with salvation, Humble, and mounted on a donkey, Even on a colt, the foal of a donkey.

The Key Chapter (14)

The Key People in Zechariah

Zechariah—prophet of Judah after the Exile; encouraged Judah to finish building the temple (1:1–14:20)

Zerubbabel—leader of the Judean exiles; carried out the work on the temple (4:6–10)

Joshua—Israel's high priest after the remnant returned to Israel (3:1–10; 6:11–13)

The Jews rebuilding the temple—who returned to Jerusalem after the Exile in obedience of God (1:16; 4:9; 6:15; 8:13)

Keys to Malachi—

A Key Word: *Try*

The Key Verses (2:17, 3:1, 4:5–6)

17 You have wearied the Lord with your words. Yet you say, "How have we wearied Him?" In that you say, "Everyone who does evil is good in the sight of the Lord, and He delights in them," or, "Where is the God of justice?"

1 "Behold, I am going to send My messenger, and he will clear the way before Me. And the Lord, whom you seek, will suddenly come to His temple; and the messenger of the covenant, in whom you delight, behold, He is coming," says the Lord of hosts.

5 "Behold, I am going to send you Elijah the prophet before the coming of the great and terrible day of the Lord. 6 "He will restore the hearts of the fathers to their children and the hearts of the children to their fathers, so that I will not come and smite the land with a curse."

The Key Chapter (3)

The Key People in Malachi

Keys In Section Eight

Malachi—prophet to Judah; last of the Old Testament prophets.

The priests—revealed their unfaithfulness by marrying foreign wives and giving false interpretation of the Law (1:7, 8; 2:1–9)

The people of Judah—married foreign wives and fell into idolatry (2:11–17)

Approximate Dates of Key Events in Sections 7, 8

586 BCE	The Babylonians take Judah captive
585	Jeremiah and others were taken to Egypt
560	Daniel's three friends survive the fiery furnace
559-530	Cyrus reigns in Persia
550	Belshazzar assumes the throne in Babylon; Daniel's visions
539	Cyrus of Persia conquers Babylon/Belshazzar's kingdom
537	The return of the Jews to Judea begins
536-534	The temple rebuilding begins then stops
522-486	Darius I reigns in Persia
520	Haggai and Zechariah begin to prophesy/the temple rebuilding resumes
516	The temple is completed
486-465	Ahasuerus (Xerxes I) reigns in Persia. Events of Esther
465-424	Artaxerxes Longimanus reigns in Persia
467	Ezra leads a group of returnees
440-425	Malachi's ministry
454	Nehemiah leads a group of returnees
453	Jerusalem's wall is reconstructed
442	Nehemiah returns to Jerusalem (last datable event in O.T.)

THIRTEEN

Restoration and Rebuilding

1 **W**e have reviewed the **CAPTIVITY**, so now it is time for a **RESTORATION** of Judah and **REBUILDING** of Jerusalem. I love this period of Old Testament.
  1.1. The *captivity* had occurred in those three stages which we reviewed:
    1.1.1. 1st in 607 BCE when Nebuchadnezzar carried off the Daniel and the sacred vessels of the Temple
    1.1.2. 2nd in 598 BCE nine years later, Nebuchadnezzar returned taking 10,000 more captives, including Ezekiel
    1.1.3. And the 3rd in 586 BCE; when Nebuchadnezzar actually tore down and burned the walls of Jerusalem, and destroyed the Temple.
  1.2. So the fall and destruction were over a twenty-year period.
2 Now the restoration which is *also* three-fold. First a summary:
  2.1. Zerubbabel in 536 BCE, when plans to rebuild were made, and the temple actual construction began. Temple was completed in 516. The beginning of a restored people.
  2.2. Ezra, in 467 with a great religious reformation, reestablishing worship of God
  2.3. Nehemiah 14 years later in 454 when the walls and city were rebuilt.
    2.3.1. So it took longer to return than it did to be taken.
    2.3.2. It's easier to slip and fall than it is to build into maturity
    2.3.3. The story of the first two returns is told in Ezra, and the third return in Nehemiah; an easy way to understand the two books.
    2.3.4. We note that Ezra, Esther, and Nehemiah, may be treated as a unit. In addition, three other books may be linked with these:
      2.3.4.1. Haggai, Zechariah, and Malachi, all which deal with the work of God subsequent to the seventy years of captivity.

Restoration and Rebuilding: Ezra

2.4. Which puts us at the book of Ezra
  2.4.1.　　The book was written by Ezra which means "Jehovah helps." Ezra and the next book we'll review, Nehemiah, were a single book in the Hebrew. Some of Ezra was written in Aramaic.
  2.4.2.　　We mentioned when we looked at the two books of Chronicles that Ezra is thought to be the author of those two books also. The first few verses of Ezra are quoted from the ending of 2 Chronicles, linking the two.
  2.4.3.　　Two different times Jeremiah stated that the exile would be for seventy years. That in itself was amazing to prophesy a fixed length.[1]

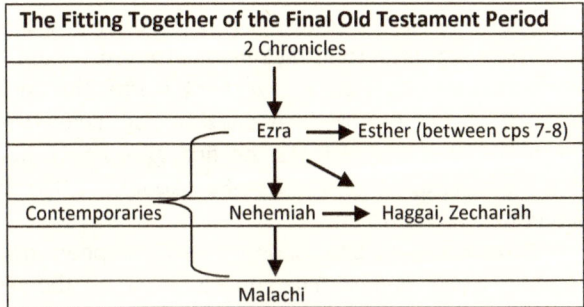

A Basic Outline of Ezra
1. The First Return Under Zerubbabel, Cps 1-6
2. The 2nd Return Under Ezra, Cps 7-10

Depth of Bible Words and Locations
A Key Word in Ezra: *Jews*
Found in 4:12, 23; 5:1,5; 6:7,8,and 14. We looked at this briefly earlier in this Section. Let's add a few comments here:

The word means "to praise." Jacob used the word in Genesis 49:8 in a blessing of his son.

We mentioned, a Jew was one from the tribe of Judah or an Israelite living in Judah. During this period of restoration, "Jew" referred to the Israelites as a group.

Jesus was called King of the Jews, then Paul clarified it for all of us in Romans 2:28 *For he is not a Jew who is one*

---

[1] Jeremiah 25:12 *'Then it will be when seventy years are completed I will punish the king of Babylon and that nation,' declares the Lord.*
Jeremiah 29:10 *"For thus says the Lord, 'When seventy years have been completed for Babylon, I will visit you and fulfill My good word to you, to bring you back to this place'"*

outwardly, nor is circumcision that which is outward in the flesh. 29 But he is a Jew who is one inwardly; and circumcision is that which is of the heart, by the Spirit, not by the letter; and his praise is not from men, but from God.

> *Jesus in Ezra and Nehemiah...He's your rebuilder and restorer of the broken down walls of human life.*

2.4.4. Cyrus was mentioned by name twenty-three times in Scripture, called by name 125 years before his birth.

2.4.5. God moved upon the heart of Cyrus and he decreed in 537 BCE that people could return to their homelands (Ezra 6:3). There was no command to return. It was the offer of a choice to be made. There was little to attract anyone to Jerusalem, for they were comfortable in Babylon. A few months after the decree, in 536 BCE, 70 years after Nebuchadnezzar had taken them to Babylon in 606, Zerubbabel leads the first group back home to Jerusalem! According to Ezra 2:64-65, about 50,000 people returned both Jew and Gentile.

2.4.6. Cyrus may have been shown Isaiah's prophecy from 200 years earlier, which named him and his releasing the Jews to return home. This certainly made him a believer in the God of the Jews.

2.4.17. Most of them were Jews from the tribes of Judah and Benjamin, the old Southern Kingdom, but there were some from the other ten tribes also. I believe all twelve tribes were represented.

Kings of Persia

Cyrus	559-530 BCE	Military emphasis; expansion to the east
Cambyses	530-522	Expansion to Egypt
Darius	522-486	Re unified Persia; different type of rule built many temples; Canon had its roots
Xerxes I, (Ahasuerus)	486-465	Called King Ahasuerus in book of Esther; Stopped funding the Jerusalem temple; Babylon revolted from Persia, defeated; economy deteriorated; battled with Greece
Artaxerxes I	474-465 rule over Jews 465-423 rule over all	Had Xerxes assassinated; Long

Restoration and Rebuilding: Ezra

	Persia	
		reign; became stagnate; no expansion
Xerxes II	423	Artaxerxes only son; Assassinated after only a 45-day rule
Darius II	423-404	Weak king
Artaxerxes II	404-359	Rebellions took place, including Egypt; had 115 sons
Artaxerxes III	359-338	Greece revolted; marched against Egypt
Arses	338-335	Son of Artaxerxes; Philip of Greece forms a league that begin downfall of Persia
Darius III	336-331	Philip of Greece father of Alexander the Greek was killed by Persian agents; Alexander marches to Persia kills most of the Persian generals
Alexander conquered Persia	330	

2.4.18.   Tradition says it took four months to make the journey of 700 miles to Jerusalem. A huge caravan was accompanied by a bodyguard of 1,000 cavalry. It is interesting, the many that stayed behind actually paid for the long trip by providing them with what they needed. (Ezra 1:6-11)

2.4.19.   This return of Babylon parallels the original Exodus. It must have been a joy for the people causing them to remember that Egyptian deliverance—both were a new start. Both showed how God preserved His people. That's what I love about this period. Indeed, this is a new start.

2.4.20.   *"The future of the world lay in this procession to Jerusalem,"* says the American scholar Mary Ellen Chase who lectured from 1926 onward. *"If there had been no return to Jerusalem, Judah would have shared the fate of Israel and become intermingled with the east and lost as a united people."*

2.4.21.   Follow what happened. When they arrived in Jerusalem, they first built an altar, kept the feast of tabernacles, and restored a unified worship of God. They built some temporary homes, however immediately laid the foundation for a re-construction of the Temple. Priority.

2.4.22. However, that work on the temple was rudely interrupted from peoples close by who didn't want a rebuilding of Jerusalem. The construction was delayed until Darius' reign, fifteen years later.

2.4.23. One of the groups, Samaritans, pretended they wanted to help build the Temple, but were rejected. The true character of these men is clearly pointed out in 4:1-2.[1] Their words were friendly, but they were "enemies." The Israelites make it clear in v. 3.[2] So those men dispatched a letter to the Persians (Artaxerxes) telling them the Jews were building fortifications and getting ready for war. A lie, but resulted in the work being halted. They were *ordered* to cease.[3] We notice the language of the letter was Aramaic, (4:6-6:8).

2.4.24. Later, due to the preaching and urging from Haggai and Zechariah, (we will review these two authors and their books later), work was resumed in 520 BCE after Darius rose to power in Persia. Darius was persuaded to examine the records of Cyrus for any confirmation of the re-building of the Temple. This was located and Cyrus commanded his governors to assist in the rebuilding![4]

2.4.25. In 516 BCE, the Temple was completed and dedicated with great rejoicing. The Scriptures record...[5]

2.4.26. We note there is a sixty-year gap between Ezra chapters 6 and 7, probably when the story of Esther took place.

---

[1] *Now when the enemies of Judah and Benjamin heard that the people of the exile were building a temple to the Lord God of Israel, 2 they approached Zerubbabel and the heads of fathers' households, and said to them, "Let us build with you, for we, like you, seek your God; and we have been sacrificing to Him since the days of Esarhaddon king of Assyria, who brought us up here."*

[2] *"You have nothing in common with us in building a house to our God; but we ourselves will together build to the Lord God of Israel, as King Cyrus, the king of Persia has commanded us."*

[3] *24 Then work on the house of God in Jerusalem ceased, and it was stopped until the second year of the reign of Darius king of Persia.*

[4] Ezra 6:7-8 *"Leave this work on the house of God alone; let the governor of the Jews and the elders of the Jews rebuild this house of God on its site. 8 "Moreover, I issue a decree concerning what you are to do for these elders of Judah in the rebuilding of this house of God: the full cost is to be paid to these people from the royal treasury out of the taxes of the provinces beyond the River, and that without delay..."*

[5] Ezra 6:15 *This temple was completed on the third day of the month Adar* (which is our Feb-March;(Refer to Jewish calendar, Volume One, Chapter ELEVEN) *it was the sixth year of the reign of King Darius* (516 BCE). *16 And the sons of Israel, the priests, the Levites and the rest of the exiles, celebrated the dedication of this house of God with joy. 17 They offered for the dedication of this temple of God 100 bulls, 200 rams, 400 lambs, and as a sin offering for all Israel 12 male goats, corresponding to the number of the tribes of Israel.*

Restoration and Rebuilding: Ezra

2.4.27. The second and third returns were similar to the first—a desire to rebuild Jerusalem was evident.

2.4.28. Ezra, still in Babylon learned that the people in Jerusalem had a Temple, but no one to instruct them in the Law of God. The Temple was an empty house, without His Word.

2.4.29. We see in the second half of Ezra, that he received permission from Artaxerxes the emperor, to lead another group to Jerusalem. In 467 BCE, over 1,700 men accompanied Ezra in the return. He took with him the Temple vessels, which had been taken to Babylonia many years earlier. This is such favor. Pause to read Artaxerxes' letter recorded in Ezra 7:6-23.

2.4.30. Interesting, chapter eight reports the names of those who traveled to Jerusalem with Ezra. Even though we are unfamiliar with these persons, each of them was important to God. Their names are recorded in the eternal books.

2.4.31. We notice in preparation for the journey, Ezra proclaimed a fast[1], the people crying to God for His guidance. Following a week of preparation, they began their journey.

2.4.32. Ezra travels to Jerusalem under this great favor; what could go wrong?

2.4.33. Don't ever ask that question! When all looks great, going smoothly, the enemy strikes. Does he ever stop?

2.4.34. When Ezra gets there, some of the people including leaders and priests had already married foreign peoples (9:2)! He was shocked and tore his garments and plucked his beard. The actions of these Jews could have destroyed the nation! We see Satan still at work in his attempt to destroy the Seed.

2.4.35. But Ezra gave himself to prayer[2] (which should be our same response today) and he persuaded many to divorce their pagan wives. This past failure would not strike again![3]

2.4.36. This shows us how vital it was to have marriages that God establishes. This was a new beginning and it must be founded with God's plan. Too many times they had failed to do this.

---

[1] Ezra 8:21 *Then I proclaimed a fast there at the river of Ahava, that we might humble ourselves before our God to seek from Him a safe journey for us, our little ones, and all our possessions*

[2] Ezra 10:1 *Now while Ezra was praying and making confession, weeping and prostrating himself before the house of God...*

[3] Ezra 10:17 *They finished investigating all the men who had married foreign wives by the first day of the first month;* Ezra 10:19 *They pledged to put away their wives, and being guilty.*

2.4.37. We conclude that Ezra had a confidence in knowing God used him to open the eyes of His people to unite in fellowship and service.

2.5. At this time, we have an example of God's continued watching over His people. The Book of Esther, took place between Ezra chapters six and seven.

2.5.1. The book's title "Esther," has always been the name. Many books we've studied had names other than what our English Bibles have. But not Esther. From the original Hebrew to the translations that have been made—it has always been Esther.

A Basic Outline of Esther
1. Esther replaces Vashti, 1:1-2:18
2. Mordecai overcomes Haman, 2:19-4:17
3. Israel survives, 5:1-10:3

Depth of Bible Words and Locations
A Key Word in Esther: *Fasting*

Found in 4:3, 14. Pretty clear meaning, "to abstain from food." At various times it meant to abstain from drinking, bathing, anointing with oil, or sexual relations.

A fast, which was very common in ancient days, varied in length. 1 Samuel 14:24 "one day"; 1 Samuel 31:13 "seven days." It could last up to forty days.

We have passages in connection with mourning for the dead, intercessory prayer, repentance, and times of distress. Isaiah told the people to always include acts of righteousness with their fasting (Isaiah 58:3-9).

Jesus in Esther...He is YOUR deliverer and preserver.

Events During Esther's Period

Darius ruled; continue to build Temple	520 BCE
Temple completed	516
Ahasuerus divorces Vashti	487
Esther marries Ahasuerus	487
Haman's plot against the Jews	482
Haman hanged	481
Mordecai made Prime Minister	481
Jews delivered	480
Ezra arrived in Jerusalem	458
Nehemiah's work begins	445

Restoration and Rebuilding: Esther

2.5.2. Penned by an unnamed author; we only know whoever it was, he had a detailed knowledge of Persia.

2.5.3. We also know it covers a period of time ending in 474 BCE and was written while Persia was still in existence. Greece conquered them in 331.

2.5.4. Esther probably takes place after the initial return under Zerubbabel, very close to 485-474. We note that a few years before the first verses of the book, Cyrus was stirred by God to issue the proclamation for people to return to Jerusalem.

2.5.5. Quite interesting, the name of God is not found or referred to in the entire book. It has been said, "although the *name* of God is not in this book the *hand* of God is plain to be seen throughout." Neither is there any reference to prayer. Perhaps this is the main reason it was not accepted into the Canon of Scripture until a later date.

2.5.6. Esther, a beautiful young Jewish girl is eventually introduced as Queen of Persia in this wonderful four-year adventure. She is instrumental in bringing about a deliverance of God's people.

2.5.7. She was raised by uncle Mordecai as his own daughter. He was a leader of Jews during this story. The Jews were delivered, and to remember God, they begin the Feast of Purim, one of the Jewish festivals.

2.5.8. Esther, an orphaned Jew, marries the Persian king Ahasuerus,[1] who is believed to be King Xerxes I, who became king following Darius in 486 BCE. He ruled a large empire for over twenty years. The wide extent of this empire in noted in v. 1, and was pictured in Daniel's dream (Dan 2) as the "silver" kingdom. At the time of this story, there were many Jews still in Babylon, even though they were free to return to Jerusalem. As mentioned, Esther chronologically falls between the sixth and seventh chapters of Ezra.

2.5.9. We might compare Esther to a chess game; God and Satan moved kings, queens, nobles; and then God moved Esther and Mordecai and was able to say "checkmate."

---

[1] Est 1:1 *Now it took place in the days of Ahasuerus* (King Xerxes, noted by author); 3 *in the third year of his reign he gave a banquet for all his princes and attendants, the army officers of Persia and Media,*

2.5.10. Ever since man fell, Satan has attempted to sever the relationship between God and man. He knew the promise of Genesis 3:15 and has always tried to destroy the coming seed.

    2.5.10.1. In Esther, we will see that Haman's scheme to kill the Jewish race, in turn, destroy the seed; Satan's plan has been consistent:

    2.5.10.2. He Killed (he thought) the seed line, Abel. The Seed grew through Seth

    2.5.10.3. Filled the earth with sin to block the seed. The Seed went on through Noah

    2.5.10.4. Deceived Abraham concerning the birth of Isaac. God preserved the Seed

    2.5.10.5. Tried to allow Esau, not Jacob, to receive the blessing. The Seed was not divided

    2.5.10.6. Murder the children. The Seed was saved in the Nile.

    2.5.10.7. He tried to murder the entire tribe of Judah, in fact, it was reduced to one person, Joash who was rescued and hidden away to protect the seed. The line to the seed was preserved.

    2.5.10.8. Caused sin in David's life to end the line. Repentance continued the Seed.

    2.5.10.9. Herod killed the infants in Bethlehem thinking Christ was among them. The seed came.

    2.5.10.10. Satan tempted the seed Himself, Christ, to denounce God. The seed prevailed.

    2.5.10.11. Peter comes beside Christ and Satan gets him to attempt to block the seed from dying on Calvary. But the seed triumphed.

    2.5.10.12. Finally, Satan entered Judas who betrayed Christ. And the seed was thought to have been buried! But all this time the seed was rising.

2.5.11. Allow me to introduce the characters in the book of Esther

    2.5.11.1. *Esther*, the main character, in the lineage of the royal family of the king of Israel. Her beauty and grace caught the attention of the officers who were to find a bride for the king.

    2.5.11.2. *Mordecai*, a descendant of Kish, the father of Israel's first king. His name means "little man" indicating his physical stature. Carried away to Babylon BCE 598. Eighty years old as chapter two of Esther begins. Uncle of

Esther who told her to conceal the fact that she was a despised Jewess.

2.5.11.3. *Vashti*, introduced in cp one. The beautiful queen of Xerxes. In fact, Xerxes would display his wife for her beauty. When she refused to appear at his order, he "put her away" and divorced to make her an example. Later, he regretted the decision, but could not change the command.

2.5.11.4. *Haman* was from the warlike people of Amalek, whom God despised. They descended from Esau. Even today, Haman is hated by orthodox Jews. Haman found favor with King Ahasuerus and was rapidly elevated. All but one person bowed before him—Mordecai.

2.5.11.5. *King Ahasuerus* was referring to Xerxes. Ahasuerus was a title, like Pharaoh.

2.5.12. Esther is a story of real survival. Haman, the king's second in command wants the Jews destroyed because of the literal "stand" that Mordecai makes. He was a man of great wealth and influence.

2.5.12.1. Mordecai no longer hides his people and his kindred—he is a Jew and lets everyone know it. We rationalize here, he could have at least bowed his head, perhaps acknowledging with hands clasped in recognition. But Mordecai knew the attitude of God toward an Amalekite.[1]

2.5.13. Haman is infuriated and vows revenge by annihilating all Jews. But Mordecai continues his stand of faith in God.

2.5.13.1. Ironside's description of this.[2]

> In this energy of faith Moses forsook Egypt; Caleb cried, "We are well able to overcome"; Gideon went forth to war with lamps and pitchers; David fought an armored giant with a shepherd's sling and stones; Jehoshaphat set singers in the van of his army where others would have set mounted troops; Daniel opened his windows to pray to the God of heaven; and Paul lived his life of devotion to the crucified, exalted Lord, and refused to conform to the demands of the men of his day and age.

---

[1] Est 3:2 *But Mordecai neither bowed down nor paid homage.*
[2] H.A.Ironside, *Joshua.Ezra.Nehemiah.Esther*, Loizeaux Brothers, Inc. Neptune, New Jersey, 1983, p. 44

2.5.14. The Jewish population was in fear—King Xerxes issued the proclamation that would annihilate them, sealed with his royal signet.

2.5.15. Esther was informed of the proclamation and was greatly grieved. Mordecai requested her to go before the king and plead for her people. Proper Persian court etiquette did not allow her to do so, under penalty of death.

2.5.16. She first requested Mordecai and all the Jews to fast for her for three days. Following the fast, she would go to the king. "If I perish, I perish."[1]

2.5.17. The queen ventures before the king with the thought of forfeiting her life for her people. We note that her beauty and attractive presence allowed her to present her case before the king. The king admired her and was willing to listen.[2]

2.5.18. Esther is used by God to save His people.[3]

2.5.19. The remainder of chapter five details the episode where Mordecai refuses to bow before Haman as he strolls down the pathway, followed by Haman's attempt to hang him on an eighty-foot gallows.

2.5.20. The extreme vanity and pride of Haman are about to destroy himself.[4] Xerxes during the night is disturbed and is led to honor Mordecai.[5] The character and deeds of Mordecai come to his remembrance and his recognition is commanded.[6]

2.5.21. The feast, which was requested by Esther as her reply to the king, was next. At Esther's request, Haman was to be included as a guest.[7]

---

[1] Est 4:16 *"Go, assemble all the Jews who are found in Susa, and fast for me; do not eat or drink for three days, night or day. I and my maidens also will fast in the same way. And thus I will go in to the king, which is not according to the law; and if I perish, I perish."*

[2] Est 5:2 *When the king saw Esther the queen standing in the court, she obtained favor in his sight; and the king extended to Esther the golden scepter which was in his hand*

[3] Est 5:6 *"What is your petition, for it shall be granted to you. And what is your request? Even to half of the kingdom it shall be done."*

[4] Est 5:9 *Then Haman went out that day glad and pleased of heart; 11Then Haman recounted to them the glory of his riches, and the number of his sons, and every instance where the king had magnified him and how he had promoted him above the princes and servants of the king*

[5] Est 6:1 *During that night the king could not sleep so he gave an order to bring the book of records, the chronicles...*

[6] Est 6:3 *The king said, "What honor or dignity has been bestowed on Mordecai for this?" Then the king's servants who attended him said, "Nothing has been done for him."*

[7] Est 7:1-2 *Now the king and Haman came to drink wine with Esther the queen. 2 And the king said to Esther on the second day also as they drank their wine at the banquet, "What is your petition, Queen Esther? It shall be granted you. And what is your request? Even to half of the kingdom it shall be done."*

Restoration and Rebuilding: Esther

2.5.22. Esther reveals she is a Jew and included in the annihilation ordered. She pleads for her people (and her own life). It must have shocked the king to hear her words.[1] The wife of the king was to be killed. King Ahasuerus continues in shock as he begins to realize that Haman had obtained a royal decree to kill his wife![2]

2.5.23. Haman is hanged and Mordecai, a Jew, becomes the prime minister. At Esther's request, the proclamation initiated by Haman, was revoked.

2.5.24. Mordecai, rather than being hung from the tall gallows, became very powerful and rose to be 2nd in command under the King of Persia, Xerxes. God certainly used Esther and Mordecai in His plan for Israel. All of God's promises to Abraham in Genesis 17 were threatened, but again I mention, God is a rescuer and preserver!

2.5.25. Although God is not mentioned in Esther—He was everywhere, blocking Satan's intervention. All of the promises to Abraham and David were in jeopardy...**but God**...God rescues His people from elimination, in this wonderful story. Checkmate!

2.5.26. Esther lived well into the reign of Xerxes' son Artaxerxes, and undoubtedly had great influence in Persia during the time of Ezra and Nehemiah.

2.5.27. We note that Esther was one of the outstanding women of the Old Testament. She was a Jewish captive in Persia who saved her people from destruction by the schemer Haman. Note the following women of the Old Testament.

---

[1] Est 7:4 *we have been sold, I and my people, to be destroyed, to be killed and to be annihilated*

[2] Est 7:6 *Then Haman became terrified before the king and queen.*

TRAVEL THROUGH THE OLD TESTAMENT

Name	Description	Biblical Reference
Bathsheba	Wife of David; mother of Solomon	2 Sam 11:3, 27
Deborah	Judge who defeated the Canaanites	Judg 4:4
Delilah	Philistine who tricked Samson	Judg 16:4, 5
Dinah	Only daughter of Jacob	Gen 30:21
Eve	First woman	Gen 3:20
Gomer	Prophet Hosea's unfaithful wife	Hos 1:2, 3
Hagar	Sarah's maid; mother of Ishmael	Gen 16:3–16
Hannah	Mother of Samuel	1 Sam 1
Jezebel	Wicked wife of King Ahab	1 Kings 16:30, 31
Jochebed	Mother of Moses	Ex 6:20
Miriam	Sister of Moses; a prophetess	Ex 15:20
Naomi	Ruth's mother-in-law	Ruth 1:2, 4
Orpah	Ruth's sister-in-law	Ruth 1:4
Rachel	Wife of Jacob	Gen 29:28
Rahab	Harlot who harbored Israel's spies; ancestor of Jesus	Josh 2:3–24; Matt 1:5
Ruth	Wife of Boaz and mother of Obed; ancestor of Jesus	Ruth 4:13, 17; Matt 1:5
Sarah	Wife of Abraham; mother of Isaac	Gen 11:29; 21:2, 3
Tamar	A daughter of David	2 Sam 13:1
Zipporah	Wife of Moses	Ex 2:21

2.6. This moves us to Nehemiah and the third return. Keep in mind, Ezra recorded the first two returns. Nehemiah has been the center for many studies and books.
    2.6.1.   Books of leadership
    2.6.2.   Books on building strong walls
    2.6.3.   This is a valuable book to study
2.7. The sacred history of the Chosen People ends chronologically with Nehemiah's final prayer *Remember me, O my God, for good (*Neh 13:31).
    2.7.1.   Nehemiah means "Jehovah Comforts." Of course, it was named after the man whom the events involved.

Restoration and Rebuilding: Nehemiah

A Basic Outline of Nehemiah
1. Nehemiah's First Term as Governor of Jerusalem, Cps 1-12
2. Nehemiah's Second Term as Governor of Jerusalem, Cp 13

Depth of Bible Words and Locations
A Key Word in Nehemiah: *Awesome*

Found in 1:5, 11; 6:14, 19. It means, "to fear," and carries the meaning of virtue. A reverence and respect for God's character. Psalms 128:1 reads *How blessed is everyone who fears the Lord, Who walks in His ways.*

Depth of Bible Words and Locations
Susa

Shushan or called Susa ("a lily"), the ancient capital of Elam inhabited by the Babylonians; later a royal residence and capital of the Persian Empire. The site is modern Shush in Iran on the Ulai River, about 250 miles east-southeast of Babylon.

Long before the time of Abraham in the Old Testament, Shushan was the center of Elamite civilization. Some scholars believe it was a cult city centering upon the worship of one of the chief Elamite gods.

Ahasuerus the king of Persia, who married Esther, held court in Shushan (Susa), one of three principal capital cities in Persia. Also, Darius I built his palace here, which was restored by Artaxerxes. Many of the events in the Book of Esther occurred here.

2.7.2. The Greek Septuagint and Latin Vulgate both named this book 2 Ezra.

2.7.3. In today's Hebrew Bible, the books of Ezra and Nehemiah are one book.

2.7.4. The events covered start in 454 BCE and run chronologically through 430.

2.7.5. Nehemiah, a cupbearer to King Artaxerxes, learns that the walls in Jerusalem were still broken down and hears of the marriages with foreigners. He gives himself to fasting and prayer.

2.7.6. Nehemiah lived in a royal palace and was a favorite of the king. Even so, we notice that his heart was directed to his people, similar to the heart that Moses had.

2.7.7. So he appeals to Artaxerxes the last king of Persia in the Old Testament. Nehemiah pleads, "Send me back to Jerusalem."

The exact words are in 2:5.[1] Artaxerxes had noticed Nehemiah was in low spirits.[2]

2.7.8. It is also probable that Esther who was the king's stepmother had some influence on behalf of the Jews. She had been Queen for sixty years.

2.7.9. He was appointed governor of Judah, and made the 1,000-mile journey from Susa, the capital of Persia, to Jerusalem. The journey took about 4 months. Nehemiah was now free to carry out the desire in his heart—minister encouragement to God's people.

2.7.10. Ezra had been in Jerusalem for fourteen years. However, Ezra *was a priest,* teaching the people from the Law of God. Nehemiah *was a builder* with authority as civil governor. He set the example of integrity by not taking any governmental allowance in food and money during his twelve years of service.

2.7.11. A few days after his arrival in 454 BCE Nehemiah goes on a secret inspection tour of Jerusalem. He sees the broken walls; God's city is in need of restoration.[3] He soon calls on the people to rebuild the walls, which had been broken down by Nebuchadnezzar.

2.7.12. 2:19 records a list of those who expressed hostility and opposed any progress. Notice God identified
    2.7.12.1. The Moabite (Sanballat)
    2.7.12.2. The Ammonite (Tobiah)
    2.7.12.3. The Arabian (Geshem), probably from Edom.

2.7.13. All were prohibited from fellowship with God's people (Neh 13:1; Deut 23:3-6). Moab and Ammon were sons of Lot, by his own daughters.

2.7.14. The Bible tells us they worked with a trowel in one hand and a sword in the other—the walls were built within two months
    2.7.14.1. Archeologists have uncovered many sections of Nehemiah's work including the "Pool of Siloam" and several important gates. (Ten are mentioned in Cp 3, two others later, 8:16 and 12:39, for a total of twelve gates in the wall.)

---

[1] Nehemiah 2:5 *I said to the king, "If it please the king, and if your servant has found favor before you, send me to Judah, to the city of my fathers' tombs, that I may rebuild it."*
[2] *So the king said to me, "Why is your face sad though you are not sick? ªThis is nothing but sadness of heart."*
[3] Neh 2:13-14 *So I went out at night by the Valley Gate in the direction of the Dragon's Well and on to the Refuse Gate, inspecting the walls of Jerusalem which were broken down and its gates which were consumed by fire.*

Restoration and Rebuilding: Nehemiah

2.7.15. Some others threatened military attack[1]
2.7.16. They lied about Nehemiah[2]
2.7.17. They wrote threatening letters[3]
2.7.18. All in an attempt to stop the work. Satan never stopped his drive to destroy the promise of Genesis 3:15.
2.7.19. In spite of all this opposition, the wall was finished in fifty-two days! The people had prayed and built.[4]
2.7.20. Immediately following the completion of the walls, cp 7 informs us of the detailed organizational skills of Nehemiah.
    2.7.20.1. Gatekeepers were to act as guards of the twelve gates.
    2.7.20.2. Singers were an appointed group to lead a spirit of praise.
    2.7.20.3. Levites were the ministry servants, with a gift of edification to the people.
    2.7.20.4. In addition, two persons were placed in charge of Jerusalem, having authority over the Gatekeepers.
2.7.21. An excellent pattern today, for every believer:
    2.7.21.1. Guard your heart against the attractions of the flesh, the world, and the devil. Guard your home against spiritual attacks.
    2.7.21.2. Always have a spirit of worship towards God
    2.7.21.3. Serve as a minister to allow God's light to shine forth in your words, actions, and deeds.
2.7.22. Then Ezra and Nehemiah, now joined by Malachi, worked consistently to bring about social and religious reforms. They wanted this to be a new nation, formed under God's direction.
2.7.23. One example recorded in Nehemiah 8 recounts the law of God being read and taught day and night by Ezra to the people gathered together.[5]

---

[1] Nehemiah 4:7 *Now when Sanballat, Tobiah, the Arabs, the Ammonites and the Ashdodites heard that the repair of the walls of Jerusalem went on, and that the breaches began to be closed, they were very angry. 8 All of them conspired together to come and fight against Jerusalem and to cause a disturbance in it.*

[2] Nehemiah 6:5-7 *then Sanballat sent his servant to me in the same manner a fifth time with an open letter in his hand. 6 In it was written, "It is reported among the nations, and Gashmu says, that you and the Jews are planning to rebel; therefore you are rebuilding the wall. And you are to be their king, according to these reports."*

[3] Nehemiah 6:19 *Then Tobiah sent letters to frighten me.*

[4] Neh 4:6 *So we built the wall and the whole wall was joined together to half its height, for the people had a mind to work.*

[5] Nehemiah 8:1-3 *And all the people gathered as one man at the square which was in front of the Water Gate, and they asked Ezra the scribe to bring the book of the law of Moses which*

2.7.24. A great gathering of unity before the gate (Water Gate) for refreshing in the Word of God. We read in Ezra, he read from morning to midday, followed by a joyful response.[1]

2.7.25. Cp 9 is the great order of proper attention to God, v. 3.
    2.7.25.1. First, attend to the Word
    2.7.25.2. Follow by prayer
    2.7.25.3. Conclude with worship.

2.7.26. The spiritual leaders then led in the longest prayer recorded in the Bible, vv. 5-37, celebrating the acts of the Lord (vv. 5-15) and reviewing the constant disobedience and rebellion of the past, along with patience (vv. 16-37).

2.7.27. They finally seemed to get it right as they renewed their covenant with God in cp 10, in particular, a separation from neighbor's women and gods.

2.7.28. The first 26 verses of cp 11 should be read as a part of cp 10. The remainder of cp 11 informs us of the feast of the dedication of the completed wall, a great occasion of rejoicing and thanksgiving to God.

2.7.29. After twelve years, Nehemiah went back to Babylonia for a visit, and it's his return to Jerusalem from that visit, in 442 BCE, which is the last datable event in the Old Testament.

	Chronology of Ezra and Nehemiah	
539 BCE	Capture of Babylon	Daniel 5:30
536	Cyrus's first year as sole ruler of kingdom	Ezra 1:1-4
536	Return under Sheshbazzar	Ezra 1:11
536	Building of altar	Ezra 3:1
535	Work on temple begun	Ezra 3:8
535-529	Opposition during Cyrus' reign	Ezra 4:1-5
529-520	Work of temple ceased	Ezra 4:24
520	Work on temple renewed under Darius	Ezra 2:2; Haggai 1:14
516	Temple completed	Ezra 6:15
467	Ezra departs from Babylon	Ezra 7:6-9
467	Ezra arrives in Jerusalem	Ezra 7:8-9
467	People assemble	Ezra 10:9
467	Committee begins investigation	Ezra 10:16
456	Committee ends investigation	Ezra 10:17
454	20th year of Artaxerxes I	Nehemiah 1:1
454	Nehemiah approaches king	Nehemiah 2:1

---

the Lord had given to Israel. 2 Then Ezra the priest brought the law before the assembly of men, women and all who could listen with understanding, on the first day of the seventh month. 3 He read from it....

[1] Neh 8:10 *...for this day is holy to our Lord. Do not be grieved, for the joy of the Lord is your strength.*

Restoration and Rebuilding: Nehemiah

454	Nehemiah arrives in Jerusalem	Nehemiah 2:11
454	Completion of wall	Nehemiah 6:15
454	Public assembly	Nehemiah 7:3??-8:1
454	Feast of Tabernacles	Nehemiah 8:4
442	32nd year of Artaxerxes	Nehemiah 5:14; 13:6
442	Nehemiah's recall and return	

FOURTEEN

Prophets of the Restoration

1 **W**e review the prophets of the restoration. During the **Captivity**, the people had Daniel followed by Ezekiel. Now in the **Restoration** period, they have three prophets sent during the rebuilding of Jerusalem--Haggai, Zechariah, and Malachi, the last of the Prophets. Haggai and Zechariah were contemporaries during this period, (refer to Ezra 5:1, 21 and 6:14). Because of the ministries of Haggai and Zechariah, the people responded to the call of God, and the Temple was completed (516 BCE).

1.1. We could call Haggai "The Temple-building prophet." The prophet's theme is the rebuilding of the Temple. He was the first prophet during the restoration of Jerusalem. From vv 2:3-9 we conclude that he was a very old man who had seen the glory of Solomon's Temple before it was destroyed.

1.2. Very little is known about the author, Haggai. Ezra mentioned him twice, and he has only two cps in his own book. It is the second shortest book in the Bible, Obadiah being shorter. He came to Jerusalem with Zerubbabel in 536 BCE, working alongside him.

1.3. He is the only person in the Old Testament with this name. From his description of Solomon's Temple in cp 2 verse 3, it is thought he must have seen it, which confirms he was an aged man when writing the book. It is clear that the period was 520 BCE, the 2nd year of King Darius of Persia.

Prophets of the Restoration

1.4. Let us glance at Psalms 137, a graphic picture of the exiles in Babylon during the period they were away from their land.[1] Jeremiah's experience:
- 1.4.1. Homesickness,
- 1.4.2. Discouragement.
- 1.4.3. That is what characterized the Israelites in Babylonia. We cannot say they were treated with cruelty, as the Northern Kingdom was treated during their Assyrian captivity.
- 1.4.4. It was not a picnic, but it was civil.

1.5. Jeremiah sent a letter to the Jews in Babylonia just before the fall of Jerusalem, which offers a little more information concerning life in exile. Read the Scripture in Jeremiah. Jeremiah 29:5-7

> 5 'Build houses and live in them; and plant gardens and eat their produce. 6 'Take wives and become the fathers of sons and daughters, and take wives for your sons and give your daughters to husbands, that they may bear sons and daughters; and multiply there and do not decrease. 7 'Seek the welfare of the city where I have sent you into exile, and pray to the Lord on its behalf; for in its welfare you will have welfare.'

- 1.5.1. We can see from Scripture, the people were reconciled to a long stay in Babylonia. This seemed to be an accepted place to live, but God had other plans. He had led them, through many years, to a promised land, and that door had never been closed. In Babylonia,
- 1.5.1.1. They bought property
- 1.5.1.2. Had a life in commerce
- 1.5.1.3. Established a religious life
- 1.5.1.4. They built synagogues
- 1.5.1.5. They had a normal life
- 1.5.2. Some rose to prominence in Babylonia
- 1.5.2.1. Daniel and his friends
- 1.5.2.2. Mordecai,
- 1.5.2.3. Ezra and Nehemiah

---

[1] Psalms 137:1 *By the rivers of Babylon, There we sat down and wept, When we remembered Zion. 2 Upon the willows in the midst of it We hung our harps. 3 For there our captors demanded of us songs, And our tormentors mirth, saying, "Sing us one of the songs of Zion." 4 How can we sing the Lord's song In a foreign land? 5 If I forget you, O Jerusalem, May my right hand forget her skill. 6 May my tongue cling to the roof of my mouth If I do not remember you, If I do not exalt Jerusalem Above my chief joy.*

1.5.3.   In fact, they became so comfortable, that at the end of the seventy years, only a relative few were willing to return and rebuild a life in Jerusalem.[1]

1.5.4.   The Jewish life had changed during the exile.

1.5.4.1.   First, their language changed as they adopted the Aramaic dialect. Nehemiah records in 8:8 *They read from the book, from the law of God, translating to give the sense so that they understood the reading.*

EXPANDED HELP PAPER
The Aramaic Dialect

A Semitic dialect formerly inaccurately called Chaldee (Chaldaic) because it was spoken by the Chaldeans of the book of Daniel (Dan 2:4-7:28). However, the term Chaldee has been abandoned.

This Babylonish Aramaean dialect supplanted the Hebrew, and became by degrees the prevailing language of the people, until in its turn was in some measure, though not entirely, supplanted by the Greek. It is commonly accepted that Jesus spoke Aramaic.

This was the language of Babylonia, and was acquired by the Jews during the exile, and carried back with them on their return to their own land.

Both Hebrew and Aramaic used the same alphabet, the one borrowed from the Phoenicians. The precise date of the invention of the alphabet is unknown, but it surely ranks as one of the most influential inventions in the history of humanity. This script quickly became adopted throughout the ancient Near East. It even served as the precursor of Greek, which in turn served as the model for Latin, the same alphabet we use today.

The Old Testament was written entirely in Hebrew, except for Gen 31:47; Ezra 4:8-6:18; Jeremiah 10:11; and Daniel 2:4-7:28, which were written in Aramaic. Scholars do not always agree why these texts are written in Aramaic instead of Hebrew. The basic reason seems to lie primarily with the language spoken by the audience originally being addressed by the biblical author. The author was in captivity in Babylonia.

Spoken from at least about 2000 BCE, Aramaic eventually replaced many of the languages of the ancient world in popularity and usage. Aramaic was the common language spoken in Palestine in the time of

---

[1] Ezra 2:1, 64-67; *1 Now these are the people of the province who came up out of the captivity of the exiles 64 The whole assembly numbered 42,360, 65 besides their male and female servants who numbered 7,337; and they had 200 singing men and women. 66 Their horses were 736; their mules, 245; 67 their camels, 435; their donkeys, 6,720.*

Prophets of the Restoration

Jesus. While the New Testament was written in the Greek language, the language, which Jesus spoke, was probably Aramaic.

    1.5.4.2. Second, they became a people of business owners and merchants. Before, they were farmers and shepherds. Since the Aramaic dialect was used in business, Daniel used it in a few comments (although I am at loss to understand why more was not used).

    1.5.4.3. Third, it seems that a definite single collection of God's Word began during this period. A number of writings are dated to this period and shows that a real desire existed to produce a "unified book."

    1.5.4.3.1. We believe that many Psalms were completed; 85, 102, 118, 126, 137, and the praise Psalms (146-150) were all collected during this period.

    1.5.4.3.2. Of course, we already stated that the books of Ezekiel and Daniel were completed and even 1 and 2 Kings are dated to this period.

    1.5.4.4. A fourth change during the Exile, the most important of all. During these years, there was a final break with idolatry! No more "there you go again."

    1.5.4.5. I've often thought this was perhaps the purpose of God in breaking apart His people, first into Israel and Judah, then allowing both to be taken away from the land; ten Northern tribes migrated northwest into Europe and two tribes alone for these seventy years, a generation.

    1.5.4.6. It is during this period that the Kingdom of God becomes universal with the Jews; and again let me emphasize, all twelve tribes were represented. The synagogue was established for the first time as a place of worship during the exile. Ezekiel had much to do with this.

2 Scripture turns to the last period of our Old Testament Travels, the three final prophetical books.

A Basic Outline of Haggai
1. Temple of God, 1:1-2:9
2. Blessings of God, 2:10-23

Depth of Bible Words and Locations
A Key Word in Haggai: *Signet Ring*

Found in 2:23, really two words in our English Bibles. We could think of this as affixing a seal or even "to seal up." When it was pressed into wax, the ring left the personal identification of the owner, the sender. Much more meaning than our ID badges. Haggai compared Zerubbabel to a signet ring. Zerubbabel restored or sealed the royal authority to the line of David.

> Jesus in Haggai...He is your Restorer

2.1. You recall, when the people returned to Jerusalem in 536 BCE, they had just one thought—get the Temple re-built. However, invaders had stopped them and quickly their attention turned to their own homes and businesses. Therefore, Haggai stirs them.[1] His total recorded ministry lasted four months--preaching four sermons over the period, and then disappeared from the record.

    2.1.1. Fifteen years into the rebuilding, Haggai comes on strong with his four messages. His reason for writing and preaching is clear.[2]

    2.1.2. The handful of people who had returned to Jerusalem had a colossal task before them of rebuilding the Temple. They started the work but lost the will to continue. They lost heart and became selfish (1:4). Poor crops, droughts, little trade, and turmoil resulted. Their joy was lost (1:6, 9-11).

    2.1.3. He preaches a message of priority. "Realize what you're doing, what's really being accomplished? Get back to building HIS House."

    2.1.4. Haggai, along side of Zechariah, joined with Zerubbabel who had led the first group back in 536 BCE, to resume the building. Haggai's message had a "quickening" effect, for the work began in less than one month. Haggai becomes God's mouthpiece for a message to Zerubbabel in an attempt to stir them to action. God informs them that the reason for their poor crops was their complacency.

    2.1.5. A second message is preached by Haggai about a month later. This was a great message of

---

[1] Haggai 1:2 *Thus says the Lord of hosts, 'This people says, "The time has not come, even the time for the house of the Lord to be rebuilt."*

[2] Haggai 1:5-6 *Now therefore, thus says the Lord of hosts, "Consider your ways! 6 "You have sown much, but harvest little; you eat, but there is not enough to be satisfied; you drink, but there is not enough to become drunk; you put on clothing, but no one is warm enough; and he who earns, earns wages to put into a purse with holes."*

Prophets of the Restoration: Zechariah

encouragement. Some thought the new Temple was too small, not enough glitter.[1] They remembered Solomon's great Temple. So Haggai offers them God's assurance in cp 2[2], and tells them not to lose heart.

2.1.6. The short book ends on an upbeat note, having linked the rebuilding of the Temple with a restoration of prosperity like that of David and Solomon.

2.2. Within two months after Haggai began to preach, Zechariah, ("Yahweh remembers") becomes an encourager to the Jews. Zechariah's ministry was a two-year period. The book is the longest of the "minor prophets," and a message urging the builders ON![3] The book of Zechariah was named after the writer. A very common name—at least 29 others of the same name in the Old Testament. Zechariah, like Jeremiah and Ezekiel before him, was both a prophet and a priest.

A Basic Outline of Zechariah
1. Eight Visions of Zechariah, Cps 1-6
2. Four Messages of Zechariah, Cps 7-8
3. Two Burdens of later writers, Cps 9-14

Depth of Bible Words and Locations
A Key Word in Zechariah: *Angel*

Found several times, 1:9; 2:3; 3:1, 5. *Angel, which* we looked at earlier in this Section.

The word could refer to angelic beings or human messengers. Both prophets and priests are mentioned as messengers from God, using this word. In Zechariah, angels

---

[1] Haggai 2:3-4 *'Who is left among you who saw this temple in its former glory? And how do you see it now? Does it not seem to you like nothing in comparison?"*

[2] Haggai 2:6-9 *"For thus says the Lord of hosts, 'Once more in a little while, I am going to shake the heavens and the earth, the sea also and the dry land. 7 'I will shake all the nations; and they will come with the wealth of all nations, and I will fill this house with glory,' says the Lord of hosts. 8 'The silver is Mine and the gold is Mine,' declares the Lord of hosts. 9 'The latter glory of this house will be greater than the former,' says the Lord of hosts, 'and in this place I will give peace,' declares the Lord of hosts.' "*

[3] Zechariah 1:16-17 *Therefore thus says the Lord, "I will return to Jerusalem with compassion; My house will be built in it," declares the Lord of hosts, "and a measuring line will be stretched over Jerusalem."' 17 "Again, proclaim, saying, 'Thus says the Lord of hosts, "My cities will again overflow with prosperity, and the Lord will again comfort Zion and again choose Jerusalem."*
Zechariah 2:5 *'For I,' declares the Lord, 'will be a wall of fire around her, and I will be the glory in her midst.'" 8 For thus says the Lord of hosts, "After glory He has sent me against the nations which plunder you, for he who touches you, touches the apple of His eye."*

bring revelations from God and interpret dreams and visions (1:14; 6:4, 5).

> *Jesus in Zechariah...He is the Reigning King.*

- 2.2.1. Haggai was the *practical* one, "you're not accomplishing much, let's get the Temple built!" His ministry was during a period of only four months.
- 2.2.2. But Zechariah was the *inspirational* one and ministered for several years.
- 2.2.2.1. Zechariah was a young prophet who stood alongside the aged Haggai and strengthened the Jews as they built the Temple. In fact, the book of Haggai and the first eight chapters of Zechariah should be read together because of the overlapping dates and similar themes.
- 2.2.2.1.1. Both center on Zerubbabel
- 2.2.2.1.2. Both lift up the priestly office
- 2.2.2.1.3. The rebuilding of the Temple is prerequisite to the receiving of the blessings of God
- 2.2.3. His first eight chapters record his side-by-side ministry with Haggai. His specific dated prophecies in the form of visions are situated in the Persian period, concerned with the rebuilding of the Temple.
- 2.2.4. The remaining six chapters are materials from a later period. They are set apart and form the second division of the book. In contrast to the first eight chapters, they have no identifiable prophecies, no night visions, and have a distinctive "flavor." They seem to have no organized structure, in contrast to chapters 1-8. This has led to a few scholars conclusion that chapters 9-14 were composed later by two additional authors. However, that theory was not given until 1653 CE.
- 2.2.5. After considerable research and prayer, the author of the work you are reading, has concluded that there is sufficient evidence to name Zechariah the author of the entire book.
- 2.2.5.1. The differences in style and material may be accounted for under close examination.
- 2.2.5.1.1. The author was a much older prophet, writing the two *oracles* (cps 9-14) concerning revelation of future events.

Prophets of the Restoration: Zechariah

2.2.5.1.2. There is no evidence that cps 9-14 ever existed except in the single book of Zechariah.

2.2.5.1.3. Similar rare expressions are found in both cps 1-8 and 9-14. For example, many references to "saith the Lord," 10:12, 12:1, and 13:2. The uncommon term "remove" or "cut off" is found in 3:4 and 13:2, strongly suggesting the same writer.

Haggai	520 BCE
Zechariah 1-8	520-518
Zechariah 9-11	c. 480-
Zechariah 12-14	c. 470
Malachi	c. 450

2.2.6. Zechariah was a member of the Great Synagogue, 120 members started by Nehemiah. This group developed into the Sanhedrin referred to in the New Testament. Zechariah came to Jerusalem with Zerubbabel. The first words date the book to 520 BCE the same as Haggai.

2.2.7. Zechariah was murdered near the temple, similar to Haggai who had been stoned to death shortly before.

2.2.8. The books of Zechariah and Haggai are like comparing a factual, straightforward commentary writer such as Matthew Henry, with Max Lucado a more poetical writer. Both were, and are still, needed.

2.2.9. Zechariah's messages are unusual, being delivered to him by an angel in conversations. The first six cps are a record of eight visions, all received in a single night! He saw with both the physical eye and with an inner vision under the Holy Spirit's inspiration. (Read about him falling asleep and the angel awakening him to continue). So much to receive in the same night! All eight of these visions span the centuries and accept the Jewish hope concerning the restoration of the Kingdom to Israel when Christ returns.

2.2.10. Zechariah pointed them to Christ, with his message, a message still glowing for us today.[1]

2.2.11. Zechariah is a beacon of hope for all of us. He represents the work of building God's spiritual house.[2]

---

[1] Zechariah 14:9 *And the Lord will be king over all the earth; in that day the Lord will be the only one, and His name the only one.*

[2] Zechariah 4:6 *Then he said to me, "This is the word of the Lord to Zerubbabel saying,*

2.2.12. He tells each of us in our day, The real builder is the Branch, Christ[1]

2.2.12.1. The first six chapters are filled with imagery, but great meaning.[2] His **eight** visions:

2.2.12.1.1. *Angelic Horsemen*, (1:8-17), watching over the earth, and nations of the earth. The red horse's rider is the presence of God, the Lord Himself. The myrtle trees are a beautiful symbol of Israel, an eternally elect nation and the object of His grace. The vision foresaw the suffering and humiliation during the extended period of Gentile rule. The question asked *"How long"* could be asked today, (for the times of the Gentile rule still remains). Read of the intensity of the Lord's passion as He cried out (1:15) *But I am very angry with the nations who are at ease* displaying His displeasure with the nations who are secure in themselves and not in Him. The return of Christ is a comforting word (1:16) *I will return to Jerusalem with compassion; My house will be built in it.*

Depth of Bible Words and Locations
Myrtle
Found in Isa 41:19; 55:13; Neh 8:15. A lovely indigenous shrub with dark green, scented leaves, star like flowers, and edible, dark-colored berries. Isaiah referred to the myrtle as one of the choice plants of the land during the future Kingdom.

Myrtle branches were used in constructing booths for the Feast of Tabernacles, the great feast remembering Israel's redemption out of Egypt (Lev 23:43).

The myrtle trees were seen in *the ravine* perhaps a display of Israel's "hidden condition" during the time of Gentiles and before the coming of Christ.

2.2.12.1.2. *Horns and craftsmen*, (1:18-21), show Israel (both nations) overthrown by four nations. The *four horns* are revealed in verse 1:19.[3] They are the four great powers of the times of the

---

'Not by might nor by power, but by My Spirit,' says the Lord of hosts...
[1] Zechariah 6:12-13 *"Then say to him, 'Thus says the Lord of hosts, "Behold, a man whose name is Branch, for He will branch out from where He is; and He will build the temple of the Lord. 13 "Yes, it is He who will build the temple of the Lord, and He who will bear the honor and sit and rule on His throne...." "*
[2] Zechariah 1:8 *I saw at night,* 2:1 *Then I lifted up my eyes and looked,*
He was wide-eyed! No sleeping (as a dream), only seeing.
[3] *These are the horns which have scattered Judah so that no man lifts up his head; but these craftsmen have come to terrify them, to throw down the horns of the nations who have lifted up their horns against the land of Judah in order to scatter it.*

Prophets of the Restoration: Zechariah

Gentiles (Dan 2:37-45)—Babylon, Medo-Persian, Greece, and Rome. The *craftsmen* were sent to punish the great powers. Therefore, we interpret the first horn as Babylon, cast down by Medo-Persia, the second horn. Accordingly, the second horn, Medo-Persia, in turn, became the first craftsman. The second horn, Medo-Persia, was cast down by the third horn, Greece, which thus became the second craftsman. The third horn, Greece, was in turn cast down by the fourth horn, Rome, which became the third craftsman. The fourth horn, Rome, the most dreadful of all, will not become a craftsman, for it will not be cast down. Instead, in its revived ten-kingdom form of the last days of Gentile world dominance, it will be destroyed by the fourth craftsman, which will be the millennial Kingdom set up by the Messiah at His coming. The fourth craftsman corresponds to Daniel's *great mountain* which will fill the earth. Daniel also "saw" a fourth beast (Dan 7:7) *terrible, powerful and dreadful, and exceedingly strong. And it had great iron teeth; it devoured and crushed and trampled what was left with its feet. And it was different from all the beasts that came before it, and it had ten horns.*

2.2.12.1.3.   *The Surveyor and Measuring line*, (2:1-13), both the current rebuilding and the future building of a great city in a prosperous Jerusalem. Jesus will be in the future city. *Another angel* is perhaps assisting the *angel of the Lord*, Christ. The message included good news for Zechariah and the others present in Jerusalem. They were struggling to rebuild the city. The message offered five promises of immediate encouragement as well as future hope. (1) Jerusalem will greatly expand with population and spiritual growth. (2) Jerusalem will experience divine protection and glory (3) future destruction of ecclesiastical and commercial systems of Babylon and the world system--so flee! (4) the nations against Israel will be judged and punished (5) the earth will be prepared for the future full Kingdom blessing.

2.2.12.1.4.   Joshua's (representing Israel) *filthy clothing*, (cp 3), removed and replaced by the Branch. A sinful people will only experience the mercy and righteousness of the Lord. The state of Israel is represented by Joshua. Joshua (the High Priest at the time of Zechariah) is pictured standing before *the Lord* (Christ) with Satan there accusing hm. The Lord responds (3:2) *The Lord rebuke you, Satan!*—showing Satan is a reality.[1] The encouragement from the Lord represents hope for anyone: *Remove the filthy garments from him. Again he said to him, "See, I have taken your iniquity away from you and will clothe you with festal robes."* This vision also foretells of a restored Israel under the branch *I am going to bring in My servant the Branch.*

2.2.12.1.5. *Golden Lampstand* and olive trees, (4:1-14), the Holy Spirit anointed nation of the future millennium period. Israel will be restored (explained in vision four), followed by her witness to the world in vision five. Notice Zechariah was awakened by the "assisting angel." He probably was exhausted from the four previous detailed visions. Zechariah did not understand the endless supply of the oil-Spirit. The *bowl, spouts* and *trees* indicate the fullness of the Holy Spirit thrusting forth a future redeemed Israel (Joel 2:28-32). Eight promises of encouragement were given in this vision. (1) The Temple would be completed by the Spirit of the Lord (His power) (2) Every obstacle will be removed (3) The Temple will joyfully be completed (4) The Temple will be completed quickly (5) Confidence that the Lord is in charge (6) Critics will be silenced (7) Joy in seeing it be built (8) God's presence will encircle the globe.

2.2.12.1.6. *Flying scroll*, God's Word (5:1-4), terrible nations cursed by God. It is again recorded of Zechariah I *lifted up my eye.* The scroll was *flying,* completely unwound and inscribed on both sides. It was approximately thirty feet long and fifteen feet wide. The roll represented God's curse against all sinners. *This is the curse that is going forth over the face of the whole land.*

2.2.12.1.7. *The woman and the Ephah,* (5:5-11). Wickedness itself is removed from the entire earth during the Millennium described in these verses. We learn from Exodus 16:36 that an ephah was a dry measurement container, which could hold approximately one bushel. In this vision, the container represented the extensive sin in the land. The woman, pictured in the container, is a personified wickedness. The final moments of this vision are concerned with the removal of wickedness before the Kingdom blessing comes. John the revelator refers to the woman and the ephah in Rev 18 and 19.

---

[1] Zechariah 3:1 *Then he showed me Joshua the high priest standing before the angel of the Lord, and Satan standing at his right hand to accuse him.*

Prophets of the Restoration: Zechariah

2.2.12.1.8. *Four chariots*, (cp 6:1-8), angels administering justice and righteousness. The last of the eight visions is connected with the first vision. The first vision found the nations lacking the condition of turmoil to which His restoration would take place. They were in a current state of relaxation and contentment. This final vision is introduced by the emphatic *and behold* with a focus on the four vehicles of divine judgment upon the nations. They will come from *between the two mountains*. The mountains likely are Mount Zion and Mount Olivet, since they are the heart of the Jewish homeland. Notice the use of chariots and their horses. They are connected to Daniel's four empires and the four horsemen of the Apocalypse. *Red* symbolizes war and bloodshed (Rev 6:4), *black* symbolizes famine and death (Rev 6:5-6), *white*, victory (Rev 6:2), and *dappled* (Rev 6:7) symbolize death from various sources. The prophet requested and immediately received an explanation. The chariots represented four angels going forth to the land. The horses symbolize the four judgments, performed by the angels.

2.2.12.2. Following the eight visions, a picture is offered concerning Christ who will build the final Temple. This *man* is referred to in several Scriptures as *behold the man, the Branch, the last Adam,* and *the second man*. He will rule and be a Priest, upon His throne. He will produce peace in a perfect Millennium and bind together both Jew and Gentile.

2.3. Cps 9-14 the last six cps of Zechariah were written at a later period— Zechariah was an elderly man when this second division of his book was penned. We read, again and again, references to Christ.

        2.3.1.   Comes on a donkey, 9:9-10
        2.3.2.   Betrayed for 30 pieces of silver, 11:12-13
        2.3.3.   Piercing of Christ, 12:10
        2.3.4.   Wounding of Christ, 13:1,6,7
        2.3.5.   In fact, next to Isaiah, he is considered the most important messenger of Christ in the Old Testament. Only Isaiah had more passages concerning Christ. We have many prophecies here. We will not read them but you can refer to them in 11:12-13; 12:10; 13:1, 6 and 14:2, 4.
        2.3.6.   Perhaps the most striking of all is in cp. 9.

9 Rejoice greatly, O daughter of Zion!
Shout in triumph, O daughter of Jerusalem!
Behold, your king is coming to you;
He is just and endowed with salvation,

Humble, and mounted on a donkey,
Even on a colt, the foal of a donkey.
10 I will cut off the chariot from Ephraim
And the horse from Jerusalem;
And the bow of war will be cut off.
And He will speak peace to the nations;
And His dominion will be from sea to sea,
And from the River to the ends of the earth.

2.3.7. This final division of cps 9-14 contains two oracles that look forward to the return of Christ and establishment of His Kingdom.

Depth of Bible Words and Locations
Oracle

The Hebrew word *massa* has a meaning of "to bear" or "to lift up." In our study, it appears as a heading above Zechariah 9:1 and 12:1 in several translations. The word is most likely used by the prophet to be an encouragement or "to lift up." It is used this way in Num 23:7; 24:3, 15-16. In the context of Zechariah, the two oracles are primarily promises of salvation. Some translations have "burden." (NKJV, NASU, ESV). The AMP uses both *THE BURDEN or oracle (the thing to be lifted up)*.

2.3.7.1. The first message in cps 9-11 pictures the conquests of Alexander the Great in contrast to that of the Messiah's future world rule of peace. Tyre is the example used by Zechariah. The island stronghold town was constructed off the mainland. A citadel of defense, which withstood a five-year siege by the Assyrians under Shalmaneser V and, years later, a thirteen-year siege by Babylonia, under Nebuchadnezzar.

2.3.7.2. Tyre is described with words such as *"a fortress," "piled up," "silver," "gold,"* and *"wealth."* A dramatic fulfillment of her destruction is announced by *Behold* in verse 1:4. The Lord judged the city, using Alexander as the human cause of the destruction. Alexander was on a march to expand a kingdom—following Tyre, three of the five principal Philistine cities states were mentioned next in his path Ashkelon Gaza, and Ekron, (Ashdod and Gath are not mentioned). Interesting, Alexander passed by Jerusalem in his quest, without laying siege to it, for God said in verse 9:8 *I will camp around My house.*

Depth of Bible Words and Locations
Tyre

A fortified Phoenician city located on the Mediterranean coast. It sent its ships all over the world, founding the city of Carthage in northern Africa. Jezebel was from here. Assyria conquered the city, later came under the domination of Persia. Ezekiel wrote his prophecy against Tyre (Ezekiel 26). Nebuchadnezzar turned against the city following his destruction of Jerusalem. Alexander the Great invaded the Persian Empire in 332 BCE, destroying the fleet of ships of Persia. He almost destroyed the city along with the mainland section and the island offshore, ½ mile away.

Depth of Bible Words and Locations
Philistine City-States

According to the Bible, the Philistines ruled the five city-states (the "Philistine Pentapolis") of Gaza, Askelon, Ashdod, Ekron, and Gath, from the Wadi Gaza in the south to the Yarqon River in the north, but with no fixed border to the east. The Bible paints them as the Kingdom of Israel's most dangerous enemy.

2.3.7.3. The Messiah will come to establish peace, in contrast to Alexander. A restoration will include:
2.3.7.3.1. The Messiah/deliverer coming on a donkey
2.3.7.3.2. A renewal of covenant relationship
2.3.7.3.3. Removal of all idolatry
2.3.7.3.4. However, Israel will reject their shepherd/king and follow another shepherd leader. Christ will be betrayed for thirty pieces of silver.
2.3.7.4. The second heavy message of cps 12-14 pictures a future war of all the nations against God.[1] God will be victorious and destroy the nations. Israel will recognize the One they pierced—they repent and are cleansed.[2] Israel's future military triumph is described in 12:6-7 using the words *a firepot among pieces of wood and a flaming torch among sheaves*
2.3.7.4.1. Chapter 14 pictures the victorious return of the Messiah as the divine King. A final attack on Jerusalem shows the Lord

---

[1] Zechariah 12:9 *And in that day I will set about to destroy all the nations that come against Jerusalem.*
14:2 *For I will gather all the nations against Jerusalem to battle,*
[2] Zechariah 12:9 *"I will pour out on the house of David and on the inhabitants of Jerusalem, the Spirit of grace and of supplication, so that they will look on Me whom they have pierced; and they will mourn for Him, as one mourns for an only son..."*

standing on the Mount of Olives. In chapter 14, we also have a description of the **Day of the Lord** when all nations gather against Jerusalem to do battle. The Gentiles will at first obtain an initial but fleeting taste of victory in Jerusalem (14:2). Half of the population will be left. However, the personal appearance of the Messiah, His feet will *stand on the Mount of Olives,* [1] will end the battle. He returns and all the holy ones with Him.

    2.3.8. The concluding images of Zechariah are those of peace, joy, prosperity, and the reign of the Lord over the entire world![2]

3 Then we arrive at Malachi the last in the group of twelve Minor Prophets and final Prophet in the Old Testament. Immediately we view the book as an Oracle (1:1; also, refer to comments on Zech 9:1 and 12:1). He delivers the final words of the Old Testament, 100 years following Haggai and Zechariah's message. Malachi is the "Holiness Preacher." His name means "my messenger." Indeed this last book of the Old Testament is *from* a messenger of God, predicting a *coming* messenger of God.

3.1. Again, as we've seen before, this book is named from it's author. We are told nothing about the prophet elsewhere in the Old Testament, however, we learn he was a devout Jew in post-exilic Judah and contemporary of Nehemiah.

3.2. With this book, God closes the Old Testament canon. The Jews identify Malachi as a member of the Great Synagogue.

3.3. The evidence inside the book, date it around the time that Nehemiah returned from his trip to Persia, 424 BCE.

A Basic Outline of Malachi
1. Past Privilege of Israel, 1:1-5
2. Present Promise to Israel, 1:6-3:15
3. Future Promise to Israel, 3:16-4:6

Depth of Bible Words and Locations
A Key Word in Malachi: *Try*

---

[1] Zechariah 14:3-4 *Then the Lord will go forth and fight against those nations, as when He fights on a day of battle.* 4 *In that day His feet will stand on the Mount of Olives,*

[2] Zechariah 14:9 *And the Lord will be king over all the earth; in that day the Lord will be the only one, and His name the only one.*

Prophets of the Restoration: Malachi

A Hebrew word meaning "to put to the test." When God uses the word in connection with His people, it means a proving in such a way that they become stronger, more established. Malachi challenged the Israelites to "try" God to test His faithfulness. It's also found in Genesis 42:15, 16; and Psalms 26:2

Jesus in Malachi...He's the Son of Righteousness with healing in His Wings!

3.4. It was a time of indifference to spiritual matters. Life was not easy. The Jews were under the political dominion of Persia. The Persian title *governor* is used in 1:8 as well as Ezra 5:3, 16, and 14. The walls had been rebuilt; the Temple now again was a place of worship. However, after these 100 years, the excitement of the new Temple and city had worn off. Where was the anticipated revival that Haggai foresaw? Houses had been reconstructed, the wall rebuilt. Most hearts were indifferent toward God. The priests and the people were violating the Mosaic Law regarding sacrifices, tithes, and offerings. Hope had dimmed. Malachi addressed this downfall. Many people were just skeptical because they had been home for 100 years, they thought the messages of Ezekiel and Zechariah were immediate. It is a series of the people's responses to those statements from God. The format is one of question and answer.
        3.4.1.   Where is this kingdom of peace?
        3.4.2.   Where is the One to rule and reign in the Temple?
        3.4.3.   I can understand how they felt.

3.5. So, they became cynical, even the priests were immoral, lazy in their duties; they offered *blind* and *lame* animals for sacrifice, rather than the best, the perfect. Seven times you find the people saying "How? How does this happen? Prove it." God shows His ongoing love throughout. Malachi's answer was decisive and clear. God was not being honored. This truth had to be taught. Those who were encouraged realized God had a book with individual names of those who honor Him. He loves the individual as a son.

3.6. With this in mind, Malachi begins with a declaration of God's love for Israel—*"I have loved you," says the Lord.* In contrast to God's love was the response of the people. They believed that because the Lord had chastised and afflicted them, He did not love them. In his book, Malachi wrote concerning six sins of the priests and people, six sins in ancient history AND in our day.
        3.6.1.   The priest's questioned God's love, 1:1-5
        3.6.2.   The priest's dishonored God's name 1:6-2:9

- 3.6.3. The people did not follow God's commands 2:10-16
- 3.6.4. The people questioned God's justice 2:17-3:6
- 3.6.5. The people robbed God's storehouse 3:7-12
- 3.6.6. The people complained about God's ways 3:13-4:6

3.7. Malachi's message is in a different presentation than other prophets. Malachi seems to take comments he heard and questions being asked, and answers each one. That is the design and method of his book.

- 3.7.1. He rebuked and condemned the abuses of the people who 100 years after their return from Babylon, had grown to disrespect God's love for them. We see again, God's people begin to fall away, lazy in serving God.
- 3.7.2. In all the answering of questions, he maintains a single standard of holiness in one's daily walk and attitude toward God.
- 3.7.3. Malachi refers to the two nations that sprang from Jacob and Esau. Both were destroyed by the Babylonians—only Judah was restored.[1]
- 3.7.4. Four times he speaks of the future *day of the Lord*[2]
- 3.7.5. Tragically, the priests disgraced God's name. Malachi addresses this in 1:11-14. A world-wide honoring of His name is foreseen, when all people in the future Kingdom will offer prayers to Him.

3.8. In chapter 2, the Lord continued His words to the priests, warning them of their spiritual relationship. In addition, the people are warned concerning their state of unfaithfulness. Malachi preaches about the matter of mixed marriages, which broke their covenant with God.

3.9. Chapter 3 is connected with 2:17 and reveals the judgment to come because of the unfaithfulness of the people in refusing God's love. *Behold, I am going to send My messenger, and he will clear the way before Me.* The speaker is the Messiah announcing John the Baptist, fulfilled by Matthew 11:10. Isaiah already announced him years before (Isa 40:3), *A voice is calling,"Clear the way for the Lord in the*

---

[1] Israel and Edom
[2] 1:11, 3:1-6, 16-18, and 4:1-6

Prophets of the Restoration: Malachi

wilderness." And the Lord (a young Jesus) *will suddenly come to His temple* (Mal 3:1).

3.10. He closes with a future day when Christ will come and cleanse the people from all sin. The last two lines in Malachi are considered by many to be later additions. The final Section of this course **will review the** 400 years of divine silence, which follow. Malachi's words will ring condemnation in their ears during those years. No direct message from God for 400 years!

    3.10.1. His final words included:
    3.10.2. A reminder to keep the Law of Moses
    3.10.3. A prophecy of John the Baptist. The next voice you hear will be John's
    3.10.4. The love of God, like a parent for children
    3.10.5. A cursed world if He does not come back
    3.10.6. We then read the first words of the New Testament in Matt 1:1 *The record of the genealogy of Jesus the Messiah, the son of David, the son of Abraham.*

3.10.6.1. He DID come.
3.10.6.2. His message was "Repent, for the Kingdom of heaven is at hand." And Jesus begins with a sermon on a mountaintop, about that kingdom which you and I live in.

    3.10.7. The last word in the Old Testament is *curse.* In our *travels,* we saw the original curse which resulted from Adam and Eve. That curse, sin, will not be totally removed until Christ returns. Until then, we can ask Him, to forgive our individual sins and give us His righteousness.

SECTION 9
Between the Old and New Testaments

Jewish Apocryphal and Pseudepigraphical writings, work of Flavius Josephus, the Dead Sea Manuscripts, and other historical records

Theme Statement: *"Behold, a people who dwells apart, And will not be reckoned among the nations.* (Num 23:9)

FIFTEEN

Silence

1. The Old Testament closed with relatively few Jews living in the land that was promised by God. At the close of the Old Testament period and the record of Malachi (*c.* 425 BCE), Judea had been a province of Persia for at least 140 years. Many Jews were scattered throughout the 128 provinces of the Persian Empire (see later comments on the dispersion). Ironside notes a foretaste of what would come, *"Malachi is witness that people may be separated from outside evils and not be separated to the Lord."*[1]
    1.1. Let's compare some differences from the time of Malachi with the time of the Gospels.[2]
        1.1.1. In the days of Malachi, the population was scanty; the cities were heaps of rubbish; the land everywhere bore the marks of long desolation; the poverty of the many was aggravated by the rapacity of the few. Within the temple, the line of priests was worshipping and carrying on the sacrifices established by the Law of Moses. The priestly line could be traced back to Aaron. The re built Temple is still the center of Jewish worship, however, many synagogues have been established and became the focal point, more than the temple.
        1.1.2. On the other hand, in early New Testament days, Palestine appears as one of the most densely populated parts of the Roman Empire. The merchants of Palestine share in and largely control the trade of the Mediterranean world. A king is now on the throne, a descendent of Esau rather than Jacob. The priests were religious figures, no longer in the accepted line of Aaron.

---

[1] H. A. Ironside, *The 400 Silent Years*, Loizeaux Brothers, New York, 1914, p. 9
[2] Raymond F. Surburg, *Introduction to the Intertestamental Period*, Concordia Publishing House, St. Louis, 1975, p. 10

1.1.3. Greek is universally used throughout the Roman Empire as the language of the New Testament. Aramaic replaces Hebrew as a spoken language. Hebrew became a dead language following the return to Palestine. At the end of the Old Testament period, Aramaic had become the language of the Persian Empire.
2. The period between the Old Testament and the New Testament began with the completion of the Book of Malachi and continued until the angel's announcement of the birth of John the Baptist (Luke 1:11-17), approximately 400 years.
   2.1. From our perspective of time, four centuries is a long....long time. Entire nations, civilizations rise and fall and are forgotten in less time than that. Some call this the "Intertestamental Period" because it is the time between the writing of the Old and New Testaments.
   2.2. It is also referred to as "The Silent Years" or "Silent Centuries." It does not mean there was an absence of Hebrew history written. In fact, a body of literature was produced that came to be called "the Apocrypha," from the Greek *apokryphos* meaning "hidden."
      2.2.1. The Biblical Apocrypha ("meaning "hidden") denotes the collection of ancient books found, in some editions of the Bible, in a separate section between the Old and New Testaments. All Apocryphal **books** are in Greek, except one, which is extant only in Latin. With the one exception, all of these books are considered "Old Testament."
      2.2.2. None was in the Hebrew-written Bible and none of the apocryphal writers laid claim to inspiration. The apocryphal **books** were never acknowledged as sacred scriptures by the Jews, custodians of the Hebrew Scriptures (the **Apocrypha** was written prior to the New Testament).
      2.2.3. For a time in the earliest centuries of the Christian church, these books of the *Apocrypha* were accepted as Scripture by some, especially in the Greek translation of the Old Testament, the Septuagint. The Septuagint also includes fifteen books that are not part of the Hebrew canon, all written following the standard Hebrew collection.
   2.3. The Septuagint was translated from the Hebrew because the emphasis was placed on using the Greek language from 330 BCE. The Jews, who had been scattered, became predominately Greek-speakers.
      2.3.1. According to Jewish legend, in 250 BCE, Ptolemy Philadelphus brought together seventy-two scholars who translated the Old Testament into Greek in seventy-two days. Thus, the Latin word for *seventy,* "Septuagint" (LXX), was the

Silence

name attached to this translation. Translated in Alexandria, Egypt, the Septuagint was the most important and widely used Greek translation of the Old Testament.

2.3.2. However, when Saint Jerome translated the Septuagint into Latin for the Vulgate in the fifth century CE, he expressed doubts about the validity of the Apocryphal books. These books were excluded from the KJV of 1611 CE, never included in the Old Testament of the Hebrew Christians, and never accepted by Calvin or Luther. They do not fit into the themes of God's Word but do make for interesting reading and historical information.

2.4. Though the voice of God was silent, the hand of God was actively directing the course of events during these four centuries, as Daniel saw in his vision of future events.

3 My endeavor in Section 9 is to trace the history of a chosen people following their return from captivity in Persia. What happened during these four hundred years? Most believers know little about these four centuries. The political and religious history of the four centuries between the Old and New Testaments should be considered by every Bible student. The developments during these centuries greatly influenced the atmosphere into which Jesus Christ entered.

3.1. Many Bible readers end their study with the prophetic records of Zephaniah and Malachi. Others stop much earlier at the wonderful Scripture record of Isaiah. Little is written about the four hundred years of silence following the Old Testament and few readers are familiar with the details of that period.

3.2. This author's information is drawn from the volumes including H.A. Ironside's "The 400 Silent Years,"[1] and Raymond F. Surburg's "Introduction to the Intertestamental Period."[2] In addition, materials are drawn from the study of Josephus' work and books of the Apocrypha (1 and 2 Maccabees in particular).

Final Years of the Old Testament

1 Nehemiah's passion and driving force attempted to establish a covenant relationship between God and His people. He directed his efforts to encourage, almost demanding, a holy separation between the Hebrews and the nations surrounding them. We have

---

[1] H. A. Ironside, *The 400 Silent Years*, Loizeaux Brothers, NY, 1914
[2] Raymond F. Surburg, *Introduction to the Intertestamental Period*, Concordia Publishing House, St. Louis, 1909

encountered this theme at various times in the two volumes of *Travel Through the Old Testament*.

1.1. I am reminded of the theme of this Section from Numbers 23:9 *Behold, a people who dwells apart, And will not be reckoned among the nations.*

1.2. The sacred history of the Chosen People ends chronologically with Nehemiah's prayer: "Remember me, O my God, for good." Ben Sira composed his work "Wisdom of Ben Sira" in Jerusalem about 190 BCE, concluding with Nehemiah's name "glorious in his memory." Therefore, even before the later Maccabean revolt (165–63 BCE), the Jews recognized that after Nehemiah and his contemporary prophets, that is, toward the end of the fifth century, in the age of Socrates, the p*ost-biblical period* of Jewish history begins, the subject of this Section.

1.3. When Jerusalem was conquered (597 B.C.E.) and, later (586), destroyed by the Babylonians, the court, the warriors, and the craftsmen were transferred to Mesopotamia. The captivity had created numerous Jewish settlements in Mesopotamia. A Babylonian historian recorded "King Nebuchadnezzar assigned places in the most convenient district of Babylonia."

2   In 538 BCE, as previously noted in this volume, in fulfillment of the prophecy of Jeremiah[1], the Jews were given permission by Cyrus to return to their native land. Ezra and Nehemiah recorded the three returns to Palestine by the Jews.

2.1. Eventually, it is estimated that 30-50,000 people made the return trip over a period of time. We would note that many chose to remain in Babylonia. These remaining exiles can be regarded as the nucleus of the permanent Jewish settlements that gradually expanded from the center to the provinces. Today, the number of Jews has dipped to below 9,000, who are committed to remaining in Iran.

2.2. Persia continued domination of those returning to Jerusalem and the surrounding territories. However, under the leadership of Ezra and Nehemiah, the returning Jews enjoyed some measure of independence. It was Ezra who restored the Law of Moses. Ezra arrived in Jerusalem as a Persian representative, with a royal letter placing "the Law of God" on the same demanding level as the law of the king.

2.2.1.   There was no established governing body, only that of the retuning 4,229 priests.[2] At this time, the High Priest crossed

---

[1] Jer
[2] Ezra 2:2-67

Silence

over to political rule. Previously a High Priest was "only" a religious leader. The Persians allowed the priests to have governmental control of the land.

3   The period of approximately 400 years includes six historical divisions.
   3.1. The Persian Era, which actually dates back to 536 BCE AND continues through 336 BCE
   3.2. The Greek Era (336–323 BCE)
   3.3. The Egyptian Era (323–198)
   3.4. The Syrian Era (198–165)
   3.5. The Maccabean Era (165–63)
   3.6. The Roman Era (63–4)
      3.6.1.   God was in "preparation" during the 400 years, for a specific time. God moved around the nations of history so that when a second Elijah came on the scene, we view an entirely different earth of nations. "The fullness of time." God had the nations ready for His plan. The time to redeem a people. Gal 4:4-6 *But when the fullness of the time came, God sent forth His Son, born of a woman, born under the Law, 5 so that He might redeem those who were under the Law, that we might receive the adoption as sons.*

4   An overview of the six periods will show the time of preparation.
   4.1. **The Persian Era (536–336 BCE)**
      4.1.1.   We know the Persians dominated the Middle East from approximately 536 BCE. They were used by God to deliver Israel from the Babylonian captivity (Daniel 5:30–31). The Jewish people seemed to be accepted by the Persians during most of this period. Daniel pictured the rise of a bear who was higher on one side than the other, signifying the division between Media and Persia, with the Persians predominant[1]
      4.1.2.   A partial destruction of Jerusalem took place because of a rivalry over the office of high priest and the Persian governor, who were both powerful political figures. During this period, Jerusalem and a strip of land around it formed a small district of Judea (Yehud). The district of Judea was about thirty-five miles long, from Bethel to Bethzur, and about thirty miles broad, the plateau between the Dead Sea and the lowland in the west. A good part of the one thousand square miles was a desert.

Depth of Bible Words and Locations
Bethzur

---
[1] Dan 7:5

Found in 2 Chron 11:7 and Nehemiah 3:16. Located a few miles south of Jerusalem, near Hebron. The Greeks later called the town Betsoura during its peak of prosperity in the Hellenistic period. In 164 BCE, during the Maccabean wars, the Battle of Beth-Zur was fought there. The battle was the confrontation between the Seleucid Greek general Lysias and the Maccabees, led by Judas Maccabeus, resulting in the defeat of Lysias and his forces. This victory was followed by the recapture of Jerusalem by the Maccabees. The site's importance lay in its strategic location on a hilltop. Josephus describes Beth-Zur as the mightiest stronghold in Judea.

4.1.3. Very little of the political history of Judea during this era is known, mostly recorded through the history of the High Priest (see later notes). The Jews were represented by "nobles" or heads of the clans. The Jews were first of all peoples we know to open wide the gates to *proselytes to join them, to seek the Lord God of Israel* (Ezra 6:21).

4.1.4. The Persian Empire fell in 333 when Alexander the Great proceeded down the coast of Syria toward Egypt.

4.2. **The Greek Era (336–323 BCE)**

4.2.1. This was a rather brief period. Philip of Macedon, the father of Alexander the Great, highly esteemed Greek culture. Alexander ascended the throne of his father at a young age, determined to continue his father's vision of the expansion of Greek ideals.

4.2.2. Alexander left Europe for Asia in 334, and never returned to Macedonia. He met a great Persian army of 600,000 under the command of Darius III. The Persian army was several times as large as Alexander's, but the Persians were put to flight and their defeat in 333 marked the beginning of the downfall of the great Persian Empire.

4.2.3. Alexander's invasion of Palestine in 332 BCE was during his great campaign to rule the world. He did treat the Jews with respect, allowing them to maintain Jerusalem. He accepted the Jews among the citizens of the new settlements founded in the East. According to Josephus, the Jews were given equal status with the Greeks. It is told that Alexander had a vision as he approached Jerusalem, of an old man robed in a white garment, who would meet him and show him events of great significance to himself. He was met by the high priest who opened the prophecies of Daniel and read them to Alexander. Alexander realized he was the goat with the horn in his forehead that would smash the power of Medio-Persia and conquer the world.

Silence

4.2.4. Physical training was the foundation of Greek life, and through the palaestra, by way of sports, the Jewish settlers became recognized members of Greek communities. After Alexander the Great conquered the Persian Empire, Greek princes and generals wrestled for the right to govern the Near East.

4.2.5. Alexander the Great conquered Persia, Babylon, Palestine, Syria, Egypt, and western India in what we would consider a very quick and powerful campaign. His invasion of Egypt was welcomed by the Egyptians, who hated the Persians. Alexander was proclaimed as the son of Pharaoh. He founded the City of Alexandra in 331, supervising its construction, settling many Jews in the city.

4.2.6. In 323, Alexander reached Babylon with an army that marched from India, traversing a land no European had ever penetrated. In the same year, Alexander the Great having determined his next conquests would be Arabia, Africa, and Western Europe, died of a fever at the age of thirty-three having reigned over Greece only thirteen years. Perhaps his most important act was the dispersion of Jews. No other person in history has been claimed in legends by so many different nations.

Depth of Bible Words and Locations
Macedonia

The earliest kingdom of Macedonia was centered on the northeastern part of the Greek peninsula. Before the 4th century BCE, Macedonia was a small kingdom outside the areas dominated by the great city-states of Athens, Sparta, and Thebes.

The reign of Philip II (359–336 BC) saw the rise of Macedonia, during which the kingdom rose to control the entire Greek world. Philip II's son Alexander the Great continued his effort to command the whole of Greece by leading a federation of Greek states, a feat he finally accomplished after destroying Thebes for their insurrection.

The name Macedonia comes from the Greek meaning "tall," possibly descriptive of the people.

4.3. The Egyptian Era (323–198 BCE)

4.3.1. Alexander left no heir to rule in his place. His son had been murdered earlier. A number of relatives of Alexander hoped to be the successor to rule his empire. Before his burial, the relatives battled for his kingdom.

4.3.2. Following the death of Alexander in 323 BCE, his four generals, Ptolemy, Lysimachus, Cassander, and Seleucus contested and divided the kingdom into various territories. These were Daniel's "four kingdoms" that took the place of the "large horn" (Daniel 8:21–22). As we will see, Ptolemy and Seleucus were the two that we are concerned with in connection to Palestine.

    4.3.2.1.   To Ptolemy, Egypt and northern Africa were assigned

    4.3.2.2.   To Lysimachus, Syria

    4.3.2.3.   To Cassander, Greece

    4.3.2.4.   To Seleucus Nicator, Babylon

4.3.3.   Ptolemy Soter, the first of the Ptolemaic dynasty, ruled Egypt and soon dominated nearby Israel. Josephus in Book XII of Jewish Antiquities, records:

> And this king seized Jerusalem resorting to cunning and deceit. For he entered the city on the Sabbath as If to sacrifice, and as the Jews did not oppose him for they did not suspect any hostile act and because of their lack of suspicion and the nature of the day, were enjoying idleness and ease. He became master of the city without difficulty and ruled it harshly. This account is attested to by another historian: "There is a nation called Jews who have a strong and a great city called Jerusalem which they allowed to fall into the hands of Ptolemy by refusing to take up arms and instead through, their untimely superstition submitted to having a hard master."

4.3.4.   He dealt severely with the Jews at first, but toward the end of his reign and into the rule of Ptolemy Philadelphus, his successor, the Jews were treated favorably. In 200, the Jewish militia helped Antiochus III of Asia to remove the Egyptians from Jerusalem. The restored nation of Israel had serious political unrest during this time. The High Priest was the political head. Also during this period, the Septuagint was authorized and completed in Egypt.

The Ptolemies, Greek kings of Egypt

Ptolemy I	Soter (Lagi); built the library at Alexandria; strong army; carried Jews to Egypt	323-283 BCE
Ptolemy II	Philadelphus; one of the richest kings in the world of his day; loved education, established a zoo, loved the Greek	283-247

Silence

	culture; died at age 62 from having lived a wild and luxurious life.	
Ptolemy III	Euergetes; loved pure science; made great advances such as measuring the circumference of the earth, the lever.	247-221
Ptolemy IV	Philopater, battled with the Seleucids, defeating them. Friendly to Palestine until they refused him entrance to the Temple. Egypt began to decline under Philopater.	221-203
Ptolemy V	Succeeded his day as an infant in 205; the kings of Macedonia and Syria, eventually defeated the Ptolemies.	203-181

4.3.5. During the period of 312-134 BCE, the Jews were under the rule of the Seleucids Dynasty. Seleucus Nicator was one of the four generals of Alexander. He founded the city of Antioch and made it the capital of his kingdom.

    4.3.5.1. The House of Seleucid hoped to expand the Greek culture and founded as many as forty cities. The names of Seleucid rulers include Antiochus (I, II, III, IV, V, VI), Seleucus (I, II III, IV), and Demetrius (I, II, III).

    4.3.5.2. There were three main groups striving for the domination in Judea

4.3.5.2.1. The dominant group brought in the Grecian ways and customs. They wanted to force the Jews to follow the customs of the Greek nation; Greek philosophy, games and religion. They were the predecessors of the infidel Sadducees.

4.3.5.2.2. A weaker group, eventually known as the Pharisees were clinging to the law, but continually adding to it making it more legalistic. Slowly they became the weak Pharisees of the New Testament. Follow the law but lacking individual spiritual discernment.

4.3.5.2.3. It is difficult to call the third group a party as were the other two. They were a feeble and afflicted people, clinging to the word of God and the promise of the coming Messiah. From this third group, eventually birthed the Essenes. They have been called the Quakers of Judea.

4.3.5.2.4. It was the son of Antiochus the Great of Syria, Epiphanes, who deposed the last rightful high priest in Jerusalem (Onias III).

4.4. **The Syrian Era (198–165 BCE)**

4.4.1. The Jews were not treated well during the reins of Antiochus III the Great (222-187) who took Palestine from Egypt in 198 BCE. The same concerning his successor Seleucus IV (Philopater (187-175). However, Antiochus III, in his attempts to expand, was no match for the Roman legions. They defeated his army in 190 BCE and made him a puppet ruler in the Roman chain of command. Palestine is the most fought over country in the world, and Jerusalem is the most captured city in all history.

4.4.2. Ben Sira, in 190 BCE, spoke of the political High Priest during this period, Simeon, in terms appropriate to a prince *"he was the glory of his people in his time."* Ben Sira informs us that the "assembly of Elders" and the popular "assembly in the gate" regulated social life and had judicial and administrative functions. He speaks of the Jews who are ashamed of the Torah and its regulations.

Depth of Bible Words and Locations
Ben Sira

Ben Sira (2nd century BCE) was a Hellenistic Jewish scribe, sage, and allegorist from Jerusalem. Sira was a scholar and scribe thoroughly versed in the Law, and especially in the "Books of Wisdom." He is the author of the Book of Sirach also known as the Book of Ecclesiasticus. Also, a medieval text, the alphabet of Sirach, has been attributed to Ben Sira. Ben Sira is also known as Jesus Ben Sira. He wrote his work in Hebrew, possibly in Alexandria, Egypt, *c.* 180–175 BCE, where he is thought to have established a school. Some commentators claim Ben Sira was a contemporary of Simon the Just although it is more likely that his contemporary was the High Priest Simon II (219–199 BCE). According to the Greek version, the author traveled extensively and was frequently in danger of death. In his writings, he speaks of the perils of all sorts from which God had delivered him. He was exposed to many false statements in the presence of a king of the Ptolemaic dynasty.

4.4.3. However, many Jews had refused to give up their form of worship and sacrifices to God. A decree was then issued that all Jews were to conform to Syrian laws, customs, and religion.

Silence

Antiochus (IV) Epiphanes (175-163) drove a herd of swine into the temple and sacrificed swine flesh on the altar dedicated to the Olympian Zeus. This was a disgrace to Jews and God. Antiochus substituted the altar dedicated to Zeus, the main Greek god. In addition, indecent orgies polluted the sacred courts of the temple. This (rightfully) outraged the religious sensibilities of the Jews. The Books of the Maccabees (see the next Era), contained descriptions of this sad situation:

> For the king had sent letters by messengers unto Jerusalem and the cities of Judah that they should follow the strange laws of the land. And, forbid burnt offerings and sacrifice and drink offerings in the temple and that they should profane the Sabbaths and festival days: And pollute the sanctuary and holy people: Set up altars and groves and chapels of idols and sacrifice swine's flesh and unclean beasts.....To the end, they might forget the law and change all the ordinances. And whosoever would not do according to the commandment of the king should die. 1 Macc. 1:44- 50.

4.4.4.　　During this time, at least they were allowed to exist under their own high priest (see list of High Priests). All went well until the Hellenizing party decided to have their favorite, Jason, appointed high priest rather than the high priest favored by the orthodox Jews. They brought this about by bribing Seleucus's successor, Antiochus (IV) Epiphanes. This set off a political conflict that finally brought Antiochus to Jerusalem in a fit of rage. In 168 BCE Antiochus set about destroying every distinctive characteristic of the Jewish faith. The program to Hellenize the Jews, while generally successful in other conquests, met with opposition in Judea. The Jews in Palestine wore Greek clothes, imitated Greek customs, and spoke Greek. Young men were seen attired in Greek caps. However, most of the Jewish people loved their Jewish faith and customs.

Depth of Bible Words and Locations
Hellenistic Culture

The Hellenistic culture was spread as Greek culture in the wake of the conquests of Alexander the Great during the 4th century BCE. Hellenistic Judaism was a form of Judaism that combined Jewish religious tradition with elements of Greek culture. Traditional Jewish followers (Judaizers) were in constant conflict with the culture (Hellenizers). The translation of the Hebrew Bible to Greek. The Septuagint was the major literary product during the second temple period. The works of Philo was one of the works of Hellenistic Jewish authors. Jewish life in both Judea and the Diaspora was influenced by the culture and language of Hellenism. The Greeks viewed Jewish culture favorably, while vice versa, Hellenism gained adherents among the Jews. While Hellenism has sometimes been presented (under the influence of 2 Maccabees, itself notably a work in Greek), as a threat of assimilation diametrically opposed to Jewish tradition.

4.4.5. The reign of Antiochus IV in Syria was a most tragic period for the Jews. He embarked in 173 BCE on the first of four campaigns against Egypt. Following this first victory, Antiochus had himself proclaimed king of Egypt. Unrest in Jerusalem caused Antiochus's soldiers to march through the city, massacring 40,000 men, women, and children, besides selling many Jews into slavery. Because of the cost of the wars and his standard of living, he was in need of funds. He decided to obtain the fiancés from various types of taxes upon the Jews. Heavy taxes such as one-third of the grain harvest, one-half of the fruit harvest, and on salt obtained from the Dead Sea.

4.4.6. The Jews experienced difficult times. However, Hellenizing, force, and brutality did not triumph over their faith. They continued to resist Hellenism and formed a party of opposition headed by the scribes whose origin is traced back to Ezra.

Syrian Kings of the United Syria, the Seleucid Dynasty

Antiochus III the Great, son of Seleucus II	222-187	
Seleucus IV, son of Antiochus III	187-175	Assassinated
Antiochus IV Epiphanes, Son of Antiochus III	175-164	Assassinated his infant son in 170 BCE
Antiochus V Eupatorm son of Antiochus IV	163-161	Appointed Syrian King by the Romans.
Timarchus	163-160	Usurper to the throne
Demetrius I Soter, son of Seleucus IV	161-150	
Alexander I Balas, son of Antiochus IV Epiphanes	150-145	Brother of Timarchus
Demetrius II Nicator, son of Demetrius I Soter	145-137	

Antiochus VI Dionysus, son of Alexander Balas and Cleopatra Thea	145-142	Did not actually rule; nominated in opposition to Demetrius II
Diodotus Tryphon	142-138	
Antiochus VII Sidetes another son of Demetrius I Soter	138-129	Became king following his brother, Demetrius II Nicator was taken prisoner
Alexander II Zabinas	129-123	Opposed Demetrius II Defeated him with the help of the Egyptian king. Ruled parts of Syria
Demetrius II Nicator, another son of Demetrius I Soter	129-126	
Cleopatra Thea	126-125; 125-121	Daughter of Ptolemy VI ruled at various times with Alexander I Balas, Demetrius II, and Antiochus VII
Seleucus V Philometor, so of Demetrius II Nicator and Cleopatra Thea	126-125	Briefly ruled with mother Cleopatra Thea. She had him assassinated in 125
Antiochus VIII Grypus, son of Demetrius II Nicator and Cleopatra Thea	125-121; 121-96	

4.5. The Maccabean Era (165–63 BCE)

4.5.1. We next find that a clash took place between the world of the Jews and their belief, Judaism, and the Greek culture world of Hellenism. The result would determine Jewish history and their religion.

4.5.2. Judea was ruled by the Hellenistic empire of the Ptolemies for 100 years. During that period, we are not knowledgeable of any clashes between the two cultures. The situation began to change for the worse following 200 BCE when Judea was conquered by Antiochus the Great.

4.5.3. The open clash between the two cultures began when Seleucus IV Epiphanes sacked the Jerusalem Temple.

4.5.4. This period was the last time for Jewish independence until 1948 CE. Thousands of Jews joined an elderly priest named Mattathias (The Maccabee family), in a demonstration to honor

God. This followed the Syrian official's attempt to force heathen sacrifice near Jerusalem. Mattathias revolted and killed a Jew who had given in and did sacrifice. They fled into the nearby mountains. Three of his sons continued the revolt and eventually took back Jerusalem and restored the worship of God. One of his sons, known as Judah the "Maccabee" became the leader following Mattathias's death in 167 BCE.

Depth of Bible Words and Locations
Maccabee
The word Maccabee in Hebrew means "hammer." In truth, there was only one Maccabee, and that was Judah. But it's a very common to refer to "the Maccabees" in the plural. Only Judah really went by that title, Maccabee.

4.5.5. The event of restored worship is commemorated today as the Feast of Hanukkah (Dedication). Whereas most of the holidays in the Jewish calendar are listed in the Bible, this is the one major holiday added by "man." A treaty with the Roman Republic in 161 BCE was the first step in receiving political independence. The treaty is recorded in 1 Maccabees. Judah died one year after the treaty was signed.

4.5.6. Fighting continued in the outlying areas of Judea, with several futile attempts by Syria to defeat these Maccabeans. Finally, under the leadership of Simon, the Jews received their full –fledged independence (142 BCE). The Hasmonean epoch then had evolved from uprising to independent statehood. They experienced almost seventy years of independence under the Hasmonean dynasty.

4.5.7. It was under the Hasmoneans we encounter for the first time separate groups that are referred to as "sects." Two of the more famous ones were known as the "Pharisees" and the "Sadducees." The books entitled First and Second Maccabees describe the Maccabean revolt and the chaos of Palestine.

4.5.8. The country was conquered by the Roman armies in the year 63 BCE.

4.6. The Roman Era (63–4 BCE)

4.6.1. After Pompey of Rome took Syria and entered Israel in 63 BCE, the independence of the Jews ended. Pompey was literally locked out of Jerusalem by Aristobulus II who *claimed* to be the king of Israel. The Roman leader, in anger, took the city by force and Israel's attempt at freedom from oppression seemed to be lost.

Silence

4.6.2. In 47 BCE Julius Caesar appointed Antipater procurator of Judea. Herod, the son of Antipater, eventually became the king of the Jews around 40 BCE. Herod the Great, as he was called, planned and carried out the rebuilding of the second temple in Jerusalem. He then proceeded to kill every descendant of the Hasmoneans, including his own wife and two sons. This was the man on the throne when Jesus was born in Bethlehem.

SIXTEEN

The High Priests

1. The historical overview of the first three centuries of the "Silent Years" may *also* be understood by briefly tracing the highlights of the High Priests. Each of the priests may be considered with the appropriate era. The government was entrusted to the high priest, which makes this a good historical reward of the periods.

The High Priests of the "Silent Years"

Jeshua (or Joshua), son of Jehozadak	c. 515-490 BCE	Following the re building of the 2nd Temple
Joiakim, son of Joshua	c. 490-470	The Persian Era
Eliashib, son of Joiakim	c. 470-433	The Persian Era
Joiada, son of Eliashib	c. 433-410	The Persian Era
Johanan, son of Joiada	c. 410-371	The Persian Era
Jaddua, son of Johanan	c. 371-320	The Persian Era
Onias I, son of Jaddua	c. 320-280	The Egyptian Era
Simon the Just, son of Onias	c. 280-260	The Egyptian Era

The High Priests

Eleazar, son of Onias	c. 260-245	The Egyptian Era
Manasseh, son of Jaddua	c. 245-240	The Egyptian Era
Onias II, son of Simon	c. 240-218	The Egyptian Era
Simon II, son of Onias	c. 218-185	The Egyptian Era
Onias III, son of Simon	c. 185-175	Last rightful high priest The Syrian Era
Jason, son of Simon	c.175-172	The Syrian Era
Menelaus	c.172-162	The Syrian Era
Alcimus	c.162-159	The Maccabean Era
Nine High Priests	c.153-37	The Hasmonean Dynasty Era
Eight High Priests	c.37-3 BCE	Herodian-Roman Era

1.1. Jeshua or Joshua was according to the Bible, the first person chosen to be the High Priest for the reconstruction of the Jewish Temple after the return of the Jews from the Babylonian Captivity. While the name Yeshua is used in Ezra–Nehemiah for the High Priest, he is called Joshua son of Yehozadak in the books of Haggai and Zechariah. Jeshua is the high priest who returned with Zerubbabel (Neh 12:10, 12, 26)

1.2. Joiakim, son of Joshua would have aided in the rebuilding of the temple, in the days of Ezra and Nehemiah. Very little else is known concerning him.

1.3. Eliashib, son of Joiakim, became the high priest during the lifetime of Nehemiah. He is regarded to have edited the available Bible Books and arranged the Psalms in the order in which they are found in the Hebrew Bible.

1.4. Joiada was the fourth High Priest of Israel, son of Eliashib. He is in the lists of Neh 12:10-11, 22 and 13:28. The only information given about Joiada is that his son married the daughter of Sanballat the Horonite for which he was driven out of the Temple by Nehemiah. This is important because the books of Ezra and Book of Nehemiah contain severe instructions against marrying foreign women.

1.5. Johanan, son of Joiada. Even though he remained a Jew, he was a godless man. His brother Jesus was promised the high priesthood. Jesus got into a quarrel with Johanan in the temple and Johanan killed him. He committed murder in order to secure his place of authority as high priest and ruler. The Jews accepted the position regardless of character and devotion.

1.6. Jaddua, son of Johanan, was a man of spotless integrity, and his name is held in great respect to the present day. He served under the kings of Persia but realized the time of Daniel's time for destruction of the second empire, had come. He recognized Alexander the Great as the he-goat with a horn between its eyes. Jaddua realized that Alexander was marching toward Jerusalem. He carried the sacred Scriptures and went to meet the conqueror. It is thought that Alexander fell to the ground as Jaddua approached him.

1.7. Onias I succeeded Jaddua, mentioned in Neh 12:11. We know little about him; he died in 300 BCE.

1.8. Simon the Just, the son of Onias I. Josephus tell us something about this man, "because of his piety toward God and his kind disposition to those of his own nation." Various works of holiness and faithfulness are credited to him. Eulogies such as "morning star" and "the rainbow giving light in the bright clouds" were given. Simon sought to block the coming Hellenizing culture. He clung to the holy writings and the sacred temple services. Simon was president of the Sanhedrim or High Council of the Jews and the first of whose great Rabbi's oral teaching was embodied in the *Mishna (or Mishnah)*. He added the final changes to the work of Ezra and helped to establish the canon of the Old Testament. He died in 291 BCE, leaving an infant son.

EXPANDED HELP PAPER
Mishna (or Mishnah)

These *oral laws* or traditions are somewhat akin to judges interpreting the law of the land based on past interpretations by other judges.

This authority to rule and make judgments on God's will likely began when Moses accepted his father-in-law's advice to share the burden of leadership with 70 elders of the community *(Exodus 18:13–26)*.

The oral law itself is thought to originate with the instructions that Adonai gave Moses on Mount Sinai. These laws were passed down orally as well as through the written word.

The first Mishna (or Mishnah) (compilation of oral traditions), Tractate Avot states: "Moses received the Torah at Sinai and transmitted it to Joshua, Joshua transmitted it to the Elders, the Elders transmitted it to the Prophets, and the Prophets transmitted it to the men of the Great Assembly. They said three things: Be deliberate in judgment, raise many students, and make a protective fence for the Torah."

Pirkei Avot, a section of the Mishna (or Mishnah) (first major written redaction of the Oral Law) devoted to ethics, traces an unbroken span of teachings that originate at Sinai. Although those teachings began to be written down nearly 1,500 years after Sinai, it is believed they have been faithfully preserved.

Judaism traditionally believes that the Torah cannot be fully understood without the oral law.

If one rejects the oral law, such as the Karaites do, it is said that one will only end up creating a new oral law that does not originate from Sinai, but from subjective interpretations or the imagination.

The oral law deals with two main categories: Halakha — legal decisions regarding the precise way a commandment is to be performed; and Haggada — nonprescriptive elements meant to inspire and edify, such as rabbinic stories, sermons, and commentaries relating to the Tanakh [Old Covenant] and Jewish life.

The Babylonian Talmud contains much of the Halakha and Haggada and was compiled in written form by AD 600 with about 2.5 million words. Within these words are a wide variety of *traditions, folklore, and laws*.

Many are at odds with one another and with Scripture; yet, there is room for this in traditional Judaism, which by its nature is based on evolving traditions and ideas.

1.9. Eleazar, son of Onias, the ninth High Priest, held the high priesthood for the next fifteen years. The Jews enjoyed relative peace during this period. It was during this important time that Ptolemy Soter and Ptolemy Philadelphus were Egyptian leaders. The first translation of the Scriptures, the Septuagint was completed. He died in 276 BCE.

1.10. Manasseh, a son of Jaddua, brother of Eleazar held the office of high priest until his own death in 251 BCE. Little is known of his years.

1.11. Onias II, son of Simon the Just was an infant at the death of his father. The son of a great man, but was *unworthy* to fill the office. However, he was high priest following Manasseh. Ptolemy Eurgetes came to the throne in 247 BCE, bringing the nation of the Jews into great danger. Onias's ignoring the rule of Eurgetes threatened the destruction of the Jews, which created panic. Joseph, the nephew of the high priest, appeased the situation by entertaining the Egyptian ambassador and pleading for mercy. He became what is known as a *Jewish Publican*, receiving money to benefit himself. He kept the post of Publican for many years, with thousands of men under his control. He enriched himself at the expense of his own people.

1.12. Simon II, son of Onias II, is mentioned in 3 Maccabees, chapter 2. He experienced peace in Judea, even though the family of Joseph, "the sons of Tobias," continued the practice of ill-gotten gains. This period is accented by the Syrian rules of Selencus Nicator, Antiochus Soter, Antiochus Theos, and Seleucus Callinicus.

1.13. Onias III, son of Simon is described in scriptures as a pious man who opposed the Hellenization of Judea. 2 Maccabees 3:1 records

> The holy city was inhabited in all peace, and the laws were kept very well, because of the godliness of Onias, the high priest, and his hatred of wickedness.

1.13.1. Onias III was the last to obtain the *rightful* high priesthood by inheritance. He was removed by Antiochus Epiphanes, brother, and successor to Seleucus Philopater. With this, the era of "rightful" high priests closed and a new era began.

1.14. Jason, son of Simon, was a deceitful man using flattery and bribery to keep the office. He had changed his name to Jason from his birth name, Joshua. He and his younger brother named Onias strived against each other for the office. Onias was temporarily outwitted and changed his own name, to Menelaus. Onias III, still living, saw the evil in the office after Menelaus robbed the temple of its golden vessels and selling them at Tyre. Onias III was murdered by Menelaus. Both Jason (Joshua) and Onias (Menelaus) were high priests at various times.

1.15. Alcimus was opposed by the Jews of Jerusalem who were led by Judas Maccabaeus. Several military attempts were made to secure Alcimus as high priest. He was established as high priest in Jerusalem, with a strong support group to uphold him. However, soon he died from a paralytic stroke.

2 We have arrived at the end of our journey. Let us close a long journey that we have taken, first with a summary scripture from the New Testament.

> Hebrews 1:1-2 *God, after He spoke long ago to the fathers in the prophets in many portions and in many ways....*

3 After all our study, our journey *Through the Old Testament*, I ask you the questions: *"What is the meaning of the Old Testament?"* and *"What is the enduring message?"*

3.1. I conclude with *my* findings.

3.2. The Old Testament has a single central truth: The Doctrine of God in seven revelations

    3.2.1. He is Creator
    3.2.2. He is Personal
    3.2.3. He Reveals Himself
    3.2.4. He is Holy
    3.2.5. He is Just
    3.2.6. He is Redeemer
    3.2.7. He is Father

3.3. It also, contrary to many people's realization, it is a book about Christ. As we have noted along the way, He is in every book of the Old Testament. We barely touched on that.

> A final verse to close. Psalms 47:6-8 pictures our King of Kings *Sing praises to God, sing praises; Sing praises to our King, sing praises. 7 For God is the King of all the earth; Sing praises with a skillful Psalms. 8 God reigns over the nations, God sits on His holy throne.*

APPENDIX

CHRONOLOGY OF OLD TESTAMENT HISTORY*			
Egypt/God's people	**Approx. Period of Book;** *date Book was written*	Approx. Date (BCE)	Babylonia, Assyria, other parts of the world. (All dates BCE)
Pre-Adam period	**Genesis Begins**	Undated Past	
		5000	Earliest evidence of civilization found near the area of Babylon. Nile River takes form.
Creation (six days)		4004 Copper Age 4500-3300	Ussher's Date of the creation
Birth of Cain		4003	
Cain kills Abel		c. 3900	
Birth of Seth		3874	
Birth of Methuselah		3500 3317	Pictographs used by Samarians
		Early Bronze Age 3300-2000	
		c. 3200	Growth of city-states in Mesopotamia
First dynasty of Egypt (King Menes); Upper/Lower Egypt unified; early hieroglyphic writing; Memphis built; trade lines w/Mesopotamia		c. 3150-2890	Invention of writing in Mesopotamia
Death of Adam		3074	
Enoch, translated by God; did not experience death		3017	
Death of Seth		2962	
Birth of Noah		2948	
		c. 2900	First dynasty of kings at Ur; first advanced civilization; Nineveh founded by Babylonia; first known use of ink; Babylon destroyed by the Flood
Great pyramids at Gizeh. Old Kingdom Period. Dynasties 3-6		2700-2200	
Dark period in Egypt		2500	Developments in India/Pak.
Birth of Japheth		2448	
Birth of Shem		2446	

Birth of Ham		2444	
Death of Methuselah; the Flood		2348 2344	
Noah leaves the Ark		2343	
		2350	Sargon I (Sargon the Great) King of Babylon
Egypt (Pepi) invaded Sargon's empire		2313	
		2300	Babylonian area repopulated; Ziggurats or temple-towers built about this time; (Sumer) Mesopotamia annexed by Akkadians (Sargon)
Birth of Eber		2281	
		c. 2230	Greece founded; earlier indications of population
Tower of Babel		2242	Ur rises to power; Cuneiform invented
		c. 2240	China, perhaps founded by Noah 2240; Took name from "yellow earth"; earliest records were written in 1500 and record back to the 1600-1046 Shang Dynasty
Birth of Terah		2126	
430 years of sojourn began		2091	Silk industry founded; Hammurabi's Code
Terah's first son, Haran, was born		2056	
		2004	The city of Ur falls
Middle Kingdom of Egypt Dynasties 11-15		c. 2000 2000-1550 Middle Bronze Age 2000-1550	Babylonians use geometry, zodiac; Indoor plumbing use in Crete; Stonehenge, England religious center; Hittites formed; Written history began
Death of Noah		1998	
Birth of Abram/Lot		1997	
Birth of Sarai		1986	
Call of Abram; death of Terah moves to Canaan; famine caused Abram to leave for Egypt		1921	
Abram and Lot		1920	

returned to Canaan			
Ishmael born to Hagar		1910	
God made a covenant with Abram; name changed to Abraham; Sodom and Gomorrah		1897	
Birth of Isaac		1896	
Ishmael jesting with Isaac; Sarah upset; suggested start of the years of slavery in Egypt		1891	
Isaac took to Mt. Mariah		1871	
Death of Sarah		1860	
		1859	Assyria starts as a tiny colony of Babylonia; lasts until 607 BCE
Isaac marries Rebecca		1856	
Death of Shem		1846	
Rebecca birthed twins; Jacob and Esau		1837	
Death of Abraham in Canaan		1821	
Death of Eber		1817	Canaanites developed sounds of an alphabet
Hyksos invaded Egypt; captured Memphis and lower Egypt		1775	
Death of Ishmael		1773	
Esau sells birthright Jacob; Jacob flees to Haran, marries Leah, Rachel; Jacob's ladder		1759	
Leah bore Reuben, Jacob's first born		1758	
Birth of Judah		1755	
Egypt has developed papyrus and ink for writing; alphabet devised		1750 1699	Old Babylonia Empire unified under Hammurabi, its sixth king. Code found in 1902 CE; the first real dynasty of Babylon; Code of Hammurabi, 282 laws written before God's law.

			c. 1750	(Many similarities)
Jerusalem established				Babylon becoming a center for commerce
Birth of Dinah			1748	
Birth of Joseph			1745	
Jacob fled from Laban; Rachel dies when Benjamin born; Esau and Jacob meet; Jacob wrestles with (Christ)			1739 1729	
Joseph sold into slavery			1728	
Joseph interpreted dreams of two officers of Pharaoh's court			1717	First Chinese dictionary
Death of Isaac in Canaan			1716	
Joseph interprets Pharaoh's dream; made ruler under Pharaoh			1715	
Jacob allows Benjamin to go to Egypt			1708	
7 years of plenty ends; migration of Jacob's family to Egypt; 70 Hebrews settle in Egypt			1706	
				Babylon Empire United 1700-648 Kassite's rule until 1160
Death of Jacob in Egypt; body was embalmed; Hyksos invade Egypt			1689 1674	
Joseph speaks of Israelites departure from Egypt; death of Joseph in Egypt	**Genesis Ends**		1635	
	Preferred time of Events in Job		c. 1625	
New Empire established in Egypt; Ahmose I; Egypt's greatest period; Hyksos expelled; Dynasties 18-20			1570 1570-1075	Hittites strike Babylon

Israelites are enslaved in Egypt			
		1582	Early settlements in Greece
Birth of Aaron		1574	
Amenhotep I orders all male babies killed; raises Moses until 18 yrs old		1573	
Birth of Moses	**Exodus Begins**	1571	
Israelites are in bondage; *Hyksos kings driven out of Egypt*		1544	
Moses raised, as a young man, under Thutmose I		1553-1536 Late Bronze Age 1550-1200	Assyrian wars with Hittites
Thutmose II sought to kill Moses		1536	
Birth of Joshua		1534	
Moses fled to Midian		1531	
Birth of Caleb		1529	
Thutmose III made Egypt a power by 17 campaigns; lost in the Red Sea?		c. 1508-1491	
		1501-1447	Early Greek Alphabet; Library of Hittites contains eight languages; Leprosy in India and Egypt
		1500	Babylon conquered, first time; Corinth founded
		1496-1446	Art of shipbuilding perfected, Mediterranean countries
Burning bush		1491	Phoenician letters brought into Greece, become Roman letters eventually used in America
Ten plagues; first Passover; Exodus from Egypt, and into the Wilderness, led by Moses	**Numbers begins**	1491	
Mount Sinai, giving of the Law; Ten Commandments	*Moses wrote Genesis, Exodus, Leviticus, Numbers c. 1491-1451 (see alternant JEDP*	1491	

305

	theory		
Tabernacle; 12 spies sent into the land		1490	
Death of Miriam and Aaron		1452	
	Exodus Ends	1451	Mexico Sun Pyramid build
		1451	Olmec culture begins in Mexico
	Leviticus (one month); *Moses wrote Psalms 90*	1451	
38+ Years of Wandering; 17 camping stops over the 38 years	**Numbers Ends**	1491-1451	
	Deuteronomy (one month) **Joshua Begins**	1451	
Moses had taken the land east of the Jordan; divided the land into 2 ½ tribes; Moses viewed all the land of promise; death of Moses	*Joshua wrote Joshua*	1451	Ethiopia, located in the Horn of Africa, becomes independent, the first independent country on the continent. Known as "Kush" by ancient Egyptians. Known to be inhabited for several previous centuries.
Weak rule in Egypt under Amenhotep II and Thutmose IV		1447-1391	
Joshua crossing the Jordan; Jericho; manna stopped;		1451	Hittites rise to power in Asia Minor
Conquest of Canaan, Joshua		1451-1445	
Land portioned to tribes		1445-44	
Hebrew alphabet developed beyond earlier form			
Death of Joshua; buried in the city he built, Timnathserah	**Joshua Ends**	*c.* 1424	
Egypt expands trade under Amenhotep III		1420	
First of 14 'judges', (1) Othniel (of Judah);	**Judges Begins**	1392	Hittites conquer Mesopotamia and Syria; at

Delivery from oppression of the Mesopotamians			height of power
Egypt's greatest splendor; Tutankhamen/ Rameses I		1380-1373	
	Judges written, perhaps by Samuel; **Ruth events,** sometime during Judges, probably late Judges	c. 1392-1050	
Judge (2) Ehud (of Benjamin) defeats Moabites		c. 1342	
		1290	Babylon conquered by Assyrians but held only for a short time
		1267	First Assyrian Empire founded under Ninus
Judge (3) Shamgar		c. 1260	
Judges (4) Deborah (of Ephraim) and Barak (of Naphthali); defeated Canaanites		c. 1260	
		1250	Shalmaneser I (of 5) first powerful king of Assyria; Trojan war in Greece
Birth of Eli		1214	
		1206	Genghis Khan unified tribes in China
		1200 Iron Age 1200-586	Philistines occupy Mediterranean coast Hercules; Hittite Empire Ends
Judge (5) Gideon (of Manasseh) defeats Amalekites and Midianites		c. 1233	
Judge (6) Tola		c. 1197	
Philistines suffer a defeat at the hands of Ramesses III		1188	
		1184	Trojan war; fall of Troy
Birth of Samson		1155	

307

			1152	Cho Dynasty in China
Judges: (7) Jair (8) Ibzan (9) Elon (10(Abdon			1146 1139 1129	
			1117	Philistines expand into Israel Beginning of Greek History, first evidence of quality civilization, revealed in discovered pottery
(11) Jephthah delivers Israel from the Ammonites; *Upper/Lower Egypt split; weakness begins*			c. 1087	
Judge (12) Samson (of Dan) delivers from Philistines, dies;			1101	
Ark moved to temple of Dagon			c. 1100	
			1114-1093	Tiglath-Pileser I rules Assyrian Empire
Birth of Samuel (Israel's 14th Judge). (Also, Eli was a Judge)	**1 Samuel Begins; 1 Chron Ends; 2 Chron Begins**		c. 1105	
Ark moved again			1096	
Saul anointed first King (41 yr reign)			1095-1056	
Civil war in Egypt			1090	
David is born			1085	
Samuel secretly anoints David as Saul's successor			1070	
David and Goliath			1067	
Jonathan visits David			1064	
David cuts off Saul's robe in Engedi; works for Philistines			1062	
Death of Eli			1061	
Death of Samuel			1060	
Israel a dominant power; Philistines took off the head of Saul; Death of Jonathan	*Many Psalms written (6,11,12,19 26, 58, 59,120,131, and several others)*		1055-1048 1055	

		1 Sam Ends		
		Judges Ends 2 Sam Begins	1050	
David king over 12 tribes; David captures Jerusalem			1048	
David brings Ark of Covenant to Jerusalem; David broke the Philistine hold			1047	
Mephibosheth restored			1040	
David and Bathsheba; Solomon is born			1037	
			1030-1018	Shalmaneser rules Assyria
Preparations to build the Temple				
Absalom revolts against David			1027	
Absalom took possession of David's kingdom			1023	
Saul's sons hung by Gibeonites			1022	
Birth of Rehoboam			1016	
Solomon marries daughter of Pharaoh		1 Kings Begins 1 Chron Ends 2 Chron Begins 2 Sam Ends	1015	
Reign of Solomon			1015-975	
Solomon marries daughter of Pharaoh			1014	
Temple built in Jerusalem			1012-1005	
Temple dedicated			1004	Mayan Dynasties founded in Central America; refrigeration developed, Chinese
Power extended from the Red Sea to Euphrates River				
		Ruth written c. 10th century, unknown author	1000	
		Song of Solomon (Songs); *written by Solomon*	c. 980	

	Ecclesiastes; possibly written by Solomon; alternate date written by others c. 450	*c. 970*	
	Many Proverbs were written	950-750	
Southern Kingdom (Judah and Benjamin Tribes) 20 kings, 1 Dynasty **Judah King/yrs** Events/Prophets			Northern Kingdom (Ten Tribes) 20 kings, 9 Dynasties **Israel King/yrs** Events
Rehoboam/17 975-959; Solomon dies; division of Kingdom; (a fixed date using 586 date for fall of Judah and Ezek 4:4-5)		975	**1st Dynasty; Jeroboam/22;** established shrines at Bethlehem and Dan 975-954
Foreign domination of Egypt, ruled by Lybia			
Egypt (Shishak) invades Judah and Israel, takes cities	1 & 2 Samuel written 930	971	Tiglath-Pileser II rules Assyria 967-935
Abijam (Abijah)/3 958-955; Abijam wars against Jeroboam, wins; highest casualty rate of any Bible battle.		958	
Asa/41 955-914		955	
Judah Wars against Israel		954	**Nadab/2 954-953** Ben-hadad I, King of Syria; war-like people build the

				Assyrian Empire; set on conquest of the world
Religious reforms			953	**2nd Dynasty; Baasha/24 953-930**
Birth of Jehoshaphat, son of Asa		949		
Ethiopia invades Judah		941		
			940	Ben-haded invades Israel, destroyed much of the Asher and Dan Tribes
	2nd Possible date Job written	930		
		930	**3rd Dynasty; Elah/2 930-929**	
		929	*Zimri/7 days; shortest "dynasty" to sit on a biblical throne*	

			Dynasties	**Events/***Prophets*
		929	**4th Dynasty; Tibni/Omri/12 929-918**	God chose him as ruler; sets up idols, Baalism; builds Samaria; conquers Moab
Asa's feet diseased		918	**Ahab/21 918-897**	Marries Jezebel; Constant war with Judah; defeated Ben-hadad; death of Omri
Jehoshaphat/25 914-889; Co-regent w/Asa Religious reform Peace with Israel/ Ahab; death of Asa		914		
		914		*Elijah's* 1st miracle; Death of Omri
Death of Jehoshaphat		c. 899		*Elijah chooses Elisha*
Joram(Jehoram)/ 8 898-884 (co-rule for six);		898		

Married Ahab's daughter; Edomites revolted; set up worship of Baal				
		897	*Ahaziah/2* *898-897*	Calf worship/war with Judah; fell out of window, dies; death of Ahab
	1 Kings Ends; 2 Kings Begins	897-889	*Jehoram/12* *897-884*	Ben-hadad invades Israel
"J" source of Pentateuch		c. 897		*Elisha 1st miracle, ministry; Homer in Greece; Elijah took to heaven*
Died of disease allowed by God		885		
		845		Israel invaded by Ben-hadad II, King of Damascus (880-842)
Made his son Ahaziah his 2nd in command. His other sons were killed		886	*5th Dynasty; Jehu/27 884-857*	Attempts reform; pays tribute to Assyria; Assyria invades; shrewdest of Israel kings suppressed Baalism for a while
Ahaziah/1; Killed by Jehu		884		
Athaliah/6 884-878; (Queen) Daughter of Jezebel/6; slays all leaders except Joash		884		
Joash (Jehoash) /40 879-839; Hidden in temple/influenced by High Priest, Jehoiada; made king at age 7; repaired the temple; Samaria founded		879		Assyrian empire extended; control of Babylonia; Syria 870; Palestine 740; Egypt 675
		858-824		Shalmaneser III rules Assyria
		857	*Johoahaz/17 857-840*	Baal worship; Marriage to Jezebel
				Alliance of peace with Judah

	Obadiah, alternate date and written date	840		Growth of Baalism/idolatry
		839		Joash visited *Elisha* on his death bed; Death of *Elisha*
				Israel/captures Moab
		843-840	**Jehoash/16 840-826**	
Amaziah/29 839-811; Invades Israel		839		Syria defeated by Assyria
Jerusalem's walls broken down Flees, hides, assassinated		784	**Jeroboam II/41 826-785**	Son of Joash; Period of prosperity; Dies in fall from window; killed by Jehu
(Best date) **Joel 835-796** (Later option in 600 BCE)	Joel writes Joel 835; alternative date is 400	830		
Uzziah born to Amaziah; Joash died		826	c. 825	Carthage founded
Uzziah (Azariah)/52 810-758; Co-regent w/Amaziah		810		
Isaiah and Joel living		808		*Jonah* living
		800		Homer "LLiad: and "Odyssey" in Greece; Assyrian power weakened
Prosperity in Judah		784	**Zachariah/6mo 772**	Israel Invaded by Assyria;
		783-773		Shalmaneser IV rules Assyria
		776		First Olympic games; Greek history begins
	Jonah written, unknown author 760; **Amos Begins**	760		
	Hosea Begins Jonah	755		Greece, Hellenic outlook emerged
			753-509	Royal period of Rome
		772	6th **Dynasty;**	Uproots Baal

			Shallum/1 mo 772	
		772	**7th Dynasty; Menahem/10 772-762**	Pays tribute to Assyria; King Pul of Assyria invades Israel
Birth of Ahaz, son of Jotham		761	**Pekahiah/2 761-760**	Turns in desperation to God
Isaiah saw the glory of God		759	**8th Dynasty; Pekah/11 759-739**	
Jotham/16 758-742; Co-regent with Uzziah (leprosy) at first; the "E" source of Pentateuch	**Micah Begins; Possible date that Joel takes place**	750		Jezebel killed, left for dogs; Idolatry on a grand scale; Great Britain settled by the Celtics
	Amos Ends Amos writes Amos	c. 750		Assyria attacked by Media
		748		Rome was founded; Babylonia (Nabonassar) under Assyrian rule; Tiglath-pileser III rules
				Takes back the cities lost by his father
Isaiah, Micah	**Isaiah Begins**	742		
Ahaz/16 742-726; Co-regent with Jotham at first (759); Idolatry; wicked King; Becomes ruler; Edom, joined by Philistines invaded Judah, took captives; Jotham dies		742		Dentistry advances made in Italy, false teeth; Rome institutes a 10-month calendar
Asks Tiglath-pileser III to help against Syria and Israel; Ahaz becomes a servant to Assyria		740-720		Assyria regains power, pushes west; Tiglathpileser III ("Pul" king of Assyria invades Israel
	Micah writes Micah c. 740-710			

Egypt captured by Assyria		c. 735			Israel invaded by Tiglath-pileser III, takes much land, captives to Assyria
		730		**9th Dynasty; Hoshea/9 730-720**	The last King of Israel; Pays tribute to Assyria; restored order in Israel
Death of Ahaz		726			
		722-721		FALL OF ISRAEL; some of the northern Israelites go south to Judah	Shalmaneser V attacks Samaria, Sargun II completes the victory; captured many Israelites, carries them away; 254 yrs following division of the Kingdom.
Hezekiah/29 726-697; reforms temple worship following death of his father, Ahaz	**Proverbs gathered**	726			
Many other reforms introduced; eventually turns from God, destroys Moses' brazen serpent; father of Manasseh		726			Greek alphabetic inscriptions written on ceramics
	Hosea Ends; Hosea writes Hosea c. 722	722			Samaria (Israel) captured
		722-705			Assyrian Empire expands; Sargon II rules
Jerusalem, full of foreigners, sees no need of God		711			
Attempted siege of Jerusalem God Intervenes!	*Isaiah writes Isaiah 700-680; two alternative writers may have written cps 40-66*	709			
Hezekiah's tunnels; rebels		705-681			Sennacherib reigned in Assyria; made war

from Assyria; Sennacherib comes to regain control; Judah survives and outlasts the Assyrian empire		705		on Egypt and Asia Sennacherib war against Judah; killed many Jews; marched to Egypt, took captives
Manasseh/54 697-642; Evil Rule, idolatry, cruelty; thought to have sawn Isaiah in half	**Micah Ends Isaiah Ends**	697 680	Assyria captured Babylonia; became united	Murdered by Hoshea Babylon rebuilt under Esarhaddon (681-669)
		690		God intervenes; Sennacherib killed by his own sons; new kingdom of the Medes
Manasseh carried captive into Babylon		677		Greek city-state emerges
Egypt conquered by Assyria		671		
		657		Assyria took the Medes
		660		Japan recognized as a country
Thebes captured by Assyrians		664		
		650-625		Damascus falls to the Assyrians
		650		*Jeremiah* born
Death of Manasseh after he returned from captivity		643		
Amon/2 642-640; Evil reign		642		
Josiah/31 640-609	**Zephaniah Begins**	640		
	Nahum Begins	635 630		All Asia joins Medes to attack Assyria
Josiah's Great religious reform comes; cleanses Judah from idolatry; Jeremiah's call		629		
	Jeremiah Begins	628		Pays tribute to Assyria
	Nahum writes			Puppet king under

	Nahum 630-620			Assyria
	Jeremiah writes Jeremiah 627-585 Zephaniah writes Zephaniah 625	626		Nabopolassar, the father of Nebuchadnezzar, rules Babylonia 626-605
Josiah finds "Book of The Law"		624		**Fall of Israel**
Ezekiel was born	**Nahum Ends; Zephaniah Ends**	622		Captured by Sargon III
Jehoahaz/3mo; taken to Egypt 609 Josiah killed at Megiddo; his son was Jehoahaz		612		
		607		
	Habakkuk Begins *Last of the Psalms written*	612		Time of Buddha; Nineveh, Haran captured by Babylonia; Temple of Artemis built in Ephesus
Many in Judah taken by Egypt		605		Nebuchadnezzar II 605-562
Jehoaikim/11 (Eliakim) 609-598; rebelled against Nebuchadnezzar (Beginning of 3 captivities) by Babylonia; Jehoiakim was chained and carried to Babylon; Daniel also was taken		607		
Reigns as vassal of Nebuchadnezzar Nebuchadnezzar, as a General, takes rule of Jerusalem; 1st	*Habakkuk writes Habakkuk c. 607;* **Daniel Begins**	606		Birth of Confucius

317

Deportation to Babylon; 70 years in Babylon begins; *Egypt falls to Assyria;* Baruch records words of Jeremiah				
Nebuchadnezzar's rule		c. 606-561		
Raruch again records the words of Jeremiah		605		
Daniel took captive to Babylon Nebuchadnezzar, Daniel have dreams		604		
				History of Japan begins
Jehoiakim rebels against Babylon; Nebuchadnezzar's army destroyed Judah		600		
Obadiah uttered a prophecy against Edom; **2nd possible date of Joel**	**Obadiah** (a possible date)	600		
Jehoiachin (Jeconiah)/3 mo 598; 2nd Deportation to Babylon Nebuchadnezzar invades Jerusalem, takes captive 10,000 including Ezekiel, Jehoiachin; Mordecai and Ezekiel took captive	**Habakkuk Ends**	598		Birth of Cyrus

Zedekiah/11 597-586; Last king of Judah, evil reign; refused invitation from Jeremiah	**2 Kings Ends**	597		
Ezekiel's vision; Baruch read all his journal to all the captives in Babylon; Ezekiel carried by the Spirit to Jerusalem and then back to Babylon	**Ezekiel Begins** in Babylonia; *Ezekiel writes Ezekiel 592-570*	594		Olive tree brought to Italy from Greece
The Glory departs the temple		592		
		589		Nebuchadnezzar's father breaks from Assyria, aligns with the Mede's, independence of Babylon; Babylon destroys much of Egypt
Zedekiah rebels against Babylonia; final siege on Jerusalem		588		
Jerusalem and the Temple destroyed by Nebuchadnezzar 3rd Deportation to Babylon; many other biblical dates are established by counting backward from this known "point"	**Jeremiah Ends; 1 and 2 Chronicles Ends**	586		
"D" source of Pentateuch	**Lamentation**	586		
Jerusalem develops subterranean water tunnels				
END OF JUDAH		586		

319

Captives to Babylon; a few Jews left in Judah	Obadiah writes Obadiah c. 586-553			
	Jeremiah writes Jeremiah c. 585-580			
Jeremiah, Baruch, and others were taken away to Egypt		585	Persian Empire 559-330 BCE;	
"P" source of Pentateuch	1 and 2 Kings written (single book); unknown author	c. 580		
Ezekiel "sees" the Israelites restored		575		
		570		Nebuchadnezzar builds Hanging Gardens; grows proud
		571		Nebuchadnezzar conquered Egypt; kills many Jews there; he dreams and Daniel explains; acknowledged the power of God; took Tyre
Daniel, fiery furnace		562		Nebuchadnezzar II died; Aesop's fables.
	Ezekiel Ends	571		
		c. 560-539	Babylon descends, Belshazzar last king; writing on the wall in 539	
Ezekiel died				
		559-530	Cyrus II (the Great) reigns in Persia	Builds battering rams; defeated Belshazzar; capture of Babylon
		550		Birth of Buddha; Birth of Confucius (one year later)
	Jeremiah writes 1 Kings and 2 Kings 560-550;	559-549 545	Cyrus the Great of Persia conquers Media; Cyrus conquers	Darius born, 549

	Jeremiah writes Lamentations c. 545		Lydia; built battering rams	
	Some Psalms were written in Babylon;	539	Cyrus conquers Babylon and adds it to Medo-Persian Empire, resulting Persian Empire is huge, powerful	Darius the Mede ruled the kingdom Cyrus gave him, Babylon; Michael the angel appears to him
		538		Darius subdues all the countries from Syria to the Red Sea
		536	Decree of Cyrus permitting Jews to return to Palestine	
Lions' den	**Ezra Begins**; Daniel writes Daniel 537-530	537	End of 70 years of captivity	
First return to Jerusalem under Zerubbabel (Sheshbazzar). As many as 43, 360 returned. Begin to rebuild temple, but held up by Samaritans Daniel dies	**Daniel Ends**	536 525	King Cyrus develops a messenger system using horses Persian Empire (Cambyses) conquers Egypt; king of Arabia made a league with Cambrysees Aramaic language begins to replace Old Hebrew in Palestine	
		529	Death of Cyrus; his son, Cambyses rules Persia 530-522; wars, conquers, Egypt	
Artaxerxes sent letter forbidding the rebuilding of Jerusalem		522	Death of Cambyses; Artaxerxes stopped the rebuilding of Jerusalem	
		521	Buddha's study of philosophy began	
Haggai encourages the	**Haggai Begins Zechariah**	520		

321

Jews to persevere in the work in Jerusalem	**Begins;** *Haggai writes Haggai c. 510*	522-485 520	Darius the Great's rule in Persia Greeks use papyrus
Darius says to continue the building of the temple		520	Edict of Cyrus located
Temple is completed by Zerubbabel	*Zechariah writes Zechariah c. 520-518*	516	
	Haggai Ends	505	
		c. 500	Rise of democracy at Athens
Esther marries King Ahasuerus		486	
Haman plots against the Jews		482	
Haman hanged/Mordecai made Prime Minister		481	Expansion/founding of the Roman Republic
Rescues her countrymen from tragic fate (in Persia)		480	Treaty between Carthage and Rome
		492-479	Graeco-Persian Wars; Persia attempts to conquer Greece
		490	Greeks Battle of Marathon
	Esther, Jewish Queen	485-474 486	Death of Darius, 486 in battle; Reign of Xerxes in Persia Persian wars; took Greece; burned many temples in Asia; Xerxes took Athens Battle of Salamis Socrates in Greece 470-399 Pericles in Greece
		480	Death of Buddha; death of Confucius

			(one year later)
	Zechariah Ends	c. 470	
		465-425	Xerxes dies; Artaxerxes Longimanus, son of Xerxes, rules Persia
Second return under Ezra and a small group	Ezra Ends; Esther written 460-400	467	Persian army driven out of Asia, Persian wars end
Begin Daniel's 70th week to Christ		454	
		450-430	Age of Pericles at Athens, golden age of Greek Art; temple of Zeus built
	Ezra writes 1 & 2 Chronicles, Ezra, and Nehemiah 430-420		
Third return to Jerusalem under Nehemiah, who is appointed Governor of Judah. Walls rebuilt. Law of Moses is read, reforms made. Feast of Tabernacles; Sanballat and Tobiah; Ezra read the law of God	Nehemiah Begins	454	20th yr of Artaxerxes reign
		448	Greece at peace with Persia
Nehemiah governor of Judah		445-430	Construction of Parthenon at Athens
Last datable events in O.T. history: Nehemiah returns to Jerusalem after visit to Persia	Ezra wrote Nehemiah written 430-420	442	

		431-404 424-404	Peloponnesian War in Greece Reign of Darius II in Persia
	Malachi; *Malachi was written, unknown author 430-420*	c. 441-425	
	Nehemiah Ends	430	
		438	Spartacus; Parthenon in Greece completed
		429-347	Plato
		425	Artaxerxes died; his son Xerxes II made king (for one year) killed in his bed
		407	Plato studies philosophy under Socrates
		404	Athens in downfall
	A 3rd possible date that Joel takes place (unlikely)	404-358	Artaxerxes II ruled Persia
The Silent Period		400	Chinese complete a wall to keep out the Hun people Plato 373 BCE
		356	Alexander The Great is born; leads Greece to a world power
		331	Persia and Egypt falls to Alexander
		323	Alexander dies

My humble attempt has been made to link events in world history with events in the Bible. Because God is sovereign, He is Lord of both sacred and secular history. Therefore, all events in history are in harmony with His plan—He is Lord of all. He created the entire world for man to live upon. The events, which took place in the world, were not by accident.

Man did not randomly appear or accidently stumble upon various sections of His world. God is in control of all!

The project of establishing biblical chronology, though well determined and contained within very certain narrow bounds, must be seen as an *ongoing* project. Additional refinements remain possible.

© Thomas L Hiegel

INDEX

INDEX

Complete/Consolidated Index of Persons, Key Words, Depth of Words and Places, and Expanded Help Papers

A Second Elijah 281
Abijah 110, 112, 113, 115, 121, 310
Abraham Covenant 119
Achan 138
Africa 148, 228, 230, 271, 283, 284, 306
Agur the son of Jakeh 49
Ahab 66, 70, 78, 79, 80, 81, 82, 84, 85, 86, 87, 88, 104, 105, 114-117, 122, 252, 311
Ahasuerus 199, 206, 208, 209, 239, 242, 246, 247, 249, 251, 253, 322
Ahaz 68, 107, 108, 117, 132, 136, 143, 201, 313, 314, 315
Ahaziah 78, 80, 110, 117, 122, 311, 312
Alexander. 192, 213, 215, 217, 243, 270, 271, 282, 283, 285, 287, 288, 289, 294, 324
Alexander the Great's Four Generals
    Cassander 215, 283, 284
    Lysimachus 283, 284
    Ptolemy ...... .215, 278, 283, 284, 285, 289, 296
    Seleucus 283, 284, 285, 286, 287, 288, 289, 296
Alexandria 148, 279, 284, 286
Alphabet of Sirach 286
Amalek 249
Amaziah .68, 69, 107, 110, 122, 129, 130, 313
Ammonites 116, 187, 227, 255, 308
Amon ..68, 107, 110, 122, 164, 176, 177, 186, 316
Amos..... 64, 69, 71, 72, 82, 83, 86, 89, 92, 93, 94, 95, 123, 127, 136, 148, 177, 187, 202, 313, 314
Amos' Series of Five Vsions 94
Angels 217, 218
Announcing John the Baptist 274
Antiochus Epiphanes 165, 296
Antiochus III 284, 286, 288
Antiochus IV 288
Antipater 291
Antiquities of the Jews 165
Apion 165
Arabic 216
Aramaic 260
Armageddon 168, 169, 171

Artaxerxes 199, 206, 208, 209, 223, 235, 236, 239, 242-245, 251, 253, 256, 257, 321-324
Asa...67, 79, 106, 107, 108, 110, 112, 113, 114, 115, 116, 121, 310, 311
Asaph 21
Asherah 74, 80, 87, 113, 114
Ashkelon 178, 270
Assyria..... 66, 70, 71, 80, 83, 90, 99, 100, 104, 108, 114, 123, 132, 135, 136, 137, 140, 145, 148, 149, 150, 151, 159, 160, 161, 162, 163, 167, 168, 171, 175, 176, 178, 180, 186, 187, 188, 203, 204, 207, 244, 271, 301, 303, 307, 309, 310, 312, 313, 314, 315, 316, 317, 319
Assyrian Empire ... 71, 83, 148, 161, 162, 169, 175, 307, 308, 310, 315
Assyrians ...71, 82, 91, 92, 108, 135, 139, 149, 156, 162, 163, 164, 175, 220, 270, 307, 316
Athaliah..... 109, 110, 116, 117, 120, 122, 312
Attempts to Destroy the Bible 181
Azariah 68, 107, 108, 110, 115, 122, 130, 197, 210, 313
Baal ... 65, 66, 68, 74, 80, 81, 82, 87, 103, 104, 107, 114, 116, 118, 121, 123, 132, 163, 171, 311, 312, 313
Babylon 74, 123, 140, 141, 147, 148, 149, 150, 151, 152, 157, 159-163, 171, 172, 179, 180, 184-190, 192, 196-201, 203-206, 210, 211, 214, 215, 225, 226, 227, 234, 239, 241, 242, 243, 245, 247, 248, 253, 256, 259, 267, 274, 283, 284, 301, 303, 304, 305, 307, 315, 316, 317, 318, 319, 320
Babylonish Aramaean Dialect 260
Baruch 157, 180, 183, 317, 318, 319
Basic Outline of 1 and 2 Chronicles 75
Basic Outline of 1 and 2 Kings 74
Basic Outline of Amos 92
Basic Outline of Daniel 210
Basic outline of Ecclesiastes 55
Basic Outline of Esther 246
Basic Outline of Ezekiel 225
Basic Outline of Ezra 241
Basic Outline of Habakkuk 187

328

INDEX

Basic Outline of Habakkuk #2 188
Basic Outline of Haggai 261
Basic Outline of Hosea 95
Basic Outline of Isaiah 141
Basic Outline of Jeremiah......................... 179
Basic Outline of Joel................................. 124
Basic Outline of Jonah 89
Basic Outline of Lamentations 193
Basic Outline of Malachi 272
Basic Outline of Micah 151
Basic Outline of Nahum 175
Basic Outline of Nehemiah....................... 253
Basic Outline of Obadiah.......................... 190
Basic Outline of Obadiah #2 190
Basic Outline of Proverbs 45
Basic Outline of Psalms 16
Basic Outline of Song of Solomon 58
Basic Outline of Zechariah 263
Basic Outline of Zephaniah 177
Battle of Beth-Zur 282
Ben Sira 280, 286
Bethlehem 152
Between the Old and New Testaments 10, 276
Biblical Apocrypha 278
Book of Ecclesiasticus 286
Book of Jubilees 212
Book of Sirach 286
Cambyses.. 205, 206, 207, 208, 242, 247, 321
Carchemish 167, 187, 188, 204
Chaldee 260
Christ in Psalms 27
Chronology of Ezra and Nehemiah........... 256
CHRONOLOGY OF OLD TESTAMENT HISTORY 10, 301
Chronology of Zephaniah, Habakkuk, and Lamentations 194
Concerning the High Antiquity of the Jews 165
Constantine.. 181
Covetousness in the Old Testament 138
Cupbearer to King Artaxerxes 253
Cush 148
Cyrus .148, 149, 199, 200, 205, 206, 207, 208, 215, 223, 225, 234, 239, 242, 244, 247, 256, 280, 318, 320, 321
Damascus.......... 108, 132, 148, 187, 312, 316
Daniel. 86, 160, 161, 163, 169, 172, 184, 188, 196-200, 202, 204, 205, 208-226, 229, 230, 231, 239, 240, 247, 249, 256- 261,

267, 269, 279, 281, 282, 284, 294, 317, 318, 320, 321, 322
Daniel's First Prophecy............................. 212
Daniel's First Vision 214
Daniel's Second Vision 217
Daniel's Seventy Weeks 221
Darius I Hystaspis..................................... 247
Darius II.............................. 206, 208, 243, 323
Darius III.................................208, 243, 282
Dates of Key Events
    586-442 BCE....................................... 199
    697-585 BCE....................................... 159
    750-709 BCE....................................... 135
    975-721 BCE... 70
David 15, 17, 19, 21, 23, 24, 28, 37, 38, 45, 47, 48, 56, 59, 65, 73, 74, 75, 77, 78, 81, 97, 103, 105, 106, 109, 111, 112, 116, 118, 134, 137, 143, 145, 166, 180, 185, 201, 237, 248, 249, 251, 252, 262, 263, 271, 275, 308, 309
Day of the Lord 123-126, 195, 272
Depth of Bible Locations
    Babylon 162
    Bethzur.. 281
    Chaldea 162
    Edom 191
    Ephraim 72
    Lachish 139
    Macedonia 283
    Moab... 148
    Philistine City-States 271
    Samaria 82
    Shechem 81
    Susa 253
    Tirzah 81
    Tyre 271
Depth of Bible Words
    Angel: Key Word in Zechariah 263
    Asherah... 114
    Awesome: Key Word in Nehemiah 253
    Baal 118
    Baal: 1 Kings Key Word..........................74
    Beloved 58
    Ben Sira 286
    Compassion: Key Word in Micah 151
    Fasting: Key Word in Esther 246
    Greed 138
    Hellenistic Culture............................... 287
    Hezekiah 139
    Heal: Jeremiah Key Word.................... 179
    Heal: Jeremiah Key Word.................... 179

INDEX

High Places: 2 Kings Key Word 74
Huldah 167
Humble: Zephaniah Key Wor 177
Image: Habakkuk Key Word 188
Jealous: Nahum Key Word 175
Jews: Key Word in Ezra 241
Judah 110
Leaven 98
Maccabeans 192
Maccabee 290
Myrtle 266
Oracle 270
Passover: 2 Chronicles Key Word 75
Praise: Psalms Key Word 22
Prepared: Jonah Key Word 90
Pride: Obadiah Key Word 190
Salvation: Isaiah Key Word 141
Seek: Amos Key Word 93
Selah 21
Seven 222
Signet Ring: Key Word in Haggai 261
Sons: 1 Chronicles Key Word 75
Son of Man: Ezekiel Key Word 225
Spirit: Joel Key Word 124
Stumble: Hosea Key Word 95
Troubler 87
Try: Key Word in Malach 272
Vanity: Ecclesiastes Key Word 55
Vision: Daniel Key Word 210
Weeps: Lamentations Key Word 193
Wisdom: Proverbs Key Word 45
Wisdom 45
Description of Nineveh 176
Diocletian 181
Ecclesiastes .16, 19, 41, 43, 45, 46, 47, 55, 56, 60, 138, 309
    Errors in the Book! 57
    Suggested Authors 56
    What is the message of Ecclesiastes 56
Edom.100, 117, 123, 129, 130, 148, 170, 187, 190, 191, 192, 201, 227, 254, 274, 314, 318
Edomite family, the Herods 192
Edomites ... 129, 132, 155, 159, 187, 192, 311
Egypt 11, 48, 69, 72, 75, 77, 99, 112, 113, 114, 123, 129, 148, 159, 160, 161, 162, 167-167, 180, 185-188, 193, 199, 203, 206, 207, 215, 228, 230, 231, 239, 242, 243, 249, 266, 279, 282-286, 288, 301-306, 308, 310, 314-317, 319, 320, 321, 324

Ehan 21
Ekron 178, 270, 271
Elam 187, 253
Eliakim 110, 122, 171, 317
Elijah ... 66, 70, 73, 84-89, 104, 116, 123, 140, 191, 238, 281, 311, 312
Elisha 66, 70, 73, 84, 88, 89, 104, 123, 138, 140, 221, 311, 312
Elkosh 175
Eloth 131
Enoch, I and II 212
Ephraim 64, 70, 72, 77, 89, 98, 270, 307
Epiphanes 286-289
Esarhaddon 161, 244, 315
Esau 187
Esdras 168
Essenes 285
Esther..12, 199, 203, 208, 209, 233, 235, 239, 240, 241, 242, 244, 246-251, 253, 254, 322
Esther, Events in the Period 246
Ethiopia 114, 148, 178, 228, 306, 311
Euphrates River 169, 202, 230, 309
Evangelical Prophet 149
EXPANDED HELP PAPER
    Angels 217
    Apocalypsis 212
    Babylon/Persia 203
    Basic Summary of End Time Events 229
    Flavius Josephus 164
    Four Covenants 119
    Information on Psalms 27
    Jezebel 80
    Mishna 295
    Seven Hebrew Words of Praise 22
    The Aramaic Dialect 260
    The Indestructible Bible 181
    The Six Related Books 73
    The Words of Our Words of our Mouth According to Proverbs 51
    What is Armageddon 168
Ezekiel 45, 47, 48, 82, 86, 148, 152, 160, 161, 172, 174, 184, 190, 196, 198, 200, 202, 210, 218, 225-229, 231, 232, 240, 258, 261, 263, 271, 273, 317, 318-320
Ezra 11, 74, 93, 111, 193, 199, 206, 207-209, 222, 223, 233-236, 239, 240-249, 251-256, 258-260, 273, 280, 282, 288, 294, 295, 320, 322, 323
Feast of Hanukkah 290
Ferdinand and Isabella 182

INDEX

First Isaiah 140
First six seals 229
First Temple in Jerusalem 166
Fitting Together of the Final Old Testament Period 241
Five Divisions of Psalms 16
Flavius Josephus 164, 165, 276
Fulfilled Prophecies from Isaiah 143
Fulfilled Prophecies in Daniel 2, 7, and 8 . 214
Gatekeepers of Nehemiah 255
Gaza 94, 178, 270, 271
Gehazi's Greed 138
Geshem 254
Gomer 70, 96, 97, 228, 252
Habakkuk 17, 21, 86, 154, 157, 158, 160, 161, 167, 174, 175, 180, 184, 187, 188, 189, 194, 210, 317, 318
Haggai 86, 199, 208, 233, 234, 236, 237, 239, 240, 241, 244, 256, 258, 261, 262, 263, 264, 265, 272, 273, 294, 321
Haman 235, 246, 248, 249, 250, 251, 322
Hannah, a prayer of 18
Har. 169, 170
Haran 90, 188, 302, 303, 317
Hasmonean 290
Hasmoneans 290, 291
Hebrew poetry 10, 17, 18, 19, 58
Hebrews 25, 29, 38, 47, 48, 75, 76, 95, 118, 150, 174, 192, 201, 202, 279, 297, 304
Hellenism 288, 289
Hellenistic Judaism 287
Heman 21
Henry VIII 182
Hermon, Mt 82
Hezekiah. 45, 47, 49, 56, 67, 68, 105, 107, 108, 110, 122, 132, 136, 137, 138, 139, 140, 143, 146, 149, 150, 161, 163, 164, 177, 315
Hezekiah's Reforms 136
High Priests of the Silent Period
    Eleazar, son of Onias 296
    Eliashib, son of Joiakim 294
    Jaddua, son of Johanan 294
    Jeshua or Joshua 294
    Johanan, son of Joiada. 294
    Joiada, son of Eliashib 294
    Joiakim, son of Joshua 294
    Manasseh, a son of Jaddua 296
    Onias I 294
    Onias II, son of Simon the Just 296
    Onias III, son of Simon 296

Simon II, son of Onias II 296
Simon the Just, the son of Onias I 294
Hilkiah the priest 166
Holy Spirit ... 48, 128, 149-151, 231, 232, 265, 268
Hosea 64, 70-72, 77, 81, 83, 86, 89, 93, 95-100, 102, 109, 123, 136, 151, 252, 313, 315
Hosea's Three Children 96
Hoshea 71, 78, 83, 122, 314, 315
Huldah 166, 167
Huldah the Prophetess 166
Idolatry ...55, 77, 80, 81, 82, 85, 94, 101, 112, 113, 114, 116, 132, 148, 164, 171, 176, 198, 204, 239, 261, 271, 312, 315, 316
Imagery in Zechariah
    Angelic Horsemen 266
    Filthy Clothing 267
    Flying scroll 268
    Four Chariots 269
    Golden Lampstand and Olive Trees ... 268
    Horns and craftsmen 266
    The Surveyor and Measuring line 267
    The woman and the Ephah 268
Images of God in Psalms 30
Intertestamental Period 278
Iran 187
Isaiah 17, 45, 56, 58, 73, 82, 86, 87, 93, 95, 108, 123, 131-152, 165, 180, 188, 191, 196, 200, 202, 206, 207, 210, 214, 218, 220, 227, 242, 246, 266, 269, 274, 279, 313-15
Isaiah 53 150
Isaiah's Description of Israel's Future Kingdom 144
Ishbosheth 77
Islam 182
Jabesh 82
Jehoahaz 78, 82, 110, 122, 157, 160, 171, 186, 317
Jehoash 69, 78, 82, 88, 110, 117, 122, 130, 312, 313
Jehoiachin 110, 122, 157, 160, 172, 186, 200, 205, 318
Jehoiada 118, 121, 123, 130, 312
Jehoiakim . 110, 122, 157, 160, 171, 172, 180, 183, 184, 186, 187, 188, 317, 318
Jehoram ..68, 78, 80, 107, 108, 110, 116, 117, 122, 129, 311, 312
Jehoshaphat. 67, 68, 107, 110, 112, 115, 116, 122, 129, 249, 310, 311

331

INDEX

Jeremiah 46-48, 55, 73-75, 82, 86, 95, 118, 120, 141, 148, 150, 152, 154, 156, 157, 159-161, 165-167, 171, 172, 174, 175, 177, 179, 180, 183-187, 190, 192, 193, 194, 196, 199, 200, 206, 210, 217, 221, 224-226, 231, 239, 241, 259, 260, 263, 280, 316-320
Jeremiah's Time 186
Jeremiah's Trials 186
Jeremiah's symbols 185
Jeroboam ... 65, 66, 69, 70, 78, 79, 81, 82, 88-90, 92, 104, 113, 121, 122, 201, 310, 313
Jerusalem....34, 36, 38, 44, 56, 66, 72, 73, 77, 79, 82, 86, 90, 92, 104, 108, 112, 116, 118, 121, 123, 124, 130, 131, 135-143, 144, 146, 148, 149-152, 159-161,169-175, 178, 179, 180, 184, 186, 187, 188, 190-194, 199, 200-209, 217, 219, 222-228, 230, 231, 234-240, 242-247, 253-256, 258, 259, 260, 262, 263, 265, 266, 267, 269, 270, 271, 272, 280, 281, 282, 284, 286-291, 294, 297, 303, 308, 309, 313, 315, 317, 318, 319, 321, 323
Jesus in Amos... 93
Jesus in Daniel... 210
Jesus in Esther... 246
Jesus in Ezekiel.. 225
Jesus in Ezra and Nehemiah..................... 242
Jesus in Habakkuk 188
Jesus in Haggai 262
Jesus in Hosea 95
Jesus in Isaiah.. 141
Jesus in Jeremiah 179
Jesus in Joel... 124
Jesus in Jonah 90
Jesus in Kings and Chronicles 76
Jesus in Lamentations 193
Jesus in Malachi 273
Jesus in Micah 151
Jesus in Nahum 175
Jesus in Obadiah 190, 193
Jesus in Proverbs...................................46, 56
Jesus in Proverbs and Ecclesiastes 46
Jesus in Psalms 16
Jesus in Song of Solomon 59
Jesus in Zechariah 264
Jesus in Zephaniah 177
Jesus quoted from the book of Psalms 39
Jews 27, 46, 47, 62, 63, 92, 110, 138, 148, 152, 164, 165, 178, 187, 191, 192, 199, 201, 202, 207-210, 212, 221, 230, 234, 235, 237, 238, 239, 241, 242, 244, 245, 246, 247, 249, 250, 254, 255, 259, 260-264, 272, 273, 277, 278, 280, 282-291, 294-297, 315, 319, 320-322
Jezebel 66, 80, 84, 87, 104, 114-117, 252, 271, 311, 312, 314
Joash 67, 69, 105, 108, 110, 117, 118, 120-123, 129, 248, 312, 313
Joel...... 86, 102, 108, 109, 122-129, 149, 178, 268, 313, 314, 318, 324
Jonah... 17, 64, 69, 70, 72, 89, 90-93, 95, 123, 175, 313
Jonah, The prayer of 17
Joram 78, 110, 116, 122, 311
Josephus 62, 164, 165, 168, 206, 228, 276, 279, 282, 284, 294
Josiah ..68, 107, 110, 122, 155, 157, 159, 160, 166-169, 171, 172, 176, 177, 184, 186, 316, 317
Jotham 68, 107, 108, 110, 122, 131, 132, 136, 143, 313, 314
Journey of a Young Man in Proverbs 54
Judah 10, 47, 49, 65-69, 73-80, 86, 92, 94, 95, 98, 99, 100, 102-113, 115-118, 121, 123, 124, 127, 129, 130, 132, 134, 136-143, 146, 147, 149, 151, 152, 154, 155, 157-168, 171, 172, 174, 177-180, 184-192, 199-205, 209, 225, 226, 231, 234, 237-244, 248, 254, 261, 266, 272, 274, 287, 290, 303, 306, 310- 319, 323
Judgment on
   Ammon 94
   Damascus.. 94
   Edom.. 94
   Gaza 94
   Israel 94
   Judah... 94
   Moab 94
   Tyre 94
Judgments against
   Damascus.. 187
   Elam 187
   Hazor 187
   Kedar 187
Julius Caesar... 291
Kandalanu 162
Kedar Hazor 187
Keeping These Sx Books Clear 76
Keys to 2 Chronicles 67
Keys to Amos 69
Keys to Daniel 197

INDEX

Keys to Ecclesiastes 42
Keys to Esther 235
Keys to Ezekiel 198
Keys to Ezra 234
Keys to First Chronicles 105
Keys to First Kings 65, 103
Keys to Habakkuk 157
Keys to Haggai 236
Keys to Hosea 70
Keys to Isaiah 134
Keys to Jeremiah 156
Keys to Joel 107
Keys to Jonah 68
Keys to Lamentations 159
Keys to Malachi 238
Keys to Micah 134
Keys to Nahum 155
Keys to Nehemiah 236
Keys to Obadiah 158
Keys to Proverbs 42
Keys to Psalms 15
Keys to Second Chronicles 106
Keys to Second Kings 66, 104
Keys to Song of Solomon 43
Keys to Zechariah 237
Keys to Zephaniah 155
King Darius of Persia 258
King of the North 169, 170
King of the South 170
Kings of Israel 78
Kings of Judah 110
Kings of Judah and Israel, side by side 121
Kings of Persia 242
Kish 248
Lachish 130, 137, 139, 151, 186
Lamech 17
Lamentations . 17, 18, 19, 154, 159, 161, 175, 192, 193, 194, 320
Last king of Persia 253
Last Word in the Old Testament 275
Latin Vulgate 59, 73, 253
Latin word for seventy 278
Levites of Nehemiah 255
Libya 114, 228
Locusts in Joel 94, 124-128
Longest Prayer Recorded in the Bible, ... 256
Maccabean revolt 280, 290
Maccabeans 192, 290
Maccabees. 11, 165, 279, 282, 287, 288, 290, 296
Maccabeus, Judas 282

Maher-shalal-hash-baz 143
Malachi 86, 199, 233, 238-241, 255, 258, 265, 272-277, 278, 279, 323
Manasseh... 68, 107, 110, 122, 137, 150, 159, 163, 164, 165, 166, 176, 177, 186, 293, 296, 307, 315, 316
Man's Relationship
  to God 53
  to Himself 53
  to Others 54
Martin Luther 25
Masada 165
Mattathias 192, 289
Medes 147, 160, 162, 203, 205, 206, 211, 213, 215, 316
Megiddo 167, 168, 169, 170, 317
Menahem 78, 82, 122, 313
Menelaus 297
Messiah...27, 34, 88, 117, 141, 143, 145, 149, 152, 222-225, 267, 270, 271, 272, 274, 275, 285
Messianic Prophecies In Psalms 28
Micah 82, 86, 108, 120, 123, 133-136, 138, 140, 150, 151, 152, 314, 315
Midianites 169
Moab 79, 82, 100, 146, 148, 170, 178, 187, 227, 254, 311, 312
Moabites 116, 148, 307
Mordecai 235, 246-251, 259, 318, 322
Moses Covenant 119
Nabopolassar 159, 162, 205, 316
Nadab .... See Kings of Israel
Nahum .. 17, 90, 154, 156, 159, 161, 174-177, 184, 316, 317
Names Of the Book of Ecclesiastes 55
Napoleon of Egypt 169
Nebuchadnezzar 140, 157, 160, 162, 163, 172, 186, 187, 188, 190, 191, 197, 198, 199, 204, 205, 211-215, 228, 240, 242, 254, 270, 271, 280, 316, 317, 318, 319, 320
Necho 167, 168, 171
Necho II 167
Nehemiah 138, 199, 208, 209, 219, 223, 233, 236, 239-242, 249, 251, 252-257, 259, 260, 265, 272, 279, 280, 282, 294, 323
New Covenant 120
Nineveh.....69, 83, 90, 91, 137, 140, 156, 162, 175-178, 187, 188, 301, 317
Northern Kingdom ..64, 65, 72, 76-84, 89, 92-95, 98, 100, 108, 109, 112, 113, 115, 116,

INDEX

130, 135, 136, 138, 148, 150, 201, 259, 310
Obadiah ... 122, 154, 159, 161, 174, 175, 184, 187, 190, 191, 193, 258, 312, 318, 319
Oded 115
Ophel Treasure Excavation 136
Oral Laws or Traditions 295
Origin of Satan 148
Palaestra 283
Parallelism 19, 146
Pekah 78, 82, 122, 201, 313
Pekahiah 78, 82, 122, 313
Pentateuch.................. 22, 166, 312, 314, 319
Pentecost 128, 129
Persia .. 11, 149, 187, 199, 200, 203-207, 209, 213, 214, 215, 217, 228, 235, 239, 242, 243, 244, 247, 251, 253, 254, 267, 271, 272, 273, 277, 279, 280-283, 294, 320-324
Persian Emperors 206
Persian Empire. 203, 206, 208, 209, 253, 271, 277, 278, 282, 283, 319, 320, 321
Pharisees 164, 285, 290
Philip II 283
Philistine 131, 151, 252, 270, 271, 308
Philistines. 117, 132, 178, 227, 271, 307, 308, 314
Philistines and Arabians 117
Philo 288
Philopater 285, 286, 296
Pompey of Rome 290
Pool of Siloam 139, 254
Pope Gregory IX 182
Pope Innocent 182
Promised Land 10
Prophetic Poetry 146
Proverbs...... .16, 17, 19, 41, 42, 45-54, 56, 60, 190, 310
Psalms.... 14-17, 19, 20-30, 32, 34, 35, 38, 39, 47, 90, 93, 120, 179, 196, 200, 212, 219, 220, 233, 253, 261, 294, 297, 308, 317, 320
Ptolemies 285, 289
Ptolemy Philadelphus 278, 284, 296
Pul...83, 313, 314
Queen of Persia 247
Reasons for Division of the Kingdom 77
References to Christ in Zechariah 269
Rehoboam . 65, 67, 76, 79, 81, 103, 106, 110, 112, 113, 121, 309, 310
Sadducees 285, 290

Salvation is extended to all Gentiles 128
Samaria .77, 79, 81, 82, 83, 92, 148, 236, 311, 312, 314, 315
Sanballat 254
Sanhedrin 116
Sargon 83, 100, 301, 302, 315, 317
Sargon II.. 83
Satan...57, 117, 166, 169, 181, 211, 218, 231, 245, 247, 248, 251, 255, 267, 268
Scope of Lfe From Proverbs 53
Second Isaiah 140
Second Shortest Book in the Bible 258
Seleucid, House of 285
Sennacherib.90, 137-140, 149, 159, 161, 175, 315, 316
Sennacherib's Prism.................................. 137
Septuagint.... 59, 73, 148, 165, 253, 278, 279, 284, 287, 296
Seven Hebrew Words of Praise................. 22
Seven Sections of Proverbs 48
Shallum 78, 82, 110, 122, 313
Shalmaneser V 83
Shamash-shumukin.................................. 162
Shaphan the scribe 166
Shear-jashub 143
Shishak..112, 310
Shortest book in the Old Testament 190
Shoshenq I 113
Shushan 253
Simon the Just... 286
Singers of Nehemiah 255
Sinsharishku 162
Sin-shumu-lisher 162
Six Periods of the Intertestament Era
   The Egyptian Era 281
   The Greek Era...................................... 281
   The Maccabean Era 281
   The Persian Era 281
   The Roman Era 281
   The Syrian Era 281
Solomon 21, 41-45, 47, 48, 49, 55, 56, 57, 59, 60, 61, 62, 65, 67, 73-78, 81, 82, 103, 106, 111, 112, 113, 166, 174, 179, 180, 252, 258, 263, 309, 310
Song of Deborah 17
Song of Solomon.... 16, 17, 19, 43, 45, 47, 50, 55, 56, 58, 59, 60, 61, 62, 81, 309
Song of Solomon Interpretations
   ALLEGORICAL 62
   Author's REALISTIC VIEW 62
   FICTIONAL 61

INDEX

HISTORICAL 61
Song of Songs.. 59
Song of the Bow 17
Songbook of the Hebrew nation 20
Sons of Asaph.. 21
Sons of Korah 21
Soter 284, 288, 289, 296
Southern Kingdom . 76, 79, 93, 103, 109, 110, 112, 121, 134, 136, 150, 155, 157, 161, 173, 201, 202, 242, 310
Spirit of God 121, 124, 128
Suffering Savior...................................... 150
Syria 80, 100, 108, 114, 132, 148, 192, 201, 215, 282, 283, 284, 285, 286, 288, 289, 290, 306, 310, 313, 314, 320
Syrian Kings of the United Syria, the Seleucid Dynasty 288
Take one-a-day for Health 47
Teachings in Psalms
   "Pilgrim Songs" of Israel....................... 38
   Delight in public worship...................... 38
   Fellowship with God.............................. 38
   Future Life 38
   God as a Personal God 38
   His Help to Each of us.......................... 38
   Nature and Existence of God 38
Teachings in the Book of Proverbs 50
Teachings in Psalms
   Nature of Man....................................... 38
Temple 39, 46, 47, 111, 120, 130, 132, 136, 138, 152, 166, 172, 174, 192, 193, 205, 208, 226, 227, 229, 230, 232, 240, 243, 244, 245, 246, 256, 258, 261, 262, 263, 264, 268, 269, 273, 277, 285, 289, 292, 294, 309, 317, 319, 321
Temple-building prophet 258
The Beautiful Sayings in Song of Solomon . 59
The Branch... 145
The Burden of Nineveh 17
The Cave of Elijah.................................... 86
The Day of the Lord..........................124, 126
The Defeat of the Assyrian army............. 147
The Kings of Judah 110
TheLamentations of Jeremiah................... 18
The Life of Flavius Josephus 165
The Prayer of Habakkuk 17
The Psalms of Hezekiah 17
The Ptolemies 284
The Reformer.........................146, 161, 163

The words of King Lemuel......................... 50
Theme of Each Psalm 30
Thutmose III 169, 305
Tiglath-pileser 83, 132, 314
Time-line of
   536-454 BCE..................................... 207
Titus 164, 165
Tobiah 254
Torah 12, 115, 152, 166, 192, 286, 295
Types of Hebrew Poetry
   Dramatic Type 19
   Funeral Song 19
   Song or Lyric type................................. 19
   Teaching Type called didactic poetry ... 19
Types of Psalms
   National 25
   Nature 24
   Penitential... 26
   Royal or Messianic 27
Tyre 80, 114, 148, 199, 227, 270, 271, 297, 320
United Kingdom 75, 76
Uriah 171
Uzziah ...68, 92, 107, 108, 110, 122, 130, 131, 136, 143, 147, 313, 314
Vashti 235, 246, 249
Vespasian 164
Vineyard, The... 147
Voltaire 182
War Scroll.. 212
Wars of the Jews 165
Wisdom Literature 46
Women of the Old Testament 251
Words of Our Mouth 51
Xerxes ...... .199, 205, 206, 208, 209, 235, 239, 242, 243, 247, 249, 250, 251, 322, 323
Yeshua 294
Yo el 124
Zechariah 82, 86, 121, 130, 170, 199, 208, 218, 231, 233, 234, 237-241, 244, 258, 262-273, 294, 321, 322
Zedekiah .. 110, 122, 157, 160, 172, 184, 186, 190, 318, 319
Zephaniah 86, 90, 148, 154, 155, 159, 161, 174, 175, 177, 178, 180, 184, 194, 210, 279, 316, 317
Zerubbabel....... .207, 234, 237, 238, 240, 241, 242, 244, 247, 258, 262, 264, 265, 294, 321

SCRIPTURE INDEX

SCRIPTURE INDEX

OLD TESTAMENT

Genesis

Gen 3:15	248, 255
Gen 4:23-24	17
Gen 6:22	119
Gen 7:5	60, 214, 281
Gen 7:5, 9, 16	119
Gen 8:17	119
Gen 9:6-7	17
Gen 10:11	90
Gen 11:3-4	205
Gen 11:29	252
Gen 12:1	81, 144, 224
Gen 12:2	119
Gen 13:14-17	119
Gen 15:6	119
Gen 15:16	120
Gen. 16:3–16	252
Gen 17:1	67, 106
Gen 17:10	119
Gen 22:1-19	119
Gen 22:15-18	119
Gen 25:13	187
Gen 27:27-29	17
Gen 29:11	193
Gen 29:28	252
Gen 30:21	252
Gen 31:11	221
Gen 31:47	260
Gen 41:45-52	72
Gen 42:15-16	273
Gen 49:2-27	17

Exodus

Ex 2:21	252
Ex 4:22	75
Ex 6:20	252
Ex 12	75
Ex 12:37	75
Ex 13:3-10	75
Ex 15	17
Ex 15:4	19
Ex 15:20	252
Ex 16:36	268
Ex 17	147
Ex 18:13–26	294
Ex 19-24 (cps)	119
Ex 19:4	119
Ex 19:5	119

SCRIPTURE INDEX

Ex 19-24 99
Ex 20:17 138
Ex 31:6 45

Ex 34:4 188
Ex 34:6 151

Leviticus

Lev 18:25 127
Lev 23:5–8 75
Lev 23:43 266

Numbers

Num 23:7 270
Num 23:9 .... 276, 280
Num 24:3 270
Num 28:16–25 75

Deuteronomy

Deut 1:30 127
Deut 5:21 138
Deut 9:4, 5 127
Deut 16:1–8 75
Deut 23:3-6 254
Deut 33:2 221

Joshua

Josh 2:3–24 252
Josh 5:13–15 127
Josh 7:25 87

Judges

Judg 2:11–15 74
Judg 2:13 118
Judg 4:4 252
Judg 5 17
Judg 13:6 221
Judg 16:4, 5 252

Ruth

Ruth 1:2, 4 252
Ruth 1:4 252
Ruth 1:9 193
Ruth 4:13, 17 252

1 Samuel

SCRIPTURE INDEX

1 Sam 1	252
1 Sam 2:1-10	18
1 Sam 2:4	95
1 Sam 8:1-2	124
1 Sam 14:24	246
1 Sam 16:14-16	124
1 Sam 31:13	246
1 Sam 43:2	87

2 Samuel

2 Sam 1:19-21	17
2 Sam 11:3, 27	252
2 Sam 13:1	252
2 Sam 14:20	220
2 Sam 22:6	91
2 Sam 23:1	14, 16, 19
2 Sam 24:16	219

1 Kings

1 Kings 2:1	75
1 Kings 3:2–4 (cps)	75
1 Kings 4:11, 15	112
1 Kings 4:32	47
1 Kings 9:4	103
1 Kings 9:4-5 (cps)	65
1 Kings 11:41	111
1 Kings 14:15	202
1 Kings 14:23	75
1 Kings 15:6	113
1 Kings 15:13	114
1 Kings 15:14	114
1 Kings 16:24	82
1 Kings 16:30	252
1 Kings 16:31	74, 80
1 Kings 16:33	80
1 Kings 17:1	85, 88
1 Kings 18:4,13	80
1 Kings 18:19	87
1 Kings 18:19, 21, 26, 40	74
1 Kings 19:5	219
1 Kings 19:15-17	88
1 Kings 22:53	74
1 Kings 28:17	86

2 Kings

2 Kings 1:8	85
2 Kings 2:9	88
2 Kings 2:15	88

SCRIPTURE INDEX

2 Kings 5:10-14	89
2 Kings 6:17-18	221
2 Kings 8:17-19	116
2 Kings 11:21	123
2 Kings 12:3	75
2 Kings 14:4	75
2 Kings 14:25	82, 89, 92
2 Kings 14:29	82
2 Kings 15:4	75
2 Kings 15:10	82
2 Kings 16:5-6	201
2 Kings 16:20	102
2 Kings 17:22–23	66
2 Kings 18-19 (cps)	147
2 Kings 18:5-6	137
2 Kings 19:35	90, 139
2 Kings 19:36	90
2 Kings 20:20	137, 139
2 Kings 21:16	165
2 Kings 21:7	74, 114
2 Kings 22:8	180
2 Kings 23	168
2 Kings 23:4	114
2 Kings 23:8, 15, 20	75
2 Kings 23:27	66
2 Kings 23:35	171
2 Kings 24:2	133, 136
2 Kings 24:3-4	163, 165
2 Kings 24:3-5	166

1 Chronicles

1 Chron 1:43	75
1 Chron 3:12	75
1 Chron 4:25	75
1 Chron 5:14	75
1 Chron 7:14	75
1 Chron 9:4	75
1 Chron 11:22	75
1 Chron 15:16	24
1 Chron 17:11–14	105
1 Chron 23:30	23
1 Chron 26:28	75
1 Chron 29:11	105

2 Chronicles

2 Chron 7:14	67, 106
2 Chron 10:8-11	112
2 Chron 11:7	282
2 Chron 11:21-22	113

SCRIPTURE INDEX

2 Chron 12:9	112
2 Chron 14:11-13	114
2 Chron 15:16	114
2 Chron 16:9	67, 106
2 Chron 16:11	111
2 Chron 16:12	115
2 Chron 18:1-2	115
2 Chron 20:15	116
2 Chron 20:19	22
2 Chron 20:32-33	116
2 Chron 21:11	116
2 Chron 21:19-20	116
2 Chron 22:3	117
2 Chron 23:13	23
2 Chron 24:20-22	121
2 Chron 26:4-5	130
2 Chron 26:5	110
2 Chron 26:15	131
2 Chron 26:16-17	131
2 Chron 26:22	146
2 Chron 27:6	132
2 Chron 29:35-36	137
2 Chron 30:1	75
2 Chron 32	147
2 Chron 32:9	137
2 Chron 32:1-26	137, 145, 157
2 Chron 32:30	139
2 Chron 32:32	146
2 Chron 32:5	138
2 Chron 33	163
2 Chron 33:11-12	163
2 Chron 33:5	163
2 Chron 34:22-28	167
2 Chron 35	168
2 Chron 35:1	75
2 Chron 35:9	75
2 Chron 35:11	75
2 Chron 35:13	75
2 Chron 35:18-19	75
2 Chron 35:23	168
2 Chron 36	172
2 Chron 36:12	172
2 Chron 36:22, 23	200

Ezra

Ezra 1:1-6	223
Ezra 1:6-11	243
Ezra 2:1	260
Ezra 2:2-67	280

SCRIPTURE INDEX

Ezra 2:64-65 ... 242
Ezra 3:12 ... 193
Ezra 4: 5 ... 208
Ezra 4:12, 23 ... 241
Ezra 4:24 ... 223
Ezra 5:3 ... 273
Ezra 5:6 ... 208
Ezra 5:13-17 ... 223
Ezra 6 and 7 (cps) ... 244
Ezra 6:1-12 ... 208, 223
Ezra 6:3 ... 242
Ezra 6:7-8 ... 241, 244
Ezra 6:14 ... 241
Ezra 6:14 ... 258
Ezra 6:15 ... 244
Ezra 6:21 ... 93, 282
Ezra 7:6-23 ... 245
Ezra 7:10 ... 234
Ezra 7:7-28 ... 223
Ezra 8:21 ... 245
Ezra 9:2 ... 245
Ezra 10:1 ... 245
Ezra 10:17 ... 245

Nehemiah

Neh 1:5, 11 ... 253
Neh 2:1-8, 13, 17 ... 223
Neh 2:5 ... 223, 254
Neh 2:13-14 ... 254
Neh 2:19 ... 254
Neh 3:16 ... 282
Neh 4:6 ... 255
Neh 4:7 ... 255
Neh 5:13 ... 23
Neh 6:5-7 ... 255
Neh 6:14 ... 253
Neh 6:15, 16 ... 236
Neh 6:19 ... 255
Neh 8:1-3 ... 255
Neh 8:8 ... 236, 260
Neh 8:10 ... 256
Neh 8:15 ... 266
Neh 8:16 ... 254
Neh 9 ... 256
Neh 9:5-37 ... 256
Neh 10 ... 256
Neh 11 ... 256
Neh 12:10, 12, 26 ... 293
Neh 12:11 ... 294
Neh 12:22 ... 208

SCRIPTURE INDEX

Neh 12:39 254
Neh 13:1 254
Neh 13:28 293
Neh 13:31 252

Esther

Est 1:1 247
Est 3:2 249
Est 4:3, 14 246
Est 4:14 235
Est 4:16 250
Est 5:2 250
Est 5:6 250
Est 5:9 250
Est 6:1 250
Est 6:3 250
Est 7:1, 2 250
Est 7:4 251
Est 7:6 251
Est 8:17 235

Job

Job 7:16 55
Job 25:3 221
Job 38:7 220
Job 38:37 46

Psalms

Ps 2 39
Ps 5:11 30
Ps 6:4 26
Ps 6:5 38
Ps 7:11 30
Ps 8 .... 24, 39
Ps 8:1, 6 30
Ps 9:17 91
Ps 16:10 39
Ps 16:10-11 38
Ps 19 24
Ps 19:1 19
Ps 19:14 15
Ps 22 150
Ps 22:1 27
Ps 22:3 24
Ps 22:16 27
Ps 22:18 27
Ps 23:4 38
Ps 24 28
Ps 26:1 30

SCRIPTURE INDEX

Ps 26:2 273
Ps 29 39
Ps 30:2 .... 30, 179
Ps 30:9 38
Ps 34:7 212
Ps 34:15. 38
Ps 34:20 28
Ps 35:5-6 220
Ps 37 200
Ps 37:39, 40. 30
Ps 38:18 26
Ps 39:9 26
Ps 40 28
Ps 41 28
Ps 42:1 38
Ps 46 25
Ps 46:1 38
Ps 47 28
Ps 47:1 .... 23, 24
Ps 47:4 39
Ps 47:6, 8 297
Ps 47:9 39
Ps 50:23 23
Ps 51 38
Ps 51:5 38
Ps 51:11 124
Ps 57:7 23
Ps 63:1 38
Ps 63:3 23
Ps 63:4 24
Ps 66:16, 20. 39
Ps 68:7 39
Ps 69 28
Ps 69:4, 9. 28
Ps 69:25 39
Ps 72 21
Ps 72:15 23
Ps 72:20 15
Ps 78:2 30
Ps 78:23–29 30
Ps 78:58 75
Ps 78:70, 71. 15
Ps 80: 8 99
Ps 84 38
Ps 84:3-4-5 38
Ps 85 .... 39, 261
Ps 86 15
Ps 88 21
Ps 89 .... 15, 21
Ps 89:9 30
Ps 90 21

SCRIPTURE INDEX

Ps 91:11-	220
Ps 94:9-10	38
Ps 96	15
Ps 98:5-65	23
Ps 101	15
Ps 102	261
Ps 103	15
Ps 103:3	179
Ps 103:20	219
Ps 105	15
Ps 105:9	39
Ps 107:2	30
Ps 107:20	179
Ps 109	28
Ps 109:8	39
Ps 110	27
Ps 110:1, 2	27
Ps 117	120
Ps 118	25, 261
Ps 118:2	30
Ps 119	19
Ps 119:10	93
Ps 119:89	183
Ps 120-134	38
Ps 122	15
Ps 124	15
Ps 126	38
Ps 126:1	233
Ps 127	21
Ps 128:1	253
Ps 132	28
Ps 134:2	24
Ps 137	39, 259, 261
Ps 137:1	259
Ps 137:7	191
Ps 139:17, 18	38
Ps 145:21	15
Ps 146-150	261
Ps 147:3	179
Ps 147:4	90
Ps 148:2	219, 220
Ps 148:5	219
Ps 150:3	24
Ps 150:6	22

Proverbs

Prov 1:5	53
Prov 1:5–7	42
Prov 1:7	53
Prov 2:5	46

SCRIPTURE INDEX

Prov 2:6 46
Prov 2:7, 8 46
Prov 2:9 46
Prov 3:1–3 54
Prov 3:3 53
Prov 3:19 .... 46, 51
Prov 3:34 53
Prov 3:5–6 42
Prov 4:1–4 54
Prov 4:24 51
Prov 5:21 51
Prov 6:2 51
Prov 6:23 53
Prov 6:9–11 53
Prov 8:17 54
Prov 8:6-7 51
Prov 10:11 52
Prov 10:19 52
Prov 10:20 52
Prov 10:22 53
Prov 10:25 53
Prov 11:2 190
Prov 11:4 53
Prov 11:17 19
Prov 12:4 53
Prov 12:13, 14 52
Prov 12:18 52
Prov 12:28 53
Prov 13:2 52
Prov 13:4 54
Prov 14:6, 8 51
Prov 15 47
Prov 15:4 52
Prov 15:11 .... 53, 91
Prov 15:16 48
Prov 15:26 52
Prov 15:28 48
Prov 16:21 52
Prov 16:24 52
Prov 16:32 53
Prov 17:3 53
Prov 17:17 54
Prov 17:22 51
Prov 18:21 .... 52, 53
Prov 19:15 53
Prov 19:27 54
Prov 20:7 54
Prov 20:11 53
Prov 20:19 54
Prov 21:1-2 51
Prov 21:23 52

SCRIPTURE INDEX

Prov 22:6	51
Prov 22:17	41
Prov 22:19	53
Prov 22:6	54
Prov 22:24	49
Prov 23:4	49
Prov 23:22	53
Prov 23:23	54
Prov 26:10, 11	53
Prov 26:18-28	49
Prov 27:1	53
Prov 27:20	91
Prov 28:13	53
Prov 28:19	49
Prov 29:11	53
Prov 29:15	51
Prov 30:2-6	49
Prov 31	19
Prov 31:2-9	54
Prov 31:10–31	54

Ecclesiastes

Eccl 2:24	43
Eccl 12	58, 126
Eccl 12:9, 10	48
Eccl 12:13–14	43

Song of Solomon

S of S 1:1–3:5	62
S of S 1:14	58, 256
S of S 2:8	58
S of S 3:6–5:1	62
S of S 4:16	58
S of S 5:2–8:14	62
S of S 6:1	58
S of S 6:10	58
S of S 7:10	43
S of S 8:7	43
S of S 8:14	58

Isaiah

Isa 1:18	142
Isa 2-5 (cps)	147
Isa 2:2-4	152
Isa 5:1-7	147
Isa 10:13	45
Isa 11-12 (cps)	145
Isa 11:9	214
Isa 12:5	142

SCRIPTURE INDEX

Isa 13:6, 9	127
Isa 14:1	151
Isa 17	148
Isa 18	148
Isa 19	148
Isa 21	148
Isa 22:1–14	127
Isa 23	148
Isa 25:1	142
Isa 25:9	141
Isa 27:1	149
Isa 30:18	142
Isa 34:16	93
Isa 35	149
Isa 37:36	149
Isa 38:10-20	17
Isa 38:20	141
Isa 39	200
Isa 4	147
Isa 4:2-3	142
Isa 4:2-6	145
Isa 4:2–6	127
Isa 5	147
Isa 5:14	91
Isa 5:6	142
Isa 6:1	131
Isa 6:1-3	147
Isa 6:2-3)	218
Isa 6:3	220
Isa 7:14, 15	142
Isa 8:3	143
Isa 9:6, 7	134
Isa 9:9	82
Isa 36-37 (cps)	137, 149
Isa 40:3	274
Isa 40:3-5	149
Isa 40:5	142
Isa 40:30	95
Isa 41:18	147
Isa 41:19	266
Isa 42:10	142
Isa 42:15	146
Isa 44-45(cps)	149
Isa 44:28	207
Isa 45:1–14	207
Isa 45:4	206
Isa 46-48 (cps)	150
Isa 49:12	202
Isa 49:6	141
Isa 53	141
Isa 53:5	142

SCRIPTURE INDEX

Isa 53:6	134
Isa 55:13	266
Isa 56:9-11	138
Isa 56-61 (cps)	150
Isa 58:3-9	246
Isa 59:1	142
Isa 60	150
Isa 60:1	142
Isa 63:13	95
Isa 65	150
Isa 66:15	142

Jeremiah

Jer 1:6	179
Jer 2:8	171
Jer 2:19	96
Jer 3:15-17	185
Jer 3:22	179
Jer 6:14	179
Jer 7:23–24	156
Jer 8:11	179
Jer 8:11–12	156
Jer 10:11	260
Jer 10:12	46
Jer 11:13	118
Jer 11:18-23	186
Jer 13	185
Jer 14:19	154, 161
Jer 15:15-21	186
Jer 15:18	179
Jer 15:20	141
Jer 18	185
Jer 18:15	55
Jer 19	185
Jer 19:4–6	74
Jer 19:5	75
Jer 20:1-18	186
Jer 20:14-18	184
Jer 22:9–11	157
Jer 23:13	82
Jer 24	185
Jer 24:1-3	95
Jer 25	200
Jer 25:11	196, 200
Jer 25:11-12	224
Jer 25:12	241
Jer 26:20-23	171
Jer 26:7-24	186
Jer 27	185
Jer 28:10-16	186
Jer 29	200

SCRIPTURE INDEX

Jer 29:10 .... 224, 241
Jer 29:5-7 259
Jer 30-33 (cps) 185
Jer 30:2 180
Jer 31 185
Jer 31:20 47
Jer 31:29 48
Jer 31:31 185
Jer 31:33 174
Jer 31:34 120
Jer 31:31-34 231
Jer 32 185
Jer 34 185
Jer 36:23 180
Jer 36:4 180
Jer 37:11-16 186
Jer 37:17-21 186
Jer 38:5 186
Jer 38:6-9 186
Jer 38:10-28 186
Jer 39:11-40:4 186
Jer 42:1-43:4 186
Jer 43:8-13 186
Jer 45:1 180
Jer 46:2–12 127
Jer 46:13-26 186
Jer 48 148
Jer 49 187
Jer 49:16 190
Jer 50-51 (cps) 187

Lamentations

Lam 1:1–2:22 127
Lam 2:5–6 159
Lam 3 194
Lam 3:22–23 159

Ezekiel

Ezek 1:1 226
Ezek 1:5 218
Ezek 1:1-24 227
Ezek 2:1 225
Ezek 3:17 .... 225, 227
Ezek 10:1 245
Ezek 10:17 245
Ezek 12:18 225
Ezek 13:1–9 127
Ezek 16:46-55 82
Ezek 18:2 47

SCRIPTURE INDEX

Ezek 28:4, 5 45
Ezek 29-32 (cps) 228
Ezek 36:24–26 198
Ezek 36:25-28 231
Ezek 36:33–35 198
Ezek 39 228

Daniel

Dan 1:8a 211
Dan 2 212
Dan 2, 7, and 8 (cps) 214
Dan 2:4-7 216
Dan 2:20-22 197
Dan 2:31-32 213
Dan 2:31-45 214
Dan 2:37-45 267
Dan 2:40-43 231
Dan 2:44 197
Dan 2:44-45 214
Dan 3 211
Dan 3:21 211
Dan 3:27 211
Dan 4:30 163
Dan 5 211
Dan 5:26-28 211
Dan 5:28 .... 205, 213
Dan 5:30–31 281
Dan 6 211
Dan 6:19-22 211
Dan 6:22 221
Dan 6:22-23 220
Dan 7-8 (cps) 215
Dan 7:10 221
Dan 7:3-4 214
Dan 7:4 215
Dan 7:6 215
Dan 7:7 .... 215, 267
Dan 7:9 216
Dan 8 217
Dan 8:1, 13 210
Dan 8:8, 9 217
Dan 8:15, 27 210
Dan 8:16 218
Dan 8:16-17 219
Dan 8:21–22 284
Dan 9 .... 217, 221
Dan 9:2 210
Dan 9:2-3 224
Dan 9:24-27 222
Dan 9:25 .... 222, 223, 224
Dan 11:40 169

SCRIPTURE INDEX

Dan 11:40-45 170
Dan 11:44 230
Dan 13 206
Dan 15:26 210

Hosea

Hos 1:2, 3 252
Hos 1:3-9 70
Hos 1:4-6 83
Hos 1:6 96
Hos 1:8 96
Hos 2:7 96
Hos 2:18–23 127
Hos 2:19 96
Hos in 3:1 97
Hos 3:4 .... 83, 97
Hos 4:1 70
Hos 4:5 .... 95, 144, 235
Hos 4:6 97
Hos 4:17 .... 64, 72
Hos 5:5 95
Hos 6:4 .... 102, 109
Hos 7:8 98
Hos 7:10 98
Hos 7:11 89
Hos 8:8 99
Hos 9:3 83
Hos 10:2 99
Hos 10:8 99
Hos 11:7–9 70
Hos 11:12 99
Hos 12:2 99
Hos 12:8 99
Hos 12:14 99
Hos 14:9 100

Joel

Joel 1:2 .... 123, 125
Joel 1:4 125
Joel 1:15 127
Joel 2:1 127
Joel 2:1, 15 126
Joel 2:2 127
Joel 2:4 126
Joel 2:11 .... 107, 125
Joel 2:13 125
Joel 2:15 126
Joel 2:19-20 126
Joel 2:28 .... 124, 128
Joel 2:28–29 107

SCRIPTURE INDEX

Joel 2:28-32 268
Joel 2:30, 31 127
Joel 2:30-32 128
Joel 2:32 127
Joel 3:12–14 127
Joel 3:16 127
Joel 10-12 125

Amos

Amos 2 148
Amos 2:6-8 94
Amos 3:1–2 .... 69, 83
Amos 3:11 83
Amos 3:15 93
Amos 3:9, 10 .... 94, 104
Amos 4:1 93
Amos 5:4 93
Amos 5:11 93
Amos 5:18–20 127
Amos 5:21-24 94
Amos 5:27 83
Amos 6:1 82
Amos 7: 14-15 93
Amos 9:11–15 127
Amos 9:8 202
Amos 8:11–12 69
Amos 9:1-10 95

Obadiah

Oba 3 .... 190, 191
Oba 10, 21 158
Oba 10-14 191
Oba 15 192
Oba 18 192
Oba 19, 21 190
Oba 21 192

Jonah

Jon 1:17 90
Jon 2:2 91
Jon 2:2-9 17
Jon 2:8–9 68
Jon 2:9 91
Jon 4:2 68
Jon 6:8 90

Micah

Mic 1:1 82
Mic 1:2 152

SCRIPTURE INDEX

Mic 3 152
Mic 4 152
Mic 4:1-5 152
Mic 4:6–8) 127
Mic 4:10 151
Mic 5 152
Mic 5:2 152
Mic 6 153
Mic 6:6-8 120
Mic 6:8 .... 135, 153
Mic 7 153
Mic 7:6 150
Mic 7:7 153
Mic 7:8 153
Mic 7:14 153
Mic 7:18 135
Mic 7:19 151

Nahum

Nah 1:1 .... 175, 210
Nah 1:7–8 156
Nah 1:14 176
Nah 2 176
Nah 2:13 176
Nah 3:1 176
Nah 3:5 176
Nah 3:5–7 156
Nah 3:7, 8 176
Nah 3:19 176

Habakkuk

Hab 1:5-6 188
Hab 1:6-11 188
Hab 1:12-2:1 188
Hab 2 189
Hab 2:2-6 189
Hab 2:4 157
Hab 2:18 .... 124, 188
Hab 3 189
Hab 3:1 187
Hab 3:2-19 17
Hab 3:17–19 157

Zephaniah

Zeph 1: 2 177
Zeph 1:7, 18 178
Zeph 2 .... 148, 178
Zeph 2:3 177

SCRIPTURE INDEX

Zeph 2:7 .... 29, 179
Zeph 3 178
Zeph 3:9-15 178
Zeph 3:12 177
Zeph 3:14-15 178
Zeph 15:3 155

Haggai

Hag 1:1 208
Hag 1:2, 4 262
Hag 1:5-6 262
Hag 1:6 262
Hag 1:7–8 236
Hag 2:3-4 263
Hag 2:3-9 258
Hag 2:6-9 263
Hag 2:23 261

Zechariah

Zech 1:1 208
Zech 1:8 266
Zech 1:8-17 266
Zech 1:9 265
Zech 1:15 266
Zech 1:16-17 263
Zech 2:1-13 267
Zech 2:3 265
Zech 2:5 263
Zech 3 267
Zech 3:1 .... 265, 268
Zech 3:1-2 218
Zech 3:2 267
Zech 3:4 264
Zech 4:1-14 268
Zech 4:6 265
Zech 5:5-11 268
Zech 6:1-8 269
Zech 6:4, 5 265
Zech 6:12- 266
Zech 8:3 237
Zech 9 269
Zech 9:1 .... 270, 272
Zech 9:9 237
Zech 9:9-10 269
Zech 11:12-13 269
Zech 12:3 231
Zech 12:9 271
Zech 12:10 269
Zech 13:1, 6 269
Zech 13:1,6,7 269

SCRIPTURE INDEX

Zech 13:2 264
Zech 14 271
Zech 14:2 272
Zech 14:2, 4 269
Zech 14:3-4 272
Zech 14:9 .... 265, 272
Zech 14:12 170

Malachi

Mal 1:11-14 274
Mal 1:1-5 273
Mal 1:8 273
Mal 2 274
Mal 2:10-16 274
Mal 2:17–3 238
Mal 2:17-3:6 274
Mal 3 274
Mal 3:1 275
Mal 3:13-4:6 274
Mal 3:7-12 274
Mal 4:1-2 244
Mal 4:6-6:8 244

NEW TESTAMENT

Matt 10:35 150
Matt 10:5-7 202
Matt 11:10 274
Matt 12:39-40 92
Matt 13:35 30
Matt 16:11 98
Matt 2:14 99
Matt 21:42 30
Matt 21:9 30
Matt 22:44 29
Matt 24:30 229
Matt 26:28 120
Matt 27:34 29
Matt 27:35–36 29
Matt 27:46 29
Matt 3:17 29
Matt. 1:5 252
Mark 14:57 29
Mark 16:19 29
Mark 16:6–7 29
Luke 1:11-17 278
Luke 10:15 91
Luke 11:29 92

SCRIPTURE INDEX

Reference	Page
Luke 17:22-36	229
Luke 21:33	183
Luke 22:47	29
Luke 23:34	29
Luke 23:35	29
John 15:25	29, 39
John 19:32–33, 36	29
John 2:17	29, 30
John 20:25, 27	29
Acts 1:15	39
Acts 1:20	29
Acts 2:16-17	129
Acts 2:27	91
Acts 2:31	39
Acts 26:7-8	202
Acts 4:23–31	39
Rom 2:28	241
Rom 4:17	88
1 Cor 14:26	39
Gal 4:4-6	281
Eph 5:19	39
Col 3:16	39
1 Thess 5:2–5	127
Heb 1:1-2	296
Heb 1:8	29
Heb 10:7	29
Heb 11	150
Heb 11:37	150
Heb 2:8	29
Heb 5:6	29
2 Pet 3:9	92
Rev 1:18	91
Rev 16	169
Rev 16:12	230
Rev 16:14	231
Rev 6:12-13	229
Rev 6:17	229
Rev 6:2	269
Rev 6:7	269
Rev 16:16	170

NOTES

NOTES

www.ingramcontent.com/pod-product-compliance
Lightning Source LLC
Chambersburg PA
CBHW032038090426
42744CB00004B/52